THE ROUTLEDGE COMPANION TO TRANSLATION STUDIES

"An excellent all-round guide to translation studies taking in the more traditional genres and those on the cutting edge. All the contributors are known experts in their chosen areas and this gives the volume the air of authority required when dealing with a subject that is being increasingly studied in higher education institutions all over the world"

Christopher Taylor,
University of Trieste, Italy

The Routledge Companion to Translation Studies brings together clear, detailed essays from leading international scholars on major areas in translation studies today.

This accessible and authoritative guide offers fresh perspectives on linguistics, context, culture, politics and ethics and contains a range of contributions on emerging areas such as cognitive theories, technology, interpreting and audiovisual translation.

Supported by an extensive glossary of key concepts and a substantial bibliography, this Companion is an essential resource for undergraduates, postgraduates, researchers and professionals working in this exciting field of study.

Jeremy Munday is Senior Lecturer in Spanish and Translation Studies at the University of Leeds. He is the author of *Introducing Translation Studies*, *Translation: An Advanced Resource Book* (with Basil Hatim) and *Style and Ideology in Translation*, all published by Routledge.

Also available from Routledge

The Routledge Companion to Postcolonial Studies
John McLeod
978-0-415-32497-7

The Routledge Companion to Postmodernism (Second Edition)
Stuart Sim
978-0-415-33359-7

The Routledge Companion to Critical Theory
Simon Malpas and Paul Wake
978-0-415-33296-5

The Routledge Companion to Semiotics and Linguistics
Paul Cobley
978-0-415-24314-8

Language: The Basics (Second Edition)
R.L. Trask
978-0-415-34019-9

Language and Linguistics: The Key Concepts (Second Edition)
R.L. Trask and Peter Stockwell
978-0-415-41359-6

THE ROUTLEDGE COMPANION TO TRANSLATION STUDIES

Edited by
Jeremy Munday

Taylor & Francis Group
LONDON AND NEW YORK

First published 2009
by Routledge
2 Park Square, Milton Park, Abingdon, Oxon OX14 4RN

Simultaneously published in the USA and Canada
by Routledge
270 Madison Ave, New York 10016

Routledge is an imprint of the Taylor & Francis Group, an informa business

© 2009 Jeremy Munday for selection and editorial matter; individual contributors their contribution

Typeset in Times New Roman by Keyword Group Ltd
Printed and bound in Great Britain by TJ International Ltd, Padstow, Cornwall

All rights reserved. No part of this book may be reprinted or reproduced or utilised in any form or by any electronic, mechanical, or other means, now known or hereafter invented, including photocopying and recording, or in any information storage or retrieval system, without permission in writing from the publishers.

British Library Cataloguing in Publication Data
A catalogue record for this book is available from the British Library

Library of Congress Cataloging-in-Publication Data
The Routledge companion to translation studies / edited by Jeremy Munday.
p. cm. – (Routledge companions) 1. Translating and interpreting. I. Munday, Jeremy.

P306.R68 2008
418′.02–dc22   2008044855

ISBN 10: 0-415-39640-9 (hbk)
ISBN 10: 0-415-39641-7 (pbk)
ISBN 10: 0-203-87945-7 (ebk)

ISBN 13: 978-0-415-39640-0 (hbk)
ISBN 13: 978-0-415-39641-7 (pbk)
ISBN 13: 978-0-203-87945-0 (ebk)

Contents

List of figures and tables	vii
List of contributors	viii
Acknowledgements	xii
Abbreviations	xiii
1 Issues in translation studies *Jeremy Munday*	1
2 The linguistic and communicative stages in translation theory *Peter Newmark*	20
3 Translating text in context *Basil Hatim*	36
4 Translation as a cognitive activity *Amparo Hurtado Albir and Fabio Alves*	54
5 Translation as intercultural communication *David Katan*	74
6 Translation, ethics, politics *Theo Hermans*	93
7 Technology and translation *Tony Hartley*	106
8 Issues in interpreting studies *Franz Pöchhacker*	128
9 Issues in audiovisual translation *Delia Chiaro*	141

CONTENTS

Key concepts 166

Bibliography 241

Index 284

FIGURES AND TABLES

FIGURES

1.1	Translation strategies as a cline	8
3.1	From register to the semiotic triad text–genre–discourse	50
3.2	Text/genre/discourse/register as Russian dolls	53
4.1	Bell's model of the translation process	57
4.2	Kiraly's psycholinguistic model	59
5.1	The iceberg representation of culture	78
7.1	Example XML tags	108
7.2	Concordance of 'infiltrate' sorted by left context	111
7.3	Concordance of 'infiltrate' as verb followed by 'into'	112
8.1	Conceptual spectrum of interpreting	132
9.1	The polysemiotic nature of audiovisual products	143

TABLES

2.1	Summary of Vinay and Darbelnet's seven translation procedures	32
2.2	Vinay and Darbelnet's seven translation procedures, with literal translations of the French examples	35
4.1	PACTE model of subcompetences	66
5.1	Japanese 'effacement' and Anglo 'self-enhancement' scripts	86
5.2	Logical levels table of context of culture and context of situation	89

Contributors

Fabio Alves is Associate Professor for Translation Studies and a leading researcher of LETRA (the Laboratory for Experimentation in Translation) at the Federal University of Minas Gerais, Brazil. He holds a PhD from Ruhr-Universität Bochum in Germany with a process-oriented study of cognitive differences and similarities observed among Brazilian and Portuguese translators. His research focuses primarily on the empirical-experimental investigation of the translation process and on the development of expertise in translation. His publications include articles in *Meta*, *TradTerm* and *Cadernos de Tradução*, as well as a range of book chapters in the Benjamins Translation Library and others.

Delia Chiaro holds a Chair in English Linguistics and Translation at the University of Bologna's Scuola Superiore di Lingue Moderne per Interpreti e Traduttori, Forlì, Italy. She is also Director of Studies of the Forlì Master's programme in multimedia translation and a European-funded international summer school in screen translation involving lecturers and students from five EU institutions. She is a renowned scholar in screen translation and humour and combines these two interests in her audience-based, data-driven work on the perception of verbally expressed humour translated for television, cinema and the internet. Her publications include *The Language of Jokes: Analyzing verbal play* (Routledge, 1992), a special issue of *Humor, International Journal of Humor Research* on humour and translation (volume 18(2), 2005) and a chapter on the subject in *The Primer of Humor Research* (ed. V. Raskin, Berlin: De Gruyter, 2008). Author of a number of articles in international journals, she has lectured on humour and translation in Europe, Asia and the USA.

Tony Hartley trained as a translator and interpreter (French and Russian), and subsequently held posts in French higher education before returning to the UK university system. He was the first to introduce commercial machine translation into the translation curriculum at Bradford, where he also taught conference interpreting, working regularly as a freelance. He then moved into cognitive science, first at Sussex and then at Brighton, designing and implementing a number of software systems, particularly in the domain of natural language generation. Now Director of the Centre for Translation Studies at the University of Leeds, he combines his twin interests in translation and computing in leading a group of researchers active in the development and evaluation of a range of translation technologies. He has been an investigator on numerous UK- and EU-funded research projects and held visiting appointments at the Universities of Laval and Sydney, as well as the Communications Research Laboratory (now NICT) in Japan.

Basil Hatim is a theorist in English⇔Arabic translation and translator/interpreter both into and out of Arabic. He has worked and lectured widely at universities throughout the world. He has published extensively on applied linguistics, text linguistics, translation/interpreting and TESOL. His authored or co-authored books include *Discourse and the Translator* (Longman, 1990), *The Translator as Communicator* (Routledge, 1997), both with Ian Mason, *Communication Across Cultures* (Exeter University Press, 1997), *Teaching and Researching Translation* (Longman, 2002) and, with Jeremy Munday, *Translation: An Advanced Resource Book* (Routledge, 2004). This is in addition to some fifty academic papers on a variety of intercultural communication issues in a diverse range of international refereed publications.

Theo Hermans is Professor of Dutch and Comparative Literature at University College London (UCL) and Director of the UCL Centre for Intercultural Studies. He edits the series 'Translation Theories Explored' for St. Jerome Publishing (Manchester) and is a co-founder of the International Association for Translation and Intercultural Studies (IATIS). His main research interests concern the theory and history of translation. He edited the collections *The Manipulation of Literature* (Palgrave Macmillan, 1985), *Crosscultural Transgressions* (St. Jerome, 2002) and *Translating Others* (St. Jerome, 2 vols, 2006). His monographs include *The Structure of Modernist Poetry* (Croom Helm, 1982), *Translation in Systems* (St. Jerome, 1999) and *The Conference of the Tongues* (St. Jerome, 2007).

Amparo Hurtado Albir is professor at the Departament de Traducció i Interpretació of the Universitat Autònoma of Barcelona and holds a doctorate in translation studies from ESIT of the Université de Paris III. She is principal investigator of a number of research projects on translation pedagogy and the acquisition of translation competence and is principal investigator of the PACTE research group. She is the author of numerous publications on the theory and pedagogy of translation, the most prominent of which are: *Enseñar a traducir: Metodología en la formación de traductores, e intérpretes* [Teaching Translation: Methodology in translator and interpreter training], (ed.), Madrid, Edelsa, 1999; *Traducción y Traductología* [Translation and translation studies], Madrid, Cátedra, 2001. In addition, she is also general editor of the *Aprender a traducir* [Learning to translate] series (Universitat Jaume I, Castellón, and Edelsa publishers).

David Katan taught at the Interpreters' School, University of Trieste for 20 years before taking up the chair in English Language and Translation at the University of Salento (Lecce), Italy, where he is now also

Director of Studies for the specialist course in Translation. He has published over 40 articles on translation and intercultural communication, both nationally and internationally. His book *Translating Cultures: An Introduction for Translators, Interpreters and Mediators* is now in its second edition (St. Jerome, 2004). He has also contributed to the revised Routledge Encyclopedia of Translation Studies (eds Mona Baker and Gabriela Saldanha, 2008). He is Senior Editor of a new journal, *Cultus: the Journal of Intercultural Mediation and Communication*, and is a member of the editorial boards of *RITT-Rivista internazionale di tecnica della traduzione* (*International Journal of Translation* and *ESP Across Cultures*).

Jeremy Munday is Senior Lecturer in Spanish Studies and Translation at the University of Leeds, UK. His research interests include translation theory, discourse and text analysis applied to translation, and the application of corpus-based tools to the contrastive analysis of language. He is author of *Introducing Translation Studies* (Routledge, first edition 2001, second edition 2008) and *Style and Ideology in Translation: Latin American writing in English* (Routledge, 2008), and co-author of *Translation: An advanced resource book* (Routledge, 2004, with Basil Hatim). Chair of the Publications Committee of the International Association of Translation and Intercultural Studies (IATIS), he is editor of *Translation as Intervention* (Continuum and IATIS, 2007) and co-editor, with Sonia Cunico, of the special issue of *The Translator* on ideology and translation (vol. 13(2), November 2007). He is also a qualified and published translator from Spanish and French to English.

Peter Newmark was formerly Head of the School of Modern Languages, Polytechnic of Central London (now University of Westminster). He holds a BA (Cantab.) and has Hon. D. Litts at Masaryk University, Brno, the Hong Kong Baptist University and the University of Westminster. His major publications include *A Textbook of Translation* (Prentice Hall, 1987), *About Translation* (Multilingual Matters, 1991) and *More Paragraphs on Translation* (Multilingual Matters, 1998). He writes a bimonthly 'Translation Now' column in *The Linguist*, the publication of the Chartered Institute of Linguistis, London. He teaches periodically at the Centre for Translation Studies, University of Surrey.

Franz Pöchhacker is Associate Professor of Interpreting Studies at the Centre for Translation Studies, University of Vienna. He was trained as a conference interpreter and has been working freelance as a conference and media interpreter since the late 1980s. Following his doctoral research on simultaneous conference interpreting (*Simultandolmetschen als komplexes Handeln*, Gunter Narr, 1994), he extended his research interests to community-based interpreting in healthcare and asylum settings and has worked in particular on general issues of interpreting studies as a discipline

(*Dolmetschen: Konzeptuelle Grundlagen und deskriptive Untersuchungen*, Stauffenburg, 2000; *Introducing Interpreting Studies*, Routledge, 2004). He has lectured widely and published over sixty papers. He is the editor, with Miriam Shlesinger, of *The Interpreting Studies Reader* (Routledge, 2002) and of *Interpreting: International Journal of Research and Practice in Interpreting*.

ACKNOWLEDGEMENTS

Thanks are due to the following copyright holders for permission to reproduce illustrations from their publications: to Editions Didier, Paris for Table 2.1, taken from page 55 of Jean-Paul Vinay and Jean Darbelnet's Stylistique comparée du français et de l'anglais; Méthode de traduction, Editions Didier 1958/2008; to Longman for Figure 4.1, from page 49 of Roger Bell's *Translation and Translating: Theory and practice*, London: Longman, 1991; to Kent State University Press for Figure 4.2, from page 105 of Don Kiraly's *Pathways to Translation: Pedagogy and process*, Kent, OH: Kent State University Press, 1995.

I would like to thank all the contributors for their enthusiasm to contribute to this project and their willingness both to keep to tight deadlines and to accept editorial recommendations; to all the editorial team at Routledge, particularly Aimée Foy, for their patience, support and tolerance; to Sylvia Potter, for copy editing; and, at home, to Cristina, Nuria and Marina, because I took time from them to work on this project.

Abbreviations

SL   Source language
ST   Source text
TL   Target language
TT   Target text

1
ISSUES IN TRANSLATION STUDIES

JEREMY MUNDAY

1.0 INTRODUCTION

This volume sets out to bring together contributions on key issues in translation studies, providing an overview, a definition of key concepts, a description of major theoretical work and an indication of possible avenues of development. This first chapter serves both as an introduction to the volume as a whole and as a discussion of how the field itself has evolved, especially since the middle of the twentieth century.

1.1 THE HISTORY OF TRANSLATION PRACTICE AND EARLY 'THEORY'

One of the characteristics of the study of translation is that, certainly initially, it was based on the practice of translating; much early writing was by individual translators and directed at explaining, justifying or discussing their choice of a particular translation strategy. In Western translation theory, which has exerted a dominance over a subject that has evolved until recently mainly in the West, these writings are traditionally felt to begin with the Roman rhetorician and orator Marcus Tullius Cicero (106 to 43 BCE) and the Bible translator St Jerome (c.347–c.420 CE). In his essay, 'De optimo genere oratorum' ('The best kind of orator', 46 BCE), Cicero describes the strategy he adopted for translating models of classical Greek oratory:

> [S]ince there was a complete misapprehension as to the nature of their style of oratory, I thought it my duty to undertake a task which will be useful to students, though not necessarily for myself. That is to say I translated the most famous orations of the two most eloquent Attic orators, Aeschines and Demostenes, orations which they delivered against each other. *And I did not translate them as an interpreter but as an orator*, keeping the same ideas and the forms or as one might say, the 'figures' of thought, but in language which conforms to our usage. And in so doing, I did not hold it necessary to render word for word, but I preserved the general style and force of the language.
> (Cicero 46 BCE, trans. H.M. Hubbell, in Robinson 1997a: 9, emphasis added)

Noteworthy is Cicero's assertion that translation here was for the benefit of his students and not for himself. It was a training and instruction exercise, rather than having any other intrinsic value of its own, and this concept of translation as furthering other ends has persisted through the centuries. But Cicero also considered a translation necessary in order to overcome misunderstandings arising from a growing cultural and linguistic divide between the Greek and Roman worlds. The italicized part of the quotation corresponds to the original Latin *non converti ut interpres sed ut orator*; here, *interpres* is to be understood as a literal, word-for-word translator (a common form of translation at the time, when the readers could generally be expected to have some competence in the source language) and *orator* as the speech maker who attempts to influence the audience by his persuasive use of language. As Robinson points out (1997a: 9, footnote 6), this distinction, novel at the time and hugely influential since, in some ways resembles that between formal and dynamic equivalence proposed by the modern-day translation theorist and Bible translator Eugene Nida (see Chapter 2).

While the Classical authors of ancient Greece and Rome exerted authority over much European thought and literature (and translation), an even more important phenomenon was the translation of the Bible itself. Translation was a means of disseminating the word of God. In this respect, the Greek Septuagint translation of the Hebrew Scriptures (the Christian Old Testament) in the third–first centuries BCE was crucial. The claim, made later by Philo Judaeus (20 BCE, in Robinson 1997a: 13), that the team of seventy-two scholarly translators each independently arrived at exactly the same wording in their translations, thus confirming their fidelity to the source) illustrates most clearly the perceived need to allay potential dangers associated with altering a sensitive text and the possible charges of misinterpretation or manipulation. The claim was repeated by St Augustine in his *On Christian Doctrine* (428 CE, in Robinson 1997a: 34) as proof that the translators were divinely guided ('inspired by the Holy Spirit') into reproducing a translation that, even if challenged by those who compared it with the Hebrew, should now be considered to have authority.

Once translation was allowed, the problem for the religious authorities was how to keep control over the different versions. This is a problem of 'rewriting' (cf. Lefevere 1992), not unique to translation, as is shown most evidently in the process of canonicity of the sacred books of the major monotheistic religions (the Torah, the Christian Bible and the Qur'ān); that is, decisions as to the material that was to be included and the exact form of the text that was authorized (see, e.g. Peters 2007). In the case of the Christian New Testament, the late fourth-century Pope Damasus commissioned St Jerome to produce a new Latin translation as a standardized version, replacing the many variants in existence and being partly a revision of the *Veta Latina* (Old Latin) version. Jerome unusually had knowledge of Hebrew as well as Greek, and so, in his later translation of the Old Testament, was able to refer to the source text (ST) itself. This also meant that he became aware of the many differences between the Hebrew and the Septuagint, realizing that the Septuagint was, indeed, a highly edited version. As far as general translation strategy was concerned, in his famous and lengthy letter to Pammachius (Jerome 395 CE, in Robinson 1997a: 23–30), Jerome defends himself against accusations of errors. Calling on the authority of Cicero, Horace and other Classical authors, and providing a judicious caveat for the sensitive area of religious texts, the letter includes the now-famous description of its author's strategy:

> Now I not only admit but freely announce that in translating from the Greek – except of course in the case of the Holy Scripture, where even the syntax is a mystery – I render, not word for word, but sense for sense.
> (Jerome 395/1997: 25)

In Western Europe this word-for-word versus sense-for-sense debate continued in one form or another until the twentieth century (see Chapter 2). The centrality of the Bible to translation also explains the enduring theoretical questions about accuracy and fidelity to a fixed source.

Some 1100 years after St Jerome, in the religious Reformation of the sixteenth century, translation most clearly showed itself as a political weapon in Europe. Against the fierce opposition of the Church, the Bible was finally translated into vernacular languages and some of those translators set out clear translation strategies. Prominent among these was Martin Luther, in his *Sendbrief vom Dolmetschen* ('Circular letter on translation') of 1530, defending his Bible translation into a modern German that was clear and everyday rather than elitist (Luther 1530/1963).

Any attempted summary of historical writings on translation would inevitably be extremely selective and, given the space constraints of the volume and this chapter, overly brief. For this reason, the reader is directed to the following, which can be used as starting points for research: Robinson (1997a) for a compilation of extracts from prefaces and other writings of 90 major figures Kelly (1979) and Rener (1989), see below for a discussion on the practice and theory from Classical to pre-modern times; Baker and Malmkjær (1998) and Baker and Saldanha (2008) for a brief overview of many traditions; Lefevere (1977) for the German tradition from Luther; Berman (1992) for the German Romantic tradition; Amos (1920/73), T. Steiner (1975), Venuti (1995/2008), Classe (2000) and France (2000) for the English tradition; Ellis (2003), Braden *et al.* (2004), Gillespie and Hopkins (2005), France and Haynes (2006) and Venuti (forthcoming) for a five-volume history of literary translation in English; G. Steiner (1975/98) for an attempt at a general (European) theory of translation. It is important to remark, however, on the historical dominance of writings by men: in Robinson's *Western Translation Theory from Herodotus to Nietzsche* (1997), only nine of the 90 extracted authors are women, which is nevertheless more than in other anthologies. There is also a dominance of European writing and languages that has only recently begun to be addressed in the publication of, amongst others, volumes on the Chinese tradition of Yan Fu (Chan 2004), the very earliest writing on translation in China (Cheung 2006) and Asian translation traditions more generally (Hung and Wakabayashi 2005). Yet, somewhat ironically, in order to be heard internationally these publications on translation appear in English, a language that dominates international scholarship and imposes its own academic conventions (Bennett 2007).

Nevertheless, what can be said is that the practice of translation remained an enduring feature of writing on the subject. Early attempts at theoretical or abstract conceptualization in the fifteenth and sixteenth centuries were based on the practice of the ancient Classics. As Frederick Rener (1989: 261) puts it in his *Interpretatio: Language and translation from Cicero to Tytler*,

> these ideas were taken from the statements and the practice of important translators of the past. In Western Europe, Cicero and Jerome held the position of *auctores principes* in matters of translation and they were consulted on questions of theory as well as practice.

The writings most often noted in the European context are those of Martin Luther (1530), Etienne Dolet (1540) and the later John Dryden (1680) and Alexander Tytler (1797, see Chapter 2). For Rener (ibid: 7),

> the many centuries between classical antiquity and the eighteenth century should be regarded as a unit which is cemented by a strong tradition. The binding element is a common theory of language and communication and an equally jointly shared idea of translation.

That theory of language was based on the Classical classifications of grammar and rhetoric and the (hierarchical) distinction and separation between *res* (thing), *verba* (sign) and style (Rener ibid: 35). Such a fixed nature of language was only really challenged from the time of the German Romantics of the early nineteenth century (Schlegel, Goethe, Schleiermacher, Humboldt, etc.) and, in the early twentieth century, in the work of Saussure in linguistics and Walter Benjamin in philosophy. Persistent revisitings of such writings have transfused translation studies in recent decades (see 1.5 below).

1.2 The rise of 'translation studies'

In comparison with many other academic disciplines or interdisciplines,[1] translation studies is a relatively new area of inquiry, dating from the second half of the twentieth century and emerging out of other fields such as modern languages, comparative literature and linguistics. The very name *translation studies* was first proposed by James S. Holmes as late as 1972 as a better alternative to *translatology* and to *translation science*, or *science of translating* (cf. Nida 1964). Versions of *translatology* have become established in languages such as French (*translatologie*); the latter, *translation science*, was a calque of the German *Übersetzungswissenschaft* (e.g. Koller 1979), but, as Holmes (1988: 70) notes, 'not all *Wissenschaften* can properly be called sciences'. Over time, just twenty years since the widespread dissemination of Holmes's paper after his death, the name *translation studies* has become established within the English-speaking world even if there remain competing terms in other languages (cf. Stolze 1997: 10). This preference is increasingly supported by its use in institutional names (e.g. 'Centre for Translation Studies') and in the titles of widely-used volumes such as *Translation Studies* (Bassnett 1980/2002), *The Routledge Encyclopedia of Translation Studies* (Baker and Malmkjær 1998; Baker and Saldanha 2008), *Introducing Translation Studies* (Munday 2001/2008), *A Companion to Translation Studies* (Kuhiwczak and Littau 2007) and the present volume. We may detect some influence of English over other languages, the calque *estudios de la traducción* in Spanish, for example.

The debate over the name of the field of study is in many ways a symbol of a more important phenomenon, what Holmes (1988: 71) saw as 'the lack of any general consensus as to the scope and structure of the discipline. What constitutes the field of translation studies?' The candidates he discusses from the 1970s include comparative/contrastive terminology and lexicography, comparative/contrastive linguistics, and 'translation theory'. The answer to the question, however, presupposes that we agree what 'translation' is.

1.3 What is 'Translation'?

There are two issues that need attention here: what we actually mean by *translation* (this section) and what disciplines or activities fall within the scope of translation studies (section 1.4). The understanding of these issues has been transformed since Holmes's tentative, yet seminal, paper. As far as the former is concerned, central to the development of translation studies, indeed canonized within its writings, is the well-known, tripartite definition of translation advanced by the structural linguist Roman Jakobson:

1. Intralingual translation or *rewording* is an interpretation of verbal signs by means of other signs of the same language.
2. Interlingual translation or *translation proper* is an interpretation of verbal signs by means of some other language.
3. Intersemiotic translation or *transmutation* is an interpretation of verbal signs by means of signs of nonverbal sign systems.

Jakobson (1959/2004: 139, emphasis in original)

'Intralingual' translation thus refers to a rewording or rephrasing in the same language (most explicitly introduced by phrases such as *in other words* or *that is*), and 'intersemiotic' to a change of medium, such as the translation that occurs when a composer puts words to music (see Chapter 2) or, even more notably, when the musical sound completely replaces the verbal code. For Jakobson, 'interlingual' translation, between two verbal languages (e.g. Chinese and Arabic, English and Spanish), is 'translation proper'. Although that may be the most 'prototypical' form of translation (cf. Halverson 1999), it is by no means unproblematic. For instance, what constitutes 'some other language', or, for that matter, 'the same language'? This may appear clear to us when we discuss, for instance, an intralingual subtitling service for the hard-of-hearing in the broadcaster's own language as compared to the various interlingual subtitling options in other languages on a DVD, but where do we site dialect in this classification? When the film *Trainspotting* (directed by Danny Boyle, 1996, UK), with its urban Scottish dialects, is subtitled for an English-speaking US audience, is this to be considered a case of intralingual or interlingual translation? Or what about an Asturian speaker subtitled for Castilian-speaking viewers on Spanish TV? Spoken in the region of Asturias in northern Spain, Asturian is considered to be a distinct language by some but does not enjoy official language status nationally. Such questions relate to language policy and to our own linguistic and research perspective and may have political or ideological import.

The subtitling in the foregoing examples is another instance of phenomena which cross boundaries. As well as being either intralingual or interlingual, subtitling is also a form of intersemiotic translation, the replacement of an ST spoken verbal code by a target text (TT) written verbal code with due regard for the visual and other acoustic signs: thus, there may be a written indication of telephones ringing, dogs barking, characters shouting; or sometimes non-translation of visual elements such as nods and head-shakes that are obvious from the image, and so on. Interest in intersemiotic translation, in the interaction of the visual and written semiotic codes in particular, has grown over the years, especially in relatively new areas of research such as audiovisual translation (see Chapter 9), children's literature (e.g. Lathey 2006), advertising translation (e.g. Adab and Valdés 2004) and in areas related to localization and multimedia translation which have revolutionized the translation profession (see Chapters 7 and 9).

Translation thus refers to far more than just the written text on the page, the product of the translation process. Defining what we mean by the word is notoriously slippery: in their *Dictionary of Translation Studies*, Shuttleworth and Cowie begin their entry for 'translation' by acknowledging this fact: '**Translation** An incredibly broad notion which can be understood in many different ways' (1997: 181), while Baker and Malmkjær (1998) do without a specific entry for 'translation' in their longer *Encyclopedia*. Hatim and Munday prefer to talk of 'the ambit of translation', defined as:

1. The process of transferring a written text from SL to TL, conducted by a translator, or translators, in a specific socio-cultural context.
2. The written product, or TT, which results from that process and which functions in the socio-cultural context of the TL.
3. The cognitive, linguistic, visual, cultural and ideological phenomena which are an integral part of 1 and 2.

Hatim and Munday (2004: 6)

As we shall see below, it is the phenomena in the third point of this definition that have attracted most attention in recent translation studies.

However, such definitions still do not answer the question of the limits on *translation*, and the boundaries between *translation*, *adaptation*, *version*, *transcreation*, etc. that have key implications for the criteria by which the target text is judged. For example, *adaptation*, again, has been variously defined as:

> a set of translative operations which result in a text that is not accepted as a translation but is nevertheless recognized as representing a source text of about the same length.
>
> (Bastin 1998: 5)

but also as:

> a term traditionally used to refer to any TT in which a particularly free translation strategy has been adopted. The term usually implies that considerable changes have been made in order to make the text more suitable for a specific audience (e.g. children) or for the particular purpose behind the translation.
>
> (Shuttleworth and Cowie 1997: 3)

Such contradictory attempts at definition highlight the difficulty, and even futility, of expecting watertight categories for what might better be viewed as a cline of strategies under the overarching term 'translation' that might resemble Figure 1.1 (see below).

The left-hand side of the cline relates to translation strategies that are based on the maintenance of ST structure, the most extreme being that of 'phonological' translation (Nord 1991/2005: 33) such as the Zukofskys' famous translation of the poems of Catullus (1969), which sought to recreate the sound of the Latin rather than render the sense. 'Formal' here refers to Nida's formal equivalence (or 'formal correspondence', Nida and Taber 1969), which 'focuses all attention on the message itself, in both form and content' (Nida 1964: 159; see Chapter 2), a kind of literal translation that is 'contextually motivated' (Hatim and Munday 2004: 41). 'Functional' is Nida's 'dynamic'

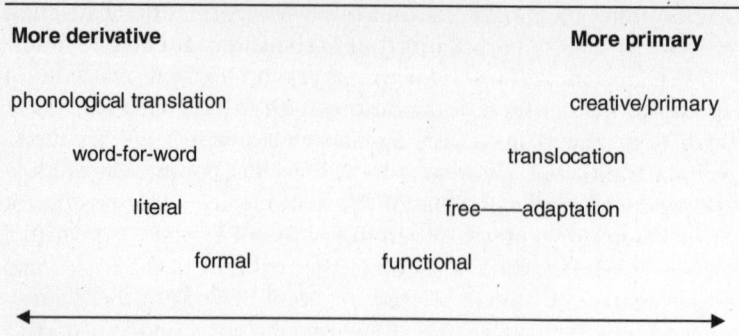

FIGURE 1.1 Translation strategies as a cline

or 'functional' equivalence, an 'orientation' that seeks to create the same response in the TT readers as the ST created in the ST readers ('equivalent effect' or 'equivalent response'). The wide implications of functional translation theories and other forms of text and discourse analysis will be considered in Chapter 3. 'Translocation' is taken from J. Michael Walton's (2006: 182–3) 'tentative series of categories' of Greek drama in English, the seventh and final in a classification which starts with the word-for-word cribs known as 'literals' and which includes 'adaptation' (e.g. Seamus Heaney's *The Cure at Troy* and Ted Hughes's *Oresteia*) as its fifth category. 'Translocation' is used in the sense of a play being relocated into a new culture (e.g. Eugene O'Neill's *Mourning Becomes Electra* and Wole Soyinka's *The Bacchae after Euripedes*) and Walton even suggests that this is the category into which most contemporary and most 'innovative' 'translations' or 'recreations' of Classical Greek drama fall.

On the extreme right-hand side of Figure 1.1 is the point 'creative/primary'. This is not because other forms of translation are not creative, although, being based more obviously on a source text, they may be more derivative. It is more because of the increasing interest from translation studies in the crossover between translation and creative writing (e.g. Perteghella and Loffredo 2006) and the phenomenon of 'transcreation', a term used by the Brazilian Haroldo de Campos (1981, in Vieira 1999: 110; see also Chapter 6). In Vieira's reading, '[t]o transcreate is not to try to reproduce the original's form understood as a sound pattern, but to appropriate the translator's contemporaries' best poetry, to use the existing tradition'. The anthropophagic, transcreative use of the original in order to 'nourish' new work in the target language breaks the notion of faithfulness to the original text as a necessary criterion for translation. Interestingly, the term 'transcreation' has recently come to be used in the very different context of video games (see O'Hagan and Mangiron 2006, and Chapter 9) to denote a type of translation that frequently rewrites the sound track in order to create new, target-culture appropriate effects of humour, especially.

Another important identitary question for the discipline is the distinction between written translation and spoken translation (often equated to 'interpreting'). Jakobson's definition (above) makes no explicit mention of interpreting, while many others (e.g. Bassnett 1980/2002, Gentzler 2001, Munday 2001/2008, Hatim and Munday 2004) deliberately restrict themselves to written translation. However, the difference between translation and interpreting cannot always be one of the written versus the spoken: for example, interpreters are routinely asked to produce TL versions of written documents such as witness statements and other exhibits in the courts and formal speeches that are written to be read, etc., thus blurring the boundaries between the modes. An alternative way of treating the question was proposed by Otto Kade (1968), who coined the superordinate German term *Translation* to cover both translation (*Übersetzen*) and interpreting (*Dolmetschen*). Kade proposed a 'far-sighted definition of interpreting' (Pöchhacker, this volume, Chapter 8), selecting as the key features (a) the single presentation of the ST which does not normally allow review by the interpreter, and (b) the time constraint affecting the target text production, which severely limits the possibility of correction and more or less excludes revision. There has been a somewhat uncertain relationship between translation studies and what is now termed 'interpreting studies' (Pöchhacker and Shlesinger 2002; Pöchhacker 2004; see also Snell-Hornby 2006: 162). For Pöchhacker (this volume), 'often referred to as a "(sub)discipline", [Interpreting studies] is both an increasingly autonomous and diversified field of academic pursuit, on a par with translation studies, and a domain within the latter, alongside such specialized fields as audiovisual translation'. In this volume, we treat the 'duality' described by Pöchhacker by giving interpreting studies, and indeed audiovisual translation, their own chapters, but also acknowledging the strong ties that link these different modalities by treating elements of the different modalities in, for example, the chapter on cognitive theories (Chapter 4) or politics and ethics (Chapter 6). Many of the translation strategies outlined in the audiovisual chapter, section 9.4, are also directly relevant for other forms of translation and interpreting.

1.4 THE SCOPE OF TRANSLATION STUDIES

The scope of the discipline of translation studies, the second issue noted in the previous section, has been transformed since James Holmes's time. Holmes's famous 'map' of translation studies, graphically represented by Gideon Toury (1995: 10; see also Munday 2008: 10), divides the discipline into a 'pure' and 'applied' side, with much the greater emphasis being placed on the former. 'Pure' is then subdivided into 'theoretical' and 'descriptive', and these in turn subdivided according to the objectives and subjects of inquiry.

The term 'translation theory' is used by Holmes (1988: 73) to refer to 'theoretical translation studies', the goal of which is 'to develop a full, inclusive theory accommodating so many elements that it can serve to explain and predict all phenomena falling within the terrain of translating and translation, to the exclusion of all phenomena falling outside it'. Such a goal, Holmes admits in an understatement, would be 'highly formalized and ... highly complex' and, in its absolute form, would be closely aligned to the concept of translation 'universals'. Hypothesized universals include lexical simplification, explicitation and standardization (Blum-Kulka and Levenston 1983; Blum-Kulka 1986/2004; Laviosa 1998). However, disproving a universal is very much easier than proving one and most theorists these days would accept that the number of situational variables in the translation process is so vast it would restrict an absolute theory (i.e. statements that hold for every case) to the very bland, such as 'translation involves shifts' (Toury 2004).

For Peter Newmark (see Chapter 2), 'translation theory' is 'focussed for an occasion on a particular set of translation tasks' that should be 'useful' for the practising and trainee translator. This is typical of the theoretical work in the linguistic and functional frameworks which has sought to answer key questions, such as equivalence, more or less prescriptively and in line with what was useful for translator training. Some of this work has itself become "canonized" by its continued influence and/or by its inclusion in translation studies anthologies (e.g. Venuti 2004): Vinay and Darbelnet's comparative stylistics of French and English (1958/2004), which is the origin of some of the metalanguage used to describe translation (see Chapter 2); Eugene Nida's seminal analysis of translation (2004) from a purportedly 'scientific' but ultimately socio-linguistic perspective in the 1950s and 1960s especially, which shifted the attention from the word to the audience in such dramatic fashion (see also Chapter 2); German attempts at setting foundations of a general theory of translation based on text type and *skopos* (purpose) and function (Reiss 1971/2000; Reiss and Vermeer 1984; Nord 1988/91/2005; see Chapter 3). These were all important developments in taking translation studies away from a static concentration on individual ST–TT word equivalence, incorporating additional elements of context, participants and 'culture' (Vermeer 1986, 1989). Snell-Hornby (2006: 55) sees this as the beginning of the 'cultural turn' in translation studies (see below, Section 1.5).

In Holmes's map, the other subdivision of 'pure' theory is the descriptive branch, championed most prominently from the late 1970s by Gideon Toury, whose *Descriptive Translation Studies- and Beyond* (1995) has become an indispensable reference point for those working in this area. Toury's early work came out of the context of polysystem theory, developed by his colleague Itamar Even-Zohar (see 1990/2004, 1997/2005), which studied translated literature as a system that interrelated dynamically with the source system (Hermans 1999). Translations were studied, not as isolated texts, but within their cultural, literary and socio-historical contexts, and as 'facts of target cultures' (Toury 1995: 29). Although *skopos* theory had also proposed a target-culture oriented definition, Toury and the descriptivists stood out by their rejection of value-laden evaluations of TTs in relation to their STs. The focus moved away from the prescriptive ('X must be translated as Y') and firmly towards the descriptive ('in text A, produced under conditions and constraints B, X is translated as Y').

In Toury's work, the central concept is one of the 'norms' that operate in the translation process, from the selection of texts to the textual choices on the page. Norms are linked to 'regularities of behaviour' (Toury 1995: 55), so the descriptive branch is geared towards the observation of translational behaviour in, a corpus of translated texts, using a replicable methodology that allows generalizations to be made. These generalizations may, with further inquiry, lead to the formulation of probabilistic 'laws' of translation that reconceive the idea of translation universals. Thus, 'in text A, produced under conditions and constraints B, X is translated as Y' becomes 'in texts of type A, produced under conditions and constraints B, X *is likely to be translated* as Y'. Toury's two proposed laws ('the law of standardization' and 'the law of interference') may be tentative and rather general, but his work has been crucial for providing a firm methodology and orientation for the vast array of empirical studies based on the examination of source and target texts, including corpus-based studies (see Pym *et al*. 2008).

1.5 Cultural and other 'turns' in Translation Studies

The 1980s and 1990s also saw the growing influence of cultural studies on translation, the so-called 'cultural turn' as it was coined in Bassnett and Lefevere's edited volume *Translation, History and Culture* (1990; see especially Lefevere and Bassnett 1990: 4; Snell-Hornby 2006: 47–67). These are described, necessarily selectively, by Theo Hermans in Chapter 6 of this volume, and include: descriptive translation studies itself; André Lefevere's work on ideology, poetics and patronage and on translation as 'rewriting'; postcolonial and feminist/gender translation theory; the concepts of norms, constraints and rules that operate in the translation system; and ethics and identity formation.

The shift in research paradigms has had several major consequences: one has been the interrogation of long-held tenets of translation, such as the very notion of ST–TT equivalence, which has been rejected, or revisited, by deconstructionists and postcolonialists. Thus, Walter Benjamin's 'The task of the translator' (1923/2004), in which he posited the role of translation (and, ideally, interlinear translation) in ensuring the persistence or 'afterlife' of a text and in generating a 'pure' language, became the centrepoint for deconstructionist readings of translation that rejected any stable, fixed meaning (e.g. Graham 1985; Niranjana 1992). The notion of the aim of translation as being one of TL 'naturalness' (e.g. Nida and Taber 1969) has also been challenged by scholars such as Antoine Berman (1992, 1985/2004) and Lawrence Venuti, who reworked Schleiermacher's (1813/2004) distinction between the translator who brings the author to the writer and the translator who brings the writer to the author. It is Venuti's terms 'foreignization' and 'domestication', his criticism of the Anglo-American literary translation scene (Venuti 1995/2008) and a call for 'resistance' from translators (Venuti 1998a), that have enjoyed popularity in recent years.

A second consequence has been the noticeable focus on the agents of translation and interpreting, especially the translators themselves, rather than the texts. Work on the sociology of translation uses Bourdieusian concepts such as 'field' and 'habitus' (see Simeoni 1998; Inghilleri 2005; Wolf and Fukari 2007) in an effort to theorize, describe and understand the socio-historical place and role of the translator. Such translator-centred research, whether it be from a socio-logical, cognitive or other perspective, promises to complement micro-studies of translated texts and the broader theorizing of the cultural context.

A third consequence is a more threatening one. With such varied developments from so many other frameworks entering translation studies, does the discipline share a sufficient basis to avoid fragmentation? Are we all studying the same phenomenon? This question initiated intense debate in the journal *Target* after the publication of Chesterman and Arrojo's paper 'Shared ground' (2000) but remained unanswered. My own opinion is that there are inevitable differences in the studies that take place under the umbrella of translation studies (the same could of course be said of many other academic subjects) but that there is enough commonality and common interest to keep the discipline together. The survey of the contents of the volume in the next section will indicate the existence of both differences and commonalities quite clearly. The problem that faces translation studies is that it has come together out of other disciplines (modern languages, comparative literature, linguistics, etc.) and for this reason it sometimes lacks a strong institutional basis and thus risks being swallowed up by larger disciplinary structures (Faculties of Arts, Departments of Languages and Intercultural Studies, etc.). The way forward for translation theorists may therefore be collaborative work in research groups on specific topics rather than by working as isolated individuals. This has begun to happen in recent years, prompted by a shift in priorities in research funding in some countries.

1.6 THIS VOLUME

The chapters in this volume are each written by an expert in the specific field of investigation. While attempting to give coherence and consistency in the editing process, I have also endeavoured to allow each author to speak with his/her voice, in many ways reflective of the theories they describe. Each chapter thus becomes an overview of the particular specialization but, within that remit, each author has been able to develop those areas that are of most interest to him/her. The list of key concepts then functions as a reference to specific ideas discussed in the chapters and as a means of covering some major concepts that have not been treated elsewhere.

However, it is important to bear in mind that there are often difficulties resulting from the inconsistent use of the terminology or metalanguage of translation studies. This is especially true of the linguistic terminology, as discussed in Chapter 2, 'The linguistic and communicative stages in translation theory', by **Peter Newmark**. Together with Eugene Nida, Newmark is the most prominent of translation theorists from the linguistic tradition. In this chapter, Newmark reviews key elements of linguistic and communicative translation theories, which he sees as being the first two 'stages' of translation theory. For him, 'linguistic' theories continued up to George Steiner's *After Babel* (1975/98), were devoted mainly to the study of literary translation and were centred on the opposition of 'word-for-word' and 'sense-for-sense' translation (see section 1.1). Newmark uses the term 'pre-linguistics' to refer to the early, pre-Tytler writings.

Those theories which fall under Newmark's 'communicative' stage include most notably the seminal work of Nida on formal correspondence and functional equivalence which brings the audience into the centre of the translation equation. Newmark later touches on links to what he terms the third ('functional') and fourth ('ethical') stages of translation theory, treated in more depth in Chapters 4 and 6 of this volume.

Newmark's concerns are with the usefulness of 'translation theory' (as opposed to 'translation studies', which he sees as 'more diluted') and the recurring question of the translator's search for the 'truth', moral and aesthetic. In this quest, he distinguishes between literary and non-literary texts, which he considers to have different characteristics and objectives, an opinion which of course is not shared by those critics who advance an 'integrated' theory of translation for all text types (cf. Hatim and Mason 1990; Snell-Hornby 1988/95).

Basil Hatim is the author of Chapter 3, which continues to look at the textual product, but in a wider, discourse context. Hatim reviews the influential text-type and *skopos* theory of Katharina Reiss and Hans Vermeer and the work of the German functionalists (notably Christiane Nord and Juliane House) that had such influence in the 1970s onwards. For over two decades Hatim has been a major proponent of register and discourse analytic models that have been imported by translation from applied linguistics. Most especially, this work builds on the Hallidayan systemic-functional tradition of register analysis and relates it both to lexicogrammatical features and to higher-order text, genre and discourse that enable communication to take place and attitude to be expressed. The overriding point is that 'no text can remain in...a state of relative isolation from facts of socio-cultural life' (Hatim, this volume). Here, we have moved beyond the consideration of individual words or phrases to an exploration of communication through conventionalized (or distorted) genres and through discourse as a 'socio-textual process', which may have ideological promptings or consequences. There are links here with the critical linguistics of Hodge and Kress (1979/93) and the critical discourse analysis school of Norman Fairclough (1989/2001). However, rather than the latter's objective of uncovering and combating inbuilt institutional ideological prejudices and pressures, in translation studies this thread of work focuses on uncovering manipulative practices and distortions in translation and teaches trainee translators how these may be avoided.

From translation as a *product*, even in the dynamic communicative sense described by Hatim, we move in Chapter 4 to a consideration of the translation and interpreting *process*. **Amparo Hurtado Albir** and **Fabio Alves** chapter, 'Translation as a cognitive activity', is a major and comprehensive overview of work in one of the most innovative fields of research in translation studies. The six processing models they discuss apply different theoretical frameworks: the interpretive theory of the Paris School; Bell's linguistic and psycholinguistic model; Kiraly's socio-logical and psycholinguistic model; Wilss' decision-making model; Gutt on relevance theory; and Gile's effort model. Just as linguistic and communicative theories of translation have drawn on a broad range of linguistic theory, so is cognitive translation studies dependent on and potentially contributing to advances in cognitive science.

What becomes clear from Chapter 4 is the huge amount of empirical-experiential work on cognitive processing and competences that is taking place across the globe using ever more sophisticated data-gathering devices: the think-aloud protocols of the 1980s and 1990s have been supplemented or supplanted by keystroke logging, eyetrackers and neuroimaging. The possibilities for understanding the cognitive processing in translating and interpreting has never been greater, while at the same time the often expensive technical equipment and requirements for such investigation are necessarily restrictive: increasingly we are talking of the need for interdisciplinary research teams equipped for the task.

Chapter 5 by **David Katan** examines translation as 'intercultural communication' and discusses what is understood by the term 'culture'. This is related to the very nature of language and has enormous bearing on how the translator operates. Katan explores the central terms of 'context of situation' and 'context of culture', coined by Malinowski in the 1920s and taken up by Halliday some thirty years later. However, rather than the discourse-based approach of Chapter 3, Katan looks at the question from an anthropological angle and concentrates on the translator as an intercultural mediator, applying a 'culture filter' to the foreign text and negotiating meanings for the target text reader.

It is interesting that similar concerns reappear in new guises: is cultural meaning 'carried' or 'negotiated' by language? Is the culture filter applied depending on the cultural distance of the audience, as Nida would claim, or depending on text type, as Juliane House proposes in her influential *A Model for Translation Quality Assessment* (1977/81)? Are the rules, norms and conventions (cf. Nord 1991/2005) that govern translation domestic rather than universal? The conclusion to this chapter illustrates how it provides a link between the word, discourse and cognitive foci of the earlier chapters and the more wide-ranging panorama of translation in later chapters. Thus, Katan provides a logical levels table for the culture of situation and culture of context, of which some of the parameters, such as 'values/beliefs', 'identity' and 'translator role/mission', relate closely to the following chapter.

Chapter 6, 'Translation, ethics, politics' by **Theo Hermans**, provides an insightful summary of the expansion of the discipline since the 1980s brought about by the broadening of the contextualization of translation/interpreting. Hermans' own edited volume, *The Manipulation of Literature* (1985), was one of the seminal early publications that introduced the study of ideological manipulation on the part of the actors in the process of literary translation, the translator being just one of these and often less powerful than the editor, commissioner, etc.

Hermans' chapter necessarily selectively touches on a vast array of work related to cultural studies (see above section 1.5), demonstrating how the 'ambit' of translation and translation studies (cf. section 1.3 above) has been transformed with the influx of ideas from other disciplines. Just as Peter Newmark (Chapter 2) emphasizes the ethical consideration of 'truth', so Hermans here stresses the centrality of 'the translator as re-enunciator and discursive subject in the text [which] also brings on questions of responsibility and accountability, and hence ethics'. The translator 'revoices' the source text author, literally in the case of an interpreter, metaphorically in written translation, and leaves a trace of his or her involvement in the textual choices made in the target text. The questions for research in translation studies centre on the ideological and ethical motivations and consequences of such choices.

Hermans also notes the metaphorical meanings of translation that are brought into play by postcolonial theories, where, for example, referring to Eric Cheyfitz's (1991) study of the colonizers' appropriation of land in North America, '[t]ranslation is...much more than a verbal transaction; it means transfer of territory into other hands, overwriting one system of thought with another, and often the eviction – translation in its most physical sense – of the original inhabitants'. The interrogation of the very meanings of translation, far beyond Jakobson's three text-based categories (see section 1.3 above), is a relatively recent phenomenon but one that is gathering strength, as is evident from Maria Tymoczko's (2006) call for the questioning of the Western-based 'presuppositions' that have so far dominated translation studies (see section 1.7 below).

Chapter 7, 'Technology and translation', by **Tony Hartley**, deals with an area that has been relatively neglected in mainstream theory of translation and yet has become indispensable for the practising translator. Hartley surveys a wide range of technology, including machine translation, corpus linguistics, translation memory systems, terminology and controlled language. The chapter is important in summarizing such a wide field and in linking specific advances in computing and communication, for example, the standardization of infrastructure and computing languages that enables data to be shared and tools to be open-access. Such developments underlie the global transformation in the commercial translation sector, affecting all aspects of translation practice including the status and identity of the translator him/herself.

One of the most interesting features of Hartley's chapter is that it provokes a revisiting of certain traditionally-held perspectives within translation studies. This goes beyond the different definitions accorded to 'pseudo-translation', 'adequacy', etc. to the actual form and objective of practice and theory: so, 'translation units' are identified as matching segments in parallel corpora which may then provide equivalents for translation memories or future translations; 'controlled language', used in much technical writing to restrict the ST author's choices and facilitate translation, in fact has its roots in the Simplified English of the 1930s that was designed to make translation unnecessary; the complexity of component translation tasks and the huge volume of work mean that today translation is in most cases a team effort, even if the individuals do not often meet or speak to the other members – ironically, such collaborative effort undermines what Tymoczko (2006) sees as the false Western supposition of individualistic translation, just as much as does her own example of Chinese Buddhist translations of the second–fourth centuries CE. Finally, Hartley's description of the move to online translation and of the possibilities inherent in wikitranslation shows that the whole practice of translation (including quality assurance) is likely to be transformed by the democratizing potential of the web.

The last chapters deal with two other specific domains or modalities that, as we indicated above, are beginning to achieve semi-autonomous status in translation studies, as evidenced by conferences, associations and/or specialized journals and monograph series specifically dedicated to them: interpreting studies and audiovisual translation.

Chapter 8 is devoted to 'Issues in interpreting studies' and is authored by **Franz Pöchhacker**. Although once more necessarily restricted by space limitations, the chapter is enlightening for the overview it gives of interpreting studies and its relation to translation studies (see above, section 1.3). Most significantly, many of the issues and trends Pöchhacker discusses have their counterparts in studies of written translation too: discourse, cognitive processing, intercultural mediation, ethics, quality, training, technology, history and so on. This suggests that translation studies and interpreting studies may be following similar paths away from the linguistic and encompassing sociological approaches.

Pöchhacker concludes with the statement that '[o]verall, methodologies in interpreting research have been gravitating from the cognitive toward the social sciences, and from quantitative toward qualitative data' but that they 'complement' each other in improving our understanding of interpreting. This is important. There has been a general move from linguistics to discourse to cultural studies, in its many forms, and a focus on the agents involved in the communicative process, both in translation and interpreting investigation. What Pöchhacker emphasizes, however, is that these different forms of investigation all have their place in furthering knowledge.

Chapter 9, 'Issues in audiovisual translation', by **Delia Chiaro**, examines a growing field of specialization that is reflective of the development of new media with different forms of text production and language communication. Initially, centred almost exclusively on the analysis of film subtitles and dubbing, audiovisual translation (sometimes also known as 'screen translation' or 'multimedia translation') now encompasses phenomena as varied as voice-over, fansubs, video games, audio description and even forms of localization, reflective of the strong involvement of new technologies in the practice and study of translation (see also Chapter 7).

Despite these new modalities, which have only really been taken seriously since the 1990s, there are clear links with other forms of translation. This chapter should not therefore be seen as being limited to audiovisual translation. Thus, section 9.4, entitled 'Translating audiovisual products', details various translation procedures to cope with the specific time, space and visual constraints of the screen. The problems Chiaro focuses on, culture-specific references (names, institutions, food items, etc.), language-specific features (dialect, forms of address, etc.) and overlaps between the two (in areas such as songs and humour) are, as the author acknowledges, elements that are also problematic in more conventional written translation and interpreting, but they are particularly in audiovisual translation problematic because of the other fixed constraints of the screen.

This last chapter is indicative of the continuing concern in audiovisual translation for the practicalities of the professional's work and for systematizing them to provide guidelines for the subtitler/dubber (see Díaz Cintas and Remael 2007 for an example of this). On the other hand, it begs the question of whether research in audiovisual translation is following the pattern of the study of written translation and interpreting in first centring on the practicalities of the work before moving on to considering cognitive, cultural, historical, sociological and other aspects of the field. This would be a legacy of the practice–theory, practitioner–scholar divide. Another possibility, which I think is quite possible, is that it is indicative of the way in which technological advances are not only revolutionizing working practices but in many ways are driving part of the research agenda: so, in order to cope with the pace of technological change, research on the functioning of technological applications is necessary to better understand the implications of the change and to test responses to it. This would also be the case for the evolution of the machine translation and computer-assisted translation tools discussed in Chapter 6.

Technology, not just restricted to localization, is indeed a new paradigm in translation studies. Far from detracting from the research into translation, it is providing it with a new vista, perhaps especially in linguistic and cognitive investigation, which have been greatly neglected since the cultural turn of the 1980s/1990s.

1.7 CHALLENGES TO PERCEPTIONS OF TRANSLATION

Since translation and interpreting, in their myriad forms, necessarily involve language use/transfer/communication, the exclusion or downplaying of the linguistic and textual study of the subject would seem as foolish now as, in decades gone by, was the overlooking of translation as an intercultural phenomenon. Indeed, the 'cultural turn' (see section 1.5 above) ushered in a stream of investigation that transformed the discipline and today continues a process of recontextualization that goes right to the core of what is understood as translation, as can be seen in Theo Hermans' remarkable two-volume *Translating Others* (2006), a collection of papers from a mainly non-Western perspective. In one of the most outstanding contributions, 'Reconceptualizing Translation Theory: Integrating non-Western thought about translation', Maria Tymoczko (2006) invokes the need to challenge 'presuppositions' that have dominated the discipline. Among these are an overemphasis:

- on translation as a mediating form between cultures, overlooking the fact that differential language use is often a marker of identity for a group;
- on the written text and on Classical Greco-Roman text types and genres;
- on the individual translator rather than the team project (e.g. Buddhist translation in China);
- on the trained, professional translator in highly literate societies rather than the more informal, oral translator in many cultures.

In addition, Tymoczko perceives an ignorance of the role of translation and cultural contact in migrations from the past; and, most importantly of all, an unnecessarily restricted conceptualization of what *translation* is.

Part of the solution, Tymoczko suggests (ibid.: 20–2), may be found in broadening the scope of the word for *translation* to include conceptualization from non-Western languages: in India, *rupantar* ('change in form') and *anuvad* ('speaking after'), in Arabic *tarjama* ('biography'), in Chinese *fan yi* ('turning over'), each indicating a different form of engagement with the process. This would have important implications for the relation between STs and TTs, for instance further challenging the prominence of the concept of equivalence in Western-based studies (see 1.3 above). Thus, if we expand what we understand by and research as *translation*, the conventional requirement of the TT to resemble the source will no longer hold. For Tymoczko (ibid.: 27), this would then entail broadening the study of translation to include different 'modes', namely *transference*, *representation* and *transculturation*: *transference*, as an alternative and broader alternative to *translation*, can be physical or symbolic and involve a different medium; *representation* entails the construction and exhibition of an image of the Other, and *transculturation*, adopted from the Cuban anthropologist and historian Fernando Ortiz (1940), involves not only the transmission but also the 'performance' of other cultural facets and forms, which may not be linguistic at all. Tymoczko's contention is that it may be possible to examine (and re-examine) translations according to whether they are predominantly aimed at transference, representation or transculturation. The response to Tymoczko's call is awaited. It remains to be seen whether or not it will herald a new 'turn', detour, byway or complete translocation of translation studies.

NOTES

1 See Snell-Hornby (1988/95, 2006), Munday (2001) and Chesterman (2002) for a discussion of translation studies as an interdiscipline.

2
THE LINGUISTIC AND COMMUNICATIVE STAGES IN TRANSLATION THEORY

PETER NEWMARK

2.0 INTRODUCTION

Translation theory is an 'operational instrument' which is, in Benjamin Britten's (1964) sense of the two words, both 'useful' (i.e. specifically required, as well as practical) and 'occasional' (i.e. focussed for an occasion on a particular set of translation tasks), and therefore to be used by the translator, the student and the critical reader as a frame of reference. I would argue that translation theory is not indispensable, since there are good translators who have had no theoretical training, but it is an essential component of any translator training syllabus. Most prentice translators have to master their skills through study, but a few gifted linguists appear to acquire them instinctively, because they know how to write well in the target language. In my view, translation theory works best when continuously accompanied by defining and illustrative bilingual translation examples which have been met in the teacher's professional experience or appear in standard textbooks on the subject. These are better than invented examples, but any example is better than none.

Translation theory in a wider sense is usually known as 'translation studies', or as 'translatology', the comprehensive study of translation (see Chapter 1). Whilst translation studies has a more extensive compass, and is concerned with diluted aspects of the subject, I see 'translation theory', or 'translatology', when the term is not used in a pretentious context, as a stricter discipline. As an interdiscipline, however, I believe it must take into account its essential components and their applications, namely a theory of writing well and of stylistic and ethical language criticism, as well as the subjects of cultural studies, applied linguistics, sociolinguistics, psycholinguistics, logic and ethical philosophy.

2.1 FOUR STAGES OF TRANSLATION THEORY

I consider that there have been four successive stages in translation theory. They are sometimes referred to, in the study of translation, as translational turns (see Chapter 1) or transfers. I classify them as follows:

1. **The linguistic stage**, up to 1950. It covers mainly literary texts, that is poetry, short stories, plays, novels and autobiography. This stage is mainly

concerned with the continually recurring discussion of the merits of word-for-word, as opposed to sense-for-sense, translation. This is the 'pre-linguistics' stage.
2. **The communicative stage**, from around 1950. This stage covers non-literary and literary texts. It is concerned with the categorization of text registers, the participation of a range of readership groups (less-educated to expert), and the identification of types of procedures for translating various segments of a text. It marks the application of linguistics to translation studies.
3. **The functionalist stage**, from around 1970. It covers mainly non-literary texts, that is, 'the real world'. It is focussed on the intention of a text and its essential message, rather than the language of the source text. It tends to be seen as a commercial operation, with the author as the vendor, the text and/or the translation as the tender, and the readership as the consumer.
4. **The ethical/aesthetic stage**, from around 2000. This stage is concerned with authoritative and official or documentary texts, and includes serious literary works. Since the turn of the millennium, I have endeavoured to establish that translation is a noble, truth-seeking profession and that a translation must not mislead readers factually nor deceive them with false ideas; if such occur in the original, they must be corrected or glossed extratextually, depending as their ethical benchmark on the United Nations Universal Declaration of Human Rights (1948) plus amendments, and not on the translator's personal ideology; in my view, the UN Declaration is the keystone of social and individual ethics today. So, where prejudiced language is used in the source text, in respect of gender, race, colour, religion, class, age, mental health or physical appearance, whether intentionally or unintentionally, it has generally to be pointed out in a translator's preface or the footnotes, unless the text is historical (e.g. in Tom Paine's *The Rights of Man*, 1791/1984). The truth is essentially twofold: (a) the correspondence of a factual text with reality; (b) the correspondence of an imaginative text with a meaningful allegory, and, consequentially; (c) the correspondence of the translation with the respective type of text (compare text-type analysis discussed in Chapter 3).

These four stages are cumulative, in the sense that they absorb without eliminating each other. The fourth stage is final, but it is dynamic, since the moral truth progresses but the aesthetic truth is permanent – no one will ever excel Shakespeare's language or Hardy's poetry. My brief is to discuss the linguistic and communicative stages, but, in order to indicate their place in this frame, I shall add in the conclusion of this essay a few words about the functionalist and ethical/aesthetic stages.

2.1.1 THE LINGUISTIC STAGE

In CE 384 St Jerome (CE 395/1997; see section 1.1) wrote his letter to Pammachius on the best method of translating, enjoining his readers to render sense-for-sense not word-for-word, but importantly making an exception of Biblical texts (and not only to protect himself from attacks from religious quarters); these have to be translated textually (that is, word-for-word). Ever since, translators, translation scholars and the general public have been arguing about the merits of literal (or close) and free (or natural or liberal or idiomatic) translation. This argument can be picked up at almost any point in translation theory history: take Sir John Denham in seventeenth century England, who said it was not his business to 'translate language into language, but poesie into poesie' (see Tytler 1797: 35; also, Sowerby 2006: 94–100); or, in the nineteenth century, consider the arguments between F.W. Newman, the staunch upholder of literal translation, and the great poet Matthew Arnold (1861), who was working his way towards the concept of the translator's equivalent response (see Venuti 1995: 118–47 and Reynolds 2006: 67–70).

Indeed, the superiority of sense over word and of context over the dictionary is the basis of the interpretive theory of translation, where 'natural' has become 'cognitive' and 'close' is rejected as 'linguistic'; this is the prevailing philosophy of translating at the École Supérieure d'Interprètes et de Traducteurs (ESIT) at the Sorbonne in Paris (see Chapter 4). The theory was first formulated as the *théorie du sens* by Danica Seleskovitch (e.g. 1968), who identified interpreting with translation. The theory neglects the fact that sometimes the source text (e.g. *'cette pomme est mûre'*) may be identical with the translation ('this apple is ripe'); further, it is artificial and misleading for a translator to replace a word with its synonym simply because, like *excellent* in French and English, it has the same form in both languages. The great Schubert scholar Eric Sams told his son Jeremy, the brilliant opera translator and director, never to translate a word, say the French *prudent*, by its synonymous English cognate, i.e. *prudent* (Jeremy Sams, personal communication), which severely impeded any accurate translation (this does not mean, however, that these two words translate each other in every context – *avisé* (Fr) and *wise* (En) respectively are obvious alternatives for *prudent*).

Certainly, the first religious writings tended to be translated literally, since they were believed to be written by or inspired by God; however, only informal translations of the Qur'an, which was revealed to the prophet Muhammad by Allah over a period of twenty-three years, were permitted and they were to be regarded as paraphrases – the Qur'an is believed to be a miracle and it cannot be imitated by man. Since the great religious texts were written (and even before), most writers of essays (from Cicero to Martin Luther and beyond) and of aphorisms about translation have preferred sense-for-sense to word-for-word translation. Translations were often seen in a bad light, for instance as traitors or as beautiful but unfaithful women (the seventeenth-century *belles infidèles*, see Perrot d'Ablancourt 1654/1997 and Zuber 1968), being either too free or too literal. In the theatre, 'literals', as they are called by directors or the established playwrights who use 'lits' as the basis for their versions, may even include the mistranslation of false friends or *faux amis* – translating *actuellement* (Fr) or *aktuell* (G) as *actually*, rather than the correct *currently* or *topical*, is the typical example. These are the source of deceptions – though in fact, like puns, they often conceal truths – but also of the precious merriment in translation.

From the Renaissance onwards, translations of poetry and of historical works achieved some prominence. From the beginning of the nineteenth century, the Romantics, with their interest in local cultures, began to take a more detailed and scrupulous interest in translation which was close and even faithful, following both the language and the philosophy of their authors. Amongst the perceptive writings on translation from that period are those by Friedrich Schleiermacher (1813), Wilhelm von Humboldt (1816) and Shelley (1821). Though Schleiermacher never sufficiently indicated the criteria for making the right choice between the two methods, his figurative distinction between literal and free translation was historic and influential: 'Either the translator leaves the author in peace as much as possible and moves the reader toward him; or he leaves the reader in peace as much as possible and moves the writer toward him' (Schleiermacher 1813/2004: 49). This dictum always influences translators, whether they are aware of it or not, since the more they value the text, ('leaving the author in peace'), the more closely they are likely to translate it.

The outstanding work on translation theory in this linguistic period was the *Essay on the Principles of Translation* by Alexander Fraser Tytler (Lord Woodhouselee) delivered as a lecture to the Royal Society in 1790 and published in successively extended editions in 1791, 1797 and 1813 – see the introduction to the critical edition by Jeffrey Huntsman (Tytler 1978). This was a prescriptive work and included Latin, French, Spanish and English literature in its discussions. Tytler defined a good translation as one in which 'the merit of the original work is so completely transfused into another language as to be as distinctly apprehended, and as strongly felt, by a native of the country to which that language belongs, as it is by those who speak the language of the original work' (Tytler 1797: 14–15, 1978: 15–16; also in Robinson 1997a: 209). From this cognitive proposition, which is close to Nida's later functional equivalence (see below), Tytler (ibid.) derives three rules:

1. That the translation should give a complete transcript of the ideas of the original work.
2. That the style and manner of writing should be of the same character as that of the original.
3. That the translation should have all the ease of original composition.

Tytler tends to assume a virtual identity in the two sets of readership: 'All the ease of original composition' indicates an elegant classical Augustan style of translating, which may be quite remote from the 'style and manner' of this or that original text. However, the strength of the book lies in its numerous witty and caustic examples. The most memorable is Tytler's criticism of Voltaire's translation of Hamlet's 'To be or not to be' soliloquy, where the original and the translation are quoted in full. The Hamlet references are not indicated in detail, but it is not difficult to spot them:

> How wonderfully has he [Voltaire] metamorphosed, how miserably disfigured him [Shakespeare]! In the original we have the perfect picture of a mind deeply agitated, giving vent to its feelings in broken starts of utterance, and in language which plainly indicates that the speaker is reasoning solely with his own mind, and not with any auditor. In the translation, we have a formal and connected harangue, in which it would appear, that the author [Voltaire], offended with the abrupt manner of the original ... has corrected, as he thought, those defects of the original, and given union, strength and precision to this philosophical argument.
>
> (Tytler 1797: 368, 1978: 376)

Tytler then lists Voltaire's numerous additions. Hamlet becomes 'a thorough sceptic and freethinker' and expresses doubts about the existence of a God; he treats priests as liars and hypocrites, and the Christian religion as a system which debases human nature:

> *Dieux justes, s'il en est –*
> *De nos prêtres menteurs bénir l'hypocrisie*
> *Et d'un héros guérrier, fait un Chrêtien timide*[1] *–*
>
> Now, who gave Mr Voltaire a right thus to transmute the pious and superstitious Hamlet into a modern *philosophe* and *esprit fort*? Whether the French author meant by this transmutation to convey to his countrymen a favourable idea of our English bard we cannot pretend to say; but we may at least affirm that he has not conveyed a just one.
>
> (Tytler 1797: 373–4, 1978: 380–81)

Tytler's criticism demonstrates a precision, a regard for the truth and a moral enthusiasm that I find exemplary. Further, Tytler is particularly acute in pursuing and discussing the generalizations about translation difficulties formulated by other writers: thus, in correspondence with Tytler and in his own book, *Preliminary Dissertations to a New Translation of the Gospels* (1789), George Campbell noted that there were words in every language that corresponded imperfectly with any word in another language, notably those which related to morals, the passions and the feelings (see also Kelly 2005: 75). Whilst the basic meanings of *virtue* (goodness), *temperance* (moderation) and *mercy* (exemption from punishment) have always been clear, the meaning of *virtus* (Latin) is (culturally) limited to 'courage in combat', the English *temperance* in time and place (e.g. *temperance hotel*) to 'abstinence from alcohol', and *mercy/misericordia* to 'pity'. The list can be extended to words of feeling which at one time or another have been associated with cultural stereotypes and which have been borrowed as neologisms by other languages: *hooligan* (English into many languages); *machismo* (Spanish, aggressively/ostentatiously male), *mañana* (Spanish, dilatoriness); *chauvinism* (French, first jingoism then sexism); *Schlamperei, Schlampigkeit* (German, sloppiness); *sympathique* (French, agreeable); are illustrative examples.

Tytler is also perceptive on such subjects as the concision of Latin (1797: 96), the translation of changes of style (ibid.: 97) and mood, idiomatic phrases (ibid.: 135), antiquated and newly coined terms, naïve humour (ibid.: 183–4), parody, comic verse and lyrical poetry (ibid.: 123–34). He believes that the genius of a translator should be akin to that of the original author – the best translations of poems have been translated by poets – but disclaims any idea that a translator should be as great as his author; a translator's particular talent is that of creative interpretation.

Over a century and a half later, Vladimir Nabokov stated that translating should be defined as 'rendering, as closely as the associative and syntactical capacities of another language allow, the exact contextual meaning of the original' (Nabokov 1964: vii–viii), but he often violated his own definition, producing such lines as 'She, to look back not daring, accelerated her hasty step'. He was complying with his concept of 'constructional translation', where the primary sense of all the words of the original are translated as though out of context, and the word order of the original is approximately retained. In fact, he stated 'to my ideal of literalism, I sacrificed everything – elegance, euphony, clarity, good taste, modern usage, even grammar' (ibid.). In return, he provided the 'pyramids of notes' for which he has become famous, which he, preceding my own insistence on notes as the translator's obligation and on a preface as the emblem of his/her identity, sees as a separate but integral part of the translation which uniquely establishes the translator's presence in the translation. I believe that Nabokov was translating for scholarly readers who knew no Russian and would be able, with the help of his notes, to construct an accurate poetic image of Pushkin's poem; he was also attempting to efface the many fanciful and romantic images of Pushkin current at the time.

It is worthwhile to highlight, amongst others, the key writings on language and translation by Walter Benjamin, Ludwig Wittgenstein and George Steiner. In his 'The task of the translator' (1923/2004), Benjamin based his theory of translation on the concept of a universal pure language which expressed universal thought; within this circumference, languages complemented and borrowed from each other when translating (such as ' "Where's the birthday child?", as the Germans say'). He favoured literal translation of syntax as well as words, but not of sentences: 'For if the sentence is the wall before the language of the original, literalness is the arcade' (1923/2004: 81). He allotted no role whatsoever to the reader.

The linguistic philosopher Ludwig Wittgenstein's famous statement (1958/73: 20) 'For a large class of cases – though not for all – in which we employ the word "meaning", it can be defined thus: the meaning of a word is its use in the language', was important in excluding any external influence on the meaning of a text apart from its context. However, he ignored the fact that a word is usually first met and interpreted by and in its context and is rarely checked for its appropriate meaning in a reliable, up-to-date dictionary, thus inviting misunderstandings or mistranslations which may persist for many years.

George Steiner's *After Babel* (first edition, 1975) included perhaps the last translation theory during the linguistic stage. He described a fourfold 'hermeneutic motion' – trust, penetration, embodiment and restitution, implicitly sexual in allusion – to represent the act of translation; he optimistically thought it would supersede the 'sterile triadic model [literalism, paraphrase, free imitation] which has dominated the history and theory of the subject' (Steiner 1975/98: 319). But it has not: the overriding model, which has been sterile, if not differentiated, as Douglas Robinson pointed out in *The Translator's Turn* (1991), has been dualistic.

Steiner writes superb translation criticism but lacks the solid Johnsonian commonsense a critic should have, for example, when, forgetting Paul Celan's poetry, he declared the German language irreparable after Auschwitz (Steiner 1967: 101). However, he was probably the first critic to observe (1975/98: 437–48) that when a composer sets music to words, she is performing an act of translation, which is in fact the third of Ramon Jakobson's three kinds of translation (1959/2004), the intersemiotic (see section 1.3). Intersemiotic translation converts one mode of communication into another, in this case retaining both modes (music and language) with singular force. Thus, the words: *Ich sinke, Ihr Lieben, ich komme* [I am sinking, you dear ones, I am coming], are given a unique, unforgettable pathos when set to music by Franz Schubert in *Totengräbers Heimweh* [Gravedigger's Homesickness] (1825).

2.1.2 THE COMMUNICATIVE STAGE

After the Second World War, language study began to morph from philology, with its connotation of the Old World, literary and classical, into linguistics, with connotations of fact, modernism, the real world and perhaps the United States. Translation gradually became mainly a recognized profession concerned with technical, specialized, non-literary texts; as a literary occupation, it was almost always freelance and generally underpaid. During the linguistic stage, translation theory was invariably literary, or 'documentary'. In the communicative stage, most translation theory became non-literary.

Notwithstanding attempts at an 'integrated' theory of translation (Snell-Hornby 1988/95; see also Hatim and Mason 1990), in my opinion a distinction has to be made between (a) 'imaginative' or 'literary' translation, which is concerned with humanistic subjects and specifically with poems, short stories, novels and plays, and may call on a single readership (for a poem) or a substantial audience (for a play) and is often related to connotative meaning; and (b) factual or non-literary translation, the domain of science and of verifiable knowledge, often related to the denotative content of the encyclopaedia. The first is figurative and allegorical and is marked by original metaphor and other tropes; the second is bound by the exterior world, which is accessed by way of more standard metaphor and literal language. Writing about the interior connotative world of the mind (a rose is beauty, freshness, a deep odour) is quite different from writing about the real exterior world of denotation ('A rose is a rose is a rose', as Gertrude Stein wrote so memorably in the poem *Sacred Emily*, 1922). In both kinds of translation, it is useful to practice 'interior thinking', in the sense of Lev Vygotsky's *Thought and Language* (1962), as well as to think aloud, checking the natural speech rhythms of what one has written. Where translators need to visualize (that is, to see in their mind) either a factual or an imaginary scene or action, often reshaping a memory of their own, they often also have to 'sonorize' an imaginary and particularly a literary action or scene. 'Sonorize' is here used to mean 'hearing the voices of the dead or the living, as well as the cries or the sounds in the mind'. Whilst translators know that the names and titles in a factual text really exist, in a literary text they have to verify the existence of any geographical and contemporary or historical names they do not recognize. They have to find out whether these names currently change in the target language (e.g. French *Lac Léman* to English *Lake Geneva*; Czech *Praha* to English *Prague*), or follow the present and 'definitive' trend of reverting to their 'native' source-language versions (e.g. French *Marseille* no longer *Marseilles* in English, but still *Marsiglia* in Italian).[2] However, if a proper name is a neologism, which would be more common in an 'imaginative' than in a factual text, it should be closely but 'neologistically' translated in accordance with:

- its likely sense, e.g. *Adam Lambsbreath* (in Stella Gibbons' *Cold Comfort Farm*, 1932) as *Lammsatem* (German translation);
- its sound, e.g. *Nettle Flitch* (ibid.) as *Nettelflitsch* (German);
- or its combination of sound and sense, e.g. *Starkadder* as *Starkwapper* (German).

In principle, a valid factual text is translated accurately where there are no feasible alternatives; alternatives only inevitably present themselves where there are plain semantic gaps in the target language. Notable examples are most idioms and slang and what seems to the English-language user the inexplicable absence in many languages of words for *policy, waist, knuckle, prim, shin* and so on. An imaginative text is interpreted and so translated in various ways, but there are always limitations to the area of choice which can only depend on the particular thought and language of the translation. In these cases, a translation error is usually easier to indicate definitely ('this is wrong'), than a correct translation choice ('this is right').

The communicative stage in translation was heralded by the worldwide showing of the Nuremberg Trials. Translation and interpreting became world news for perhaps the first time. It was also in this period that 'linguisticians', notably Eugene Nida in the USA, J.C. Catford in the UK, the Leipzig School in East Germany (Otto Kade, Albrecht Neubert and the contributors to the journal *Fremdsprachen*) and J.-P. Vinay and J. Darbelnet in Quebec, began to turn their attention to translation as a form of applied linguistics. Most prominently, Eugene Nida, a well-known American linguist(ician) and Bible translator, was the first writer on translation to apply linguistics to translation. With his theory of 'dynamic', later 'functional', equivalence, he introduced into translation a third player, namely the readership, which had previously been virtually identified with the translator, or with a vague, imaginary person. Nida (1964: 160) contrasted two types of translation:

1. **Functional equivalence**. 'The message of the original text is so transported into the receptor language that the response of the receptor is essentially like that of the original receptors'. The standard Biblical example is 'He gave them a hearty handshake all round'.
2. **Formal correspondence** (Nida and Taber 1969).[3] The features of the form of the source text are mechanically reproduced in the receptor language. Typically, formal correspondence distorts the grammatical and stylistic patterns of the receptor language, and so potentially distorts the message and misinforms the reader. The standard example is 'He gave each of them a holy kiss'.

Note that 'equivalence' implies close resemblance, whilst 'correspondence' indicates a matching of identity between ST and TT. The latter immediately creates syntactic/semantic distortion; a translation of the French *J'adore la beauté*, for instance, would not normally be *I adore the beauty*.

In his two seminal works, *Toward a Science of Translating* (Nida 1964) and *The Theory and Practice of Translation* (Nida and Taber 1969), Nida pointed out that both dynamic equivalence and formal correspondence could vary, the first in strength of effect, the second in degree of resemblance, and that they could overlap where the form in one language approximately followed the form in the second. He overlooked the significance of the familiarization effect which, through numerous repetitions and some background knowledge, can make a strange translation sound natural in the target language (e.g. that of Shakespeare's Sonnet 18, *Shall I compare thee to a summer's day,* the pleasant connotation of which may not initially work in a language such as Arabic, where the concept 'summer's day' tends to connote excessive, uncomfortable heat).

In formulating functional equivalence, Nida, who is the most influential world figure in translation, produced the first important theory of communicative translation. He has made numerous other contributions to translation theory, particularly in the fields of socio-linguistics, grammatical and discourse analysis, and componential analysis. In his *Componential Analysis of Meaning* (1975), Nida usefully discriminates between the general and the distinguishing components of lexical items. The technique can be of use to a translator, and may become intuitive and instinctive in the many cases when a descriptive word in the source language (e.g. German *stürzen*) is not adequately translated by a single word in the target language (a fact often overlooked in the dictionaries), and is better split into an idiom or two or three words (*fall+suddenly/heavily/dramatically*). In cases, particularly in imaginative texts, where emphasis or ellipsis appears to distort the word order, theorists such as Tesnière (e.g. 1959), Helbig (e.g. Helbig and Schenckel 1969) and Newmark (1988) have shown that the sense can be sourced when the grammatical terms are 'semanticized'. An example from Heinrich Mann's great *Der Untertan* [Man of Straw]:

Und gefällig schrie das Häuflein mit. Diederich aber, ein Sprung in den Einspanner und los, hinterdrein.
[And obligingly shouted the little crowd at the same time. Diederich however, a jump into the one-horse carriage and away, behind there]
The little crowd obligingly echoed Diederich's cry, but he, jumping into the one-horse carriage, started off in pursuit.

Note that, in the 'natural' translation, the noun *Sprung* ['jump'] and the adverbs *los* ['away'] and *hinterdrein* ['behind there'] have been transposed into the verb forms *jumping* and *started off in pursuit*.[4]

Some years later, Juliane House (1977; see also Chapter 3) produced her theory of (a) 'overt' translation, where the emphasis is on the 'universal' meaning of the text, and the reader is not being specifically addressed, and (b) 'covert' translation, where the translation has the status of an original source text in the target culture, and a 'cultural filter' focussed on the target culture has been passed through the original in the process of translating. A cultural filter (see also Chapter 5), which anticipates the modern-day concept of 'localization' (see Chapter 6), can be crudely exemplified as the translation of French *vin* by German *Bier* or English *beer* as the national drink, though this instance is rather old-fashioned. House's *Model for Translation Quality Assessment* (1977) was followed by her comprehensive *Translation Quality Assessment: A model revisited* (1997), which, in its scathing review of the extenuating, consumer-oriented German translation of Daniel Goldhagen's *Hitler's Willing Executioners* (1996), puts a particular emphasis on the ethical aspect of translation.

In *Approaches to Translation* (Newmark 1981), I introduced the concepts of (a) semantic translation, defining it as translation at the author's level, the attempt to render, as closely as the semantic and syntactic structures of the target language allow, the exact contextual meaning of the original; and (b) communicative translation, which is, at the readership's level, an attempt to produce on its readers an effect as close as possible to that obtained on the readers of the original; it renders the contextual meaning of the original in such a way that both content and language are readily acceptable and comprehensible to the readership.

Note that Nida's functional equivalence and my communicative translation are identical, but that House's covert translation, which is similar, stresses the different culture in each of the two languages, rather than the effect on the reader. Nida's formal correspondence is a distortion of sensible translation; House's overt translation and my semantic translation resemble each other, but I put more stress on the possibilities of literal translation. In these theoretical pairs, the text typology is important: Nida bases his theories on Biblical texts, but they are not intended to be confined to them; House's covert translation uses scientific, tourist and financial texts as examples; her overt translation has religious (Karl Barth), political (Churchill) and literary texts, the latter a lovely excerpt from Sean O'Casey's *The End of the Beginning*. I use an extract from Proust for semantic translation and a political column for communicative translation. I stress that the language in semantic translation is serious and authoritative; in communicative translation, facts and ideas are more important than language, but if the original is well written it should be closely translated, whatever the text.

Nida's, House's and my dualistic theories covered literary and non-literary texts. In their choice of appropriate examples, they were influenced, as was Katharina Reiss, an important figure for popular text translation, and Christiane Nord (1991/2005) (documentary and instrumental translation), by the psychologist Karl Bühler, who distinguished the three functions of language as the expressive, the descriptive and the appellative. Reiss (1971/2000) links these functions to 'expressive', 'informative' and 'appellative' text types and to topic or domain text 'varieties' or genres (a novel, a scientific report, an advertisement, etc., see Chapter 3). Whilst this typology encouraged translators to use appropriate language, it incurred the risk, particularly in the 'Americanized' business and tourism areas, of promoting the overuse of typically stale, standardized expressions in translation.

Later, in *About Translation* (Newmark 1991) and many later publications, I attempted to soften the rigidity of such schemes by suggesting a series of translational correlations, such as:

1. The more important/serious the language (keywords, collocations, emphases) of the original, the more closely it should be translated.

2. The less important the language of a text, the less closely it need be translated.

This second correlation refers to factual texts, where a variety of directional synonyms or paraphrases (e.g. *indicate, refer to, show, demonstrate*) may be used fairly freely, provided that the essential qualities of the action, the facts and the ideas are accurately rendered.

Probably the most important book on translation that appeared during this communicative stage was *Stylistique comparée du français et de l'anglais* by the French Canadian linguists J.-P. Vinay and J. Darbelnet (1958), translated (1995) as *The Comparative Stylistics of French and English* by Juan Sager and M.-J. Hamel. Its influence on the literature, and on the teaching of translation, was enormous in North America and Europe. It was followed, almost as a model, by Alfred Malblanc (1963), and by Gerardo Vázquez Ayora (1977). It also influenced W. Friederich's excellent *Die Technik des Übersetzens* (1977).

Vinay and Darbelnet were concrete, clear and even dramatic:

> The story begins on the New York–Montreal highway...KEEP TO THE RIGHT — NO PASSING — SLOW MEN AT WORK ... and it finishes in Paris .... And here, before our delighted eyes, the desired translations pass us by: PRIORITÉ À DROITE — DÉFENSE DE DOUBLER — RALENTIR TRAVAUX.
>
> (Vinay and Darbelnet 1958/1995: 1, 6)

Note that the literal English versions of the French, which would have helped the student, are ignored: 'Priority on right – It is forbidden to overtake – To slow down. Jobs/works'.

All terms used are explained in the key concepts and the book is abundantly indexed, as all reference books should be, for quick consultation. Vinay and Darbelnet insist that translation is 'an exact discipline' (ibid.: 7) and only partially an art, but they appear unaware that they are only discussing non-literary translation and that their references to literary translation, copious but not exemplified, are confined to the contents of their bibliographies. Further, they often ignore the valid alternatives to their suggested translations, so that their discipline, though it aims to be 'scientific', linking with Nida and therefore partly influenced by Chomsky, only ends up as an approximation.

The heart of the book is its seven translation procedures exemplified in tabular form (Table 2.1). This general table of translation procedures, the first of its kind, has been much discussed and criticized. I have to some extent attempted to bring its versions up to date by replacing *Before you can say Jack Robinson* with *In next to no time* and U.S. *Hi!* with *Enjoy your meal!* (idioms and slang are often class- and time-bound). Note that these are examples

TABLE 2.1 Summary of Vinay and Darbelnet's seven translation procedures

Procedure	Lexis	Collocation/Group	Message
1. Loan / Borrowing	Fr. *Bulldozer* En. Fuselage	*Science-fiction* *à la mode*	*Five o'clock tea* Bon voyage
2. Calque	Fr. *Économiquement faible* En. Normal School	Lutetia Palace Governor General	*Compliments de la saison* Take it or leave it
3. Literal translation	Fr. *L'encre* En. (The) ink	*L'encre est sur la table* The ink is on the table	*Quelle heure est-il?* What time is it?
4. Transposition	Fr. *Expéditeur* En. From	*Depuis la revalorisation du bois* Since timber has increased in value	*Défense de fumer* Thank you for not smoking
5. Modulation	Fr. *Peu profond* En. Shallow	*Donnez un peu de votre sang* Give a pint of your blood	*Complet* No vacancies
6. Équivalence	Fr. (mil) *La soupe* En. (mil) Tea	*Comme un chien dans un jeu de quilles* Like a bull in a china shop	*Château de cartes* Hollow triumph
7. Adaptation	Fr. *Cyclisme* Br En. Cricket US En. Baseball	*En un clin d'œil* In next to no time	*Bon appetit!* Enjoy your meal!

Source: translated from Vinay and Darbelnet (1958: 55), adapted from Vinay and Darbelnet (1958/1995: 41).

Note: See the Appendix at the end of the chapter for a back translation of the French examples.

of translation procedures; only Nos. 3, 4 and 5, and the second and third examples in 6 and 7, translate each other; the first examples in 6 and 7 might in one or two contexts be used as examples of equivalent national characteristics, but they could not be used as translations, and 'adaptation', which is commonly used in drama translation to represent cultural transfer, is only used by Vinay and Darbelnet to represent equivalence of situation. Some translation theorists refer to loans or borrowings as 'transference'; to calques as 'through-translations', 'loan-translations' or 'collocational translations'; and to transpositions, which retain the same grammatical structure in the target language or exchange one with another, as 'shifts'. In this context, see J.C. Catford's pioneering work, *A Linguistic Theory of Translation* (1965), which introduced Halliday's influential systemic-functional terminology and concepts into translation theory.

According to Vinay and Darbelnet, modulations may denote the replacement of the abstract by the concrete (e.g. *le dernier étage* ['the last floor'] > *the top floor*); cause by effect (e.g. *échappe a l'analyse* ['escapes analysis'] > *baffles* or *defies analysis*); the means by the result (*firing party* > *peloton d'éxécution* ['execution platoon']); the part by the whole, or other part (e.g. *envoyer un mot* ['send a word'] > *send a line*); a change of point of view (e.g. *bière sous pression* ['beer under pressure'] > *draught beer*; reversal of terms (e.g. *je vous le laisse* ['I leave it to you'] > *you can have it*). However, its standard category is a positive translated by a double negative, such as St Paul's *I am a citizen of no mean city*. This negated contrary, is instanced in *peu profound* ['little deep'] > *shallow*, where *shallow* is a lexical gap in French, or in *il n'a pas caché que ...* ['he did not conceal that'] > *he made it plain that ...*; however, there are also plenty of other positive or double negative options. The double negative is always semantically weaker than the positive, unless the emphasis of speech shines through it.

Vinay and Darbelnet opened up a huge area of debate – the details and the essence – as no authors had previously done in translation, discussing, with a wealth of texts and their annotated translations, cultural impacts on five different regional dialects: British English, American English, Canadian English, metropolitan French and Canadian French. If we accept, as I do, Ladmiral's (1979) distinction between *ciblistes* ('targeteers'), translators inclined towards the target language, and *sourciers* ('sourcerers'), translators inclined towards the source language, then Vinay and Darbelnet, who are inclined to the former, though they make no distinction between imaginative and realistic texts or language, are open to both.

2.1.3 *The Functional and Ethical Stages of Translation Theory*

I conclude with a few more remarks about the third and fourth stages of translation theory. Functionalism (see Chapter 4) set in as a practical reaction against the academic detail of extensive linguistic analysis. It simplified translation and emphasized keywords. It concentrated on satisfying the customer or readership, treating the text, whatever its nature, as a business commission (see Holz-Mänttäri 1984), and, in Reiss's classic *Möglichkeiten und Grenzen der Übersetzungskritik* (1971, translated as *Translation Criticism: Potential and limitations*, 2000), offered a blithe romance called *Daddy Long-Legs* (Webster 1922) as its token literary text; the aesthetics and the sounds of language were ignored. In the post-modern way, Reiss does not differentiate between high and low culture.

Now, at the fourth, and, I believe, final stage of translation theory, the situation is transformed. The world has become driven by mass economic and political migrations – intercontinental, intracontinental and transcontinental. The scope and the size of the international organizations, the United Nations and the European Union, continue to increase. International non-governmental organizations, such as Amnesty International, and global charities, such as Oxfam, Action Aid and *Médecins sans Frontières,* have become more politicized. 'Intervention' has replaced 'interference' as a political term, and 'moral' and 'ethical' are no longer embarrassing or priggish epithets. Since 1945, the number of nation states, to a large extent based on national languages, has increased significantly, but the power of the nation state is declining. The result has been a universal increase in the importance of both general language competence and social and authoritative translation, as well as of the availability and the necessity of a global lingua franca, usually English.

Foreign language learning can no longer be regarded as a special gift or skill, but is a necessity. In my opinion, translators also have to become aware – note this is a looser variation on the age-old dualism – that there are basically two kinds of translation: (a) social and non-literary translation, the conveyance of messages, where the injunction and the information are the essential components, where the target language text may be more concise in some places (say, to eliminate waffle) and more explicit in others, say to clarify technical and/or cultural references; and (b) authoritative and serious translation, where the focus may range from the literary, the imaginative and the aesthetic, to the ethical, the non-literary and the plain. Here, in both kinds of translation, the translator establishes her identity, outside the text, first by commenting on the text and her interpretation in a preface and, where necessary, in footnotes, ensuring that mis-statements, prejudiced language, illogical conclusions and irrelevancies, in Gutt's (1991) comprehensive sense of relevance (see Chapter 4), are clearly shown up; second, by using fresh language in social texts, and by fusing her own style with the original's in imaginative texts. She pursues the grace and elegance that appears to be uniquely stressed in Chinese translation theory, notably by the influential polymath Yan Fu (Chan 2004) and by Liu Miqing (Chan and Pollard 1995), who insist on the close link between aesthetics and translation. In creatively translating serious imaginative texts, the translator observes the stresses and pauses signalled by the punctuation system and the word order of the source language text and respects peculiarities of syntax and lexis within the bounds of common sense, transforming the inevitable semantic gaps in her own way – but there are no rules and there is a place for surprising intuitive solutions. In both social and imaginative texts, the translator's endeavour is to modify her own style, which appears in her most commonly used keywords, idioms, epithets and connectives, and to abate the buzz words and the cultural marks of her time, though neither can be eliminated. However, she is responsible for ensuring in her rendering that the readership absorbs as much of the author's mind and intention as is possible.

In both kinds of translation, the pursuit of the truth is the translator's supreme obligation.

Appendix

Table 2.2 Vinay and Darbelnet's seven translation procedures, with literal translations of the French examples

Procedure	Lexis	Collocation/Group	Message
1. Loan / Borrowing	Fr. *Bulldozer* En. Fuselage	*Science-fiction* à la mode [*in the fashion*]	*Five o'clock tea* Bon voyage [*Good journey*]
2. Calque	Fr. *Economically weak* En. Normal School	*Lutetia Palace* Governor General	*Compliments of the season* Take it or leave it
3. Literal translation	Fr. *The ink* En. (The) ink	*The ink is on the table* The ink is on the table	*What time is-it?* What time is it?
4. Transposition	Fr. *Sender* En. From	*Since the revaluing of wood* Since timber has increased in value	*Prohibition to smoke* Thank you for not smoking
5. Modulation	Fr. *Little deep* En. Shallow	*Give a little of your blood* Give a pint of your blood	*Full* No vacancies
6. Equivalence	Fr. (mil) *The soup* En. (mil) Tea	*Like a dog in a game of skittles* Like a bull in a china shop	*House of cards* Hollow triumph
7. Adaptation	Fr. *Cycling* Br En. Cricket US En. Baseball	*In a blink of the eye* In next to no time	*Good appetite!* Enjoy your meal!

Notes

1 Literally, 'Just Gods, if there be any –
Of our lying priests to bless the hypocrisy
And of a warrior hero, makes a timid Christian –

2 On this point, see also the discussion on voice in Mossop (2007: 30) and the alternative place-name translations *Quebec/Québec* and *Bombay/Mumbai*.
3 In Nida (1964) this is termed 'formal equivalence'.
4 See Newmark (1988: 127) for further discussion.

3
TRANSLATING TEXT IN CONTEXT

BASIL HATIM

3.0 INTRODUCTION

Textuality is a multifaceted phenomenon, and textual practices are as varied as the contexts they serve, subsuming a wide range of structures beyond the single sentence. In translation studies, the challenge for years has been to identify these macro-structures and to define their precise role in the process of translation and interpreting. This has specifically meant that we first need to differentiate between such contextual templates as the 'register' membership of texts (in terms of field, tenor, mode), on the one hand, and, on the other,

- the variety of rhetorical purposes served by 'texts';
- the range of conventional 'genres' systematically utilized; and
- the various attitudes conveyed in and through 'discourse'.

Text and the notion of rhetorical purpose, and genre as a conventionally recognized 'communicative event', are ultimately seen as facilitators 'enabling' discoursal 'attitudes' to be realized and appreciated. Discursive activity is defined in terms of the perspectives taken on such issues of language in socio-cultural life as globalization, the environment, racism, gender, the commoditization of education and so on.

In this chapter, these various communicative resources are examined specifically from the vantage point of the translator[1] and in terms of how the effectiveness of activities such as reading and writing (which are crucial to any act of translating) can only be enhanced by a context-sensitive approach to texts.

3.1 OVERVIEW

For decades, applied linguists have devoted a great deal of time and effort to examining such aspects of the communicative process as the register membership of texts (Ghadessy 1988), the text as a unit of communication (Halliday and Hasan 1989), discourse as an aspect of language use (Coulthard 1985) and genre as a conventionalized 'communicative event' (Swales 1990). However, overuse and the varied applications of these concepts seem to have contributed to a state of unsettling confusion regarding how the various categories might best be understood and used. This chapter is an attempt to disentangle from the perspective of the translator some of the ramifications surrounding the use of these terms and the interrelationships that obtain among them, seen as distinct yet complementary elements of both the communication and the translation process. In the following discussion, it is suggested that situational appropriateness established by registers, together with textual well-formedness, generic integrity and a discourse perspective, may more helpfully be seen as layer upon layer of 'socio-textual practice', in which language users constantly engage in their attempt to create or make sense of texts.

With this aim in mind, a heuristic (and necessarily hypothetical) language processing model is discussed. This is informed by a range of approaches to the study of language in use, prominent among which are text linguistics (Beaugrande 1980), systemic-functional linguistics (Halliday 1985/94; Halliday and Matthiessen 2004), critical discourse analysis (Fairclough 1989/2001, 2003) and contrastive rhetoric (Connor 1996).

3.2 Text in Context

Contexts tend to shape and are in turn shaped by texts. With 'text' seen as 'language' and 'context' as 'social structure', Fowler describes the relationship in the following terms:

> There is a dialectical interrelationship between language and social structure: the varieties of linguistic usage are both products of socio-economic forces and institutions – reflexes of such factors as power relations, occupational roles, social stratifications, etc. – and practices which are instrumental in forming and legitimating the same social forces and institutions.
>
> (Fowler 1981: 21)

Thus, in subtle and intricate ways, context (subsuming socio-economic forces and institutions and a set of practices legitimating these) acts on and interacts with text (i.e. language in use). This interaction is set in motion by what is aptly called 'textualization', a process which impinges on both the production and reception of texts and which at one and the same time involves a set of procedures (i.e. strategies) and a diverse range of products (artifacts) generically known as 'texts'.

But to use 'textual' in this all-purpose manner cannot be helpful for the practitioner in many an applied linguistic pursuit, including, of course, translating. To see this specifically from the perspective of the translator, there seem to be at least four distinct yet related senses of 'textuality', yielding four different macro-structures which we seek to examine here: register (primarily addressing the need to communicate appropriately across professional boundaries), text (organized on rhetorical lines), discourse (negotiated on attitudinal, ideological grounds) and genre (framing the communicative transaction).

3.2.1 REGISTER MEMBERSHIP

Through the process of 'textualization', then, we generally aim to produce language that communicates efficiently, effectively and appropriately. But what exactly is it that we textualize? What is the process part of? What is it ultimately driven by? What is it ultimately intended to achieve? To answer these questions, it might be helpful to consider how textualization has gone wrong in the sample of concocted language use shown in Box 3.1, and reflect on what it is that disorients the reader in dealing with a sequence of sentences 'textualized' in this way. At some level, this sample exhibits a semblance of 'textualization', and the outcome is certainly 'cohesive' (for example, look at how the various elements in italics establish continuity of surface forms). Yet the text does not make sense (i.e. is not coherent). The text is conceptually fragmented and underlying logical connectivity is lacking. This is the kind of problem that can be dealt with by invoking the notion of 'register'.

Register refers to consistent variation according to the 'use' of language (Halliday *et al.* 1964). It is a kind of 'restricted language' (Firth 1957), seen within a specific 'universe of discourse' (Pike 1967). In Sample 1 (Box 3.1) for example, the rather 'peculiar' wording of *the vehicle was seen proceeding down the main street in a westerly direction* is accounted for in terms of a particular subject matter and a particular level of formality which we associate with the 'language' of police reporting. This 'register' differs from that of *leading to a spacious and well-appointed residence with considerable potential* (the language of estate agents), which in turn differs from a hairdressers' register embedded within a 'fictional' register: *She went to work, mixing up the six-ten with two parts of 425, and dabbing the mixture through 6 ezimeshes*, and so on.

Different 'uses of language' are thus involved in this example. These differences may be identified in at least three areas of contextual activity:

Box 3.1 Sample 1

The vehicle was seen proceeding down the main street in a westerly direction *leading to* a spacious and well-appointed residence with considerable potential. *She* went to work, mixing up the six-ten with two parts of 425, and dabbing the mixture through 6 ezimeshes. '*This one* has a fine shaggy nose and a fruity bouquet with a flowery head', *she said. He* managed to get into a good position, just kissing the cushion. *He* said 'Just pop up onto the couch and we will see what we can do'. *She* pulled down the menu, chose the command by using the cursor, then quit. *She* said to knead well, roll into a ball and leave overnight to rise. *Instead, he* mulched well, turned over and left the beds to settle. *Good progress made, but* concentration sometimes rather poor; more effort required if success is to be expected in the important months ahead.

Carter *et al.* 1997 (emphasis added)

what is actually taking place (e.g. reporting an incident versus advertising a property), who is taking part (e.g. police reporter versus estate agent) and what part language is playing (e.g. written-like versus spoken-like) (Halliday 1978: 31). These aspects, respectively referred to as 'field' (or subject matter), 'tenor' (related to level of formality) and 'mode' (involving various aspects of textuality such as cohesion), collectively make up the register membership of a text. Rudimentary as these categories may seem, they have nonetheless underpinned much valuable work under what has come to be known as LSP, or Language for Specific Purposes. Translation studies has followed suit and, according to Hatim and Mason (1990: 83), for example, the working assumption has been that:

> [a]ny change in any of the parameters which define the register membership of a text (e.g. field, tenor) will produce changes in the language used in that text, and consequently will have to be reflected in the translation.

However, the debate has continued to this day regarding whether translating activity consists solely of matching SL and TL registers in accordance with intuitively perceived or externally defined 'stylistic' conventions (legalese, journalese, etc.), and whether texts can be reduced to compilations of situational variables (field, tenor and mode values), recognition of which is sufficient to establish equivalence.

In posing such questions, many translation scholars (e.g. Baker 1992; Fawcett 1997) have taken traditional register analysis to task, and the general trend has veered more towards texts seen as the minimal units of translation. Before we deal with the various revisions which register theory has undergone. Since the 1960s, it is perhaps instructive to cast a glance at the related issue of text type and text function. This is a distinction recognized by a functionalist trend which questions the validity of the register-inspired equivalence paradigm of the time and is best represented in the early stages by the work of Katharina Reiss and Hans Vermeer and by *skopos* theory.

3.3 TEXT FUNCTION AND TRANSLATION *SKOPOS*

Functionalism has been an influential trend in modern translation studies. The new focus on translation purpose advocated by functionalists emerged in Germany in the 1980s under the general designation of '*skopos* theory' and is associated most notably with Hans Vermeer (e.g. 1978, 1989; Reiss and Vermeer 1984).

Skopos (Greek: 'purpose', 'goal'), is an appropriate name for a theory which focusses on such aspects of the translation process as interactional dynamics and pragmatic purpose. The theory holds that the way the target text eventually shapes up is determined to a great extent by the 'function', or '*skopos*', intended for it in the target context. Such a strategy can and often does run counter to orthodox equivalence-based procedures since, under *skopos*, the end essentially justifies the means.

The *skopos* idea relies on key concepts in pragmatics, such as intention and action. Two basic assumptions are entertained:

Skopos Rule 1: Interaction is determined by its purpose.
Skopos Rule 2: Purpose varies according to the text receiver.

Such a framework for translator decisions is governed by a number of factors, both textual and contextual. One such is audience design, which accounts for the way a target text is intended to be received. This largely determines which translation strategy is most appropriate. Different purposes may be served by different translation strategies: translation proper, paraphrase (thin glossing) or re-editing (thick glossing), may attend to different communicative needs.

But who actually decides what the *skopos* of a particular translation is? A straight answer to this question has been 'the client', who initiates the process in cases where translation is done by assignment, and supplies the translation instructions or 'brief'. But 'translation briefs' are not always sufficiently detailed regarding what strategy to use, what type of translation would be most suitable, etc. To deal with such problems, *skopos* theory entertains the general assumption that there will generally be a 'standard' way (sanctioned by the professional community of translators, for example) of proceeding to accomplish a particular translation task. This is also the case where no 'client' is particularly envisaged and where no purpose is specified.

Thus, discussions of 'purpose' in recent translation studies (e.g. Nord 1991, 2005) have tended to concentrate on the notion of the purpose of the translation to hand as stipulated by the translation commission. But, as Reiss foresaw many years ago, this kind of *skopos* is just one element in a configuration of purposes involved in the process of translation or interpreting. To identify the range of purposes, we must invoke rhetorical, functional and translational criteria and relate these (and the range of purposes which emanate from them) to such categories as 'context of situation', 'context of culture', 'rhetorical purpose' and so on. This gave rise to the notion of a text typology, originally intended by Reiss as a set of guidelines for the practical translator. As we shall see shortly in greater detail, three basic types of text are proposed and are distinguished one from the other in terms of factors such as 'intention', or rhetorical purpose, and 'function', or the use to which texts are put:

- 'informative' texts, which convey information
- 'expressive' texts, which communicate thoughts in a creative way
- 'operative' texts, which persuade.

(Reiss 1971/2000)

These types and the contexts served are said to have a direct consequence for the kind of semantic, syntactic and stylistic features used and for the way texts are structured, both in their original form and in the translation.

3.4 THE PROCESS OF TEXTUALIZATION

In the context of the evolution of register analysis, we now see textualization as the specific task of 'mode', an area at the interface between text and context, and one where functional variation of language use is ultimately negotiated. That is, in addition to establishing the spoken-like or written-like character of language use, as the traditional register analyst would have us do, 'mode' may be more helpfully seen in terms of the crucial role which it performs in defining 'what part language is playing' in the interaction. This orientation, treated cursorily by early register theory and practice, must be recognized as vitally important: how else are we to distinguish, for example, between the 'informative' mode of *the vehicle was seen proceeding down the main street in a westerly direction* and the 'persuasive' mode of *leading to a spacious and well-appointed residence with considerable potential*?

In connection with this, it is worth noting that the distinction 'informative' versus 'persuasive' (or 'operative', to use Reiss's term), if properly defined, can account for the bulk of what writers and readers do with texts, and consequently for what we mostly translate. Such distinctions must therefore be more widely and explicitly adopted as the basis of the selection, grading and presentation of translator training materials in areas such as specialized translation of academic or business communication.

To push communication forward, then, mode must be seen as functioning in tandem not only with such contextual variables as field and tenor, but also with various textural and structural mechanisms, the sole purpose of which is the construction of cohesive and coherent texts. Within the register membership of a text, mode tends to join forces with tenor, determining the appropriate level of formality, and with field, regulating the level of technicality and thus serving subject matter concerns. Together, the three variables develop what may be called the 'register profile' of a text, a catalogue of features representing the numerous areas of interface between text and context that collectively capture the sense of communicative appropriateness on such grounds as occupation, social distance, rhetorical purpose and communication channel.

3.4.1 REGISTER PROFILE IN TRANSLATION QUALITY ASSESSMENT

This notion of register, enriched by pragmatics, radically changed the way we approached the translation process. A notable attempt in this direction is the model of translation quality assessment proposed in the late 1970s by translation theorist and linguist Juliane House (see also Chapter 2). This model is informed by a theory of register and pragmatic function and is thus primarily concerned with contextual meaning in translation. From this perspective, conveying information, ideas or experience (i.e. 'field', subsuming 'ideational meanings') and using language to establish particular relationships (i.e. 'tenor', subsuming 'interpersonal meanings') form an important part of source and target 'textual profile'. Equivalence is now established on the basis of:

- analysis of the linguistic and situational particularities of source and target texts
- a comparison of the two texts
- an assessment of their relative match.

House (1977/81)

Within this scheme, an important distinction is made between language function and text function. Language function captures how language is used to convey information, express feelings, persuade, etc. This may be illustrated by Karl Bühler's (1934/65) well-known categories relating to the representational, expressive and persuasive functions which underpin Reiss's text types and Halliday's systemic functional grammar. Halliday's ideational, interpersonal and textual components also represent language functions.

As we will see under 'text typologies' shortly, such distinctions have provided the basis for a number of text classifications (e.g. Reiss's 'informative' text). In such typologies, however, language function tends to be equated with text function. In other words, the assumption is entertained that the text is a longer sentence, and what applies to sentences individually can apply to entire texts. According to House (1977/81), this is overly simplistic. Rarely, if ever, do we encounter texts that are purely of this or that type (that is, purely 'ideational' or purely 'interpersonal', for example). The way texts function may thus be more helpfully seen along a cline between two extremes.

Nevertheless, the possibility that one function of language or of text might be predominant in a given sequence of sentences is not ruled out. In her original analysis, House (1977) chose her translation data from texts which were either predominantly ideational (essentially referential) or predominantly interpersonal (non-referential) in function. Eight translations were analysed and found to have been dealt with in different ways. The analysis revealed that two kinds of translation method were at work: covert and overt translation (1977/81: 188).

Covert translation is a mode of text transfer in which the translator seeks to produce a target text that is as immediately relevant for the target reader as the source text is for the source language addressee. Functional equivalence (see Chapter 2) is the goal, and anything which betrays the origin of the translated text is carefully concealed. This strategy is said to work well with source texts which do not rely for their relevance on aspects of the source language and culture such as traditions, societal mores or institutional structures. Examples of texts which lend themselves to a covert translation strategy include advertising, journalistic writing, technical material and, interestingly, a great deal of Bible translation.

Overt translations, on the other hand, cater for situations in which the source text is specifically directed at source culture addressees and can thus be dealt with only within the socio-cultural setting of the original. In dealing with this kind of text, the translator would aim for a narrowly defined form of equivalence, with the target addressee being quite 'overtly' sidelined (1977/81: 188). The target text would be a 'translation' and not a 'second original'; it does not hide the fact that it is a translation. Historic sermons, great political speeches and a substantive body of good literature provide us with examples of this kind of overt translation strategy at work.

The position held by translation theorists such as Christiane Nord (1997) on instrumental versus documentary translation, or Lawrence Venuti (1995) on foreignizing versus domesticating translation, can now be usefully reassessed in terms of whether such dichotomies have really advanced the debate which originally started with distinctions like covert versus overt translation or Peter Newmark's (1981) semantic versus communicative translation. To date, the debate on these and related issues has been far from conclusive. This underlines the need for what James Holmes (1988) called 'research into research', which will evaluate the various models constructed. Such an examination would most probably reveal that the parallels between the various schemes outlined above are so striking that any differences are likely to be merely a matter of focus.

3.5 THE UNIT 'TEXT'

In order for a sequence of sentences to be properly considered a 'text', the sequence would have to function in ways that go beyond register profiles defined exclusively in terms of field's technicality, tenor's formality and mode's spoken versus written orientations, important as these factors are. As suggested above, we need to see mode in terms of higher-level textual criteria which, although still driven by such register variables as formality and technicality, additionally involve a level of 'intentionality' that regulates the overall communicative thrust. To capture this, two options seem to be available to the language user: a situation may either be 'monitored' in a fairly detached and unmediated fashion (serving an informative/reporting function), or 'managed' by attempting to steer the text receiver in a direction favourable to the text producer (serving a persuasive/operative function) (Beaugrande 1980; Reiss 1977).

This level of intentionality (which is pragmatic and negotiable, not an either/or option) yields two basic text types associated in their most idealized forms with the 'informative' kind of detached 'exposition' and the 'persuasive' kind of involved 'argumentation'. The evolution of these text types is regulated by 'intertextuality', a standard of textuality which all well-formed texts must meet.

At a global level, intertextuality relates to the capacity of a text to function as an 'actual' token of a 'virtual' type, in other words, carrying within it traces of the general type to which it belongs. In this way, texts would be intended to serve a particular contextual focus and would be accepted as such, a situation managed by the competent language user on the basis of knowledge of texts in interaction. We immediately recognize a counter-argument when one unfolds (e.g. *Of course tomorrow's meeting of OPEC is formally about prices. The real purpose of the meeting, however, is to salvage the cohesion of the organization;* see Hatim and Mason 1997). This recognition builds on our ability to recall other instances of counter-argumentation we have come across and stored in some textual repertoire.

In addition to intentionality, acceptability and intertextuality, a number of other standards must be met for a sequence of sentences to attain the status of a well-formed text. For example, there are the minimal requirements of cohesion and coherence. Register would thus be just one of many contextual layers regulating language use and, through a judicious deployment of vocabulary and grammar, mediating between 'language in the raw' and a sequence of language elements that serves a particular rhetorical purpose (i.e. language that is 'textured' and 'structured' in a particular goal-directed way). In all of this, there will also be a balanced distribution of known and new information, or so-called 'informativity'. At both clause and text levels, this ensures that texts are effective, efficient and appropriate to a given context (Beaugrande and Dressler 1981).

3.5.1 TEXT TYPOLOGY AND TRANSLATION

These standards of textuality have formed the basis of a number of text typologies in current use within translation studies. We have already alluded to one of the earlier text classifications, the one proposed by translation theorist Katherina Reiss (1976). In this typology, informative, expressive and operative intentions (or rhetorical purposes) and functions (or the uses to which texts are put), are said to have a direct consequence for the kind of semantic, syntactic and stylistic features used and for the way texts are structured, both in their original form and in the translation. Furthermore, Reiss posits a correlation between a given text type and translation method, to ensure that the predominant function of the text is preserved in translation. Thus, what the translator must do in the case of informative texts is to concentrate on establishing semantic equivalence and, secondarily, on connotative meanings and aesthetic values. In the case of expressive texts, the main concern of the translator should be to try and preserve aesthetic effects alongside relevant aspects of the semantic content. Finally, operative texts require the translator to heed the extralinguistic effect which the text is intended to achieve, even if this has to be undertaken at the expense of both form and content.

Another influential text classification is the one originally proposed by Werlich (1976) and subsequently developed and used by a number of translation scholars as the cornerstone of context-sensitive models of translation (e.g. Hatim and Mason 1990). This text typology has certainly avoided the pitfalls of text categorization suffered by earlier approaches, which lean heavily towards the strict end of objective criteria for assessing translation quality. As an approach to translation, Hatim and Mason's (1990) text type model is underpinned by the idea of 'predominant contextual focus' and thus confronts boldly the issue of 'text hybridization' being the norm rather than the exception. With the emphasis on contextual focus, the multifunctionality of all texts is no longer seen as a weakness in text classification, nor indeed as a licence for an 'anything goes' attitude in the production or analysis of texts or translations. For example, it is recognized that, while a distinction may usefully be made between 'expressive' texts and 'informative' texts, texts are rarely if ever one or the other type, purely and simply. On the other hand, it is equally important to recognize that, unless there is a good reason to do otherwise, metaphors in predominantly expressive texts are best rendered metaphorically, while those encountered in predominantly informative texts can be modified or altogether jettisoned, with no detrimental effect on the overall function of the text in translation (Reiss 1971: 62).

3.5.2 THE INSUFFICIENCY OF THE TEXTUAL APPROACH

So far, then, textualization is seen as a process of turning fairly dormant register input (e.g. technical vocabulary) into cohesive and coherent texts, intended to fulfil a variety of rhetorical purposes that may be grouped intertextually under such general headings as 'exposition' and 'argumentation'. The process, however, is still restricted to a number of processes that, by themselves, are simply insufficient to enable a text to take part in the larger interaction entailed by the use of language in social life, and involving a wider range of discursive practices. Within the limitations of mode, textualization is still restricted to:

- determining a set of interactive acts
- establishing sequential relationships between and among these acts
- developing an overall structure for a rather artificial suprasentential entity we call 'text'.

Candlin (1985: viii)

These are necessary but not sufficient conditions for a process as complex as the production and reception of texts that are not only well-formed but also functional, not only cohesive but also coherent. How is it possible, for example, to tell whether *wide-ranging* in the following example means 'varied and interesting' (positive connotations) or 'not focussed and aimless' (negative connotations):

> *the examples that they and other scholars use to illustrate the concept are wide-ranging.*

To bring out the positive or the negative connotations, different lexical forms are available in Arabic, for example, and to make an appropriate choice between the positive *mutanawi'a* [lit. 'varied'] and the negative *'ashwaa'iyya* [lit. 'ad hoc'], the translator would need to invoke not only lexical semantics but a pragmatics of text and, as we will see shortly, of genre and discourse.

3.6 Genre Shifts in Translation

It is not so much the rhetorical purpose of texts that would be compromised in the translation process, although this is always bound to suffer, of course. What is more problematic are the conventional do's and don'ts regulating what we do within a given communicative event: how, for example, the selection of a subjective and intimate personal style which constantly refers to and engages the 'visitor' in a tourist guide (e.g. *The visitor will..., The visitor will...*) is an acceptable genre norm in Arabic but is shunned in English.

At the level of genre, language tends to serve a particular focus on norms surrounding how certain communicative events are conventionally dealt with (e.g. the language of cooking recipes, the academic abstract). In these ritualistically sanctioned text formats, the intention is certainly to serve a range of rhetorical purposes (say, to inform, etc), which is a requirement that must be met for language to function properly at all. The rhetorical purposes catered for, however, are sometimes not ends in themselves, but a means to other communicative ends beyond the specificities of the text type in question. For example, Mills & Boon stories are intended not so much to narrate just any story as to uphold the conventional requirements of a given communicative event, in this case a heart-warming tale of requited love as a 'genre'.

Like text shifts, genre shifts in translation are also relatively common, at times leading to serious language use and translation errors. In dealing with genre, it is particularly important to recognize that changes haphazardly introduced in the translation can irreparably dislocate the text from its intended genre and thus distort the rhetorical structure of the original, a case of what Carl James calls 'genre violation' (1989: 31; see also Bhatia 1993). The solution to this kind of problem must thus obviously be to provide the translator with genre-based experience. Contextual specifications are often regrettably neglected in our training of translators and the focus on (indeed the obsession with) the 'words on the page' must give way to instilling in the trainees an awareness of larger discourse structures and genre specificities.

3.7 DISCOURSE AS SOCIO-TEXTUAL PRACTICE

Seeing text production and reception only in these highly idealized terms of text organization and mapping and even of conventional genre requirements, however, is a methodological convenience at best. In practice, no text can remain in such a state of relative isolation from the facts of socio-cultural life. To be closer to the life world of the language user and to communicate anything meaningful regarding social, cultural or political issues, texts must involve more than organization and mapping procedures or simply the need to uphold conventionality. Texts must be seen as macro-structures through which the language user can take a 'stance' on an issue or a set of issues. In language use of this kind, the 'function' or 'value' of an utterance (i.e. illocutionary force) is negotiated and not taken for granted. For example, the only way to appreciate what *wide-ranging* actually means in the above example (reproduced in Box 3.2 embedded within a text) is to see it in terms of higher level values. These socio-textual values have to do with the researcher's 'attitude' ('a new look at modulation'), with the Abstract as a conventionalized genre, and finally with the way sentences are mapped to serve a particular rhetorical purpose in a text along something like the following lines:

(a) the support which the clause in which *wide-ranging* occurs (3) lends to the previous clause about 'definitions being rather vague';

Box 3.2 Sample 2

ABSTRACT

(1) When we investigate a large corpus of translations, we find many instances where a source text expression is translated in a large number of different ways. (2) One way to interpret these findings is to use the concept of MODULATION defined by Vinay and Darbelnet (1958) as 'un changement de point de vue'. (3) Their definition is rather vague, and the examples that they and other scholars use to illustrate the concept are **wide-ranging**. (4) By analyzing various translations of the same expression, however, it is possible to define the concept more restrictively and to shed light on the data.

Salkie (2001: 433; sentence numbers and emphasis added)

(b) the contrast between the sentence containing *vague* and *wide-ranging* (3) and the following sentence (4) which ushers in a more satisfactory definition and thus highlights the negative connotations of the initial *wide-ranging*.

It is thus only when textual input is seen within a proper genre and discourse specification that language can become a mouthpiece of institutions. Under these constraints (which build on textual mapping and the conventionality of genre but are not restricted to them), we enter the domain of 'discourse'. Within this new orientation, 'field' extends beyond 'subject matter' to serve such requirements as the need to 'represent' the world from a particular perspective. This is realized by 'ideational' choices in the linguistic system of 'transitivity' which among other things clarify (or camouflage) who is affected by whom (e.g. passivization, nominalization). This is a set of lexicogrammatical resources which must be heeded and assessed for functionality by the translator. Texts dominated by structures such as

She was institutionalized because of poor memory[2]
She was discovered to have severe visual agnosia

mark a register (and consequently the text, the genre and even the discourse) with a distinct preference for a passive '*-ed*' role in representing 'agency' (Hasan 1985: 46). Compare this with texts produced within the same disciplinary field (neuropsychology) but which opt for more active '*-er*' roles:

He could remember incidents without difficulty
He could quote the original visual descriptions.

Similarly, 'tenor' extends beyond formality or informality to serve discursive requirements of 'power' or 'solidarity' through 'interpersonal' choices in the linguistic systems of 'mood' and 'modality' (e.g. unmodulated declarative sentence, Halliday 1985/94). Sparseness or proliferation of 'declarative' sentences or 'usuality' modals, for example, marks a register as serving a particular set of attitudes and not others within one and the same field and even at roughly the same level of formality. These are subtle layers of text meaning that need to be preserved in translation.

In the area of 'mood' (type of sentence structure opted for), we as readers warm to and interact meaningfully with an author who constantly keeps wondering: *How could he, on the one hand, mistake his wife for a hat and, on the other, function as a teacher at the Music School?* This kind of interaction, which must be reflected in any translation, would be lacking if we were to deal with an author who saw his task primarily as that of imparting information. Modality in the latter, information-imparting kind of texts would also be seen as least interactive, dominated by such 'usuality modality' adjuncts as *often, frequently and usually,* and 'caused modality' verbs as *suggest, indicate*. The translator must always be alert to such fluctuations in the expression of certainty.

Likewise, the register element 'mode' now acts on a much richer set of resources than is possible when 'field' is seen simply as serving subject matter concerns and 'tenor' simply as accounting for formality relationships. Mode now avails the language user of 'discursive' resources for structuring texts and negotiating genre membership in a much more dynamic and goal-directed manner. Cohesion, 'theme-rheme' organization, etc., now play more than a facilitative role, with intertextuality giving way to the deeper level of what may be termed 'interdiscursivity', where texts become vehicles for the expression of ideology and power relations. These relations, as Fairclough (2003) points out, build, on the one hand, on the reader's accumulated social experiences and, on the other hand, on lexicogrammatical and textual resources variously oriented to the multiple dimensions of social life. Features of texts thus conspire with discursive practices and collectively act on society and culture. This is how texts of the interactive kind illustrated above are likely to be highly evaluative:

> *What had been funny, or farcical, in relation to the movie, was tragic in relation to real life.*

This kind of 'intensification' would be missing in texts dominated by abstractions, not human agency (e.g. *The fluctuation of visual function in our patient*). The various interrelationships that have emerged from the way field, tenor and mode evolve in texts may now be represented as in Figure 3.1.

Discursive processes are therefore both interactive and procedural, informed by such basic pragmatic-semiotic premises as:

- Meaning is always interpretable but only in a context of negotiation.
- The communicative function of the message may best be assessed in the light of background knowledge, inference, etc.
- Utterance 'function' or 'value' is processed not as a 'product' of intuitive understanding but as a 'process' of interaction among a variety of contextual factors.

Candlin (1985: viii)

3.7.1 DISCOURSE, GENRE AND TEXTUAL REGISTER IN TRANSLATION

Translation shifts may occur at the level of register where, for a variety of reasons (some innocent, some not so innocent), informality and solidarity give way to formality and power. Shifts are also fairly common at the level of 'text', where the contextual focus may be shifted, often in a motivated manner, from one rhetorical purpose to another (say, from reporting to argumentation) within the parameters of such cognitive orientations as monitoring versus

```
REGISTER (home to >
CONTEXT OF SITUATION (regulated by >
SITUATIONALITY (regulating >
FIELD (WHAT IS TAKING PLACE OR SUBJECT MATTER) (realized by >
IDEATIONAL MEANINGS/LINGUISTIC RESOURCES (e.g. TRANSITIVITY) (and >

TENOR (WHO IS TAKING PART OR LEVEL OF FORMALITY) (realized by >
INTERPERSONAL MEANINGS/ LINGUISTIC RESOURCES (e.g. MOOD and
MODALITY) (and >

MODE (WHAT PART LANGUAGE IS PLAYING OR TEXTUALITY) (realized by >
TEXTUAL MEANINGS/ LINGUISTIC RESOURCES (e.g. COHESION,
THEME-RHEME ETC.)

ACTING ON THE TEXTUAL AND EXTRA-TEXTUAL ENVIRONMENT THROUGH
PRAGMATICS (home to >
INTENTIONALITY (regulated by >
SPEECH ACTS >
INFERENCE >
IMPLICATURE >

BECOMING SIGNS AMONG SIGNS WITHIN
A SEMIOTICS (home to >
CONTEXT OF CULTURE (regulated by >
INTERTEXTUALITY (regulating the activity of >
MICRO-SIGNS (promoting >
MACRO-SIGNS (finding expression in >
DISCOURSE (enabled by >
TEXT (and >
GENRE
```

FIGURE 3.1 From register to the semiotic triad text–genre–discourse

managing. And as we have seen in the discussion of genre above, generic integrity is another vulnerable area of text reception and production, and must be upheld unless there is a good reason to do otherwise.

When motivated, such register, text or genre shifts in translation inevitably involve 'discourse' and are almost always bound up with attitudinal statements. It is in this way that language becomes an ideological tool, ultimately serving as the voice of societal institutions. Appreciate the role of discoursal factors as the driving force behind register, text and genre shifts in the way translations are made and received, it is pertinent at this point to pose the question: how do cultural context and linguistic expression become intertwined? More specifically: in what way do translations become impoverished if the texts to be translated are stripped of intellectual or emotional overtones?

Critical text linguistics can certainly help answer some of these questions. However, the analytic model would have to be more focussed on the wider context of power and ideology, and the contribution of cultural studies has been a welcome addition to existing analytic procedures. In a collection of papers edited by Bassnett and Lefevere, the subject of language and identity occupies Mahasweta Sengupta (1990) in her study of the Bengali poet Tagore's autotranslation. The study outlines the pitfalls of a translation in which faithfulness is exclusively shown toward the target language and culture. To mimic the dominant discourse of English, Tagore (winner of the Nobel Prize for literature in 1913) would translate his own work, changing not only the style of the original but also the imagery and tone of the lyric. An entirely different register emerges, matching as closely as possible the target language poetics of Edwardian times.

In fact, it was Tagore's emulation of Western values which earned him approval in the West. Acceptance was granted on the grounds that he translated his works 'in a manner that suited the psyche of the colonizer' (Sengupta 1990: 61). This was not to survive the onslaught of time, and, in the words of Sengupta (ibid.: 62), 'he was forgotten as fast as he was made famous'. That was when he began to lecture against nationalism, thus challenging an important Orientalist superstructure, and the master–servant relationship with which he had imbued his poems was no longer there.

Manipulating texture (and consequently shifting register and overall pragmatic effects) is thus always heavily implicated in the kind of discursive practices which drive ideologies. In a study in the same collection of papers as that on Tagore, Piotr Kuhiwczak (1990) discusses a form of manipulation not intended to protect the reader from an indigenous ideology (as Tagore tried to do), but mainly to protect the reader from a poetics. Discussing Czech writer Milan Kundera's *The Joke*, Kuhiwczak points out that the English translation of the novel is both inadequate and distorted, 'an appropriation of the original, resulting from the translator's and publisher's untested assumptions about Eastern Europe, East European writing, and the ability of the Western reader to decode complex cultural messages' (1990: 124). Specifically, *The Joke*'s plot is not particularly complex; it reflects the writer's belief that novels should be about 'themes' served by narratives which are 'polyphonic, full of seemingly insignificant digressions and carefully crafted repetitions' (ibid.: 125). These are textual manifestations which only a form of discourse analysis relying on a richer cultural dimension would adequately uncover.

The translator into English saw in this mosaic of features a bewildering array of irrelevancies which had to be 'tidied' for the prospective reader to make sense and discover a reasonably structured chronological order. For example, an important 'theme' – the folk music cultural festivity – is jettisoned, sweeping away with it the very thing which Kundera intended by this particularly long digression: 'to illustrate the fragility of culture' (1990: 126).

Finally, a study by Canadian translation theorist and cultural analyst Donald Bruce (1994) is particularly noteworthy in this regard. The study focusses on the reasons for the state of neglect suffered by the French writer Jules Vallès's trilogy *L'Enfant*, *Le Bachelier* and *L'Insurgé*, and shows that the reasons are essentially discoursal. Central to the trilogy on all levels (thematic, formal and functional) is an intense rejection of the oppressive ideological apparatus of the state's educational system. To achieve these discourse aims, Vallès puts the entire gamut of linguistic and textual form to work, from neologisms to juxtaposition and irony, from syntax to discourse. As Bruce points out, this must have constituted sufficient grounds for excluding Vallès from the French canon 'in part for revenge, in part lest the virus spread' (1994: 51). It is interesting to note that this intentional exclusion was not restricted to France, as the strategic neglect was almost immediately echoed in French literature curricula around the globe, particularly in non-francophone countries where the *Lycée* model had been adopted.

The primary reason for neglecting Vallès's works is certainly ideological: the writer's anarchist links with the commune, his less than favourable attitude towards the educational establishment and the critical stance he adopted towards the oppressive humanist culture were probably enough to qualify him as a subversive element that must be suppressed. Part of the ideological reason is also the way the French critical establishment signalled its displeasure, banishing Vallès from anthologies and literary histories, a move that was not lost on non-French users of French literature.

But there are other possible reasons for the 'ghettoization' of Vallès's writings:

- in terms of style, the rather heavy use made of journalistic devices was seen by Vallès's critics as 'inferior' and not 'belletristic';
- rhetorically, the texts were strongly 'referential' (inaccessible when portraying the explosion of the Commune, for example);
- politically, the texts were morbid, problematizing social conflict instead of providing an escape from it;
- in the intellectual climate of the times, Vallès's exclusion from the canon meant that the taste for his writing was not generally cultivated, another pernicious aspect of the delegitimization process.

3.8 CONCLUSION AND IMPLICATIONS FOR THE TRANSLATION ANALYST

In this chapter, we have examined the complexity surrounding four basic suprasentential entities with which writers and readers of English and translators into and from English constantly engage: register, text, genre and discourse. It might be helpful now to see this process of interaction schematically represented (see Figure 3.2). It is discourse that is shown to enjoy a privileged status: it subsumes (and is expressed through) genre, which in turn subsumes texts and is thereby enabled to exist. Texts revolve round the idea

```
Register          →          Situationality
   ↘                            ↗
     Discourse   →          Ideology/perspective
        ↘                      ↗
          Genre   →          Communicative event
             ↘                ↗
               Text   →     Rhetorical purpose
```

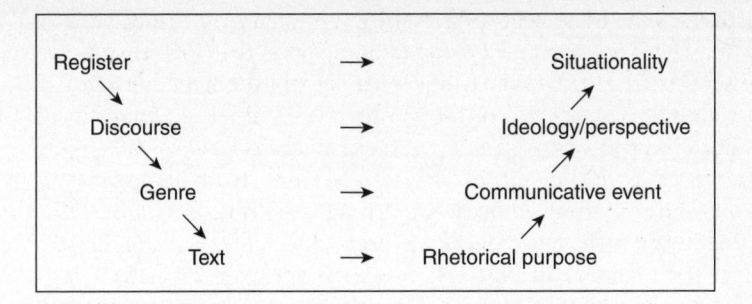

FIGURE 3.2 Text/genre/discourse/register as Russian dolls

of a rhetorical purpose (hence their organizational function). Genres, on the other hand, are conventionalized communicative events and, in tandem with texts, serve as vehicles for the discursive expression of ideologies and value systems.

Within a given register configuration (e.g. academic writing within neuropsychology), there will be variations in the degree of proximity not only between text producer and receiver (a function of tenor formality) but also between the producer/receiver and the utterances produced or received (a function of field technicality). Such an orientation has implications for the way we 'texture' our texts through mode (e.g. suppressed or unsuppressed agency) and for the way utterances and texts are shaped within a compositional plan or structure. That is, since the overall aim of such structural and textural designs is always to convey a set of attitudes, the way texts are put together in sequences within particular prose designs is never innocent. Discourse- and register-based analysis assists in uncovering and understanding the attitudes conveyed and, when used in translation practice, is a valuable tool in enabling these attitudes to be communicated appropriately in the target text.

NOTES

1 The interpreter generally works with an oral text, and has less opportunity to plan and revise (see Chapter 8). Nevertheless, many of the concepts discussed in this chapter are still as relevant for oral texts as they are for translated texts. Hatim and Mason (1997), for instance, give specific examples of the analysis of interpreting texts.
2 These and other examples of writing in neuropsychology are taken from the excellent study by Gill Francis and Anneliese Kramer-Dahl (1992).

4
TRANSLATION AS A COGNITIVE ACTIVITY

AMPARO HURTADO ALBIR AND FABIO ALVES

Apart from being an act of communication and a textual operation, translation/interpreting is also the result of the cognitive processing carried out by translators/interpreters. Therefore, one has to take into consideration the mental processes involved in the course of a translation task as well as the capacities translators/interpreters are required to possess in order to do it adequately (translation competence). These issues have been studied in cognitive approaches to translation which have gained renewed impetus over the past few years, leading Muñoz (2007) to advocate in favour of a cognitive translation studies (*traductología cognitiva*) in line with recent developments in the field of cognitive science.

4.1 THE TRANSLATION PROCESS

The analysis of the translation process entails a great deal of complexity. It is constrained by intrinsic difficulties inherent in studies which aim at tapping into any kind of cognitive processing: it is not amenable to direct observation. Furthermore, the difficulties related to the investigation of the translation process are magnified by the different phases through which the process unfolds and by the complexity of the interwoven abilities and forms of specialized knowledge which play an integral part in it.

4.1.1 MODELS OF ANALYSIS OF THE TRANSLATION PROCESS

Researchers have put forward several models of analysis about the mental processes carried out by translators/interpreters. Six of the most representative models are described here in chronological order (for a more complete account of such models, see Hurtado Albir 2001: 314–62).

4.1.1.1 THE INTERPRETIVE THEORY OF TRANSLATION

The theory of sense or the interpretive theory of translation (ITT) is pioneering in the cognitive approach to the study of translation. Its leading researchers, Seleskovitch and Lederer, at the École Supérieure d'Interprètes et de Traducteurs (ESIT) in Paris, produced ground-breaking work on the analysis of interpreting (see especially Seleskovitch 1968, 1975; Lederer 1981, 1994/2003; Seleskovitch and Lederer 1984; Delisle 1980).

ITT identifies three interrelated phases of the translation/interpreting process, namely (1) understanding, (2) deverbalization and (3) re-expression:

1. **Understanding** is conceived of as an interpretive process geared to the generation of sense. According to ITT, experience in translation and interpreting has shown that linguistic knowledge alone does not suffice and it needs to be supplemented by other cognitive inputs (*compléments cognitifs*): encyclopaedic knowledge (*bagage cognitif*) and contextual knowledge (*contexte cognitif*), a type of storage which builds up from the beginning of the process of understanding. Additionally, ITT highlights the role of memory in the process of understanding and distinguishes between immediate memory, which stores words for a short time, and cognitive memory, which stores the whole range of knowledge possessed by an individual. The end product of the process of understanding is called sense and it results from the interdependence of all linguistic and non-linguistic elements which play a role in the process. Understanding among translators and interpreters is different from understanding among normal receptors, since it is a deliberate and more analytical act of communication which requires the apprehension of sense in its totality so that sense matches the intended meaning (*vouloir dire*) of the sender of the source text.
2. **Deverbalization**. For ITT, sense is the non-verbal synthesis resulting from the process of understanding. Therefore, ITT postulates the existence of an intermediate phase of deverbalization resulting from the phase of understanding and the beginning of the phase of re-expression. This phase plays a fundamental role in the scope of ITT since it considers that re-expression is achieved through deverbalized meaning and not on the basis of linguistic form.
3. **Re-expression**. In a similar way to the process of understanding, re-expression involves the whole cognitive apparatus of an individual and generates an association between linguistic and non-linguistic knowledge. This phase presupposes a non-linear movement from a non-verbal level (the phase of deverbalization) to verbalization in a natural language and it is considered to be similar to the process of expression in monolingual communication: from the sender's intended meaning to its linguistic formulation. Intended meaning is the preverbal origin of linguistic form and, therefore, of sense. In the context of translation, the intended meaning of the sender of the source text is the point of reference aimed at by the translator.

As far as written translation is concerned, Delisle (1980) adds a final phase of the translation process which entails a second interpretation: a phase of justified analysis which aims at verifying the exactness of the provisional solutions found earlier. In other words, this phase entails the process of interpreting the equivalence found in order to guarantee that it expresses exactly the meaning conveyed by the source text.

Interpretive translation unfolds as a triangular process encompassing signs, a non-verbal phase and reverbalization. This is different from the interlingual translation process called 'transcodification', also called 'correspondence' from 1986 onwards (Seleskovitch 1986), referring to decontextualized equivalences which preserve in the text the meaning they had at the linguistic level. ITT therefore differentiates between interpretive translation (carried out between texts) and transcodification (carried out between linguistic elements); each of them entails different processes. Seleskovitch (1975) investigated a corpus of speeches in English and their consecutive interpretations and analysed the notes taken by the interpreters. She showed that they took notes of certain elements such as numbers, lists and technical terms. These are 'transcodifiable' elements which have to be written down by the interpreter since they can be isolated from context and, additionally, intervene specifically in memory retrieval more as a process of recognition rather than interpreting.

According to ITT, every translation is a mixture of both types. However, interpretive translation takes precedence over transcodification since it conveys equivalence of meaning.

4.1.1.2 BELL'S LINGUISTIC AND PSYCHOLINGUISTIC MODEL

Bell (1991) builds on linguistic and psycholinguistic perspectives to present a model which is divided into the phases of analysis and synthesis. It employs elements of artificial intelligence in its structural organization and adopts the framework of systemic-functional linguistics for its conception of language.

Bell's model accounts for translation in terms of information processing and requires both short-term and long-term memories for the decoding of source language input and the encoding of target language output. The model follows a top-down/bottom-up structure: it starts with the visual recognition of the words of the source text; then undergoes syntactic parsing in combination with mechanisms of lexical search processed by a frequent structure analyser; this is followed by semantic and pragmatic processing to generate a semantic representation supported by an idea organizer and a planner. Once the decision to translate is taken at the level of semantic representation, the input is reprocessed by synthesizers distributed in pragmatic, semantic and lexico-grammatical levels to be encoded in a new writing system and gives rise to a target text (Figure 4.1). Although input must be processed at syntactic, semantic and pragmatic levels, no fixed order is established a priori and there is always the possibility of regression, which allows for constant online revision and changes in previous decisions.

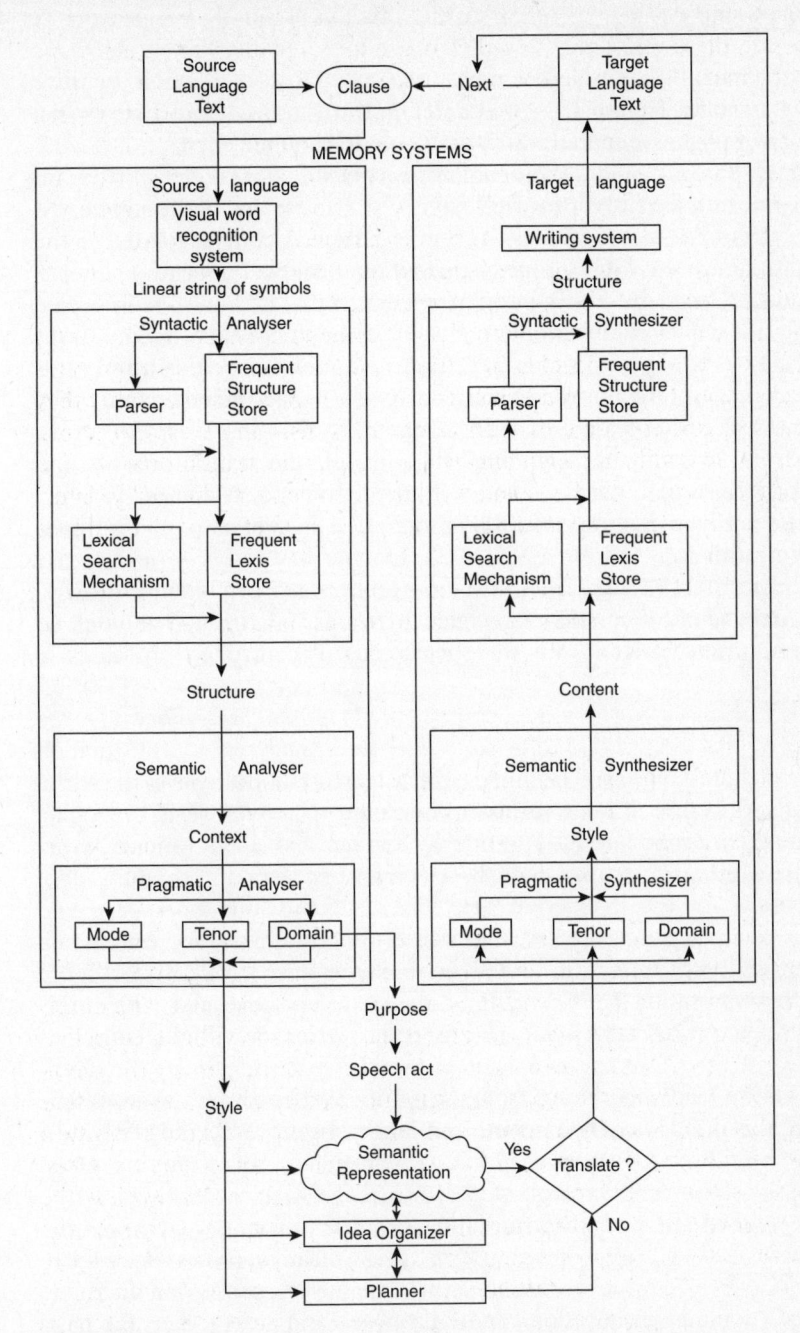

FIGURE 4.1 Bell's model of the translation process (Bell 1991: 55)

4.1.1.3 KIRALY'S SOCIOLOGICAL AND PSYCHOLINGUISTIC MODEL

Kiraly (1995) considers translation both as a social (external) and a cognitive (internal) activity. He presents two models of the translation process: a social model and a cognitive model which draws on psycholinguistics.

In Kiraly's social model, the translator is considered an active participant in three interrelated situational contexts (SCs), namely that of the source text (SC1), that of the target text (SC2), and a particular context related to the translational activity (SC3). This last situational context is located between SC1 and SC2 and, due to its internal, mental traits, it cannot be observed directly. It is in SC3 that translation-specific competences and related forms of knowledge are to be found. These are externalized by the translator's self-concept, which relates to the translator's self-image and its related social role in terms of responsibility as a social agent.

In Kiraly's cognitive (psycholinguistic) model, the translator's mind is 'an information-processing system in which a translation comes from the interaction of intuitive and controlled processes using linguistic and extralinguistic information' (Kiraly 1995: 102). On the basis of a series of case studies, Kiraly shows that the translation process is a combination of controlled and uncontrolled, non-observable processes and, through think-aloud protocols, offers insights into the specificities of controlled processes in translation.

Kiraly's psycholinguistic model consists of (1) *information sources;* (2) *the intuitive workspace; and* (3) *the controlled processing centre.* Information sources include long-term memory (which stores cultural, physical, social schemata; discourse frames; translation-related schemata; lexico-semantic knowledge; morpho-syntactic frames), source text input and external resources (reference books, data bases, native-speaker informants, etc.). Kiraly draws on the distinction between a subconscious workspace and a controlled processing centre. He insists that these do not operate in isolation and proposes an intuitive (or relatively uncontrolled) workspace in which information from long-term memory is synthesized with information from source text input and external resources without conscious control.

Translation problems emerge from the intuitive workspace when automatic processing does not yield a tentative translation output. According to Kiraly, these problems are then considered in the controlled processing centre and a strategy is chosen and implemented in an attempt to deal with them. In the case of a failed strategy, the translation problem can be sent back to the intuitive workspace, together with information which had not yet been taken into account. And, if the workspace is still unable to produce an adequate solution, a tentative translation can be proposed and accepted on the basis of the inadequate information available or the element in question may be dropped and the search procedure starts again.

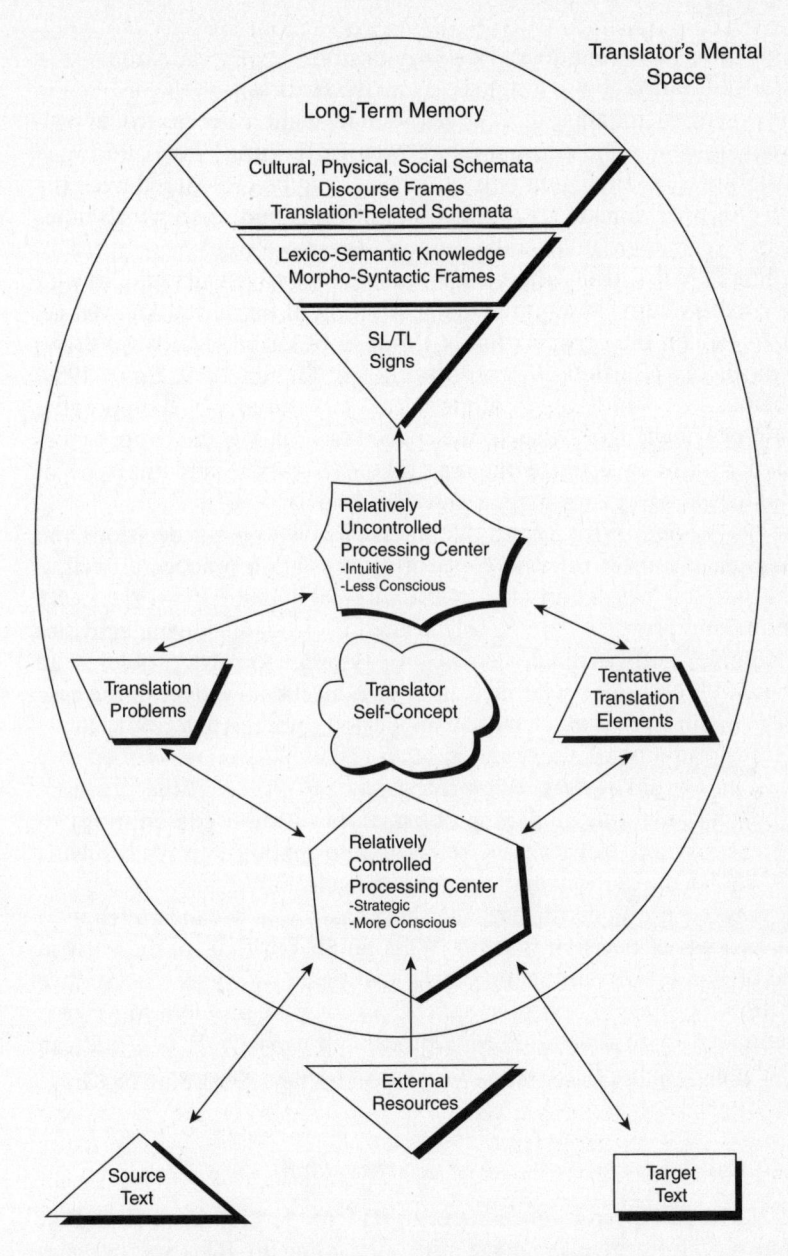

FIGURE 4.2 Kiraly's psycholinguistic model (Kiraly 1995: 101)

4.1.1.4 WILSS AND TRANSLATION AS A DECISION-MAKING TYPE OF BEHAVIOUR

Wilss (1996) considers cognitive psychology the most appropriate framework for the study of translation as a cognitive activity. He draws on the distinction between two complementary types of knowledge, namely declarative knowledge (knowing what) and procedural knowledge (knowing how), to argue that translation is an intelligent type of behaviour to be considered from the perspective of problem-solving and decision-making and upon which other mechanisms, such as creativity and intuition, also play a role.

According to Wilss, translation is a knowledge-based activity and, as with all kinds of knowledge, it requires the acquisition of organized knowledge. In order to explain the organization of this type of knowledge, Wilss draws on schema theory (Bartlett 1932; Neisser 1967; Tannen 1979; Spiro 1980; etc.). Schemas are cognitive units, hierarchically structured, which support the acquisition of knowledge. As such, the central task of cognitive approaches to translation is to investigate the way schemas operate and the type of interaction observed in knowledge-related schemas.

On the other hand, Wilss argues that knowing how to make decisions and how to choose is a most relevant element in translation practice as well as in the teaching of translation (see, above all, Wilss 1996: 174–191; 1998). Decision-making processes are closely related to problem-solving activities (a more complex and far-reaching concept). In order to solve problems, an individual builds on both declarative and procedural knowledge. In the case of translation, this issue is much more complicated since it is a derived activity (i.e. the transformation of a text into another text).

Building on Corbin (1980), Wilss recognizes six phases in the decision-making process: identification of problems; clarification (description) of problems; search and retrieval of relevant information; problem-solving strategies; choice of solution; and evaluation of solution.

There may be problems in each of the phases which can interrupt or delay the process of decision making. Wilss points out that, particularly in the scope of translator training, one must investigate processes of cognitive simplification, i.e. the process of simplifying a complex problem to make it more compatible with the translator's processing capacity. Thus, one can consider cognitive simplification as a tool which reduces inaccuracies.

4.1.1.5 GUTT AND A RELEVANCE-THEORETIC APPROACH TO TRANSLATION

Gutt (1991) builds on relevance theory (RT) to develop an account of translation as interpretive language use. According to RT (Sperber and Wilson 1986/1995), human inferential processes are geared to the maximization of relevance. The notion of relevance is defined in terms of effort and effects involved in ostensive-inferential communication to generate cognitive/contextual effects. On the one hand, the communicator ostensively manifests his/her intention to make something manifest, with ostension being defined as intentionally 'showing someone something' (Sperber and Wilson 1986: 49). On the other hand, the audience makes an effort to infer what is ostensively communicated on the basis of evidence provided for this precise purpose. For RT, human communication is a case of ostensive-inferential communication in which 'inferential communication and ostension are one and the same process, but seen from two different points of view: that of the communicator who [sic] is involved in ostension and that of the audience who is involved in inference' (Sperber and Wilson 1986: 54).

In its framework, RT also presupposes two types of use for mental representations – descriptive and interpretive; each of them refers to a corresponding type of resemblance. Descriptive resemblance establishes a correlation between an object or state of affairs in the world and a mental representation, while interpretive resemblance does this between two mental representations. According to Gutt, translation is a case of optimal interpretive resemblance in which 'two utterances, or even more generally, two ostensive stimuli, interpretively resemble each other to the extent that they share their explicatures and/or implicatures' (Gutt 1991: 44). In other words, the translator's task is to ostensively manifest to his/her audience all relevant aspects which are ostensively and inferentially conveyed by the source text.

Gutt (2000) argues that, by applying the RT framework to translation, it is possible to understand and explicate the mental faculties that enable human beings to translate, in the sense of expressing in one language what has been expressed in another. He argues that, once these faculties are understood, it is possible to understand not only the relation between input and output, but also, and perhaps more importantly, the communicative effects they have on the audience. This also applies to situations where communicator and audience do not share a mutual cognitive environment. In such cases, called 'secondary communication', Gutt (2005b) suggests that additional sophistication is needed for communication to succeed, namely the capacity of human beings to meta-represent what has been communicated to them. Gutt claims that the capacity to generate meta-representations is, therefore, a cognitive prerequisite for the capacity of human beings to translate.

4.1.1.6 GILE'S EFFORT MODEL

Gile (1995a, 1995b) builds on the notion of processing capacity stemming from cognitive psychology to propose a model of efforts and relate it to simultaneous and consecutive interpreting, as well as to sight translation and simultaneous interpreting with text. The model presupposes a distinction between automatic and non-automatic mental operations, which consume part of the processing capacity available. Gile emphasizes the non-automatic character of the mental operations made by interpreters and focuses on three types of effort in simultaneous interpreting:

1. Efforts related to listening and analysing. Gile argues in favour of a probabilistic account for listening and analysing linguistic input which interacts with time constraints, attention or information treatment capacity, and short-term memory capacity. The process of understanding is non-automatic, with short-term memory information being contrasted with elements stored in long-term memory to allow for decision making in interpreting.
2. Efforts related to discourse production in reformulation. These are also non-automatic and entail the background knowledge of the interpreter (usually weaker than that of the speaker), the need to keep pace with the speaker (usually different from the interpreter's own pace), the need to start reformulating the input without knowing how the speaker is going to complete his/her reasoning, and the need to counteract constant linguistic interference between two different languages.
3. Short-term memory efforts. These are similarly non-automatic with a storage rhythm heavily dependent on the pace imposed by the speaker.

Gile postulates a model which integrates efforts on the three different types mentioned above, each of which has specific treatment capacities that must be balanced according to the total treatment capacity available. The effort model varies slightly, depending on the mode of operation, in consecutive interpreting being broken down into two clearly marked phases (listening/analysing and reformulation). In sight translation and in simultaneous interpreting with text, listening effort is replaced by reading effort.

4.1.2 *Main Characteristics of the Translation Process*

Such cognitive models of the translation process highlight the following fundamental traits:

1. The existence of basic stages related to understanding and re-expression. Additionally, some of the models postulate a non-verbal stage such as the ITT's deverbalization phase, Bell's semantic representation or Gutt's interpretive resemblance.
2. The need to use and integrate internal (cognitive) and external resources. To that extent, Kiraly (1995) points to internal and external sources of information and Alves (1995, 1997) refers to internal and external support.
3. The role of memory and information storage.
4. The dynamic and interactive nature of the process, which encompasses linguistic as well as non-linguistic elements.

5. The non-linear nature of the process. It neither follows a linear textual progression nor is it constrained to the sequential development of its basic stages. Therefore, it allows for regressions, i.e. recursive movements in text production, and alternations between the phases of understanding and re-expression.
6. The existence of automatic and non-automatic, controlled and uncontrolled processes. Translation/interpreting requires a special type of information processing which encompasses more conscious and controlled processes and more intuitive and automatic processes.
7. The role of retrieval, problem-solving, decision-making and the use of translation-specific strategies in the unfolding and management of the process.
8. The existence of specific characteristics, depending on the type of translation. For example, in written translation (and this also applies to audiovisual translation) some authors point to the existence of a phase in which the provisional solution found is verified and controlled for accuracy. This is called 'justified analysis' by Delisle (1980) or 'revision' by Bell (1998). Another example is Gile's proposal of different effort models for consecutive interpreting, simultaneous interpreting and sight translation. The specific constraints of each translation modality generate specific problems which require specific competences from translators or interpreters, as well as the use of specific strategies and the development of specific decision-making processes.

Such traits lead Hurtado Albir (2001: 375) to define the process of translation as a complex cognitive process which has an interactive and non-linear nature, encompasses controlled and uncontrolled processes, and requires processes of problem-solving, decision-making and the use of strategies.

4.2 Translation competence

Another issue related to cognitive aspects of translation is the competence that underlies the work of translators/interpreters and enables them to carry out the cognitive operations necessary for the adequate unfolding of the translation process: this is known as translation competence (TC). One of the first definitions of TC, in Bell (1991: 43), is the 'knowledge and skills the translator must possess in order to carry it [the translation process] out'. He considers TC as an expert system guided primarily by a strategic component. This concept became more prominent in the literature of translation studies in the 1990s and is used by some of the authors mentioned here. Other terms used for this concept include translation ability, translation skills, translational competence, translator's competence and translation expertise.

4.2.1 MODELS OF TRANSLATION COMPETENCE

Most proposals relating to the modelling and functioning of TC are componential models which focus on the description of components (or subcompetences) of written translation. Some of the most representative studies are Wilss (1976), Bell (1991), Kiraly (1995), Gile (1995a), Hurtado Albir (1996, 1999), Risku (1998), Presas (2000, 2004), Neubert (2000), PACTE (2000, 2003), Gonçalves (2005), Kelly (2005), Shreve (2006), Alves and Gonçalves (2007). A few proposals are concerned with the specific functioning of TC in inverse translation (Beeby 1996; Campbell 1998).

These proposals highlight the fact that TC consists of several components (linguistic and extralinguistic knowledge, documentation skills, etc.), located at different levels (knowledge, abilities, etc.). In addition, some authors argue that TC also entails a strategic component geared to problem solving and decision making.

Pym (1992b, 2003), however, criticizes the componential models of TC, arguing in favour of a minimalist concept based on the production then elimination of alternatives. Pym (2003: 489) identifies two skills needed for TC, namely (1) the ability to generate a series of more than one viable target text (TTI, TT2 ... TTn) for a pertinent source text, and (2) the ability to select only one viable TT from this series, quickly and with justified confidence.

It should be stressed that most of the proposals concerning TC have not been empirically tested and only a few of them have attempted to validate their models from an empirical-experimental perspective (Gonçalves 2005; PACTE 2005; Alves and Gonçalves 2007; etc.).

4.2.2 MODELLING AND FUNCTIONING OF TRANSLATION COMPETENCE

The most relevant aspects in the current debate concern (1) the definition and main features of TC, (2) its components, (3) the process by which it is acquired and (4) those of its traits which are related to expert knowledge. As we shall see, these aspects have been analysed from different perspectives.

4.2.2.1 DEFINITION AND MAIN FEATURES

From a didactic perspective, Kelly (2005: 162) defines TC as the set of knowledge, skills, attitudes and aptitudes which a translator possesses in order to undertake professional activity in the field.

The PACTE group (Process in the Acquisition of Translation Competence and Evaluation) from Universitat Autònoma de Barcelona (2000, 2003, 2005, 2007), in turn, builds on the notions of expert knowledge and declarative/procedural knowledge used in cognitive psychology (see 4.1.1.4 above) to consider TC a type of expert knowledge. TC is defined by PACTE (2003: 58) as the underlying system of declarative and predominantly procedural knowledge required to translate. It has four distinctive characteristics: (1) it is expert knowledge that is not possessed by all bilinguals; (2) it is mainly procedural rather than declarative knowledge; (3) it is made up of several interrelated subcompetences; and (4) the strategic component is of particular importance, as in all types of procedural knowledge.

Shreve (2006) draws on expertise studies to focus on TC as translation expertise and defines it as the ability of an individual to use multiple translation-relevant cognitive resources to perform a translation task. He suggests that this competence could be seen as declarative and procedural knowledge from a variety of cognitive domains accumulated through training and experience and then stored and organized in a translator's long-term memory.

From a relevance-theoretic perspective, Alves and Gonçalves (2007) differentiate between a *general translator's competence* (GTC) and a *specific translator's competence* (STC). GTC is defined as all knowledge, abilities and strategies a successful translator masters and which lead to an adequate performance of translation tasks. STC, however, operates in coordination with other subcompetences and works mainly through conscious or meta-cognitive processes, being directly geared to the maximization of interpretive resemblance.

These proposals all view TC as a particular type of expert knowledge encompassing declarative and procedural knowledge (abilities, skills, etc.), the latter being predominant.

4.2.2.2 Components

The model proposed by PACTE (2003, 2005, 2007) comprises five subcompetences (bilingual, extralinguistic, instrumental, knowledge about translation, and strategic) as well as psycho-physiological components which interact together during the translation process. These subcompetences are explained in Table 4.1.

PACTE considers that the subcompetences specific to TC are the strategic, the instrumental and knowledge about translation, the strategic subcompetence being the most important due to its role of guaranteeing the efficiency of the process.

Kelly (2005: 33–4) describes the components of TC as communicative and textual competence, cultural and intercultural competence, subject area competence, professional and instrumental competence, attitudinal or psycho-physiological competence, strategic competence and interpersonal competence (ability to work with other professionals involved in the translation process), including team work, negotiation and leadership skills.

Shreve (2006), in turn, argues that TC implies having access to (1) L1 and L2 linguistic knowledge, (2) cultural knowledge of the source and target culture,

TABLE 4.1 PACTE model of subcompetences

- The bilingual subcompetence is made up of pragmatic, socio-linguistic, textual and lexico-grammatical knowledge in each language.
- The extra-linguistic subcompetence is made up of encyclopaedic, thematic and bicultural knowledge.
- The translation knowledge subcompetence is knowledge of the principles that guide translation (processes, methods and procedures, etc.) and knowledge of the professional practice (types of translation briefs, users, etc.).
- The instrumental subcompetence is made up of knowledge related to the use of documentation sources and information and communication technology applied to translation.
- The strategic subcompetence is the most important, solving problems and guaranteeing the efficiency of the process; it intervenes by planning the process in relation to the translation project, evaluating the process and partial results obtained, activating the different subcompetences and compensating for deficiencies, identifying translation problems and applying procedures to solve them.
- The psycho-physiological components are cognitive and attitudinal components (memory, attention span, perseverance, critical attitude, etc.) and abilities such as creativity, logical reasoning, analysis and synthesis.

including knowledge of specialized subject domains, (3) textual knowledge of source and target textual conventions and (4) translation knowledge – knowledge of how to translate using strategies and procedures, amongst which are translation tools and information-seeking strategies.

These proposals assume similar components for TC although they differ in their terminology and distribution in terms of sub-components. Kelly's proposal, however, is characterized by the introduction of an interpersonal subcompetence.

4.2.2.3 THE ACQUISITION OF TRANSLATION COMPETENCE: FROM NOVICE TO EXPERT

Although there are empirical studies which compare the performance of a professional translator and a translation student, there has been no empirical study of the TC acquisition process as a whole. There have, however, been several attempted descriptions of TC acquisition. All these agree that TC is an acquired skill which evolves through different phases, from novice to expert knowledge levels.

Harris (1977, 1980) and Harris and Sherwood (1978) point out that there is an innate ability for *natural translation* which all bilingual speakers have and which would be one of the fundamental bases of TC. In view of this innate ability, Shreve (1997) sees TC as a specialization of communicative competence, the development of which is a continuum between 'natural translation' and 'constructed translation' (professional translation).

Chesterman (1997a) refers to TC acquisition as a process of gradual automatization based on the five stages of skill acquisition put forward by Dreyfus and Dreyfus (1986): novice (recognition of predefined features and rules), advanced beginner (recognition of non-defined but relevant features), competence (hierarchical and goal-oriented decision-making), proficiency (intuitive understanding plus deliberative action) and expertise (fluid performance plus deliberative rationality).

Postulating a similar continuum, ranging from 'novice knowledge' (pre-translation competence) to 'expert knowledge' (translation competence), PACTE (2000) considers TC acquisition as a process of reconstructing and developing TC subcompetences and psycho-physiological components.

In line with expertise studies, Shreve (2006) suggests that, with practice, declarative knowledge (i.e. what is known about the task) is converted into production rules which lead to proceduralization and, therefore, to less effortful processing and to greater automaticity. Building on the notion of expertise trajectory (Lajoie 2003), Shreve argues that TC acquisition can be developed differentially, depending on variations in how further practical experience is acquired. Thus, there can be different kinds of translation experts, some having highly developed linguistic skills and subject area knowledge, while others, compensating for possessing no more than adequate background knowledge in a specific subject domain, excel in information-seeking skills.

Alves and Gonçalves (2007) consider the gradual development of cognitive networks, based on connectionist approaches, and distinguish between two cognitive profiles: (1) narrow-band translators who work mostly on the basis of insufficiently contextualized cues (i.e. dictionary-based meaning of words instead of contextualized meaning) and fail to bridge the gap between procedurally, conceptually and contextually encoded information, and (2) broadband translators, who tend to work mostly on the basis of communicative cues provided by the ST and reinforced by the contextual assumptions derived from their cognitive environments. In this way, expert translators are able to integrate procedurally, conceptually and contextually encoded information into a coherent whole to encompass higher levels of meta-cognition.

4.2.2.4 TRANSLATION COMPETENCE AS EXPERT KNOWLEDGE

As we have seen, several authors consider TC a particular type of expert knowledge (Bell, PACTE, Shreve, etc.). Shreve (2006) suggests that TC should be analysed in the scope of expertise studies which have shown that expert performance:

1. is demonstrably an acquired skill;
2. requires a high level of meta-cognitive activity;
3. entails proceduralization of knowledge related to domain specificities;

4. requires self-regulatory behaviour in terms of monitoring, resource allocation, and planning;
5. shows no necessary relationship of domain expertise to general cognitive capacities such as intelligence or memory.

Therefore, it would seem that studies into TC need to establish a closer dialogue with expertise studies in an attempt to identify common and different cognitive patterns between expert translators and other kinds of experts.

Finally, cognitive research into TC may be complemented by behavioural research into TC and research focusing on professional translators' behaviour, namely the factors related to the work of translators/interpreters and the tasks they perform in the work market (Gouadec 2005, 2007; Rothe-Neves 2005, 2007; Kuznik 2007; etc.). Evidence about the cognitive functioning of TC (that is, what is needed to be a translator) and the behavioural functioning (what the translators do) can help throw light on the professional profile of translators/interpreters and distinguish them from the profiles of other similar types of professional.

4.3 EMPIRICAL-EXPERIMENTAL RESEARCH ON TRANSLATION PROCESSES AND TRANSLATION COMPETENCE

Empirical-experimental research in translation studies has been carried out on translation as a cognitive activity. This kind of research allows for the gathering of data on translation processes and translation competence and thus enables their study from an inductive perspective. However, empirical-experimental research does not have a long-standing tradition in the field and this has a negative impact on the development and validation of research designs.

As far as written translation is concerned, some of the research topics are: the unity of translation; the role of linguistic and non-linguistic knowledge; the use of dictionaries; the role of awareness and automatic processes; creativity in translation; and issues related to problem-solving and decision-making (both in direct and inverse translation). Most of these studies correlate them with quality assessment of the product of their translations.

As far as interpreting is concerned, research has been carried out on the ear–voice span and the temporal distance between speakers and interpreters, the speed of reformulation, the role of anticipation, segmentation of ST input, pause analysis, neurophysiologic aspects (memory span, attention, etc.), quality and so on.

4.3.1 FIRST STEPS

Empirical-experimental research in written translation started in the early 1980s with a line of inquiry based primarily on think-aloud protocols (TAPs) based on Ericsson and Simon (1984). Sandrock's pioneering study (1982) was followed by the seminal work of Krings (1986) and those by Königs (1987), Gerloff (1988), Tirkkonnen-Condit (1989), Lörscher (1991), Kussmaul (1991, 1995), Fraser (1993), Alves (1995), Kiraly (1995), etc. Some studies added other techniques of data collection, such as questionnaires, video, interviews, etc. (Krings 1986; Séguinot 1989; Dancette 1994; Alves 1995; Kiraly 1995; etc).

TAPs have been used in translation process research for a disparate series of case studies involving different types of subjects (language students, translation students, bilinguals, professional translators and other language professionals), different language combinations and directionality (direct or inverse translation), and different topics (aspects of problem-solving and decision-making, the role of creativity, etc). However, TAPs proved to be problematic in translation process research for many different reasons, the strongest objection being that they showed what the subjects believed to have happened during the translation process and not necessarily what actually occurred. Subjects also knew that they were being observed and performed two tasks simultaneously (translation and verbalization). Additionally, TAPs did not provide access to unconscious or automatic processes and interfered in the flow of text production. However, due to the lack of other tools for data collection, TAPs remained as the main source of process-oriented information until the late 1990s.

During this period, samples used in research were not always representative of the performance of professional (expert) translators since they quite often used language or translation students. Experimental designs lacked systematization and clear objectives, used small samples (case studies) and, therefore, were unable to allow for generalizations. Additionally, research designs differed significantly, both conceptually and methodologically among researchers. Therefore, as shown by Fraser (1996), the picture emerging from those studies was quite varied and results could not be generalized.

As far as research in interpreting is concerned, Gile (1995b) points out that the first experimental studies (mostly on simultaneous interpreting) were carried out in the 1960s and early 1970s. These studies were carried out by researchers from other disciplines, such as psychology and psycholinguistics. They focused, among others: on the temporal distance between speakers and interpreter; the speed of reformulation on the comparison between rhythmical patterns in speech and pauses in spontaneous speech; the segmentation of input; the speed of speaker delivery; on background noise; anticipation. Gile criticizes these studies, arguing that they analyse very specific problems, show methodological shortcomings (subjects were not professional interpreters, input was not authentic, etc.), and, furthermore, lack specific knowledge about the reality of interpreting practice. Gile also notes that, in the late 1980s, following the *International Symposium on the Theoretical and Practical*

Aspects of Teaching Conference Interpreting, held at the University of Trieste in 1986, empirical research into interpreting gained renewed impetus with more rigorous methodological studies on pause analysis (Cenková 1989), on comparisons between sight translation and simultaneous interpreting (Viezzi 1989, 1990), on differences between bilinguals and interpreters (Dillinger 1989, 1990), among others.

4.3.2 DEVELOPMENT AND CONSOLIDATION

In the mid-1990s, empirical-experimental research moved into a second stage, striving for more systematic accounts of translation processes and translation competence, allowing also replication of experiments in an attempt to provide stronger claims for generalization. This second phase placed emphasis on multi-methodological perspectives, namely triangulation. This builds on research carried out in the social sciences and other disciplines (see, among others, Denzin 1970; Cohen and Manion 1980), and uses various data elicitation tools to 'locate' the process of translation from different yet complementary vantage points (Hurtado Albir 2001: 179; Alves 2003; etc.).

Research into written translation focused on issues concerning, among others:

- the use of TAPs (Jakobsen 2003);
- contrastive performance between novice and expert translators, between expert translators, bilinguals and other language professionals, etc. (Hansen 1999, 2002; Jääskeläinen 2000; PACTE 2005, 2007);
- the mapping of translators' cognitive rhythms (pause analysis) and of the different phases of the translation process (Jakobsen 2002; Alves 2005);
- sources of disturbance in the translation process (Hansen 2006);
- analysis of components of TC and characteristics of expert translator performance (PACTE 2003, 2005, 2007; Alves and Gonçalves 2007; Englund-Dimitrova 2005), etc.

The main instruments used were TAPs, interviews, questionnaires and psychophysiological measurements. In the late 1990s, research gained renewed impetus with the spread of computers (Neunzig 1997a, 1997b) and the development of different software packages: the Translog software developed by Jakobsen and Schou (1999) at the Copenhagen Business School allowed for the key-logging of the translation process and, therefore, for the online observation of the flow of text production. Translog2006 (http://www.translog.dk), the latest version of the software, has two interdependent components – a Supervisor and a User component – which complement each other and allow for the creation of experimental designs (projects), the replay of logged information, provision for recording retrospective protocols and the generation of xml or csv files, which can be used for statistical analysis of logged data (cf. Section 7.1).

Alternatively, Proxy (http://www.proxynetworks.com), used by PACTE, is a piece of software designed for monitoring computer users. It enables researchers to view other computer screens linked within the same network and to generate recordings which can be analysed at a later stage. Differently from Translog, Proxy recordings thus capture not only the flow of text production (what is typed by the translator) but also the other software and search engines which the translator uses to search for translation equivalents, etc.

Camtasia software (http://www.techsmith.com) also allows for recordings of computer screens and has been used in conjunction with Translog or Proxy as a resource to record actions that take place outside the range of key-logging or screen monitoring software.

More recently, a new trend has been spearheaded by the use of eye-tracking as a data elicitation tool capable of tapping into reading processes (O'Brien 2006) and, therefore, shedding light on cognitive processes related to the understanding of input which have not previously been amenable to scientific investigation. Eyetracking will be able to provide information on gaze plots, mapping saccadic movements and regressions online, as well as on hot spots, areas in the STs and TTs where fixation is stronger. By means of software which analyses the recordings of gaze patterns provided by eyetrackers, it will be possible to synchronize eyetracking data and keystroke data, which will be accessible in xml or cvs formats for subsequent statistical analysis. Additionally, a new version of Translog, called Premium Edition, will fully integrate eyetracking information with the logging of text production.

Research into interpreting has seen a significant development from the 1990s, focusing on various aspects related to the performance of interpreters such as:

- neurophysiological aspects (Gran and Fabbro 1988; Darò 1989; Lambert 1989; Green *et al*. 1990; Ilic 1990; Kurz 1993; etc.);
- the role of memory and attention (Darò and Fabbro 1994; Darò, Lambert and Fabbro 1996; Darò 1997; Padilla and Bajo 1998; etc.);
- intonation and fluency (Shlesinger 1994; Pradas Macias *et al*. 2004; etc.);
- quality (Collados Aís 1998; Collados Aís *et al*. 2003, 2007; etc.);
- remote interpreting and remote learning (Moser-Mercer 2005; etc.).

Other research strands based on modern techniques used to investigate brain activation are represented, among others, by electroencephalography (EEG) (Kurz 1993, etc.) and neuroimaging (fMRI) (Buchweitz 2006).

Several authors (Gile 1995b, 1998; Moser-Mercer 1997; Pöchhacker 1998; Jiménez 2000; etc.) have discussed the methodological problems concerning research into interpreting. Due to its specific nature, these are rather different from the methodological problems concerning research into written translation. Among the methodological problems they highlight are: (1) the impossibility of using TAPs for data collection, since it is impossible to interpret and verbalize at the same time; (2) the mistakes which may derive from the use of retrospective TAPs, since it is impossible to recall automatic cognitive processes, which are not amenable to introspection; (3) the difficulty of performing direct observation given the working conditions of interpreters; (4) the difficulty of carrying out experiments given the impossibility of replicating all the factors that play a role in the course of real-life interpreting.

4.3.3 CHALLENGES AHEAD

Empirical-experimental research is now in a position to use different data elicitation techniques as a way of capturing the process-product interface in translation and interpreting. This would thereby strengthen the potential for providing more robust evidence as to what actually takes place in the cognitive operations involved in translation/interpreting. Progress and innovation is noticeable in the work of several research groups involved in empirical-experimental research in these fields. CRITT (Copenhagen Business School), EXPERTISE (University of Oslo), LETRA (Federal University of Minas Gerais, Brazil), PACTE (Universitat Autònoma de Barcelona) and PETRA (Universidad de Granada), among others, are consolidated research groups carrying out state-of-the-art empirical-experimental investigation in written translation. GRETI and ECIS (Universidad de Granada), SSLMIT (University of Trieste) and ETI (University of Geneva) are, among others, leading research groups and institutions producing groundbreaking research in interpreting. There are also studies on methodological issues aimed at helping researchers deal with methodological problems in experimental research (Gile 1998; Neunzig 2002; Williams and Chesterman 2002; Gile and Hansen 2004; Neunzig and Tanqueiro 2007; etc.)

However, there is still a tendency in the field to use tools borrowed from other disciplines. The major problem faced by empirical-experimental research is precisely the validation of its own instruments of data collection. Other disciplines, such as psychology, have a long-standing tradition of empirical-experimental investigation and this has enabled them to obtain validated instruments capable of collecting reliable data (intelligence tests, reaction times, reflex capacity, etc.). Translation studies lacks such a tradition. Therefore, it needs to design its own instruments for data collection (questionnaires, standard charts, etc.) and to put them to the test in exploratory and pilot studies in order to guarantee the reliability of data to be collected (see, for instance, Orozco and Hurtado Albir 2002).

There is therefore still a great deal to be done in terms of empirical-experimental research in translation and interpreting. The field needs to put more effort into refining experimental designs and fostering the replication of studies, thus allowing for validation or falsification of previously found evidence. This would then allow researchers to carry out studies with a much greater power of generalization.

5
TRANSLATION AS INTERCULTURAL COMMUNICATION[1]

DAVID KATAN

5.0 INTRODUCTION

It was E. T. Hall (1959/1990) who coined the term 'intercultural communication' (Rogers *et al*. 2002). In working with US departmental administrators and Native Americans, he noticed that misunderstanding arose not through language but through other, 'silent', 'hidden' or 'unconscious' yet patterned factors. In short, cultural differences. Bennett (1998: 3) explains that the fundamental premise of 'the intercultural communication approach' is that 'cultures are different in their languages, behaviour patterns, and values. So an attempt to use [monocultural] self as a predictor of shared assumptions and responses to messages is unlikely to work' – because the response, in our case to a translation, will be ethnocentric.

That translation is 'an *act of communication*' (Blum-Kulka 1986/2004: 291, emphasis in the original) has been a given since Steiner (1975/1998: 49), but not all agree about the existence or relevance of cultural differences in translation. There are three interrelated problem areas.

The first area of controversy is in the definition of culture itself. By 1952, Kroeber and Klockhohn had recorded 165 definitions, and today lobbies are still vying for authority over the meaning of 'one of the two or three most complicated words in the English language' (Williams 1976/83: 87, also in Jenks 1993: 1).

Originally, culture was simple. It referred exclusively to the humanist ideal of what was civilized in a developed society (the education system, the arts, architecture). Then a second meaning, the way of life of a people, took place alongside. Emphasis at the time was very much on 'primitive' cultures and tribal practices. With the development of sociology and cultural studies, a third meaning has emerged, related to forces in society or ideology.

Hence, also, the way culture is acquired varies according to theory. For the humanists, culture is technically learnt through explicit instruction. Anthropologists believe that culture may be learned through formal or unconscious parenting, socialization or other inculcation through long-term contact with others. It then becomes unconsciously shared amongst the group (cf. Chesterman's *Memes of Translation* 1997a). In sociology and cultural studies, culture is a site of conflict for authority or power. When it is acquired, it is through the subliminal and enforced norms of, for example, capitalist and colonialist action.

Second, there is a fairly clear historical division between those who perceive language and culture as two distinct entities, and those who view language as culture. In the first case, translation is seen as a universalist encoding-decoding linguistic activity, transferring meaning from the SL to the TL, using what Reddy (1973/1993) called the 'conduit metaphor of language transference'. Here, culture and any cultural differences can be carried by the language without significant loss. Others, such as Nida (2002: 29), believe that 'the context actually provides more distinction of meaning than the term being analyzed'. Hence, meaning is not 'carried' by the language but is negotiated between readers from within their own contexts of culture. Each readership is hence bound to receive the text according to their own expectations, and translation is necessarily a relativist form of 'manipulation' (Hermans 1985), 'mediation' (Katan 1999/2004) or 'refraction' (Lefevere 1982/2004) between two different linguacultures (Agar 1994).

Third, and closely related to both the above is the importance of 'the culture filter' in translation.

5.1 THE CULTURE FILTER

House (1977, 1981), Hervey and Higgins (1992) and Katan (1993) talk in terms of a 'culture filter' or 'cultural filter'. Katan (1999/2004) discusses four perception filters, based on neurolinguistic programming (NLP) theory, each of which is varyingly responsible for orienting or modelling our own perception, interpretation and evaluation of (to use Goffman 1974) 'what it is that is going on'. The filters are: 'physiological', 'culture', 'individual' and 'language'.

All the filters function in the same way through modelling. A model is a (usually) useful way of simplifying and making sense of something which is complex, such as 'reality'. All models, according to Bandler and Grinder (1975), make use of three principles: deletion, distortion and generalization. In the case of human modelling we cannot perceive all of 'what it is that is going on' (deletion); we tend to focus selectively or fit what we see to what we know expect, or what attracts our attention (distortion), and we tend to fill details in from our own model or level out salient differences (generalization), to make the resulting 'map of the world' useful.

Hence, cultural filters (for Katan) are one of the four particular, but related, ways in which groups organize their shared (limited, distorted and stereotypical) perception of the world. This follows Goodenough's (1957/1964: 36) definition of culture as 'an organization.... It is the form of things that people have in mind, their model of perceiving, relating, and otherwise interpreting them'. For House (2006: 349), on the other hand, 'A cultural filter is a means of capturing cognitive and socio-cultural differences' to be applied by translators, which for Katan is more closely related to the translator's capacity to mediate.

To what extent one filter prevails over another in translation is then the third area of controversy. With 'the cultural turn' (Lefevere and Bassnett 1990: 1), and Bassnett's proclaiming (1980/2002: 23) that 'the translator treats the text in isolation from the culture at his peril', the culture filter appeared to take the central stage. However, for Newmark (in Schäffner and Kelly-Holmes 1995: 80) there is 'an over-emphasis on going from one culture to another [due to] universal issues that go beyond culture. They're sometimes dressed in cultural clothes, but that's as far as it goes'. His views coincide with many professionals (Katan forthcoming). Others, again, believe that the filter should operate selectively. House (2006: 347), herself states that the 'cultural filter' should be 'inserted' only for certain text types, such as tourist information books and computer manuals. For Nida (1964: 130), on the other hand, the degree of intervention depends less on the text type itself than on the cultural and linguistic distance or gap between the languages concerned.

5.2 CULTURE AS A SYSTEM OF FRAMES

There are three related ideas which can help clarify the apparently contradictory views of culture: context(ing), frames and logical typing.

5.2.1 CONTEXT(ING)

We have already mentioned Nida's view of the crucial importance of context. Yet, as others have noted, context is not always important. In fact, a phone book, an invoice and an instructions leaflet hardly need any context for the full meaning to be understood or to be translated. Yet what Hall (1983: 61) noted was that at all times, and in any communication, there is a process of 'contexting', whereby interlocutors negotiate *how much* of the meaning is to be retrieved from the context, *how much* of the context is shared, and if not shared: 'it can be seen, as context is lost, information must be added if meaning is to remain constant'. For Hall, this constituted 'membershipping'; Relevance theory (cf. Chapter 4) operates on the same principle. Also, even with regard to instructions, *what* is relevant cannot be assumed to be universal (see Katan 1999/2004).

'Context' is a convenient if fuzzy term, first applied to translation by an anthropologist Malinowski, whose treatise, though focussing on 'primitive' cultures, is still relevant today. He studied the inhabitants of the Trobriand Islands and their language, and noted that he would have to make a number of changes in translating their Kiriwinian conversations into English. He used the following literal translation as an example: 'We run front-wood ourselves; we paddle in place; we turn we see companion ours. He runs rear-wood behind their sea-arm Pilolu'. Malinowski realized that he would need to add a commentary for an outsider reader to make explicit the layers of meaning that would be implicit for the Trobrianders, what Geertz would later call a 'thick description'. In translation studies, this has now become popularised by Appiah (1993/2004) and Hermans (2003) as 'thick translation'. First, a reader would need not only lexico-grammatical help to follow the story, but also 'to be informed about the situation in which ... words were spoken' (Malinowski 1923/1938: 301), the 'context of situation'. A version for outsiders might have sounded something like this:

> In crossing the sea-arm of Pilolu (between the Trobriands and the Amphletts), our canoe sailed ahead of the others. When nearing the shore we began to paddle. We looked back and saw our companions still far behind, still on the sea-arm of Pilolu.

The extract now makes sense; and with more of the context, the extract may be viewed as part of a story that a Trobriander is telling while sitting round with a group of eager listeners, recounting the end of a day's fishing trip.

However, to fully understand 'what it is that is going on' the reader would need to be aware 'that language is essentially rooted in the reality of culture ... the broader contexts of verbal utterance' (Malinowski 1923/1938: 305), which Malinowski later called the 'context of culture' (1935/1967: 18; cf. Halliday and Hasan 1989: 47). Malinowski noted the use of two words in particular: 'front-wood', which contained 'a specific emotional tinge only comprehensible against a background of their tribal ceremonial life, commerce and enterprise', as in 'top-of-the-range leading canoe'; and 'paddle', which *here* signals the fact that the sail is lowered as shallow water is reached. It now becomes clear that we are witnessing a triumphal recount of a fishing expedition which finished in a race to the shore and which by now is all but over.

Many scholars have since discussed and classified the context of situation, in particular Halliday and Hasan (and see also House 1997). But as Halliday and Hasan (1989: 47) themselves point out, very little had been done in terms of developing the context of culture, which we will now discuss.

5.2.2 LOGICAL TYPING

The anthropologist Bateson (1972: 289) noted that context, if it were to remain a useful concept, must be subject to what he called 'logical typing': 'Either we must discard the notion of "context", or we retain this notion and, with it, accept the hierarchic series – stimulus, context of stimulus, context of context of stimulus, etc.'. By logical typing he meant that each context represents a 'type' (such as the different context types of 'situation' and 'culture'), and each 'type' frames, or logically informs, the next in a hierarchy of (often paradoxical) types. Goffman (1974) in *Frame Analysis*, explains that a frame tells us 'What is it that is going on here?' Each frame contains its own reality in much the same way as an area of black and white stripes on a white wall may be called a painting when framed. The labelling of the frame (e.g. 'Night and Day') affects our interpretation. If we then frame the whole exhibition as 'Reflections on Prison' we change perspective, and understand more of what it is that is going on (according to the exhibition organizer).

We can now move back to the competing definitions of culture and present them as essential parts of a unified model of culture or rather a system of frames which compete in their influence over what, when, how and why we translate.

5.2.3 THE LOGICAL LEVELS OF CULTURE

The levels themselves are based on aspects of NLP logical level theory (e.g. Dilts 1990; O'Connor 2001: 28–32) and the anthropological 'iceberg model', popularized in Hall's 'triad of culture' (1959/1990). The logical levels serve to introduce one dimension of the system, dividing aspects of culture (the iceberg) into what is visible (above the waterline), semi-visible and invisible (Figure 5.1). The frames below the water line are progressively more hidden but also progressively closer to our unquestioned assumptions about the world and our own (cultural) identities. A further, sociological, dimension may be described as operating on the iceberg itself.

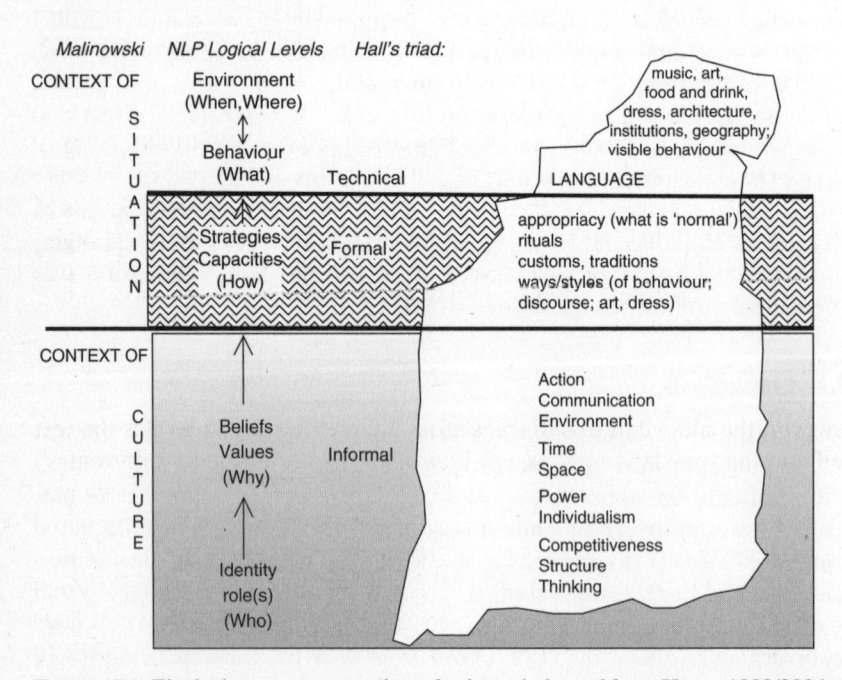

FIGURE 5.1 The iceberg representation of culture (adapted from Katan 1999/2004: 43)

The extent to which a translator should intervene (i.e. interpret and manipulate rather than operate a purely linguistic transfer) will be in accordance with beliefs about which frame(s) most influence translation. Translation scholars tend to focus on the more hidden levels, while practitioners are more concerned with what is visible on the surface.

5.3 Technical Culture: Shared Encyclopaedic Knowledge

The first cultural frame is at the tip of the iceberg and coincides with the humanist concept of culture. The focus is on the text, dressed (adapting Newmark) in its best civilized clothes of a particular culture. At this 'technical' level the language signs have a clear WYSIWYG (what you see is what you get) referential function, and any associated hidden values are universal. The task of the translator at this level is to transfer the terms and concepts in the source text abroad with minimum loss (from literature and philosophical ideas to software manuals), so that 'what you get' in the source text is equivalent to 'what you get' in the target text. As long as the two cultures 'have reached a comparable degree of development', there is no reason why meaning, reader response and uptake should not be universal (Seleskovich in Newmark, 1988: 6; see also Wilss 1982: 48).

This is what Newmark (1981: 184–5) called 'the cultural value' of translation, and indeed is embedded in the bylaws (2007) of the International Federation of Translators (Fédération Internationale des Traducteurs, FIT): 'to assist in the spreading of culture throughout the world'. The chapter headings in *Translators through History* (Delisle and Woodsworth 1995) give us an idea of what is involved: the invention of alphabets and the writing of dictionaries; the development of national languages and literatures, and the spread of religions and cultural values. Depending on the asymmetries of power, spreading the new terms and concepts might be perceived as enlightenment, 'the white man's burden', an affront, the wielding of hegemony or a much-valued addition to intellectual debate.

5.3.1 Culturemes

However, the main concern of translators intervening at this level is the text itself and the translation of 'culture-bound' terms, for example 'culturemes': formalized, socially and juridically embedded phenomena that exist in a particular form or function in only one of the two cultures being compared (Vermeer in Nord 1997: 34 and Nord 2000: 214). These 'cultural categories' (Newmark, 1988: 95, after Nida) cover a wide array of semantic fields: from geography and traditions to institutions and technologies. Scholars since Vinay and Darbelnet (1958/1995) have offered a plethora of strategies to compensate for the lack of cultureme equivalence. Kwieciński (2001: 157) has summarized these into four groups: 'exoticising procedures', 'rich explicatory procedures', 'recognised exoticisation' and 'assimilative procedures'.

'Exoticising procedures' allow the foreign term into the target language (*falafel, macho, Weltanschauung, burka*). For Newmark (e.g. 1988: 82), this procedure offers local colour and atmosphere, though this approach has been criticized by Berman (1985/2004: 286), who claims that making a text 'more authentic' (the inverted commas are his) insidiously emphasizes and exoticizes a certain stereotype. Clearly, we need to be aware of the difference between the utility of the resources available for a translator and the slavish use of any one irrespective of context or translation purpose.

The second grouping is 'rich explicatory procedures'. The aim is to slide in an extra term or two which will cue readers to enough of the context, often through a local analogy, to guide them towards a more equivalent cognition. Two of the many possible procedures are the use of explanatory brackets, such as '*Knesset* (the Israeli Parliament)', or through adjectivizing the source term, as in 'hot *cotechino* sausage'. Newmark, amongst others (e.g. Nida 1975), suggests the need here for componential analysis to analyse the semantic properties, connotations or culture-bound components of terms in the SL and the TL.

When, where and how to explicate depends on the translator's acute sensitivity to reader uptake. The following Harry Potter translation into French by Ménard is a good example of a translator's balanced member-shipping decisions (shown here in bold):

Viewers as far apart as Kent, Yorkshire and Dundee have been phoning in (Rowling 1997a: 12)
*Des téléspectateurs qui habitent **dans des régions** aussi éloignées les unes des autres que le Kent, le Yorkshire et **la côte est de l'Ecosse** m'ont télephoné* (Rowling 1997b: 11)
[Viewers who live **in regions** as distant from one other as Kent, Yorkshire and **the east coast of Scotland** have phoned me].

The third grouping is 'recognized exoticism'. Some well-known geographical and personal names and titles have 'accepted translations' according to language: *Geneva* (English) is *Genève* (French), *Genf* (German) or *Ginevra* (Italian), not to be confused with *Genova*, which is Italian for the English *Genoa*. The Italian painter *Tiziano Vecelli* changes to *Titian* only in English; *Charlemagne* (French) is *Karl der Große* (German), *Carlo Magno* (Italian) and either *Charlemagne* or *Charles the Great* (English); and *La Gioconda* (Italian) is the *Mona Lisa*. There are more exceptions than rules concerning exoticism, and 'recognition' is not only debatable but also ever changing. Thirty years ago the English used to holiday in *Apulia* while Italians went to *Nuova York*. Today they go to *Puglia* or *New York*. Americans, however, still prefer *Apulia*. So the translator will always need to check how recognized the exoticism is.

Finally, 'assimilative' procedures transform text from the original into close functionally equivalent target terms, or it is even deleted if not considered central. So, *premier ministre* and *presidente del gobierno* are French and Spanish cultural equivalents of *prime minister*, even though their powers and responsibilities are not exactly the same. And the same goes for equivalent idioms. As Nida and Taber note (1969/74: 4) *white as egret's feathers* may be as effective as 'white as snow' as long as 'snow' is not a leitmotif in itself in the target language. Alternatively, a translator can decide to 'reduce to sense', which would reduce the evocative power of the simile to a more prosaic description, as in *very, very white*. The fact, though, that partial or even complete equivalents exist does not in itself mean that assimilation or domestication is the best translation strategy. Like all the other procedures above, they form part of the resources available from which a translator may choose.

5.3.2 ALLUSIONS

While still at the level of shared context, we move away from the 'seeing' part of WYSIWYG to more context-based communication, such as Leppihalme's 'key-phrase allusions', which include clichés and proverbs (e.g. 'Apparently taxis all *turn into pumpkins at midnight*'). She proposes 'a metacultural capacity' (1997: 20), one that is able to comprehend 'the extralinguistic knowledge of the source language culture' and which can also 'take into account the expectations and background knowledge of potential TT readers'. In fact, Akira Mizuno (in Kondo and Tebble, 1997), a practising broadcast interpreter in Japan, states that translation of popular culture presents one of the greatest challenges to Japanese broadcasters. He gives a list of some recurring American favourites which have caused him the most difficulty to translate for his Japanese audience. These include, for example, 'Superman', 'the tooth fairy' and 'Kilroy was here'.

Not all allusions have such clear exophoric and exportable referents, but rather carry with them 'cultural baggage', opening up frames or schemata more specifically related to what is appropriate or valued in a particular culture, which we shall look at now.

5.4 FORMAL CULTURE: FUNCTIONALIST, APPROPRIATE PRACTICES

Hall's second, 'formal', level of culture is part of the anthropological definition, usually described in terms of what is normal or appropriate. This floats under the visible part of the iceberg because appropriacy and normality are rarely formally taught. They are more fuzzy concepts and only come to our notice when they are absent or performed maladroitly. As Agar (2006: 5) explains: 'Culture becomes visible only when differences appear'. Many translation scholars have taken up Bhabha's (1994) *Location of Culture* as the space 'in between' as a stock metaphor for translation (e.g. Wolf 2000; but see Tymoczko 2003: 186–7 for a criticism).

Vermeer's own definition, based on the first part of Goodenough's (1957/1964: 36), belongs to this level: 'Culture consists of everything one needs to know, master and feel, in order to assess where members of a society are behaving acceptably or deviantly in their various roles' (in Snell-Hornby 2006: 55). According to Snell-Hornby, it is also accepted by German-speaking translators as 'the standard'. Intervention at this level focuses on the *skopos* of the translation (Vermeer), and tailoring the translation according to reception in the target culture.

At this level of culture, linguistically we are no longer able to point to universal features that change label, or to culturemes that may require technical explication, but, as Sapir (1929/1958: 214) emphasized, 'distinct worlds'. So, cultures, here, are plural, and texts require mediating rather than conduit translation. Though Leppihalme restricts the term 'culture bumps' to 'the allusion [which] may remain unclear or puzzling' (1997: 4), the 'bump' can apply to any communication problem. It was coined by Archer (1986) as a mild form of 'culture shock', which has been defined as the 'emotional reactions to the disorientation that occurs when one is immersed in an unfamiliar culture and is deprived of familiar cues' (Paige 1993: 2).

Two examples below demonstrate the real-world problem bumps of transferring 'normal practice' with the conduit approach. A 1996 fax[2], written in English from a firm in Pakistan to a well-known Italian fashion house with the intent of becoming a supplier, began as follows:

Attn: [name and department]
I made samples for you in 1994 for the summer and we had received orders for about 20,000 blouses to be shipped in 1995 but due to a plague in our country these orders were cancelled by you. The contact was made by (full name and full address).

This is not 'the normal' way to write a business letter of introduction in English. The introductory statement is too direct, personal and accusatory. Bentahila (2004) reports on a study of university students (Tetouan, Morocco) who used a similar more personal and emotive style to write a letter of application for study grants in the UK. Optimum relevance clearly comes from another local norm: 96 per cent, for example, expressed a desire to pursue personal ambitions (e.g. 'I don't exaggerate if I say that it is my dream').

Clearly, texts with a persuasive function, as above, must be manipulated if they are to function persuasively in the target culture. As Nida (1997: 37) puts it: 'Many translators believe that if they take care of the words and grammar, the discourse will take care of itself, but this concept results from an insufficient understanding of the role of discourse structures in interlingual communication'. He continues by noting that it is the 'intelligent secretaries in North America' who

> know how to delete overtly complimentary statements from Latins, and to add appropriate expressions of greeting and friendship from their North American bosses. Otherwise Latinos will think that American businessmen will be reluctant to do business with Latinos who appear to be too flattering and insincere.

The fact that he does not mention translators is striking but belies a fundamental issue: who actually acts as a cultural mediator? The 'translator', paradoxically, does not have the freedom a secretary has to facilitate communication, due both to domestic fidelity-to-the-text norms and to the (limiting) beliefs that professional translators themselves have about their role.

Pragmatically speaking, a target reader is bound within an 'environmental bubble' (Cohen 1972: 177; Katan 2001) of his or her own normality, or model of the world, and in general can only have at most a technical understanding of another culture. If there is understanding of the formal level of culture, it will usually be an ethnocentric one (Bennett 1993, 1998; Katan 2001). As Chesterman (1997a: 54) informs us: 'Norm flouters threaten normality, produce difference and are quickly ostracized or punished'.

Useful technically oriented communication preference models are now becoming available, thanks to the study of contrastive rhetoric (Connor 1996). These can help in the mediation between culture specific accepted practices (e.g. German/English, House 2003b: 31; Italian/English, Katan, 1999/2004: 261–2); see also Ventola (2000); Candlin and Gotti (2004).

As noted above regarding Nida's comment, translation norms dictate the extent to which these models can be put into practice. Also, as descriptive translation studies have shown (Chesterman 1993; Toury 1995; Pym *et al.* 2008 amongst others), the rules and conventions guiding appropriate translation decisions are domestic rather than universal. They govern all translation practice, from decisions regarding which texts are acceptable or accepted for translation, to the type of translation and assimilation/compensation strategies to employ, and to the criteria by which a translation is judged.

5.5 Informal Culture: Cognitive Systems and Values

Hall's third level of culture he terms 'informal' or 'out-of-awareness' because it is not normally accessible to the conscious brain for meta-cognitive comment, while, as we have seen, the formal level can be technically analysed and modelled. At the informal level, there are no formal guides to practice but instead unquestioned core values and beliefs, or stories about self and the world. As such, culture, inculcated, for example, though family, school and the media, becomes a relatively fixed internal representation of reality, Bourdieu's 'habitus', which then both guides and constrains an individual's orientation in the real world.

Psychological anthropology defines culture in terms of a *Weltanschauung:* a shared model, map or view of the perceivable world (Korzybski 1933/1958); 'mental programming' (Hofstede 2001); 'the form of things that people have in their mind' (Goodenough 1957/1964: 36), which orients individual and community ways of perceiving and doing things. These are 'core, primary ethical values' (Chesterman 1997a: 149) and guide formal culture choices. Wierzbicka (1992: 63) gives an example of a Russian core value *duša* lacking in 'the universe of Anglo-Saxon culture'. The repetition of the term in Vasily Grossman's (1980) novel *Zizn'i sud'ba*, *Life and Fate*, is an essential feature of the ST. Yet the 'faithful translation ["soul"] leads to an oddness for the target text reader'. Wierzbicka's advice is to use other partial synonyms and/or eliminate some of the references to *duša* altogether.

However, not all interculturally-aware translation scholars agree with this form of active distortion of the form. For Venuti (1998a), the main issue is exactly the opposite: the loss of the foreign and an over-domestication, pandering to Anglo value systems. House, herself, warns against actively manipulating the culture filter for written language, particularly literature, as, in her view, the ST text form has its own 'worth' (and here mediators would agree); and also because 'context cannot be regarded in translation as dynamic' (2006: 343).

Nevertheless, readers at this level of culture will evaluate the use of language (behaviour) not so much in terms of 'oddness' of style but through attributing features of personality (identity) according to their *own* value system. The universal modelling filter here not only distorts the meaning of behaviour but also generalizes in terms of 'type'. So, limited information about 'the other' easily slips into generalized negative stereotyping regarding type of person. The following text from Italo Calvino's *L'avventura di una moglie*/*The Adventure of a Wife* (1993: 116) provides a good example (see Katan 2002). Stefania, the well-mannered wife, has just walked into 'a bar' for the very first time and goes up to the counter. Her very first move is to make the following bold request (highlighted):

Un ristretto, doppio, caldissimo, – disse al cameriere.
'**A concentrated, double, very hot**', she said to the barman.

Initially, this foreignized translation will leave the Anglophone reader bewildered, as none of the words directly cue 'coffee'. More serious is the fact that we have a projected directive, which the English language and cultural filters are likely to distort into a flouting of negative politeness norms; and Stefania's unassuming behaviour (for an Italian addressee) is likely to be 'typed' as 'brazen' or 'rude'.

Katan (2002) suggests a number of mediating strategies, including couching the projecting directive within an explicit request frame, thus leaving the politeness to the context so that there is no distortion of the target text within the projection. This will allow the readers (and, in reality, the barman too) to add the politeness from their own expectancy frame:

> She asked the barman for an espresso, 'thick, double and really hot'.

This solution allows the readers to glimpse, from the safety of their own environmental bubble, something of the foreignness of Italian directness in projected requests – without distorting the illocutionary intent. The choice of the foreignizing 'thick, double', rather than the domestic 'large, strong', takes the reader away from the domestic towards the look, feel, taste and aroma of an *espresso*. In so doing the reader is likely to experience a richer perlocutionary effect, and will have begun to learn something new.

At this level of culture, no word is entirely denotative. Hence, even seemingly technical words can have 'cultural baggage' attached to them according to readership. Bassnett (1980/2002: 18–19, 28–9), for example, notes how global products, such as butter, whisky and Martini, can change status and connotation once translated or transferred to a new readership, due to culture-bound practice differences. Díaz-Guerrero and Szalay (1991), furthermore, show how the same term can be associated with almost polar-opposite values and beliefs. Their free-association experiment demonstrated that Americans related *United States* to patriotism and government while Mexicans associated *Estados Unidos* with exploitation and wealth. As Allen (2000: 17), taking his cue from Bakhtin, puts it: 'Meaning ... is unique, to the extent that it belongs to the linguistic interaction of specific individuals or groups within specific social contexts'.

In monocultural communication, this 'uniqueness' does not usually require clarification of the performative, as Leech points out (1983: 174–5, 325). Intercultural communication mediators, on the other hand, will always need to consider how anchored the intended meaning is to its 'specific social context' and hence value system; and also how clear it is to the target reader that the meaning is framed within a *different* model of the world. The humble chrysanthemum, for example, has little specific connotation within the Anglo cultures, but strong symbolic meaning in most of the rest of the world. It is often the 'flower of the dead'. So a text which states 'These autumn classic chrysanthemums will make for a warm, wonderful feeling any time', taken from an American catalogue, will need to have the speech act framed with a performative, which answers the question: 'According to whom/which context?', e.g. 'In America ...', 'As *they* say ....' (See also Katan 1999, 1999/2004: 145–8).

Finally, the original writer's individual stance is also likely to be distorted or simply deleted in translation through lack of astute membershipping of the target reader. As Dillon (1992: 39–40) notes, insider and outsider reading will be very different because:

> Insiders have large funds of special information about other relevant claims, received opinion, and previous positions of the writer, in addition, they have an interest in the matter under discussion: they themselves have positions against which they test the argument ... they are in a position to evaluate what is said in terms of what is alluded to, obliquely touched on, or even unsaid.

5.5.1 CULTURAL GRAMMARS

Ethnographers have talked about the creation of a 'cultural "grammar"' (see Duranti 1997: 27; Goodenough in Risager 2006: 45), which Wierzbicka (1996: 527) describes as 'a set of subconscious rules that shape a people's ways of thinking, feeling, speaking, and interacting'.

The values and beliefs that form the basis of the subconscious rules can be teased out in two particular ways, emically and etically.[3] Wierzbicka's emic ethnographic approach (e.g. 1996, 2006) is to spell out subjective beliefs about appropriacy using semantic universals to provide 'cultural scripts'. The 'universals' contain a strictly limited use of language, free of cultural baggage, such as the adjectives 'good' and 'bad'. Table 5.1 is an example of her analysis of the difference between the 'vague, undefined' Japanese 'effacement' and Anglo 'self-enhancement'.

TABLE 5.1 Japanese 'effacement' and Anglo 'self-enhancement' scripts

Japanese 'self-effacement' script	Anglo 'self enhancement' script
It is good to often think something like this:	It is good to often think something like this:
'I did something bad	'I did something very good
I often do things like this	I can do things like this
Not everyone does things like this	Not everyone can do things like this
Other people don't often do things like this'	Other people don't often do things like this'

Source: Adapted from Wierzbicka (1996: 537).

Alternatively, either through ethnographic fieldwork or through extensive questionnaire research, attempts have been made to distil the subjective scripts into etic classifications to model the basic orientations, such as 'self-effacement'. Kroeber and Klockhuhn (1952) were the first to introduce value orientations, suggesting that there were a limited number of responses to universal human needs or problems and that cultures tended to prefer one response over another (for a summary see Katan 1999/2004).

E.T. Hall (1976/1989), for example, through his 'contexting theory', distinguished between a culture's preference to communicate in a WYSIWYG way ('low context') or through more context-based channels ('high context'). This general cline of preference helps to clarify the relative values of verbal/written contracts across cultures (Hampden-Turner and Trompenaars 1983: 123–4), website design differences (Würtz 2005), the relative importance and detail of public signs (e.g. the 'Caution HOT!' take-away coffee cups – a necessity in low-context communication cultures) and, indeed, the Anglo concern for clarity in translation (Katan 1999/2004: 234).

In a study of insurance brochures offered by banks in Britain and Italy, Katan (2006) analysed the frequency of words that logically indicate orientation alternatives, as outlined by Hofstede (1991, 2001). The frequency of terms, appertaining for example, to 'security/*sicurezza*' and to 'comfort/*tranquillita*' was significantly different, as were the use of time markers and interrogatives/declaratives, to the extent that 'Basically it would seem that the British reader is being sold an independent and comfortable life, whereas the Italian reader is being sold security and certainty' (Katan 2006: 69).

See also Mooij's (2004b) work on advertising, and Manca (forthcoming) for a corpus-driven perspective.

5.6 Outside the Iceberg: Societal Power Relations

Sociologists and cultural studies scholars focus on the influence of culture at the level of society, institutions and prevailing ideologies. Culture, here, is the result of the 'pressures that social structures apply to social action' (Jenks 1993: 25). These pressures mould, manipulate or conflict with the individual but shared models of the world discussed above.

There are two other fundamental differences compared to the pure anthropological model. First, individuals (and texts) cannot be assigned to 'a culture'. This is seen as 'essentialist' (Green in Bhabha 1994: 4). Also, Verschueren (2003: 7) believes that 'any attempt to compare cultures' is 'risky', and believes that Hofstede's 'decontextualise[d] idealised parameters of variability' are 'a particularly deplorable example'. Wierzbicka (2006: 24) agrees, stating 'there is no common, no set list of categories invented by the researcher and then "applied" to various human groups'. Instead individuals will have many cultural provenances. Within this frame of culture, the idea of a 'useful simplified model of reality', with neat ready-made classifications, begins to fall apart. Cultures are seen to be variously privileged or suppressed, and individuals will negotiate a position within a set of complex cultural systems jockeying for power. Within translation studies, scholars drawing on polysystem theory (e.g. Even-Zohar 1990/2004), postcolonial theory (e.g. Bassnett and Trivedi 1999) and narrative theory (e.g. Baker 2006) all share this assumption.

Secondly, the system in which the translator works is itself under question (as is the validity of cultural relativity). At this level, translators intervene between competing (and unequal) power systems, no longer to facilitate but to take sides, aware that texts (and they themselves) are carriers of ideologies (Hatim and Mason 1997: 147). The decision to translate Salmon Rushdie's *The Satanic Verses* (1988) or *Did Six Million Really Die?* (Harwood 1977) are clear cases in point. The translator at this level is no longer a disassociated mediator but is conscious of being 'an ethical agent of social change' (Tymoczko 2003: 181), or 'an activist' involved in re-narrating the world (Baker 2006). In a similar vein, Venuti, for example, rails against *The Translator's Invisibility* (Venuti 1995/2008), preferring to let the reader come into direct contact with the difference of 'the other'. This stance, as he says, 'stems partly from a political agenda ... an opposition to the global hegemony of English' (Venuti 1998a: 10), a hegemony that communicates and normalizes specific (e.g. capitalist, colonial) cultural values.

Intervention at this level obviously raises many ethical questions, but there is also clearly a fine practical line between a successful foreignized translation which resists the domestic generic conventions to introduce a new way of writing or way of thinking, and an unread translation because 'even breaches of canonical storylines have to be effected within circumscribed, normative plots [i.e. formal culture] if they are to be intelligible at all' (Baker 2006: 98). Also, many scholars confuse the utility of etic classifications designed to encourage mindshifting out of an ethnocentric mindset with mindless stereotyping, the opposite of what translation as intercultural communication represents.

Ultimately, though, culture has to be understood not only as a set of levels or frames but as an integrated system, in a constant state of flux, through which textual signals are negotiated and reinterpreted according to context and individual stance.

5.7 The cultural mediator

It is the mediator's task to negotiate the various signals, contexts and stances. According to Taft:

> A cultural mediator is a person who facilitates communication, understanding, and action between persons or groups who differ with respect to language and culture. The role of the mediator is performed by interpreting the expressions, intentions, perceptions, and expectations of each cultural group to the other, that is, by establishing and balancing the communication between them. In order to serve as a link in this sense, the mediator must be able to participate to some extent in both cultures. Thus a mediator must be to a certain extent bicultural.
> (Taft 1981: 53)

As Bennett (1993, 1998) makes clear, to be bicultural means having passed through a number of developmental stages towards 'intercultural sensitivity'.

One of the later stages is termed 'contextual evaluation', which is at the same competence level as Pym's (2003) definition of translation: 'the ability to generate a series of more than one viable TT [and] the ability to select only one viable TT from this series quickly and with justifiable confidence'.

To 'select', the mediator will need to ' "mindshift" cultural orientation' (Taft 1981: 53); to be able to do this, a mediator needs another point of reference. This is known in NLP as the 'third perceptual position' (DeLozier & Grinder, 1987; O'Connor, 2001: 33–4; Katan 2001, 2002), disassociated from both the contexts of the ST and from those of the virtual TT. From this third position the mediator (informed also by the other stakeholders in the translation process) can 'objectively' manipulate the text.

Of course, Hatim and Mason (1997) and Baker (2006), amongst others, are entirely correct to suggest that mediators feed their own (and are fed) knowledge and beliefs into the processing of the texts. However, the beliefs we are principally concerned with here are of a different 'type'; not those of a mediator's ideological position but rather beliefs about the (communicative) needs inherent between texts and their readers. Compare the work of Gutt (1991/2000) from a relevance theory perspective (see Chapter 4).

Table 5.2 below shows how the various 'types' frame each other. It is a logical levels table that asks at each level what it is that is going on within the context of culture and in that particular context of situation.

TABLE 5.2 Logical levels table of context of culture and context of situation

LEVEL	What is going on?	Potential differences to be accounted for in the text	Potential differences to be accounted for between cultures
Environment	Where and when is this 'going on'? In what context of situation?	Lexicogrammatical resources, genre, intertextual links, specialized language	Physical, political, social environment: period, people, setting, artefacts; culturemes, encyclopaedic knowledge, allusions, culture bumps
Behaviour	What is it that is 'going on'? What is to be translated?	Semantics: visible text, locution, cohesion	Visible action/ descriptions: (non) verbal behaviour, proxemics

Continued

TABLE 5.2 Continued

Strategies	How are these things 'going on'? How is it to be translated?	Pragmatics: illocutionary intent/force, register, organization of discourse, house rules, individual style, coherence	Communication preferences: development of ideas. spoken/written styles, habits, customs; Norms, appropriacy, rules; linguaculture
Values Beliefs	Why are these things 'going on'? What is the purpose of the translation?	Intentions: message, hidden message, assumptions, presuppositions	The hierarchy of preferred value-orientations: Beliefs about identity and about what is 'right' 'standard' or 'normal'
Identity	Who is involved in this 'going on'? - original author - reader(ships) - commissioner - translator as copier/ manipulator	Actors in the text: personalities, animated subjects,	National, ethnic, gender, religious, class, role; individual personality and cultural provenance(s)
Role, mission in society	Is this 'going on' coherent with my role/mission and the relevant social forces? How do I need to act with regard to the social forces?	Text as agent of change or status quo: esteem, ethics (of actors), long-term perlocutionary effects	The social forces. power issues: hegemonies, ideologies; moral issues, professional issues

The first two columns delineate the frame at which intervention will take place, directing the mediator through specific questions to the focus at that level. The third and fourth columns consider the (source and target) texts, contexts of culture and situation, and show which aspects of culture are relevant at each level.

To a large extent, the table synthesizes the discussion of the iceberg and the forces acting on it. So, for example, when translating a text, all translators will need to have an idea of the type of text they have to translate and what culture-bound features it may manifest. They will then, at the level of 'behaviour', need to account for 'what it is that is going on', the sense immanent in the individual sentences. Moving away from technical culture to the formal, the mediator becomes concerned with appropriacy: how the text has been written and how the text operates (or might operate) in the target culture. At the level of 'values and beliefs', mediators, taking the third perceptual position, will focus on the out-of-awareness levels of culture: what beliefs and values are implicitly carried by the ST, how these are likely to be filtered by the intended target reader; and what the (likely) intentions of the ST author were compared to the actors involved in the translation. In short, 'why are these things going on?' Hence, at the level of identity we have a variety of actors involved, both within and outside the text, who embody a cluster of values and/or beliefs which will favour a set of text strategies, visible as the text itself, produced within a particular environment. At this level of 'identity', the mediator will take into account the needs or requirements of the other actors, such as the ST author, commissioner and intended reader; and last, but not least, the mediator's own beliefs about how to mediate.

Finally, the level of 'mission' is concerned with the way roles relate to society and how translating affects the status quo, and questions the profession itself. It answers the larger more existential question as to 'why' the mediator should decide to accept (or not) a particular commission at a particular time, and what it is that has guided an individual to act as a mediator. This level, too, brings into question the whole system within which power relations, roles, values, strategies and behaviours underpinning intercultural communication are sanctified.

5.8 Conclusion

To conclude, translation as intercultural communication requires treating the text itself as only one of the cues of meaning. Other, 'silent', 'hidden' and 'unconscious' factors, which when shared may be termed cultural, determine how a text will be understood. In translating, a new text will be created which will be read according to a *different* map or model of the world, through a series of different set of perception filters. Hence the need to mediate. The translator should be able to model the various worlds, through, for example, the Logical Levels model, and by switching perceptual positions gain a more complete picture of 'What it is that is, could or should be, going on'.

Notes

1 This chapter is a much expanded version of the author's 'translation as culture' entry in Baker and Saldanha (2008).

2 In my personal possession.
3 These terms were coined by Pike (Headland *et al.* 1990) to distinguish the unframed, subjective and personal (emic) from the framed (etic) typing or classification. The etic approach will be the result of (ideally) objective and generalized empirical study.

6
TRANSLATION, ETHICS, POLITICS

THEO HERMANS

6.0 INTRODUCTION

In his opening address to the post-apartheid South African parliament in 1994, President Nelson Mandela said that a word like 'kaffir' should no longer be part of our vocabulary. Its use was subsequently outlawed in South Africa. Imagine you are asked to translate, for publication in that country, an historical document from the pre-apartheid era which contains the word. Should you write it, gloss it, omit it or replace it with something else – and if so, with what, with another derogatory word or some blander superordinate term? Are you not duty-bound to respect the authenticity of the historical record? Would you have any qualms about using the word if the translation was meant for publication outside South Africa?

In Germany and Austria, denying the Holocaust is forbidden by law. In November 1991, in Germany, Günter Deckert provided a simultaneous German interpretation of a lecture in which the American Frederic Leuchter denied the existence of gas chambers in Auschwitz. Deckert was taken to court and eventually convicted. Was this morally right? Was Deckert not merely relaying into German someone else's words, without having to assume responsibility for them? Is it relevant that Deckert is a well-known neo-Nazi, and that he expressed agreement with Leuchter's claims? If Deckert's conviction was morally justified, should we not also accept that Muslims who agreed with Ayatollah Khomeiny's 1989 fatwa against Salman Rushdie were right to regard the translators of *The Satanic Verses* as guilty of blasphemy too?

The examples (from Kruger 1997 and Pym 1997) are real enough, and they involve, apart from legal issues, moral and political choices that translators and interpreters make. While translators and interpreters have always had to make such choices, sustained reflection about this aspect of their work is of relatively recent date. It has come as a result of growing interest in such things as the political and ideological role of translation, the figure of the translator as a mediator, and various disciplinary agendas that have injected their particular concerns into translation studies.

Making choices presupposes first the possibility of choice, and then agency, values and accountability. Traditional work on translation was not particularly interested in these issues. It tended to focus on textual matters, primarily the relation between a translation and its original, or was of the applied kind, concerned with training and practical criticism, more often than not within a linguistic or a literary framework. A broadening of the perspective became noticeable from roughly the 1980s onwards. It resulted in the contextualization of translation, prompted a reconsideration of the translator as a social and ethical agent, and eventually led to a self-reflexive turn in translation studies.

To get an idea of the kind of change that is involved, a quick look at interpreting will help. Early studies were almost exclusively concerned with cognitive aspects of conference interpreting, investigating such things as interpreters' information processing ability and memory capacity (Pöchhacker and Shlesinger 2002; see also this volume, Chapter 8). However, a study of the Iraqi interpreter's behaviour in the highly charged atmosphere of Saddam Hussein being interviewed by a British television journalist on the eve of the 1991 Gulf War showed very different constraints at work; they were directly related to questions of power and control, as Saddam repeatedly corrected a desperately nervous interpreter (Baker 1997). Over the last ten years or so interpreting studies have been transformed by the growing importance of community interpreting, which, in contrast to conference interpreting, usually takes place in informal settings and sometimes in an atmosphere of suspicion, and is often emotionally charged. As a rule, these exchanges involve stark power differentials, with on one side an establishment figure, say a customs official, a police officer or a doctor, and on the other a migrant worker or an asylum seeker, perhaps illiterate and probably unused to the format of an interpreted interview. The interpreter in such an exchange may well be untrained, and have personal, ideological or ethnic loyalties. Situations like these cannot be understood by looking at technicalities only; they require full contextualization and an appreciation of the stakes involved.

6.1 Decisions, decisions

To put developments like these into perspective, we should recall the functionalist and descriptive approaches that emerged in the 1970s and 1980s. If traditional translation criticism rarely went beyond pronouncing judgement on the quality of a particular version, functionalist studies (Nord 1997) pursued questions such as who commissioned a translation or what purpose the translated text was meant to serve in its new environment (see Chapter 3). Descriptivism (Hermans 1985, 1999; Lambert 2006; Lefevere 1992; Toury 1995) worked along similar lines but showed an interest in historical poetics and in the role of (especially literary) translation in particular periods. Within the descriptive paradigm, André Lefevere, in particular, went further and began to explore the embedding of translations in social and ideological as well as cultural contexts. His keyword was 'patronage', which he understood in a broad sense as any person or institution able to exert significant control over the translator's work. Since patrons were generally driven by larger economic or political rather than by purely cultural concerns, Lefevere claimed that what determined translation was firstly ideology and then poetics, with language coming in third place only. In this vein he studied the ideological, generic and textual 'grids', as he called them, that shaped, for instance, nineteenth-century English translations of Virgil. Individual translators could differentiate themselves from their colleagues and predecessors by manipulating these grids and, if they did so successfully, acquire cultural prestige or, with a term derived from Pierre Bourdieu, symbolic capital (Bassnett and Lefevere 1998: 41–56).

More recent studies have taken this line a step further and show, for example, how translation from Latin and Greek in Victorian Britain, the use of classical allusions in novels of the period, and even debates concerning metrical translation of ancient verse, contributed to class-consciousness and the idea of a national culture (Osborne 2001; Prins 2005). Still in the Victorian era, translators contributed substantially to the definition of the modern concept of democracy (Lianeri 2002).

Lefevere's early work had been steeped in literary criticism but he ended up delving into questions of patronage and ideology. The trajectory is in many ways symptomatic for the field as a whole. The collection *Translation, History and Culture*, edited by Susan Bassnett and Lefevere in 1990, confirmed the extent to which translation was now approached from a cultural studies angle. It contained postcolonial and feminist chapters alongside pieces on translation in oral traditions and the literary politics of translator prefaces in Canada. It made the point that translation, enmeshed as it is in social and ideological structures, cannot be thought of as a transparent, neutral or innocent philological activity. The study of translation had thus readied itself for the new impulses deriving from cultural materialism, postcolonial studies and gender studies that would hit the field in the 1990s.

6.2 Translation and Ethics

The new approaches shared a concern with ethics that went beyond the tentative steps in this direction that the functionalist and descriptive line had been taking. Functionalism and descriptivism asked who translated what, for whom, when, where, how and why. Adopting the point of view of the practising translator faced with continually having to make decisions about whether or not to accept a commission, what style of translating to pick and what syntactical structures and lexical choices to put down in sentence after sentence, researchers found in the notion of translation norms a useful analytical tool. Norms could be understood as being both psychological and social in nature. They were a social reality in that they presupposed communities and the values these communities subscribed to; they were psychological because they consisted of shared and internalized expectations about how individuals should behave and what choices they should make in certain types of situation.

Gideon Toury (1995), who was among the first to apply the concept to translation as decision making, saw norms primarily as constraints on the translator's behaviour. He also pointed out the relevance of the concept: the totality of a translator's norm-governed choices determines the shape of the final text. Others subsequently improved the theoretical underpinning by invoking the interplay between translator and audience (Geest 1992; Hermans 1991; Nord 1997). Norms possessed a directive character that told individuals what kind of statements were socially acceptable; thus, making the desired choices would result in translations deemed by the relevant community to be valid or legitimate, not just as translations but as cultural texts. In this sense norms functioned as problem-solving devices. Andrew Chesterman (1997a, 1997b) related norms to professional ethics, which, he claimed, demanded a commitment to adequate expression, the creation of a truthful resemblance between original and translation, the maintenance of trust between the parties involved in the transaction and the minimization of misunderstanding. Drawing on the ethical codes of conduct of professional organizations, Chesterman went on to propose a Hieronymic oath for translators and interpreters worldwide, on the model of the medical profession's Hippocratic oath (Chesterman 2001b).

Chesterman's proposal appeared in a special issue of the journal *The Translator*, entitled 'The Return to Ethics', edited by Anthony Pym (2001). Pym's introduction stressed that ethics are concerned primarily with what particular individuals do in the immediacy of concrete situations; abstract principles are secondary. Pym himself has written at length on ethical aspects of translation (1992a, 1997, 2002, 2004). He argues that, since translation is a cross-cultural transaction, the translator's task is one of fostering cooperation between all concerned, with the aim of achieving mutual benefit and trust. Focusing, like Chesterman, on professional translators, Pym sees them as operating in an intercultural space, which he describes as the position of the skilled mediator whose business it is to enable effective interlingual communication. The ethical choices which these intercultural professionals make extend beyond translation to language facilitation as such. For example, Pym argues, given the expense of producing translations over a period of time, the mediator may advise a client that learning the other language may be more cost-effective in the long term. Decisions like these mean weighing benefits for all participants and are motivated by the translator's individual and corporate self-interest.

The idea of translators as not so much hemmed in by norms as actively negotiating their way through them and taking up a position in the process, is helped along when the translator is seen as re-enunciator (Mossop 1983 and especially Folkart 1991). In this view translators do not just redirect pre-existing messages but, giving voice to new texts, they cannot help but intervene in them and, in so doing, establish a subject-position in the discourse they shape. As a result, translation is inevitably coloured by the translator's subjectivity, generating a complex message in which several speaking voices and perspectives intermingle. The assumption, incidentally, that the translator's 'differential voice' (Folkart's term) will necessarily have its own timbre and ambience was later vindicated with the help of forensic stylistics: a study analysing a computerized corpus of translations by two different translators found that each left their linguistically idiosyncratic signature on their translations, regardless of the nature of the original text (Baker 2000). The relevance of such data does not lie in the mere recognition of the translator's linguistic tics being strewn around a text. As Mikhail Bakhtin had already suggested (1981, 1986) in his discussions of dialogism and heteroglossia, the translator's own position and ideology are ineluctably written into the texts he or she translates. At the same time, the translator as re-enunciator and discursive subject in the text also brings on questions of responsibility and accountability, and hence ethics.

A decisive shift of emphasis in translation studies may be discerned from this. For Toury, norms guided the translator's textual decision making and hence determined the shape of the resulting translation; since he took it as axiomatic that the relation between translation and original was one of equivalence, norms determined equivalence, and there the matter ended. Seeing the translator as re-enunciator still has him or her making textual choices, but the relevance of these choices is now that they are read as profiling a subject-position which is primarily ideological. As a result, translators acquire agency in the evolving social, political and cultural configurations that make up society. A number of recent studies have focused on the role of translators in the context of cultural change, political discourse and identity formation in a variety of contexts (for a sampling: Bermann and Wood 2005; Calzada Pérez 2003; Cronin 2006; Ellis and Oakley-Brown 2001; House *et al.* 2005; Tymoczko 2000; Tymoczko and Gentzler 2002; Venuti 1998b, 2005a). Considering in particular the role of interpreters and translators in contemporary situations of military and ideological conflict, Mona Baker (2006) has turned towards the theory of social narrative to frame her analyses. Jeremy Munday (2008) has harnessed critical discourse analysis and the linguistics of M.A.K. Halliday to analyse the ideological load of translated texts.

6.3 Representation 1

A 'return' to ethics suggests that the question of ethics has been raised before, as indeed it has, but from a different angle. As early as the 1980s Antoine Berman linked literary translation with ethnocentrism and otherness. In his study of German Romanticism (1992), he traced Herder's ideas on the intimate link between language and culture, Wilhelm von Humboldt's insistence on the need for translations to retain the foreignness of the foreign original, Schleiermacher's call on translators to take the reader to the foreign author rather than vice versa, and the uncompromising literalness of

Hölderlin's German translations from the Greek. Berman saw it as an ethical imperative to counter what became known as the violence of ethnocentrism, the imposition of the conventions and values of the translating culture on imported texts, with the effacement of their cultural difference as a result. His remedy was to advocate a word-for-word translation that would respect the original in its radical alterity.

In the English-speaking world Lawrence Venuti has championed Berman alongside the 'abusive fidelity' preached by Philip Lewis (1985). Venuti, too, speaks of an ethics of difference, but adds a political and ideological dimension. Statistics based on UNESCO's *Index Translationum* show a marked imbalance in global translation flows, especially as regards the position of English in recent decades. English is primarily a donor, not a receptor language. Many languages translate extensively, and mostly from English. Even when they also translate from other languages, English tends to account for a large proportion. In most West European countries, for example, translations make up between twenty and forty per cent of all published books, and up to seventy-five per cent of these translations are from English. The figures reflect the current economic, military and political dominance of the USA in the first instance, and the global weight of Anglophone culture more generally. The flow is overwhelmingly one-directional. In the English-speaking countries of the industrialized world, translations typically comprise under five per cent of published books.

For Venuti (1995/2008, 1998a) this low percentage of translations into English is problematic. A relative dearth of translations in countries already averse to learning foreign languages signals, and in turn fosters, a lack of openness to cultural diversity and especially to the very different modes of thinking and expression contained in texts that have grown up in other tongues. But there is another factor. As Venuti sees it, the danger of a closing of the Anglophone mind is exacerbated by what he calls the fluency of most existing translations into English. Fluency here means the tendency to render translations indistinguishable from texts originally written in English. Fluently translated texts make easy reading because they conform to familiar patterns of genre, style and register. The ease of reading however comes at a cost. It erases the otherness of the foreign text, and this domestication – the term is aptly chosen, suggesting both smugness and forcible taming – has harmful consequences. Its main ideological consequence is that it prevents an engagement with cultural difference because foreign texts, whatever their origin, are uniformly pressed into homely moulds. Not only that, but since foreign novels, for instance, when translated fluently, end up sounding like any other average English novel, the impression will grow that other cultures think, feel and write very much like Anglophone culture anyway – and if that is the case, why bother reading them? For Venuti, non-translation aggravated by fluency breeds isolationism and its attendant evils.

If the effect of fluency is to marginalize translated works and to make them invisible among the mass of other works, it also makes the translator invisible, in a double sense. As a translating strategy, fluency requires the translator to withdraw into discreet anonymity. But this very discretion, Venuti argues, locks translators collectively, as a professional group, into an economically disadvantageous position. Literary translators in particular – the main group Venuti is talking about – may be underpaid and routinely overlooked in book reviews or on the title pages of translated books, but they only have themselves to blame for their lack of clout and bargaining power. Their willingness to remain invisible in their texts renders them socially invisible as well.

To counter the detrimental ideological effects of fluency, Venuti proposes, and practises in his own translations from the Italian, a form of resistant or 'minoritizing' translation, initially also called 'foreignizing' ('defamiliarizing' might be a better term). The inspiration is drawn from Schleiermacher, Lewis and Berman, but Venuti has more strings to his bow than the dogged literalism that Berman was after. He is prepared to exploit all the registers of English, including anachronisms and slang, to inscribe difference in the translation itself, leave on the text a translator's imprint, and tap what he calls the 'remainder', a term borrowed from Jean-Jacques Lecercle (1990) to mean all those linguistic features that cannot readily find a place in the neatly ordered grammars of standard usage, the homogenized standard language through which dominant social classes exercise control. How the reader is to distinguish between the translator's invention and usage that reflects peculiarities of the original remains an open question. The ultimate aim of Venuti's translations is to challenge linguistic and ideological hegemonies and to contribute to a change in mentality. He realizes, though, that literature has only a limited reach and that defamiliarization needs to be practised with caution if the reader is to continue reading. His academic work has unearthed a historical genealogy of 'resistant' translation that informs his own endeavours as a translator but that has also illustrated the diversity of historical conceptions of translation in the Anglophone tradition.

Drawing on feminist, postcolonial and poststructuralist theorizing, Gayatri Spivak (1993/2004, 2005) makes a case that chimes with Venuti's and especially Berman's, except that her reflections stem from her experience translating a woman novelist writing in Bengali. Spivak wants the translator to go beyond transferring content and to surrender instead to the original, entering its textual protocols and retaining the intimacy of that encounter in a literal English version. For all the theoretical sophistication of her discourse, Spivak ends up evoking the traditional association of translation with inadequacy and loss; she admits that she never teaches texts she cannot read in the original.

Kwame Anthony Appiah (1993/2004) suggests that translations from traditions remote from the Western sphere of knowledge should be extensively annotated, a strategy he designates as 'thick translation', after the 'thick description' recommended for ethnography by Clifford Geertz (1973). Thick description seeks to provide in-depth accounts of cultural practices on the basis of detailed contextualization – the line taken also by New Historicism, for instance, and, in translation studies, by research into community interpreting (see Chapter 8).

6.4 INTERVENTIONS

The stance adopted by theorists cum translators such as Venuti and Spivak may be described as interventionist. They argue that if creative translation is a cultural practice, so is academic work. Research and teaching, like the production of wayward translations, are meant to make a difference in a social, political and ideological sense. This interventionist line, and the ethical issues it throws up, has been a constant theme in the study of translation since the 1990s. It is at its most outspoken in feminist and postcolonial approaches.

Broadly speaking, the feminist engagement with translation has been concentrated on four areas (Flotow 1997; Simon 1996). In the first place, and in parallel with work in other fields such as literary studies and art history, research has focused on uncovering female translators and their role in history. Women, by and large, were not meant to participate in public discourse but sometimes they could translate, as a form of secondary speaking. Some women even felt more comfortable translating than writing in their own name (Stark 1999). Another line of enquiry has traced the historical and ideological construction of translation and its remarkable correlation with traditional gender constructions. It has documented the association of translation with submission, reproduction, loyalty and femininity, always in opposition to the creative primacy of original speech and writing (Chamberlain 1988/1992; Johnson 1985). The parallel works both ways, as it puts both women and translation in their place. The translation of gendered language, a third area of interest, has exercised researchers and translators alike. At first the issues centred on the translator's responsibility when confronted with gender bias in texts (Levine 1991); subsequently attention shifted from ethical to technical questions, as translators struggled to cope with the explosion of experimental writing by feminist authors seeking to forge a language of their own.

The most controversial area of work has been the practice of feminist translation and criticism. For Susanne de Lotbinière-Harwood (1991), translation can only be a demonstrative rewriting in the feminine, a political act that makes language speak for women. Feminist critics have turned in particular to the textual strategies and self-positionings by female translators such as Aphra Behn, and to translations of female authors, from Sappho to Simone de Beauvoir.

The Beauvoir case is instructive. Howard Parshley's English translation of *The Second Sex* (1953, French original 1949) has been roundly condemned by feminist critics for misunderstanding some of Beauvoir's philosophical terminology and for making a number of cuts, especially in the lists of women's historical achievements in the sciences (Simons 1999). No doubt the errors and omissions are there, and they affect the book's tenor. The criticism however tends to ignore evidence in favour of the translator. Parshley greatly improved the accuracy of Beauvoir's cavalier referencing, he tried his best to seek clarification from an unresponsive author, he obtained her permission for the cuts he made, and anyway it was the publisher who suggested that the book's numerous repetitions be reduced (Bair 1990). At issue in a case like this is the fairness of the criticism and the danger of double standards, as indeed Rosemary Arrojo (1994) has charged. Feminist translators can manipulate texts, but other translators cannot? What determines whether reconfiguring a text's tenor qualifies as an objectionable distortion or as an act of political defiance?

Part of the feminist answer has been that, for them, translation is reparation. In a world of power imbalances, the violence that resists patriarchal oppression is not to be equated with the violence exercised by the system. It is this awareness of power differentials that links feminist work most closely with postcolonial approaches. Both approaches also share an interest in questions of social inclusion and exclusion (who can or must translate, on whose terms, and who benefits?), and in the deployment of translation both as part of a knowledge-controlling apparatus and as a vehicle of either complicity or resistance. The postcolonial view of translation has, in addition, delved into notions of hybridity and made translation into a cipher for something much larger than interlingual traffic.

One area of postcolonial research deals with the role of translation in colonial and postcolonial contexts (Bassnett and Trivedi 1999; Cheyfitz 1991; Niranjana 1992; Rafael 1993, 2005; Simon and St-Pierre 2000; Tymoczko 1999). Richard Jacquemond (1992), for instance, comments on the significant differences between translation from and into dominant and dominated languages respectively, both during and after periods of colonial rule. For the colonizer, translation into the hegemonic language amounts to bringing home an anthropological exhibit which adds to the centre's knowledge of the colonies, and knowledge is power. For the colonized, translation from the master tongue introduces the high-prestige commodities which symbolize the assimilation process they are meant to aspire to; or, more routinely, it serves as an instrument to increase the local efficiency of colonial control. Jacquemond also shows why in each case the postcolonial world presents the more complex picture, as the legacy of colonialism lingers among the ex-colonizers as well as the ex-colonized.

As we saw above, earlier work, not indebted to the postcolonial paradigm, had edged already towards the recognition of not just asymmetries but inequalities between cultures, and had developed an interest in the translator as a cultural agent positioned in institutional and other networks. Postcolonial theory, however, has vastly accelerated these developments, added a self-reflexive moment to them and highlighted the political and ideological dimension not only of the material studied but also of the studies themselves.

Among the new ideas that postcolonial theory, aided in this case by poststructuralist thinking, has brought to the fore, is the notion of hybridity. If early anti-colonial writers like Frantz Fanon (1952/1967, 1961/1963) operated with concepts such as *négritude*, authenticity and roots, the complexity of the cultural impact and aftermath of colonialism would later be captured in the image of the rhizome; the term, derived from Gilles Deleuze and Félix Guattari (1988), signalled the impossibility of retracing one's path to a solid, pure origin. Hybridity is the condition that, for Homi Bhabha (1994), enables cultural translation, a term he uses in a broad sense to speak of the continual displacement that comes with migration, transformation, re-inscription and in-betweenness, and which he regards as characteristic of postcolonial societies. In a more textual sense, hybridity has also proved to be a useful if somewhat fuzzy concept to grasp the dynamics of textual interweavings, heteroglossia and diverging subject-positions that manifest themselves in translations.

Etymologically, the term translation is closely tied up with metaphor, being derived from a Latin calque of a Greek word meaning 'transfer'. For Aristotle, metaphor represented an alien, deviant speech which displaced familiar usage but could be explicated and thus normalized by a process of translation. Postcolonial readings play the literal and more metaphorical meanings of translation off against one another. Eric Cheyfitz (1991), for example, analyses how European settlers in the New World effected a lawful translation of native property by rewriting native attitudes to the land in terms of the settlers' concepts of title and ownership and then holding the natives to these concepts. Translation is here much more than a verbal transaction, it means transfer of territory into other hands, overwriting one system of thought with another, and often the eviction – translation in its most physical sense – of the original inhabitants. Michael Cronin (1996) and Maria Tymoczko (1999) trace all of these meanings and uses across the long history of translation in Ireland.

6.5 Representation 2

The opening chapter of Tymoczko's book invokes metonymy as well as metaphor. If metaphor operates on the basis of similarity, metonymy relies on contiguity, in this case the part standing for the whole. Translation is metonymic in that it catches certain aspects of an original while representing the original as a whole; and for someone on this side of a language barrier, translations of a small number of works from a foreign culture create an image of that entire culture. The issue of the representation of otherness thus emerged in postcolonial translation studies as well (Brisset 2003).

In ethnography the 'crisis of representation' had come to a head in the *Writing Culture* debate of the 1980s (Clifford and Marcus 1986; Marcus and Fischer 1986). The debate concerned both the context and the procedures of ethnography as a discipline. It recalled ethnography's imperial origins and was critical of the traditional idea of the ethnographer's account of another people as an unproblematic 'translation of culture'. Its result was an explosion of experimental writing and some intense critical reflection on the nature and politics of ethnographic work (Sturge 2007).

While translation studies kept these debates at arm's length (just as, for that matter, ethnography remains oblivious to academic work on translation), its engagement with its subject – that is, intercultural traffic – acquired a marked self-reflexive aspect. It led, among other things, to the realization that the study of translation itself cannot help but translate. Like ethnography, the study of translation not only handles material in other languages and thus continually translates in the conventional sense of the word, it also transposes its findings into its own conceptual and disciplinary jargon. But if translating is not an ideologically neutral activity, how can the study of translation be? Like ethnography also, the study of translation has begun to ask questions about its own goals and procedures, especially as the discipline becomes increasingly international and multicultural.

This broadening out and opening up to other traditions has been dramatic, even if to date attention has focused mostly on India and China (Bandia 2007; Cheung 2006; Dingwaney and Maier 1995; Hermans 2006; Hung and Wakabayashi 2005; Liu 1995, 1999; Pollard 1998). The research reveals a remarkable range of different practices of translation and modes of conceptualizing them – insofar as 'translation' is still the appropriate rubric under which to gather them.

Eva Hung (in Hung and Wakabayashi 2005), for instance, has documented the pre-eminence of collaborative translation throughout the Chinese tradition, upsetting the Western vision of the lone translator as the key agent in the process. Other studies have shown Chinese translators in the early twentieth century appropriating Western texts with the express aim of turning the newly acquired knowledge against the West. The vision of the appropriation of foreign cultural goods as a form of cannibalism has been championed by several Brazilian writers and poets, notably Haroldo de Campos, who converts the European horror of anthropophagy into the positive image of a postcolonial culture no longer subservient to the colonial master and now ingesting, on its own terms and for its own purposes, what it chooses to take from abroad (Vieira 1999). Among the many neologisms with which de Campos describes his reworkings of other texts is 'transcreation', a term also used by P. Lal in the Indian context, and in a roughly similar sense of adaptation and mutation (Mukherjee 1996).

The idea that such investigations represent a welcome expansion of the horizon of translation studies is open to challenge (Susam-Sarajeva 2002;

Trivedi 2006). Covering a handful of India's many languages, Harish Trivedi (2006) explores the meanings and etymologies of various terms that could be aligned with the concept of 'translation' as understood in English. But he doubts (as Mukherjee 1996 had done) that they can be readily translated as 'translation', and goes on to wonder if such explorations, conducted in English and thus serving Anglophone translation studies, do not reduce research on local languages and traditions to the native informancy familiar to old-style imperial anthropology. The geopolitics of these academic pursuits is captured in the image of a Third World supplying raw materials for refinement in the First World's resource-hungry intellectual economy. The critiques themselves obviously impinge on the position of English in the contemporary world; paradoxically, they must be conducted in English to be heard on the international stage.

The issues of otherness, representation and the rationale of cross-cultural comparison in a postcolonial world reappear throughout the accounts of practices and theorizings that do not match the category 'translation' pure and simple. They raise questions that do not admit of easy answers, since neither incommensurability nor ready transposition will do. If different cultures are to be understood on their own terms, translating becomes problematic. Negotiating these problems, however, does not necessarily have to aim at assimilating the alien concepts into one's own vocabulary. It can serve to gauge the nature and presuppositions of that vocabulary, and thus to interrogate translation studies as currently constituted in a language such as English. This in turn might help to make Western academia a province of a larger intellectual world, not its centre. Maria Tymoczko (2006, see Chapter 1) has already listed a number of presuppositions translation studies needs to shed and proposed various avenues the field might want to take if it is to reinvent itself in a globalizing world.

The current global scene, with its economic inequality, increased interconnectedness and urbanization, and with the pre-eminence of English, only makes these issues more pressing. In an attempt to sidestep the crude binaries of national versus global and provincial versus cosmopolitan, Michael Cronin (2003, 2006) advocates micro-cosmopolitanism, which seeks to develop an eye for the myriad fractal complexities of the local while remaining aware of larger contexts. Attention to detail, he argues, will confront us with the limits of our understanding. If much proves untranslatable, so much more remains to be translated. To the apocalyptic combination of forever standardizing translation and equally relentlessly standardizing globalization, Cronin opposes a view of translation as actually fostering diversity. Translation, as he sees it, negotiates meanings and thus creates an intermediary zone of mediation which is socially necessary in densely populated multicultural centres. Without it, communities remain partitioned and shut up in their own mental worlds, and proximity will breed alienation and violent conflict. Instead of the monolingual thesis which regards ethnic diversity as a threat to cultural and political coherence and insists on speedy wholesale integration and the adoption of a common language, Cronin projects a vision in which translation helps to increase the totality of humanity's knowledge base without undermining cultural specificity. There is, it must be said, grandeur in this view of translation.

7
TECHNOLOGY AND TRANSLATION

TONY HARTLEY

7.0 INTRODUCTION

Since the 1990s, translation as a commercial activity has become a global business whose growth outstrips that of world trade as a whole (Boucau 2006). This is a natural consequence of the globalization of trade in general. The rapid expansion of the internet has been a major factor in allowing even smaller companies to market and sell their products internationally. And the demand from consumers for product information, software, user manuals, games, educational materials and so on in their own language has fuelled in its turn the demand for translation.

As the translation market grows, so does the share taken by translation companies, or 'language service providers' (LSPs). This means in effect that the practice of individual translators working directly with clients is in relative decline. It is not uncommon for a large multinational to be processing 1.5 billion words per annum for up to 500 products in over 30 languages, with the requirement that the different language versions be released simultaneously in their respective markets. Since time-to-market is so crucial to profitability, the time available for the translation of a given product may be only a matter of days. Of necessity, translation is therefore a team effort, and the members (e.g. project manager, terminologist, translator, reviser, DTP specialist, software engineer) will often be dispersed around the world. If the product itself is a software application, the text to be translated may appear in a range of contexts – printed manual, user interface, online help, website FAQ – and in a corresponding variety of file formats. Where content is constantly updated, 'the translation process must be truly integrated with the overall content lifecycle' (Esselink 2006: 28).

These trends are both enabled and driven by technology. Some of it, such as the internet and the semantic web, forms the general fabric for communicating and sharing information globally. Meanwhile, there is a continual evolution of other technologies designed to support language processing in general and translation in particular. These are the focus of the present chapter, briefly outlined in the next paragraph.

Only one of these technologies, machine translation (MT) is intended to automate the core task, i.e. the production of a string of words that will count as a translation of the source text. Others, grouped under the heading of computer-aided translation (CAT) tools, are designed to increase productivity while leaving the core task to the human translator. Upstream of the translation task, we can identify various technologies that facilitate the management and sharing of the very large volumes of text that are not only processed by CAT and MT tools but required to make these tools effective in the first place. These provide a 'platform' or infrastructure to support translation proper. Further technologies permit the mining of terminology and its organization and storage such that it can be retrieved by humans or by tools, including authoring applications intended to ensure that source texts are 'translation-friendly'. Overall, technology is central to managing large translation projects from quote to invoice and to verifying the quality of the end product. Finally, unless we have principled ways of evaluating a technology, we will be unable to decide sensibly whether to adopt it at all or to choose the best tool for a given task.

Before returning to these topics in greater detail, we need to clarify some important terms in widespread use in the translation industry. First, internationalization (i18n)[1] describes the process of designing both documents and software (programs or websites) in such a way that they can accommodate different linguistic and cultural requirements and options without the need for redesign (Esselink 2000, 2003). This includes ensuring that the required character sets (Arabic, Chinese, Russian, etc.) can be displayed and the corresponding keyboard layouts supported, that numbers and dates are correctly formatted, and that there is enough space on a page to fit the (often longer) translated text next to artwork, whose size and position must remain the same across all language versions of a document.

Localization (l10n) then entails adapting a product to the linguistic and cultural expectations of the target locale (region plus language, hence France and Québec are different locales). In the industry, this is seen as a 'special kind of translation' that takes into account the culture of the location or region where the translated text is expected to be used. However, in the translation studies community, this is simply a commonly accepted definition of translation itself. Accordingly, in this chapter we use 'localization' only in respect of software; in all other contexts the generic term 'translation' is preferred (Clark *et al.* 2006). We also restrict globalization (g11n) to the implementation of the internationalization and localization processes necessary for operating in a global marketplace.

The wider impact of globalization on the translator is debated at length in Cronin (2003) and Gouadec (2007) (see also Chapter 6). Technology reviews appear regularly in the *ITI Bulletin* (http://www.iti.org.uk) and *Multilingual* (http://www.multilingual.com). Some websites offer daily updates on translation technologies (e.g. http://www.babelport.com and http://www.globalwatchtower.com).

7.1 INFRASTRUCTURE TECHNOLOGIES

'Technology' is not only hardware and software tools; it includes collections of techniques that enable humans to produce goods and services and, more generally, control the environment. This section describes some of the less 'visible' technologies that underpin the globalization environment by making it possible to create and share translation data. Without them the emerging trend towards massive online translation (section 7.7) would be simply impossible.

7.1.1 XML AND FAMILY

One of the most powerful technologies providing a platform for globalization is eXtensible Markup Language (XML – http://www.w3.org/XML). The reason it is so important is that it is increasingly the medium in which text is delivered for translation and in which translation resources are shared.

While HTML indicates how information is to be displayed in a browser, XML describes what pieces of information mean. The tags that mark up the information are designed to be self-explanatory, as shown in Figure 7.1. By separating data from its display and from proprietary formats and by assigning it meaningful labels, XML simplifies the transport and sharing of content across otherwise incompatible platforms. It also makes content more accessible by making it available, for example, to devices that can 'publish' it as text for the Deaf and as speech for the blind. Thus, XML is at the heart of the semantic web (http://www.w3.org/2001/sw/).

The set of tags is not closed but extensible, allowing communities of users to agree on the definition of new tags for particular applications. In other words, XML is a metalanguage, used to create many new languages in different domains of knowledge and activity. Among the most important of these for globalization are XLIFF, TBX, TMX and DITA (section 7.3.1) – all actively promoted by the Localisation Industry Standards Association (http://www.lisa.org) and OASIS (http://www.oasis-open.org).

XLIFF (XML Localisation Interchange File Format) is designed to overcome problems of interoperability between the many tools that have a place

```
<?xml version="1.0" encoding="ISO-8859-1"?>
<!DOCTYPE note SYSTEM "Note.dtd">
<note>
<to>Sam</to>
<from>Jo</from>
<heading>Meeting</heading>
<body>This takes place at 12 today.</body>
</note>
```

FIGURE 7.1 Example XML tags (http://www.w3schools.com)

in the complex translation workflow. It provides for the clear separation of translatable content from program code and formatting tags. In so doing, it not only protects the integrity of the program or document layout from inadvertent corruption by the translator, it also frees the translator from responsibility for software engineering or DTP tasks, which have infiltrated themselves into the translator's job description over recent years. Metadata can record a trace of the persons, resources and tools involved in the content's creation and translation, to the benefit of all parties – content publishers, language service providers (LSPs) and tools vendors. TBX (Term Base eXchange) makes it possible to consistently reuse the same terminology in CAT and MT tools as was used in the original authoring process. TMX (Translation Memory eXchange) is the standard for the exchange of translation memory (TM) data created by CAT and software localization tools. TMs are, in essence, databases of source language sentences paired with their target language translations (section 7.4.1). In larger organizations the total volume of such pairs may number many millions, representing a costly and valuable asset.

These standards offer publishers and freelances alike independence and future-proofing, freeing them from being locked into a commercial relationship with a sole LSP or tool provider.

7.1.2 UNICODE AND OPEN SOURCE

To be stored, processed and displayed by a computer, every character – alphabetic letter, ideogram, punctuation, number, symbol – needs to be represented by a number. What Unicode (http://www.unicode.org) does is to assign a unique number to every different character, currently over 100,000 of them. This avoids possible conflicts between different encoding schemes which represent the same character by different numbers or different characters by the same number, leading to corruption as data is passed from one application to another. Unicode is the character encoding standard for XML and has been widely adopted by global organizations, since its use can hugely facilitate software localization.

Open source (http://www.opensource.org) extends this concern with sharable, reusable resources to program code. While open-source activity in translation technology remains relatively low, there are some notable exceptions in MT and TM and we can expect this model of software development to become more widespread in translation, to the benefit of translators in developing countries among others (see section 7.7).

7.1.3 CORPUS DATA AND TOOLS

Simply put, a corpus (plural *corpora*) is 'a collection of naturally occurring language data' (McEnery 2003: 449). To be exploitable for the purposes of translation technology a corpus must be machine-readable – which is typically the case whatever the purpose – and large, consisting of tens of millions rather than tens of thousands of words. There are corpora of text data, speech data and multimodal data (such as subtitled film or sign language interpretation); this section focuses on corpora of written language.

Corpora are the raw resource for many applications described in the following sections: mining terminology, creating authoring and MT systems, and reusing previous translations. Since translation strategies and choices at all linguistic levels are highly sensitive to the particular conjunction of genre and subject matter realized in a given source text, it follows that if a corpus is to adequately serve any such purpose, it cannot simply be compiled from a random collection of data. Rather it needs to be designed as a representative and balanced sample of the data that exists (it is rarely possible to build a corpus that includes everything). If, for example, the goal is to create an MT system for pharmaceutical texts, then the selection of data for the corpus must represent that domain and not the domain of chemistry. Moreover, it must strike a balance between the various types of text that talk about pharmaceuticals – patient information leaflets, research papers, etc. – and between data from the various major manufacturers.

A corpus which has been a model for much development in the field is the British National Corpus (BNC – http://www.natcorp.ox.ac.uk), which consists of 100 million words of contemporary written and spoken English covering a range of domains and genres. While monolingual corpora of this kind do have a role to play in translation, the most widely used resource is parallel corpora, which consist of source texts and their translations into one or possibly many target languages. One parallel corpus publicly available in 22 languages is that of the European Union's *Acquis communautaire*, the total body of law applicable in the 27 Member States (http://langtech.jrc.it/JRC-Acquis.html). Parallel corpora become even more useful when they are aligned, usually sentence by sentence, to facilitate the identification of translation equivalents. Yet, outside of big multilingual institutions or companies with translation resources, large parallel corpora are hard to find and expensive to create. It is much easier to build bi- or multi-lingual comparable corpora, that is, a series of monolingual corpora collected over a similar time span and with a similar balance of text types, domains and readerships. On the other hand, finding translation equivalents in a 100 million word corpus without the benefit of alignment can be like looking for a needle in a haystack, a challenge that researchers are now tackling (Rapp 1999; Sharoff *et al*. 2008).

'Harvesting' BNC-size corpora in other languages from the internet can now be done largely automatically (Sharoff 2006). A list of 500 frequent content words, or 'seed' terms, is created to generate some 5,000–8,000 queries to Google using random four-word combinations from the list. The top ten URLs from each query can then be downloaded and duplicates removed to yield a reasonably balanced corpus. Variants on this technique, using only 50–80 seeds, enable the collection of domain-specific corpora.

Other tools exist to enhance the value of corpora by adding linguistic information, or annotations, such as part of speech taggers that mark up the part of speech of each word, or parsers that label the structural constituents of each sentence. For languages where there are no whitespaces between words, such as Chinese and Japanese, tokenisers must first split the strings of characters between punctuation marks into individual words. Lemmatizers reduce inflected forms of words in the corpus context to their base, dictionary form. These tools will themselves have been previously 'trained', using statistical or machine-learning techniques, on corpora which have been reliably annotated for the very same linguistic features a particular tool is intended to identify. Although they inevitably assign some wrong annotations, the best taggers have an error rate as low as 3–4 per cent while processing some 60,000 words per second. With such volumes of data, automation is the only feasible solution and the good analyses drown out the bad.

The annotations can then be used to constrain searches of a corpus for information on the patterning of actual word forms (tokens) or lemmatized forms (types). For example, it is possible to retrieve only those occurrences of 'bill' where it is a verb, or to find all nouns that appear as subject of 'delete' in the passive. If the results of these searches are to be viewed by a human, they are often presented as concordances, which typically display a specified number of occurrences (say, one hundred) of the target expression highlighted and centred in a context of a specified number of characters or words to the left and right. Sorting the occurrences of 'infiltrate' by its left context reveals its distinct uses as verb and noun (Figure 7.2), while retrieving only its occurrences as verb followed by *into* again reveals a distinct difference between its transitive and intransitive uses (Figure 7.3).

Bilingual concordances display in parallel the corresponding contexts in the target language. The collocational patterns that emerge from corpora can be used by humans and by other computer tools in creating dictionaries or building MT systems. Further discussion of the design and use of corpora for translators can be found in Austermühl (2001), Bowker and Pearson (2002), Laviosa (2003), McEnery (2003), Zanettin *et al.* (2003), Olohan (2004) and

laws that will permit undercover policemen to	**infiltrate**	gangs and commit crimes as part of their duties.
fundamentalists were believed to be preparing to	**infiltrate**	the security zone; it was reported that
make sure that he or she is not in a position to	**infiltrate**	the immigration service and pass information back
are disguising themselves in an effort to	**infiltrate**	positions of power. They are everywhere ...
and very able bowmen. Their natural ability to	**infiltrate**	woods and move quickly through dense undergrowth
atrophy with a mixed severe mononuclear cell	**infiltrate**	consistent with a clinical diagnosis of coeliac
showed a predominantly T cell mononuclear cell	**infiltrate**	and although the possibility of lymphoma was
cross lipid cell membranes. The inflammatory cell	**infiltrate**	and its chemical products may influence
disease, however, where the mononuclear cell	**infiltrate**	is both transmural and patchy, the neutrophils,
is characterised by an inflammatory cell	**infiltrate**	oedema, ulceration, epithelial cell loss,

FIGURE 7.2 Concordance of 'infiltrate' sorted by left context (source: BNC)

the contradictions of trying to	**infiltrate intelligence into**	the world of teenpop
We	**infiltrate informants into**	the underworld
how could they hope to	**infiltrate two impostors into**	the country on their passports?
These cells	**infiltrate into**	the colonic mucosa
which would allow the Soviets to	**infiltrate more KGB agents into**	the United Kingdom under diplomatic cover.
The KGB managed to	**infiltrate an agent into**	the British factory
His specific task was to	**infiltrate criminal elements into**	the ANC

FIGURE 7.3 Concordance of 'infiltrate' as verb followed by 'into' (source: BNC)

Somers (2008). Online resources can also be found (http://corpus.leeds.ac.uk and http://www.federicozanettin.net).

7.1.4 ALIGNMENT

While aligned corpora serve a range of purposes in research and in training language processing systems, the goal of aligning parallel texts in commercial translation is to create resources that increase productivity. The texts are typically an organization's previously translated or 'legacy' documents. However, automatically pairing the corresponding segments – sentences, headings, bulleted items – of the source and target texts may not be simple, as Somers (2003a: 34–7) explains. This is because the delimitation of the segments in the first place usually relies on punctuation, but punctuation conventions and even the notion of sentence vary from language to language. So, alignment tools allow the user to specify how punctuation should be taken into account. Even so, inconsistencies – both 'UN' and 'U.N.' – can result in wrong segmentation. More fundamentally, the translator may have distributed the content of a long source sentence over two or more target sentences or merged several source sentences into one, to conform to target language norms. Moreover, the ordering of the segments may be different in the translation.

For these reasons, current commercial alignment tools take their cues not only from punctuation and sentence length but from document structure and the presence of names, dates and numbers or even matching entries in a terminology database. These serve as anchors which contribute to calculating the probability of a particular segmentation. Some alignment technologies are capable of matching tens of thousands of documents before aligning the segments within them.

The contributions to Véronis (2000) provide an overview of research in this area.

7.2 TERMINOLOGY TOOLS

Terms are lexical items which have specialized reference within a particular subject domain. 'Terminology' is both the process of identifying, organizing and presenting terms to users and the product of this process – collections of domain-specific expressions, often multi-word expressions (MWEs). In translation applications, terminology can be massively multilingual.

In company documentation and websites, terms communicate both content and brand. The impact of defective terminology on customer satisfaction can be incalculable, from impairing the usability of a product through inconsistent usage of terms in the accompanying manual to compromising health and safety. For instance, using 'shadow cursor', 'grid cursor' and 'scale cursor' to refer to one and the same object is confusing and wasteful. The translation process can simply propagate these defects to the localized versions or compound them through mis-translation. The fact that globalization has turned authoring and translation into team activities only heightens the risk of inconsistencies. The concomitant increasing human reliance on authoring, CAT and MT tools means, therefore, that terminology needs to be unified across all these applications. The benefits include a possibly significant cut in time spent on research and revision, and a gain in accuracy.

The clear implication is that terminology – process and product – needs to be managed centrally and delivered locally. This is the rationale behind TBX, already described, and the emergence of powerful tools for identifying and managing terms.

7.2.1 TERM EXTRACTION

Extracting, or 'mining' terminology from monolingual or parallel corpora may be done by a language service provider (LSP) in preparation for a job or, in the case of an MT vendor, prospectively to extend the system's domain coverage. The technology exploits two main approaches for finding candidate terms: linguistic approaches require part-of-speech tagged data to identify word combinations that match predetermined patterns (e.g. NOUN+NOUN – *water pressure*), while statistical approaches rely on the fact that the component parts of terminological MWEs tend to co-occur more often than would be predicted by chance (e.g. *dialogue* and *box*). A particular tool may combine elements of both approaches.

Searching for patterns such as NOUN+of+NOUN (e.g. *part of speech, best of breed*) or ADJECTIVE+NOUN (*hard drive*) will successfully find matching terms however infrequent, but tends to return also many false or irrelevant candidates that need to be eliminated manually (e.g. *cup of tea, long walk*). So the initial list of candidates may be filtered according to various statistical criteria and the survivors ranked according to their likely 'termhood'. A further disadvantage of the linguistic approach is that the patterns need to be redefined for every language processed. Purely statistical methods escape this drawback and are language-independent, but overlook terms whose frequency of occurrence is below some preset threshold.

Bilingual term extraction usually proceeds by first identifying the candidates monolingually in the two corpora and then pairing them using statistical techniques. The corpora are not necessarily aligned at the sentence level.

7.2.2 TERM MANAGEMENT

Term storage mechanisms for translation range from a simple two-column table or spreadsheet holding simply the paired terms to a complex relational database capable of presenting equivalents across any or all of a large number of languages. Such databases typically contain a wealth of other data: linguistic (synonyms, variants, equivalents and so on), conceptual (e.g. domain, definition, related concepts), pragmatic (usage restrictions), bibliographic (source) and management (such as date, creator and reliability). To avoid being swamped with information, individual users can customize their view of the contents of the database according to their role – author, translator – and working languages. One such 'term bank' is the EU inter-institutional terminology database IATE (http://iate.europa.eu), containing over 1.4 million multilingual entries. Various UN and other term banks can be reached via the International Telecommunications Union website (http://www.itu.int/terminology/index.html).

For productivity, an organization's term management system is integrated with the translation environment to scan the source text for known terms and propose them for insertion at the press of a key, avoiding error-prone retyping. Indeed, it is commonplace for a workflow to impose the automatic insertion of all known terms in a 'pre-translation' stage in an attempt to eliminate inconsistencies.

Sager (1990) discusses the principles of term management. Austermühl (2001), Bowker and Pearson (2002), Bowker (2002) and Jacquemin and Bourigault (2003) describe tools for extraction and retrieval.

7.3 AUTHORING TOOLS

The awareness that linguistic quality must be assured as early as possible in the document lifecycle is not new – poor source documents have long been the bane of the translator's life. Two major developments are making the integration of authoring and translation, announced by Sager (1993: 271), a growing reality. First, the exchange standards described in sections 7.1.1 and 7.1.2 permit authors and translators to reuse shared resources – not only terminology but also translation memories. Second, the mantra of 'only ever translate a given segment once' is echoed by 'only ever author a given content once', an ambition made achievable by the advent of content management systems (CMSs). Translatable web content in particular is being updated so rapidly – with FAQs, bug fixes, time-sensitive data – that the serial model of periodically retranslating revised versions of the whole document set is being overtaken by continuous publishing.

7.3.1 SINGLE-SOURCE CONTENT MANAGEMENT

'Content' designates any resource used to build a website or a document – text, graphics, links – the emphasis here being on text. Single-sourcing follows the principle of separating content from format, so that a single piece of content can be published as, for example, a Word document (.doc), a web page (.html) or online help (.chm). It also aims to write content only once and maintain it in a single place while publishing it in many places, thus reducing redundancy. This requires a modular, topic-oriented 'architecture' for writing such that the content 'works' in a range of contexts – help screen, tutorial, ready reference. Modules may be as small as a paragraph, a sentence, a phrase or even a word that appears in a page template. The advantage is that only modified content needs to be re-translated, and the CMS keeps track of this workflow; time-to-market can be reduced as authoring and translation run in tandem. The disadvantage for the translator is being confronted with linguistic fragments without any clarifying context.

Modularization on this scale entails significant design and implementation costs, but DITA (Darwin Information Typing Architecture – http://dita.xml.org) provides an increasingly widely adopted infrastructure. Designed for developing technical product documentation, it specifies three basic topic types: 'concept' (for background information), 'reference' and 'task'. A task topic, for example, is intended for instructional procedures and is itself modularized into sub-elements containing content for prerequisites (e.g. preparation of ingredients before cooking begins), steps, options, results and post-requisites (e.g. resetting or cleaning equipment after a process), among others, each instance potentially reusable in many places.

Such metadata could allow the translator to recover useful context when presented with an isolated segment from a CMS. It could even be used to govern the translation choices of an MT system; for example, where *creating a document* is tagged as occurring in the title of a sequence of steps, a nominalizing translation of the form *creation of a document* may be more appropriate for many TLs.

7.3.2 CONTROLLED LANGUAGE CHECKING

A controlled language (CL) is a version of a human language that embodies explicit restrictions on vocabulary, grammar and style for the purpose of authoring technical documentation. With roots in the Simplified English of the 1930s, the initial objective was to minimize ambiguity and maximize clarity for human readers, including non-native speakers of English, and so to avoid the need for translation altogether (Ogden 1932). Today such

Anglo-centricity is unsustainable politically and economically, so there is a certain irony in the widespread acceptance that adherence to CL principles can improve the quality of human- and, in particular, machine-translated text. There are CLs based on French, German, Spanish and Swedish, among other languages. Probably the best-known CL is AECMA Simplified English (http://www.aecma.org), which is a *de facto* standard in the aerospace industry; the concept has also been widely adopted in the automotive and IT sectors. Even within the same sector, CLs vary from one company to another while respecting the same general principles.

Thus, at the lexical level, a CL will specify the approved technical terms and often explicitly list any 'unapproved' terms which authors tend to use in error. Moreover, the prescriptions extend to non-technical expressions. For example, AECMA restricts the use of *about* to 'concerned with', specifying that *approximately* should be used for the other frequent sense; *support* can only be used as a count noun (*Put a support under the item* but not *Offer support*), and when a verb is required to express this idea it must be *hold* (*Hold the item* but not *Support the item*). At the syntactic level, typical rules limit the number of words in a sentence (to 20 in instructions or 25 in descriptions), and enjoin authors to 'Write more than one instruction per sentence only when more than one action is done at the same time'. The principle of avoiding undue complexity is complemented by that of avoiding ambiguity: 'Do not omit words to make your sentence shorter'. So, for example, *Water pump drive belt loose* is deprecated and *The drive belt of the water pump is loose* is preferred.

Several commercial tools are available for checking automatically that a technical author's text conforms to the rules of the particular CL in use. These tools can be customized to the company's lexical, syntactic and stylistic rules, which might include detecting typical errors made by non-native writers of the authoring language. Yet, while it is simple to detect that a sentence contains 26 words or some recurrent non-native construction, checking that there is 'only one topic per sentence' is impossible. If fully automatic checking remains hard, then even limited automatic correction is harder, since it entails not only recognizing that there is an error but also offering one or more correct alternatives. Consider the ungrammatical sentence "The train depart"; only the bigger context may tell us whether to add an "s" to "train" or to "depart"'. Despite the fact that CL checkers do not necessarily endear themselves to users, since they flag 'errors' that are actually CL-compliant usage while missing true errors, research and development will undoubtedly continue. The consequences of inconsistent and poor-quality content at source in the CMS make the translation workflow unmanageable.

Kittredge (2003) and Nyberg *et al.* (2003) offer detailed accounts of CL for authoring and translation. CLs can be likened to style guides with teeth, and numerous style guides for translators are available online (for example, http://ec.europa.eu/translation/language_aids). The Simple English Wikipedia (http://simple.wikipedia.org) offers advice for writing for children and learners of English.

7.4 Computer-Aided Translation (CAT) tools

CAT tools for translation and software localization nowadays offer, almost without exception, a bundle of functions that tend to include alignment, concordancing and term extraction already described, and quality assurance and even workflow management described later in this chapter. The notion of an integrated suite of tools is captured by the common label 'workstation'. This section focuses on the distinctive features of translation and localization tools, as well as tools for subtitling, that support the translator's core task.

7.4.1 Translation Memory (TM) tools

Based on the insight that existing translations contain solutions to many of the problems faced daily by translators, TM tools enable the efficient creation and searching of databases of translated documents and their originals. These memories comprise translation units (TUs), consisting of corresponding source and target segments. While the segments may often be full sentences, a TU can also pair captions, headings, list items, contents of individual table cells or even single words, for example, a label on a user interface button. TMs are designed to increase productivity by detecting that the segment currently being translated matches wholly or partially the source side of one or more TUs and then presenting to the translator the corresponding target segment or segments. The translator is free to accept or adapt any proposal as the translation of the current segment, so leveraging previous efforts by avoiding translating from scratch. Novel TUs are added to the memory and thus the volume of reusable TUs grows progressively. Large companies often have TMs numbering millions of units. The TM used for a particular job can be created by importing TUs from existing sources (hence the importance of TMX), by aligning legacy documents, or during the very process of translation, having been initially empty.

Translation memory is most effective with documents – such as manuals or catalogues – with a high degree of internal repetition or of external repetition relative to previous releases of the same document or, for example, documents describing related products.

At the core of a TM application is the algorithm that determines the match between the current segment and the stored TUs. An exact match is one where a TU source segment is identical in wording, punctuation and formatting to the current segment. A full match is one where the two segments differ only in terms of recognized variable (<u>underlined</u> in the example below), or 'placeable' elements, such as names, numbers, dates and currency values; moreover, many systems automatically reformat dates and numbers according to the conventions of the target locale. A fuzzy match is one where the non-placeable elements of the two segments are only partially the same (emboldened in the example below); nevertheless, the existing translation may be highly reusable, as with this example:

Current: Version 2.0 released on 2008/01/01 features 100 Gb RAM.
TM unit: Version **1.0** released on **2007/01/07** comes with **10** Gb RAM.
La version 1.0 lancée le 01/07/2007 est équipée de 10 Go de RAM.

The matching algorithm assigns a score to each match, usually as a percentage, to reflect its closeness. The score is then used to rank the translation suggestions displayed to the translator. The basic principle is to compute the string–edit distance – the minimum number of deletions, insertions and substitutions required to transform one string of symbols (here, characters or words) into another, relative to the length of the string. However, different implementations of the principle may take into account only characters or only words or both, and variously weight the calculations in favour of deletions, insertions or substitutions, or even according to the provenance of a TU (e.g. from the same or a different product line). As a result, no two TM tools are guaranteed to report the same results when a source segment or whole document is analysed against a given memory.

The translator's interface varies from tool to tool. Many tools support pre-translation, which automatically inserts the translations of all exact matches into the draft target text. Some offer a WYSIWYG (what you see is what you get) display of the target, others not. All seem to offer the possibility of 'locking' the formatting so that a translator cannot inadvertently corrupt it by deleting tags. They again vary in showing which expressions in the current segment are in the terminology database and in allowing new terms to be entered. Generally, they highlight the non-matching words in fuzzy matches and distinguish the different categories of match (e.g. by colour coding).

Clearly the success or otherwise of the tool in placing the most readily reusable suggestion at the top of the list will affect the translator's productivity. But it can affect remuneration also. An LSP will analyse an individual translator's source text against the TM provided for the job and will know the number of matching segments and the number of words in each category – exact, full and fuzzy (with associated scores). Only segments below a set threshold (85 per cent, say) will be paid at the full price per word, the price decreasing as the match crosses intermediate thresholds until, for exact matches, it is only 20 per cent, say, of the full price. From the translator's perspective, the reasonable contention is that even exact matches need to be checked to confirm that they are appropriate for the new context; this of course takes time which, in the translator's eyes, should be remunerated.

However, some tools claim to identify 'perfect' or 'guaranteed' matches which are not only exact in themselves but share identical neighbouring segments.

Much effort is being devoted currently to more sophisticated matching techniques that can propose the solution to a translation problem by detecting parts of the solution in different TUs and combining them, as illustrated in this example from Somers (2008):

> Current: The operation was interrupted because the file was hidden.
> TM Unit a: The operation was interrupted because the Ctrl-c key was pressed.
> TM Unit b: The specified method failed because the file is hidden.

The first task is to establish that, between them, the source sides of these two TUs (a and b) 'cover' the current segment being translated. The second is to identify in the translation memory the relevant portions of the target side of the TUs (not shown), which amounts to an alignment task. The third and final task is to recombine these target language sub-segments into a grammatically correct whole, a potentially demanding task further complicated by requirements of number, gender and case agreement in many languages. The successful automation of these tasks was the goal of a line of research known as Example-Based MT (EBMT) (Carl and Way 2006/7), but this label has been 'poached' by TM developers and is used alongside other descriptions such as 'advanced leveraging'. The more sophisticated the matching, the greater the potential benefits, but the greater also the risk of translators wasting time scanning unusable suggestions before having to translate from scratch. One consequence of such technologies and of the growing use of CMSs is that the translator may receive only modified segments, with little or no context in which to grasp their function or the circumstances in which the translation will be read and acted upon.

However, such centralization does have advantages. It is more and more the case that all translators working on the same project access the same terminology and TM resources on a shared server, rather than downloading a copy of a TM to their own machine. This means that translations of internal repetitions become immediately available to the rest of the team for automatic insertion wherever they occur. While it does present risks for maintaining quick response times over a network and the integrity of the shared TM, this mode of operation is gaining favour over post-project validation of individual translators' TMs and their integration into the central repository.

The growing emphasis on consistency at source has seen the recent release of authoring memory tools offering an auto-complete functionality which suggests possible continuations to authors as they type, based on source language segments in the TM. If the suggested completion meets the author's intended communicative purpose, it can be accepted in the knowledge that a translation also exists.

7.4.2 Software Localization (L10N) tools

In addition to the terminology, TM matching and pre-translate functions, software localization tools add specialized functions that reflect their prime use in translating text embedded in computer programs. Just as TM tools protect the formatting, so localization tools protect the program code by extracting the translatable text – mostly text that appears in the user interface, often called 'strings' – for translation in a safe environment and eventually reinsert the translated version in the right places in the right files.

In localization contexts, the term 'pseudo-translation' is a feature for coping with the fact that translations of the concise and often terse English of interface messages tend to be longer in many target languages – e.g. French TT *enregistrer* is almost three times longer than English ST *save*. To test the possible consequences of such cases, the project manager can specify an expansion factor (of, say, 50 per cent) and the tool will populate a notional TT with commensurately longer nonsense text in the appropriate character encoding. The tool can then simulate the actual 'translated' interface and will report any instances where the text overflows a button, box or window. Even though, in order to resolve any problem instances, the tool may allow the translator to re-size objects to accommodate an expanded translation, this responsibility is probably better left to a software engineer.

7.4.3 Subtitling tools

TM is not used in literary translation, nor is it common to incorporate it into the subtitling process, no doubt because of the relatively low incidence of repetitions within this genre and the context-bound nature of the equivalence between subtitles in different languages. So, dedicated subtitling tools provide no help for the core task of finding the right words. Their specificity is to display the draft subtitles as the viewer will see them and to alert the subtitler to any violations of timing constraints. These are imposed jointly by the assumed reading speeds of different viewers (adult, child, hard-of-hearing), the medium (film, DVD, TV) and the rhythm of shot changes (see Chapter 9). The tool flags subtitles which are too long to be read in the time they are displayed or whose separation from the next subtitle is too short. Some tools provide spectrographs to locate visually the onset of speech. Tools vary in respect of the number of previous and following subtitles that can be seen by the subtitler to assist in checking the flow of dialogue. Specialized modules provide access to news scripts for subtitling news broadcasts or an interface to speech recognition devices for live subtitling.

More detailed descriptions of TM and localization tools are given in Austermühl (2001), Bowker (2002), Esselink (2000, 2003), Somers (2003, 2008). A wealth of explanations, illustrations, exercises and TMs in multiple languages can be found on the websites of two EU-funded projects, eCoLoRe (http://ecolore.leeds.ac.uk) and eCoLoTrain (http://ecolotrain.uni-saarland.de). A third EU project, eCoLoMedia (http://ecolomedia.uni-saarland.de) gives access to tools and resources for subtitling.

7.5 Machine Translation (MT) tools

There are two basic approaches to building an MT system: (1) encode linguistic knowledge about the morphological, lexical, syntactic and functional structures of the source and target languages and the mappings between them; (2) provide enough aligned data to 'train' it to 'learn' the statistically most likely mappings between strings of characters in the two languages. The first approach is that of rule-based MT (RBMT) and the second that of statistics-based MT (SMT). If there is a new enthusiasm nowadays among content publishers and LSPs alike about the potential of MT, it is largely due to the advent of commercial and free online SMT – from Language Weaver and Google, respectively – thanks to the availability of very large corpora of aligned data, including TMs. SMT systems can be built in days or weeks rather than months or years, hence much of the excitement, even if the quality of the output has not necessarily improved. The rest of this section investigates the implications for the translator of the availability of large volumes of cheap but imperfect translations.

7.5.1 Current use and deployment of MT

The overwhelming use of MT today, certainly of free online MT, is for assimilation – the understanding of incoming information. Errors and lack of fluency may be tolerated provided the translation is good enough for the user to get the gist and extract specific information, especially in the case of time-sensitive documents, such as financial market bulletins, where waiting even hours for a human translation is not an option. MT used in this way enabled the Global Public Health Intelligence Network to detect the outbreak of SARS from Chinese reports in late 2002, two months before the first media reports in English (Blench 2007). The European Patent Office is deploying MT to enable affordable browsing of patent content. This is no threat to the employment of professional translators, since the demand for translation outstrips supply. MT can satisfy needs that were only latent before its evolution to its current state, as anticipated by Sager (1993: 262).

However, there is a growing use of MT for dissemination – the publication of outgoing information. Of the 860,000 pages produced in 2005 by ECMT (European Commission MT) some twenty per cent were requested by the Directorate-General for Translation, that is, as a first-draft translation to be edited by translators to the required quality standards. ECMT has been in use since 1976. The Pan American Health Organisation is another international body to have long used MT for publishing purposes, while in the commercial sector many larger companies are following SAP in integrating MT into their translation workflow. This starts with controlled authoring of documents which are analysed by the TM system. Fuzzy matches that fall below a set threshold are routed to the MT engine and back into the translator's workstation in their correct place in the text alongside the other segments, colour-coded to show their origins. Here, they are manually post-edited (revised) or re-translated conventionally before being added to the TM. All processes share the same terminology and TM resources. In such settings MT has proven to be a time-saving and cost-effective solution for certain text types and language directions.

Reports on the European Commission's usage of MT and TM are updated regularly on its website;[2] PAHO's experience is also documented online.[3]

7.5.2 ARCHITECTURES AND LIMITATIONS ON IMPROVABILITY

The predominant RBMT model is the transfer architecture (Arnold *et al.* 1994; Hutchins 2003). An initial analysis stage is intended to result in identifying the constituents of the input sentence and the functional relations – predicate, subject, object, etc. – between them, as well as sentential features such as tense, aspect and modality. Analysis relies on knowledge of the source language (SL) only, expressed as far as possible in terms of generalizations about combinations of part-of-speech categories rather than individual lexical items. The following transfer stage relies on a bilingual dictionary and mappings between the abstract structure describing an SL sentence and a structure underlying the corresponding target language (TL) sentence. The final generation stage aims to linearize this TL structure as a grammatically correct sequence of TL words.

The strategy of generalization and abstraction avoids many pitfalls of word-for-word translation. It also facilitates the independence of the analysis and generation modules such that they can be reused regardless of, respectively, the ultimate TL and the original SL, reducing the time and cost of building systems for new pairs of languages.

The translator can directly improve system performance by creating user dictionaries that remedy defects in the MT dictionaries supplied. These may be expressions that are simply not recognized – new terms, for example – or homonyms for which the sense used in the current context is not in the MT dictionary, for example *attachment* as 'emotional tie' rather than 'appended file'.

SMT systems rely on two models of statistical probabilities, the translation model and the (target-)language model, both calculated on the basis of a large bilingual corpus (preferably of millions of words). The translation model is 'the set of probabilities for each word on the source side of the corpus that it corresponds to ... each word on the target side of the corpus' (Somers 2008). In this model, readily usable translation equivalents are expected to have a high statistical probability. The (target-)language model is the set of probabilities of the relative ordering of a given set of TL words. These two models are then used in conjunction by a so-called decoder, whose task 'consists of applying the translation model to a given sentence S to produce a set of probable [TL] words, and then applying the language model to those words to produce the target sentence T' (ibid.), such that the probability of T is the highest possible. Recent approaches include phrases in both models, with improved results.

The main challenge for RBMT is ambiguity at any linguistic level (Arnold *et al.* 1994; Arnold 2003), hence the attraction of controlled languages. For SMT the main challenge is data sparsity – words in the current source text which have been encountered only rarely (or even not at all) in the training data. Of course, the corrections made to SMT output by the translator are added to the TM so that the available training data constantly improves. The hunger for more data to train SMT systems has encouraged major content publishers, particularly in IT, to pool their hitherto jealously guarded TM assets within the TAUS Data Association created by the Translation Automation Users Society (http://www.translationautomation.com).

Yet SMT systems are prone to run into difficulties when used on data different from that on which they were trained – to translate email correspondence rather than technical reports, for example. In these circumstances RBMT systems are judged more robust in maintaining their translation quality. While SMT errors may more often be unfathomable, the errors made by RBMT systems tend to be more consistent and, as a result, easier for post-editors to find since they are the product of a rule-based process. For example, a given MT system might regularly insert the definite article before abstract nouns ('*the* love conquers all') when translating from Romance languages. Similarly, instructional steps beginning *You must* in an English manual might be more appropriately translated into many languages by an impersonal construction such as *it is necessary to*. Specialized companies are already offering post-editing services to other LSPs. MT tools are rarely good at supporting the post-editing process but this new niche market may drive the development of better technologies (Allen 2003).

7.6 PROJECT MANAGEMENT TOOLS

Many translators find a spreadsheet or a generic project management application perfectly adequate for planning and managing their workflows. But, in response to the technological and human complexity of larger projects, specialist translation management tools have appeared. They cover every step from costing and quoting to invoicing. They interface with TM tools to be able to import the results of source text analysis – word counts for each category of match – and come populated with features peculiar to translation, such as setting rates for defined roles (translator, reviser, reviewer, etc.), SL–TL pairs or subject specialisms. Moreover, they can be used to enforce certain workflows by requiring one process to be signed off before the next begins, which could be advantageous in applying for certification under the EN-15308 European Quality Standard for Translation Services, for example. The eCoLoTrain website (http://ecolotrain.uni-saarland.de) provides an illustrated overview of translation project management, with exercises.

The need for quality assurance (QA) has resulted in tools which seek to automate parts of this process, available either as standalone tools or, more commonly, as plug-ins for different TM workstations. The kinds of checks they offer include: identifying untranslated or partially translated segments, detecting inconsistent translations of words or segments, punctuation, numbers, approved terminology and tags. A recent survey revealed quite widespread use but also dissatisfaction, due largely to installation difficulties, a lack of coverage of many languages and a tendency to falsely report errors (Makoushina 2007). Like the controlled language checkers already mentioned, these QA tools will continue to improve.

7.7 Collaborative Translation Tools

This chapter began with the assertion that translation is increasingly a collaborative activity. Management of the collaboration has been tacitly assumed to be top-down – a workflow where content authored in a 'master' language is periodically 'pushed' out for translation. Yet there are signs of an emerging 'pull' model of translation on demand by and for communities of users of the content. This brings a shift towards continuous publishing and, where content is user-generated, multiple source languages. Apart from questioning the traditional business model of LSPs, this movement challenges translation tools providers to find ways of supporting this new way of working.

Collaborative translation in this new sense is done by self-organizing communities of committed enthusiasts. This model has worked well in the open source software community alluded to in section 7.1.2, not only for writing program code but also for authoring and translating documentation. OpenOffice has provided guidelines to facilitate voluntary translation (into over 40 languages) and the World Wide Web Consortium has done the same.[4] Even producers of proprietary software, such as Sun and Adobe, have adopted this model for at least some of their documents, like bug reports, developers' notes and short articles.

Since it is the user community that decides what is translated, the emphasis of content producer and other 'brokers' switches from controlling to facilitating. Beyond the IT industry, Worldwide Lexicon (http://www.worldwidelexicon.org) tries to enable community-driven translation on any website, Traduwiki (http://traduwiki.org) aims to help bloggers and authors to get translations done by their readers, while dotSUB (http://www.dotsub.com) provides a very simple interface for subtitling video. Possibly the best-known source of user-generated content is Wikipedia, which likewise provides guidance on good practice and a mechanism for flagging translations in progress (http://meta.wikimedia.org/wiki/Translation). Quality assurance depends quite simply on how much the community cares about the content; potentially there are many pairs of eyes to spot and correct errors that matter.

If the open standards of Unicode and XML (sections 7.1.1–2) are critical to the growth of this movement in enabling the pooling of community resources, so are the platforms that build on them, such as the Very Large Translation Memory Project,[5] which offers free access to a collective TM (albeit while imposing the use of a particular TM tool). OmegaWiki (http://www.omegawiki.org) is a collaborative project to produce free multilingual terminology and thesaurus information.

Clearly the functionalities of existing technologies will need to be extended. From an anthropological perspective, many-to-many collaboration is a qualitatively different 'ecosystem' from the current command and control hierarchy and requires special support. At a technical level, Désilets et al. (2006) point out a number of novel challenges to maintaining wiki-style content in many languages, of which perhaps the greatest is synchronization. Content may originate in any language and then be translated, possibly with corrections and additions, into any other languages. Désilets and colleagues sketch a prototype environment which alerts authors, translators and community facilitators to language versions that have been or need to be updated, automatically locates discrepancies between versions in any two languages, and helps translators preserve the structure of intra-language links in the different languages.

The introduction to this chapter noted the growing market share of LSPs at the expense of individual translators. It remains to be seen whether this new model of collaborative translation will turn the tide.

7.8 Evaluation Techniques

There are many reasons for evaluating translation technologies: determining whether a tool is fit for purpose, tracking its performance on different kinds of data and measuring its cost-effectiveness over time are just three of them. Since translation tools are software, there are many generic quality attributes to evaluate, such as reliability, efficiency, maintainability and usability. But the focus here is on those attributes which specifically characterize the successful performance of a translation-related task.

For tasks where humans can readily agree on what is the correct result – detecting all source segments with conflicting translations, identifying all unapproved terms in a document, for example – the procedure is straightforward. First, a panel of human judges – translators, say – draws up an agreed list of right answers to serve as a gold standard against which to gauge the tool's performance. This performance can then be measured in terms of precision (the percentage of answers proposed by the tool that are correct answers) and recall (the percentage actually found of the total possible number of correct answers). Low precision means a high proportion of false positives (answers proposed that are incorrect), while low recall means many true positives (correct answers) are missed. The two measures can be weighted to reflect the user's actual needs.

Translation, however, is precisely a task where, for most segments, there is no single correct answer; on the contrary, many variants may be acceptable as legitimate. The absence of a gold standard for a whole text makes the evaluation of translation quality a hard task, open to subjective variation between judges. Several judges are then required to provide enough data points to support reliable general conclusions about the translation capabilities of a person or of a system.

There are several methods for evaluating intrinsic properties of MT output. Judges can be asked to score segments for fluency (the degree to which a text reads naturally in a given language, without regard to its content) or adequacy (the degree to which the content of the original is conveyed in the translation, regardless of how grammatically imperfect the translation is). Extrinsic measures include measuring the impact of machine-translated versus human-translated data on the performance of some task. An example would be sorting a collection of documents according to topic, a not unusual application of MT for gathering commercial and military intelligence. Performance-based evaluation foregrounds the requirements of usability and fitness for purpose, just as with the evaluation of human translation of advertising copy or safety-critical instructions. Where MT is being used to produce a first draft for subsequent human revision, the best performance measure is precisely to calculate the post-editing effort and whether it cuts or increases overall costs.

Much effort has been expended since 2001 in the search for a reliable automated metric for MT output quality that would spare the time, expense and subjectivity of human evaluations. Most of these attempts have been predicated on using measures such as string–edit distance, described in section 7.4.1, to calculate the distance between the MT output and a reference translation produced by a human professional – the fictional gold standard that results in legitimate variations being treated as errors. The consensus now seems to be that it is performance-based metrics that are best suited to MT evaluation.

Human evaluation of MT systems and output is discussed in Arnold *et al.* (1994), Hirschman and Mani (2003) and White (2003). FEMTI (Framework for the Evaluation of MT in International Standards in Language Engineering – ISLE) offers an interactive tool for suggesting appropriate metrics for different quality attributes (http://www.issco.unige.ch/femti).

Evaluation is the key to progress in all things. Evaluating technologies requires agreement on which are their important attributes and a shared understanding of the appropriate metrics for assessing them – the test data and tasks, the procedure for measuring the presence of an attribute, and the interpretation of the scale of measurements recorded. Evaluating language technologies is complicated by the subjectivity surrounding much of language usage. This subjectivity and a neglect of common standards for conducting evaluations can be seen, both in the sometimes unverifiable claims by vendors about the strengths of their product and in reviews which do not allow the comparison of competing tools. This said, the collaborative dimension of translation with the emergence of active online communities of practitioners who share protocols for evaluation is increasingly forceful in bringing to the attention of the software developers the wisdom of the crowds of translator users. This may finally ensure that 'in their own interests as well as those of their customers, [developers] should never be asked to provide an engineering solution to a problem that they only dimly understand' (Kay, 1980: 1).

NOTES

1 i18n, l10n and g11n are commonly used abbreviations for internationalization, localization and globalization respectively.
2 http://ec.europa.eu/translation/reading/articles/tools_and_workflow_en.htm
3 http://www.paho.org/English/AM/GSP/TR/MT_Docs.htm
4 http://l10n.openoffice.org/localization/translation.html;www.w3.org/Consortium/Translation
5 http://www.wordfast.com/products_vltm.html

8
ISSUES IN INTERPRETING STUDIES

FRANZ PÖCHHACKER

8.0 INTRODUCTION

The position of interpreting studies within the broader discipline of translation studies is curiously ambiguous. Often referred to as a '(sub)discipline', it is both an increasingly autonomous and diversified field of academic pursuit, on a par with translation studies, and a domain within the latter, alongside such specialized fields as audiovisual translation. This duality is also reflected in the present volume, which subsumes interpreting studies under translation studies and, at the same time, gives coverage to this field in a chapter of its own rather than under the various themes dealt with in Chapters 2 to 7.

Though subject to fundamental principles and insights concerning translation in general, interpreting studies is clearly distinguished by its unique object of study, that is, 'real-time' human translation in an essentially shared communicative context. (Interpreting is commonly referred to as 'oral' as opposed to 'written' translation, i.e. as the activity of rendering spoken messages in another language, but this simple definition fails to accommodate a number of important phenomena, as explained in section 8.2). In addition, this field of study has evolved rather differently from that of written translation, as will be described in section 8.2. Moreover, the recent diversification of interpreting as a professional practice and object of research, which has given rise to many new areas of interdisciplinary interface, has made it even more difficult to accommodate the field of interpreting studies within the boundaries, however fuzzy, of translation studies.

The case for an 'autonomous subdiscipline' notwithstanding, interpreting studies is bound up with translation studies in many ways: aside from its shared theoretical underpinnings as a form of translation, differentiated with such foresight by Otto Kade (1968), interpreting is often part of a joint 'T & I' curriculum and practised by professionals engaged (also) in written translation. It makes sense, therefore, for students and practitioners, as well as for scholars of translation, to take an interest in interpreting, just as interpreters and interpreting researchers stand to gain from a deeper understanding of 'issues in translation studies' as dealt with in other chapters of this book.

8.1 EVOLUTION AND STATE OF THE ART

8.1.1 BEGINNINGS

While interpreting as an activity has been practised since ancient times (with pictorial evidence dating back to the middle of the second millennium BCE), it seems to have been viewed as too common and unspectacular to deserve special mention, let alone sustained scholarly interest. Even when interpreting became a 'profession', essentially in the early twentieth century, considerable time elapsed before it came to be viewed as an object of study. (An interesting exception is a paper by a Spanish psychologist [Sanz 1931] on the work and skills of early conference interpreters at the League of Nations and the International Labour Organization in Geneva).

Two main sources can be identified as fuelling the early development of interpreting studies. One is the body of insights gained by practitioners reflecting on their craft. While this is also true for 'theorizing' on translation, interpreters have described their work, not so much in order to defend and justify it (as was often the case in the history of translation), but in order to explain *how* they work, often with a view to passing on their know-how to the next generation of professionals. Prime examples include Jean Herbert's (1952) *Interpreter's Handbook* and Danica Seleskovitch's (1968) classic monograph on the profession of international conference interpreting.

The other major source has been work done from the vantage point of other disciplines. Unlike the study of written translation, which owes much of its formative input to linguistics and literary studies, research on interpreting has been sourced predominantly by psychology. The crucial trigger for this was the increasing use of simultaneous interpreting, which came of age at the 1945/46 Nuremberg Trial (see Gaiba 1998) and gained further attention and prestige through its adoption by the United Nations and the fledgling European institutions. It was the skill of simultaneous listening and speaking, considered impossible according to psychological theories of the day, which spurred experimental psychologists in the 1960s to study this unique cognitive feat. Focusing on such issues as the time lag between input and output (also referred to as 'ear–voice span') and on the effect of various input conditions (e.g. speed, noise, text type), psychologists such as Henri Barik (e.g. 1975) and David Gerver (1969) carried out classic experiments that left a lasting imprint on the field and, at the same time, ushered in the next stage in the evolution of interpreting studies.

8.1.2 ACADEMIC FOUNDATIONS

In the 1960s, several personalities with a professional background in interpreting worked towards establishing the study of interpreting (and translation) as a subject in academia. One of them was Otto Kade, a teacher of Czech and Russian and a self-taught conference interpreter, whose work at the University of Leipzig (then Karl Marx University, in East Germany) made him the most influential pioneer in the German-speaking area.

Kade and his colleagues had links with the Soviet School of interpreting research, chiefly represented by Ghelly V. Chernov (e.g. 1979). Neither Chernov, who spent a dozen years as a conference interpreter at the United Nations in New York, nor his East German colleagues, were able to match the eminence of the so-called Paris School around Danica Seleskovitch. Seleskovitch played a pioneering role both in the profession (more specifically, in the International Association of Conference Interpreters – AIIC) and in the university-level training of conference interpreters at the *École Supérieure d'Interprètes et de Traducteurs* (ESIT) in Paris. It was there, at the University of Paris III/Sorbonne Nouvelle, that Seleskovitch managed to establish a doctoral studies programme in '*traductologie*' in 1974. Several fellow professionals and trainers, such as Marianne Lederer and Karla Déjean Le Féal, went on to obtain doctoral degrees, their work reinforcing an emerging paradigm of interpreting research that was built upon Seleskovitch's 'interpretive theory of translation', or *théorie du sens*, and a bias against experiments in the psychologist's laboratory.

Well into the 1980s, the Paris School paradigm held sway in matters of research on interpreting as well as the training of conference interpreters, and the monograph by Seleskovitch and Lederer (1989) describing the ESIT teaching approach remains highly influential to this day.

8.1.3 INCREASING DEPTH AND BREADTH

The *théorie du sens*, which goes back to the early 1960s, essentially holds that interpreting is not linguistic transcoding but a process based on knowledge-based comprehension. Though innovative at the time (when lexical correspondences and grammatical structures were busily fed into early machine translation systems), the interpretive theory championed by the Paris School did not open up, or prove open to, many new avenues for research. These were explored in the course of the 1980s by second-generation conference interpreting researchers, such as Daniel Gile and Barbara Moser-Mercer, who were dissatisfied with the established truths about their profession and adopted a more inquisitive approach, aspiring to greater scientific rigour and advocating closer interdisciplinary co-operation. At the University of Trieste, where representatives of the Interpreters' School collaborated with neurophysiologist Franco Fabbro to explore the neurolinguistics of interpreting, an international symposium in late 1986 marked the beginning of a new era in interpreting studies. The subsequent launch of a Trieste-based journal, *The Interpreters' Newsletter*, in conjunction with the untiring efforts of Daniel Gile to gather and disseminate information and promote networking, facilitated the emergence of a distinctly international community of researchers in the field of (conference) interpreting by the early 1990s. Efforts to co-operate with psychologists in studying the cognitive process of (simultaneous) interpreting were stepped up, and the first international peer-reviewed journal devoted to 'research and practice in interpreting' was launched, in 1996, by Barbara Moser-Mercer and cognitive psychologist Dominic Massaro.

Though its editorial team was clearly biased toward the cognitive sciences, *Interpreting* was expressly open to 'all areas of interpreting', including court interpreting, community interpreting and signed language interpreting. This broad scope of the field's dedicated journal points to the second major development of the 1990s – the extension of research interests to include previously marginal domains of the profession.

As hinted at in the preceding paragraphs, interpreting research up until the mid-1990s was largely focused on conference interpreting, and, with few exceptions, on the simultaneous mode. Interpreting as practised within social institutions, such as courtrooms, hospitals, immigration offices, schools and social service agencies, was hardly noticed by the international interpreting research community – until a milestone event in 1995 placed the 'intra-social' dimension of interpreting firmly on the map. The international conference entitled *The Critical Link: Interpreters in the Community*, and the follow-up events held every three years (see Carr *et al*. 1997; Roberts *et al*. 2000; Brunette *et al*. 2003; Wadensjö *et al*. 2007 and the website at http://www.criticallink.org), have provided a worldwide forum for practitioners and researchers to address profession-related concerns, such as training, standards of practice and codes of ethics, as well as conceptual issues of interpreter-mediated communication that arise in particular in face-to-face settings.

By the end of the twentieth century, the discipline of interpreting studies, while 'still based on a number of different paradigms', had thus taken shape as 'an independent, self-respecting research community' (Garzone and Viezzi 2002: 11) – to quote from the proceedings volume of the *Forlì Conference on Interpreting Studies* in 2000, which could be said to mark the 'coming of age' of the discipline.

8.1.4 UNITY IN DIVERSITY

Given the diverse origins and sources reviewed above, interpreting studies in the early twenty-first century presents itself as a thriving and increasingly diverse discipline, in which a set of largely complementary research approaches are brought to bear on a highly multidimensional object of study. This is reflected, for instance, in the collection of texts published in *The Interpreting Studies Reader* (Pöchhacker and Shlesinger 2002) and in the successive volumes of the journal *Interpreting*.[1]

Judged by these and other publications, the field has clearly undergone consolidation as well as growth, not least thanks to a broad perspective on the notion of interpreting. Aside from a comprehensive definition of interpreting (see also section 8.3.1), the discipline's shared conceptual foundation can be seen in a view of interpreting that ranges from international contexts, in which participants of comparable (high) status act in a professional role and/or as representatives of an institution, to community-based ('intra-social') settings, in which an institutional representative or service provider interacts with an individual speaking and acting on his or her own behalf. The format of interaction in these two broadly distinguishable spheres typically corresponds to multilateral conference-like settings with the use of simultaneous interpreting, on the one hand, and face-to-face communication mediated by a dialogue interpreter, on the other (see Figure 8.1).

international   *intra-social/*
                   COMMUNITY
           LIAISON/DIALOGUE
   CONFERENCE

─── INTERPRETING ───

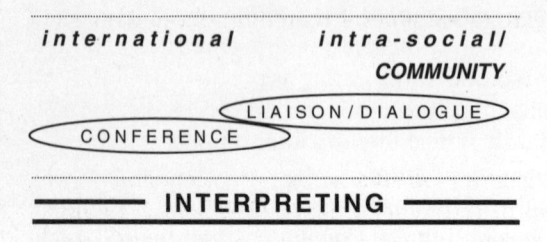

FIGURE 8.1 Conceptual spectrum of interpreting

It is important to stress, however, that the twofold distinction – between international versus community-based, and between conference and liaison interpreting or dialogue interpreting – must not be collapsed into one: there is dialogue interpreting in the international sphere (as in high-level diplomatic interpreting) just as there can be community-based conferences in which interpreters (e.g. signed-language interpreters) are at work.

This shared conceptual base notwithstanding, research into interpreting has followed a variety of different pathways, shaped by tradition as well as by the demands of newly emerging phenomena and scientific viewpoints. In a liberal use of Thomas Kuhn's notion of 'paradigm' (1962/1970/1996) (defined as a set of basic assumptions, models, values and standard methods shared by all members of a given scientific community), one could identify five paradigms of interpreting research (as described in detail in Pöchhacker 2004, chapter 4):

1. the classic paradigm of the Paris School, based on its interpretive theory (IT paradigm);
2. the (often experimental) study of interpreter's cognitive processing (CP paradigm);
3. the highly interdisciplinary approach relying on neuropsychological experiments and neuro-imaging techniques to investigate the neurolinguistics of interpreting (NL paradigm);
4. the view of interpreting from target-text-oriented translation theory (TT paradigm);
5. the study of interpreting as discourse-based interaction (DI paradigm).

Unlike paradigms in the original Kuhnian sense, the paradigms of interpreting studies listed above are not meant to be mutually exclusive or in direct competition with one another. Rather, they can be seen as approaching their shared object of study from different viewpoints, with different research questions and different methods, while ultimately working together to provide as rich an account of the phenomenon as possible. As much as the image of several paradigms mapping out the disciplinary space of interpreting studies (see Pöchhacker 2004: 80) may help to illustrate the range of approaches and perspectives, the emphasis should be on the field's unity in diversity, and the increasingly rich repertoire of ideas and models that interpreting scholars have put forward to account for their multi-faceted object of study.

8.2 MEMES AND MODELS

As suggested in previous chapters of this book, translational activity can and has been understood in different terms, variously foregrounding particular aspects of the phenomenon. Inspired by a similar effort in translation studies, these alternative 'ways of seeing' have been described as 'memes' of interpreting (Pöchhacker 2004: 51–61). Over and above five individual 'memes', or key ideas (i.e. interpreting as verbal transfer, cognitive information processing, making sense, text/discourse production and mediation), the three most fundamental conceptualizations can be singled out as 'supermemes' of interpreting, namely, interpreting as translation, interpreting as processing and interpreting as communicative activity. The first of these will be taken up below for a more elaborate definition of interpreting, while the other 'ways of seeing' and ways of modelling interpreting will be described more summarily as a backdrop to the review of major research issues (section 8.3).

8.2.1 INTERPRETING (DEFINED) AS TRANSLATION

As early as the 1960s, Otto Kade (1968) defined interpreting as a form of translation (in the wider sense) in which (a) the source-language text is presented only once and thus cannot be reviewed or replayed, and (b) the target-language text is produced under time pressure, with little chance for correction and revision.

This far-sighted definition avoids the usual reference to spoken messages and elegantly accommodates also interpreting from, into or between signed languages, as well as such variants of interpreting as 'sight translation' and live subtitling. Foregrounding the aspect of immediacy, or real-time performance, interpreting could be described more succinctly as a translational activity in which a first and final rendition in another language is produced on the basis of a one-time presentation of an utterance (or text) in a source language.

8.2.2 TEXT AND DISCOURSE

The idea that interpreting involves texts, in the broader, semiotic sense – or acts of discourse, depending on one's theoretical framework – is central to much theorizing in interpreting studies. Unlike earlier views based on the notion of linguistic (lexical/syntactic) transfer, the study of interpreting as text production can draw on insights from text linguistics and discourse studies (see Chapter 3), both for describing relevant features of the interpreter's input and textual product and for analysing the determinants and constraints of text and discourse processing. Examples of efforts at modelling interpreting in this perspective, including such features as the interpreter's prior knowledge and cognitive representation, can be found in Pöchhacker (2004: 94ff).

8.2.3 COGNITIVE PROCESSING

The most popular perspective on interpreting by far, at least for international conference interpreting, has been the view from cognition (see also Chapter 4). Charged with the comprehension and production of verbal messages, the interpreter has been conceived of as an information processing system relying on memory structures (working memory, long-term memory) and a number of cognitive subskills, such as anticipation, inferencing and macro-processing (for some classic examples of cognitive processing models of simultaneous interpreting, see Moser-Mercer 1997 and Pöchhacker 2004, Chapter 5).

8.2.4 INTERCULTURAL MEDIATION

Rather than as a set of mental structures and processes, interpreting is also conceptualized, most evidently, as mediated interaction between two or more communicating parties with different linguistic and cultural backgrounds, foregrounding issues of communicative purpose, role, trust, status and power (e.g. Anderson 1976). Viewed from a social rather than a cognitive-psychological perspective, the interpreter is seen as a mediator not only between languages but also 'between' cultures and value systems. Hence, the role of the interpreter, as prescribed in codes of ethics and professional conduct, has emerged as a particularly controversial issue (see section 8.3.4), especially in dialogue interpreting within community-based institutions.

8.3 MAJOR ISSUES

Against the backdrop of the field's evolution, its various research approaches and conceptual models, this section presents some of the thematic focal points of research in interpreting studies (as described more extensively in Pöchhacker 2004, Part II). The list of major issues is obviously not exhaustive.

Rather, an effort has been made to label the main themes in parallel with the 'issues' addressed in other chapters of this book. In any case, it should be pointed out that the various research topics are not clearly separable but inherently interrelated (as holds true also for the conceptual and modelling perspectives reviewed in section 8.2).

8.3.1 COGNITIVE PROCESSING

In line with the influential view of (simultaneous) interpreting as a cognitive processing activity (see section 8.2.3), and given the unquestionable centrality of human mental faculties in carrying out whatever type or variant of this complex communicative task, the basic component processes of comprehension and production in two different languages are fundamental to any account of interpreting (see Pöchhacker 2004, Chapter 6). Drawing on insights and methods from such fields as cognitive psychology, psycholinguistics and cognitive pragmatics, research has explored both the cognitive substrate (i.e. memory) and the various strategies employed in processing verbal messages and their paralinguistic and non-verbal components (see Poyatos 1987). Given the limitations of human working memory, a crucial concern is the high cognitive task load generated by the simultaneity of the main processing operations – concurrent source-text comprehension and target-text production in the simultaneous mode, but also source-text comprehension, memorizing and note taking in consecutive interpreting. As highlighted in Daniel Gile's (1997) Effort Models, concurrent processes competing for limited attentional resources lie at the heart of performance problems in (conference) interpreting, making attention management the interpreter's essential skill (see also Chapter 4).

A related focus of interest is the strategies used by interpreters to cope with such processing constraints as high source-text presentation rate (speed), high information density, scripted style and unusual accents. They include on-line strategies such as anticipation, compression and syntactic restructuring as well as off-line strategies preceding the real-time task (e.g. background research, study of documents, preparation of glossaries). Most of the latter are designed to enhance the interpreter's thematic and contextual knowledge and thus to aid 'top-down' (knowledge-driven) processing of linguistic input. At the same time, interpreters are guided by communicative (listener-oriented) considerations, so that features of the situated interaction become an integral part of their cognitive processing activity.

8.3.2 QUALITY

Producing an interpretation that fulfils the communicative needs and expectations of the intended addressee is arguably the interpreter's primary task – and the principal yardstick for measuring the quality of an interpreter's product and performance (see Pöchhacker 2004, Chapter 7). This client-centred ('functionalist') view of performance quality is easily adopted in interpreting, where the service users – as opposed to readers of a translation – are generally on site (exceptions being media interpreting and various forms of remote interpreting).

For conference settings, survey research among users has yielded a rather stable pattern of quality criteria, in which fidelity to the source, cohesion, fluency and correct terminological usage rank above delivery-related features such as pleasant voice and native accent (see Kurz 1993/2002). Nevertheless, experimental studies have shown such non-verbal components of the interpreter's output to have a significant impact on the quality judgements of interpretation users (see Collados Aís 1998), who are by definition unable to check the target text reliably against its source. Establishing such source–target correspondence, often in terms of omissions, additions and translation errors (e.g. Barik 1975), has rather been left to researchers and examiners, albeit tempered by the recognition that quality implies not (only) equivalence on the linguistic level but an equivalent effect of the interpretation on the listeners.

This 'pragmatic' perspective on quality is particularly salient for dialogue interpreting in institutional settings, where an interpreter's performance in face-to-face interaction can shape, for instance, jurors' impressions of witness testimony (see Berk-Seligson 1988); patients' satisfaction with clinical interviewing, and thus the quality of medical service delivery; or an adjudicator's assessment of an asylum seeker's claim and credibility. It is no coincidence that the debate about 'good interpreting' and 'best practice' is conducted so vociferously in relation to legal and healthcare interpreting, where the interpreter's role in the interaction invariably exceeds that of transmitting information and encompasses a co-construction of interactive discourse (e.g. Wadensjö 1993 and section 8.3.4) that is liable to impact, for better or worse, on legal proceedings and clinical outcomes.

8.3.3 TRAINING

Given the high demands on interpreters' performance and professional responsibility, training has been an overriding concern in the literature of interpreting studies ever since Herbert's (1952) pioneering *Handbook*. Fuelled by the growth of international conference interpreting, the demand for professional interpreters led to the creation of university-level training institutions as early as the 1940s (Geneva, Heidelberg, Vienna). And with organizations such as the United Nations and the European institutions, as well as the interpreting profession (AIIC) taking an active interest, the training of conference interpreters, at postgraduate level, has long been consolidated and institutionalized, most recently in the form of a European model curriculum (see http://www.emcinterpreting.net). Its core includes: consecutive interpreting with the aid of (more or less systematic) note taking; simultaneous interpreting in the booth, for which various preliminary exercises have been suggested (see Seleskovitch and Lederer 1989); and a variable dose of sight translation, either as a simultaneous mode of its own or in the booth ('simultaneous with text').

No such 'training paradigm' has been established for (spoken-language) interpreting in community-based settings. Rather, community interpreters in many countries are still striving for professionalization, often in the absence of sustained institutional demand and in the face of widespread *ad hoc* interpreting by untrained volunteers. Where training in public service interpreting (legal, healthcare and social-service settings) does exist, it is usually offered at undergraduate level, if as a degree course at all. This also applies to the training of signed-language interpreters in many countries, even in the USA, where interpreting in this modality attained an impressive degree of professionalization, not least thanks to the Registry of Interpreters for the Deaf (RID), but where the statutory demand for interpreters in educational settings far exceeds the supply of highly qualified professionals.

In either modality, the education of community interpreters is often significantly different from that of international conference interpreters. Rather than text-processing skills, the focus is on managing the dynamics of interpersonal interaction, including issues of culture and unequal status, and the interpreter's fraught position 'in-between'.

8.3.4 ETHICS AND ROLE

One of the hallmarks of a profession, as a community of practitioners with a special body of expertise and a commitment to serve society at large, is a set of rules stipulating what is deemed professional behavior. AIIC adopted a Code of Professional Ethics for conference interpreters as early as 1957, with a 'Code of Honor' consisting of five articles, chief among them the principle of professional secrecy. The RID Code of Ethics, dating back to 1965, went considerably further by addressing such principles as impartiality and faithfulness, which intersect with the much-discussed issue of the interpreter's role. American signed-language interpreters have indeed been at the vanguard of shaping the concept of role, moving from the view of the interpreter as an uninvolved ('neutral') 'conduit' to that of a more visible 'communication facilitator' and of a 'bilingual, bicultural specialist' (see Roy 1993), more recently calling into question the 'myth of neutrality'.

Among spoken-language community interpreters, particularly in healthcare settings, a widely known conceptualization of the interpreter's role is the pyramid model, according to which an interpreter's baseline function is that of 'message converter', complemented when necessary by the incrementally more 'visible' roles of 'message clarifier', 'cultural broker' and even 'advocate'.

To the extent that court interpreting is subsumed under the broad notion of community-based ('intra-social') interpreting, such high degrees of 'visibility' are problematic in the judicial sphere, where the standard of 'verbatim translation' often remains the favoured, if fictitious, norm. The fact that legal professionals are wary of granting interpreters more licence in dealing with meaning (i.e. 'interpreting') brings the issue of role and ethics back to the socio-professional or even political level: rather than a matter of practitioners and scholars agreeing on a definition of role, interpreters' role boundaries may be defined by professionals in other, more powerful social fields.

8.3.5 TECHNOLOGY

A major impact on the interpreting profession has always come from technological developments. As early as the mid-1920s, newly developed electro-acoustic transmission systems were employed in experiments with simultaneous interpreting. And, even though conference interpreters may have disliked the loss of status and visibility resulting from being moved from the rostrum to a booth in the back of the room, it is modern simultaneous interpreting equipment that has ensured the smooth and widespread incorporation of interpreters into conference proceedings.

Aside from interpreters' increasing online access to IT and telecommunications tools, the biggest technological revolution upon them is undoubtedly the spread of remote interpreting, that is, a situation in which the interpreter is not in the same location as the communicating parties. Rather than face-to-face, the interpreter interacts via some form of telecommunications technology, in audio or video modes. Most basically, this is implemented as (audio-only) telephone interpreting, which has been used for many years, particularly in community-based settings. With the advent of digital media and higher data transmission capacities, remote interpreting in web-based video mode has become increasingly feasible, for community-based as well as international communication scenarios.

The adoption of remote interpreting has been of particular significance in healthcare and judicial settings as well as in the domain of signed-language interpreting, where what is known as video remote interpreting (as distinct from 'video relay service', which links video access with a telephone call) is vastly expanding Deaf persons' access to interpreting services.

No less fundamental is the impact of remote interpreting in international conference settings, where experiments using satellite-based transmission date back to the 1970s. Institutional employers of conference interpreters like the UN and the European Commission and Parliament have conducted several trials of videoconference interpreting and remote (simultaneous) interpreting. While the technical set-up has undergone significant improvement (including the use of large screens and multiple camera views), 'visual access' remains a problem and has been associated with increased eye strain and fatigue. Most critically, interpreters' lack of a sense of 'presence' poses the risk of alienation and reduced motivation.

8.3.6 HISTORY

Though clearly a millennial practice, the evanescence of the spoken word (and of gestures, for that matter) has left historians with little evidence on which to construct a history of interpreting. Nevertheless, some intriguing sources have been used to shed light on interpreting practices in the past (see Bowen 1995). These include Egyptian hieroglyphics and tomb decorations (see Hermann 1956/2002), chronicles and travel writing, legal provisions and memoirs, all of which have been mined for insights into the settings in which interpreters have been used (e.g. war and diplomacy), the variable social status of the linguistic mediator, and the question of interpreters' qualifications, including their loyalty and cultural identity.

Although interpreting did not, for the most part, gain general social recognition as a profession before the twentieth century, even its subsequent history is far from fully established. Among the most significant contributions are the archival research by Baigorri-Jalón (2004) on the origins of simultaneous interpreting, Gaiba's (1998) study on interpreting at the Nuremberg Trials and the account of translation and interpreting in Germany by Wilss (1999). Clearly, though, there is ample scope for further investigations focusing on other institutional and geographic contexts.

8.4 TRENDS

The first five themes discussed in the previous section – cognitive processing, quality, training, ethics, technology – are likely to remain among the foremost issues in interpreting research and practice. Aside from various interrelations (e.g. technology in teaching or the impact of training on service quality), a number of aspects would deserve more detailed attention. Within the space available, however, the review of major issues can be complemented here only by shining the spotlight on some ongoing and future developments in the field.

8.4.1 BILATERAL MARKETS

As in previous periods in history, the widespread use of a lingua franca is a key factor shaping interpreting needs and practices. After a period of thriving multilingual conferencing (involving mainly English, French and German but also languages such as Russian and Spanish), the emergence of 'Global English' has tended to limit the demand for (conference) interpreters in international business, diplomacy and technical and scientific co-operation, while focusing it on interpreting between English and the vernacular, not least in the media.

This is true also for modern-day military interpreting, where communication among allied troops or peacekeepers may well proceed in English but where interpreters are needed in dealing with the local population.

The shift from UN-style multilingual conferencing to interpreting into and out of international English is illustrated, in particular, by the rising geopolitical status of China, where interpreting largely means working between Mandarin Chinese and English. This tends to weaken the Paris School orthodoxy on generic rather than language-pair-specific skills, and on directionality (i.e. the claim that simultaneous interpreters should work only into their A language).

Extending the focus beyond interpreting between Indo-European languages is likely to increase research interest in linguistic (language-pair-related) issues, especially involving Asian and African languages, which will also imply greater attention to underlying cultural differences. Moreover, the trend towards increasingly 'bilateral' interpreting needs should facilitate the convergence between the international and community-based domains of interpreting, with signed-language interpreting – between the national language and the respective sign language(s) of the country – serving as a well-established paradigm case: though sign-language interpreters are vitally important in public services and other community-based settings, increasing educational opportunities for the Deaf also create a need for simultaneous interpreting in conference-like situations (e.g. Turner 2007).

8.4.2 Qualitative methods

Across its various paradigms, interpreting studies has built up a rather extensive conceptual and methodological repertoire, including cognitive-psychological experiments, corpus-linguistic quantification, web-based surveys, sociolinguistic discourse analysis, sociological modelling of institutions and interaction, and ethnographic work inspired by cultural anthropology. Research on community interpreting, in particular, has favoured empirical work based on qualitative data, often in the form of case studies involving transcriptions of discourse, triangulated with ethnographic techniques such as participant observation and informal interviewing (e.g. Wadensjö 1998). Overall, methodologies in interpreting research have been gravitating from the cognitive towards the social sciences, and from quantitative towards qualitative data, fortunately with the pragmatist consensus that either approach is valid and needed, and that different viewpoints complement rather than compete with one another in the interest of further progress in interpreting studies.

Notes

1 http://www.benjamins.com/cgi-in/t_seriesview.cgi?series=INTP.

9
ISSUES IN AUDIOVISUAL TRANSLATION

Delia Chiaro

9.0 Introduction

Audiovisual translation is one of several overlapping umbrella terms that include 'media translation', 'multimedia translation', 'multimodal translation' and 'screen translation'. These different terms all set out to cover the interlingual transfer of verbal language when it is transmitted and accessed both visually and acoustically, usually, but not necessarily, through some kind of electronic device. Theatrical plays and opera, for example, are clearly audiovisual yet, until recently, audiences required no technological devices to access their translations; actors and singers simply acted and sang the translated versions. Nowadays, however, opera is frequently performed in the original language with surtitles in the target language projected on to the stage. Furthermore, electronic librettos placed on the back of each seat containing translations are now becoming widely available. However, to date most research in audiovisual translation has been dedicated to the field of screen translation, which, while being both audiovisual and multimedial in nature, is specifically understood to refer to the translation of films and other products for cinema, TV, video and DVD.

After the introduction of the first talking pictures in the 1920s a solution needed to be found to allow films to circulate despite language barriers. How to translate film dialogues and make movie-going accessible to speakers of all languages was to become a major concern for both North American and European film directors. Today, of course, screens are no longer restricted to cinema theatres alone. Television screens, computer screens and a series of devices such as DVD players, video game consoles, GPS navigation devices and mobile phones are also able to send out audiovisual products to be translated into scores of languages. Hence, strictly speaking, screen translation includes translations for any electronic appliance with a screen; however, for the purposes of this chapter, the term will be used mainly to refer to translations for the most popular products, namely for cinema, TV, video and DVD, and videogames.

The two most widespread modalities adopted for translating products for the screen are dubbing and subtitling.[1] Dubbing is a process which uses the acoustic channel for translational purposes, while subtitling is visual and involves a written translation that is superimposed on to the screen. Another, less common, acoustic form of screen translation is voice-over.

Translating for the screen is quite different from translating print. Books, newspapers and other written products are simply meant to be read. Although they may contain illustrations (pictures, photographs, graphs, diagrams, etc.), these generally serve to complement and/or enhance the verbal content. Comic books are an interesting exception as they are made up of images and words that are closely interconnected so as to create a narrative whole. While not being *audio* visual in nature, they are both read and 'watched' simultaneously as the dialogues contained in the speech balloons connected to each speaker attempt to emulate spoken language. This 'oral' element is especially evident in the conventions attached to conveying emotions, e.g. the use of words such as 'swoon', 'gasp', 'sigh', etc. as well as those pertaining to an array of physical sensations such as 'aaagh!', 'ouch', 'zap' and 'pow'. Furthermore, the visuals in comics consist of series of sequential captions that are reminiscent of stills of a film on celluloid. In a sense, readers of comics are privy to a narrative event that gives the impression of unfolding in motion. As a genre, comics could be placed on the interface between print texts and audiovisual products, as the reader is able to imagine sounds and noises, and although images are static, because they appear within a sequential framework of continuous and interconnected images and captions, the overall perception can be likened to that of watching a film (Zanettin 2008). Unsurprisingly, from the mid-twentieth century, traditional Japanese comics, known as *manga*, developed into a flourishing animated cartoon industry, *animé* (e.g. *Sailor Moon, Pokemon* etc.).

Conversely, products for the screen (i.e. films, TV series and serials, sitcoms, documentaries, etc.) are completely audiovisual in nature. This means that they function *simultaneously* on two different levels. Screen products (from this point onwards SP) are polysemiotic; in other words, they are made up of numerous codes that interact to produce a single effect (see Figure 9.1).

We talk of 'watching' films and of tele*vision*; thus, primarily, these products are made to be seen. Accordingly, at one level, SP will be made up of a complex visual code comprising elements that range from actors' movements, facial expressions and gesture to scenery, costume and use of lighting and colour. However, this visual code will also include verbal information in written form that will comprise features such as signposts and street signs and also items such as banners, newspapers, letters, notes, etc. This arrangement of visuals is united to an acoustic code that consists not only of the words in the dialogues but also of a series of non-verbal sounds such as background noise, sound effects and music. Thus, SP are both seen and heard by audiences. Screen translation is concerned mainly with conveying the verbal audio codes of an audiovisual product into other languages.

	VISUAL	ACOUSTIC
NON-VERBAL	SCENERY, LIGHTING, COSTUMES, PROPS, etc. Also: GESTURE, FACIAL EXPRESSIONS; BODY MOVEMENT, etc.	MUSIC, BACKGROUND NOISE, SOUND EFFECTS, etc. Also: LAUGHTER; CRYING; HUMMING; BODY SOUNDS (breathing; coughing, etc.)
VERBAL	STREET SIGNS, SHOP SIGNS; WRITTEN REALIA (newspapers; letters; headlines; notes, etc.)	DIALOGUES; SONG-LYRICS; POEMS, etc.

FIGURE 9.1 The polysemiotic nature of audiovisual products

To my knowledge, there is no complete overview of screen translation in terms of its exact spread and impact on a global level. However, traditionally western Europe has been roughly divided into two major screen translation blocks: the UK, Benelux, Scandinavian countries, Greece and Portugal, which are mainly 'subtitling nations', and central and southern European countries stretching from Germany down to Spain (so-called 'FIGS', France, Italy, Germany and Spain, but also Austria), which are mainly 'dubbing nations'. Both translational methods present advantages and disadvantages, not only of a practical nature but especially of a sociolinguistic and political kind. In other words, countries which originally favoured dubbing tended to do so for protectionist reasons and it is not surprising that the 1930s saw the birth of dubbing in Italy and Germany both to inhibit English and to exalt national languages, as well as to censor content. Conversely, a preference towards subtitling in Scandinavia, for example, does not simply reflect a more open attitude towards other languages but an inexpensive form of screen translation for a relatively restricted number of spectators. However, although traditional dubbing strongholds stand firm, there too subtitling markets are in rapid expansion: DVD technology, satellite and cable TV channels and digital television have produced the need for vast numbers of screen translations. Furthermore, world markets demand that products are screened soon after being premièred in the USA (products that are mainly of US origin and thus translated from English into other languages; see Dries 1996; Eurobarometer[2]). In fact, subtitling is commonplace across the whole of Europe, chiefly because of its cost-effectiveness (Chiaro 2005). Although, outside Europe, dubbing enjoys a strong standing in mainland China, Japan, Latin America and Québec, just as subtitling does in Israel, Hong Kong and Thailand, the screen translation map is less clear-cut than it seems. For example, subtitling is indeed usually preferred in countries with small populations, but political entities such as Wales, the Basque country and Catalonia opt for dubbing as a way of promoting and/or standardizing a minority language (O'Connell 1996; Izard 2000). Furthermore, even in subtitling countries, children's films and programmes are almost always dubbed, while the possibility for cinema and TV users to choose between one modality or another is becoming ever more common through interactive pay TV stations. Cinema theatres screening in the original language with subtitles are becoming commonplace in traditionally dubbing countries, while countries such as Denmark and Greece now also dub to audiences other than children (Gottlieb 2001a; Díaz Cintas 1999). Finally, the general tendency in English-speaking countries is to subtitle the few foreign language feature films that actually enter these markets, for highly educated, 'élite' art-house cinemas audiences, while TV products in languages other than English are virtually non-existent (Kilborn 1989). In 2006, foreign language films represented 3.5 per cent of the total UK gross box office revenue, of which 1.8 per cent were in Hindi and presumably played almost exclusively to an Asian audience. In the same year, 2 per cent of all films broadcast across terrestrial TV channels were in a foreign language.[3]

This chapter will present and discuss the different ways in which SP are translated from one language to another. SP include full-length feature films for cinema, TV, video and DVD and the entire spectrum of TV products (i.e. series, serials, sitcoms, documentaries, news programmes, advertisements, etc.), many of which are also available in home video and DVD formats.[4] Following this brief overview of how screen translation fits in within the wider field of multimedia translation, the two major modalities adopted for translating SP, namely dubbing and subtitling, will be described and discussed in detail, especially in terms of the advantages and disadvantages of each specific mode. The modalities of voice-over and TV interpreting will also be presented and discussed. Finally, a detailed discussion of the specific translational constraints of screen translation will close the chapter.

9.1 DUBBING

Dubbing is a process which entails 'the replacement of the original speech by a voice track which attempts to follow as closely as possible the timing, phrasing and lip-movements of the original dialogue' (Luyken *et al.* 1991: 31). The goal of dubbing is to make the target dialogues look as if they are being uttered by the original actors so that viewers' enjoyment of foreign products will be enhanced.

9.1.1 THE DUBBING PROCESS

There are traditionally four basic steps involved in the process of dubbing a film from start to finish. First, the script is translated; second, it is adapted to sound both natural in the target language and to fit in with the lip movements of the actors on screen; third, the new, translated script is recorded by actors; and finally it is mixed into the original recording. The first translation is usually word for word. Some companies employ translators simply to provide a literal translation of the script, after which it is the adaptor or 'dubbing translator' who subsequently adjusts the rough translation to make it sound like natural target-language dialogue. By tradition, the dubbing translator need not be proficient in the source language, but creative and talented enough in the target language to create fresh dialogue that is convincing. As well as rendering talk natural, care is taken to ensure that the dialogue fits into visual features on screen such as lip movement, facial expressions and so on. Furthermore, the new dialogue also needs to take the emotive content of each utterance into account. However, with the awareness that a thorough understanding of the source text is a crucial asset for a translator, it is becoming ever more common for the two processes (the translation itself and the adaptation) to merge and be carried out by a single translator who is proficient in both languages (Chaume 2006).

While the script is being translated and adapted, the dubbing director, a project manager who supervises the entire dubbing process, including economic aspects such as negotiating time scales and costs with the commissioner, will choose the dubbing actors (known as 'voice talents' in the USA) that best suit the parts. The director may choose an actor according to his or her voice quality, which may closely match that of the original actor. However, in the case of well-known actors, it is common in Europe for one person to dub the same actor for his or her entire career. For example, Woody Allen has at least three European counterparts who have dubbed him in all his films: Wolfgang Draeger in Germany (Pisek 1994), Oreste Lionello in Italy and Joan Pera in Spain. While the dubbing director carries out these administrative tasks, his or her 'dubbing assistant' will divide up the film track (traditionally in videotape form) into 'takes' or loops (*anelli*, literally 'rings', thus reminiscent of celluloid) and mark them with a time code at the beginning and end of each. These short tracks of film are organized according to the combination of characters appearing in each one in order to arrange recording shifts in the studio for the different actors involved. Recordings are carried out with the actors watching the film and listening to the dialogues contained in each original take through headphones while they rehearse the translation that they read from the script. As soon as the actors' utterances are in sync with the original, recording begins. The new voices are processed by a synthesizer so that they are coordinated as precisely as possible with the original lip and facial movement (Paolinelli and Di Fortunato 2005).[5] Significantly, actors are free to adapt the new screenplay when they begin recording. In fact, they will often have the freedom to manipulate utterances as they think fit according to artistic or other criteria. Furthermore, the dubbing director may intervene in the translation of the dialogues wherever he or she wishes. In practice, a single person often carries out more than one of the four steps in the process. For example, the same person may double up as both dubbing director and dubbing translator or an actor may also double up as dubbing director (Chiaro 2005). Finally, once recording has been completed, the dubbed tracks are mixed with the international track and musical score so as to create a balanced effect.

So far we have considered an 'artisan' approach that has been common across Europe since the outset of dubbing. Nowadays, however, digital technology is beginning to replace this more traditional approach, mainly for reasons of cost-effectiveness. One of the advantages of digital technology is that it allows actors more freedom during the recording process. Push-button technology eliminates the bother of having to continually wind reels of tape back and forth. Moreover, the dubbing assistant no longer needs to slice up a reel into takes because there is no need to arrange actors into numerous and complex shifts. Thanks to electronic formats, each dubbing actor can simply record their part on their own. The complicated and time-consuming traditional artisan approach forced actors to physically work together in all the scenes in which the original actors appeared together; hi-tech allows each actor to perform his or her part in the film, not necessarily in the presence of other actors. Separate pieces of footage will thus be edited into a whole by means of software and/or computer appliances.

As well as simplifying technical and organizational aspects of the dubbing process, new technology is also able to modify lip sync and voice quality. Software is now available that can automatically modify footage so that an actor mouths words that he or she did not actually speak in the original; in other words, the original sequence can be modified to sync the actors' lip motions to the new soundtrack.[6] Other programmes allow a dubbed voice to be readily assimilated to that of the original actor, irrespective of the source language, by recording first a sample of the original voice and then the dubbed dialogues. The software matches the first recording with the second, giving the impression that the original actor is speaking the target language with its characteristic quality and intonation patterns.[7]

Finally, it is worth briefly mentioning the idiosyncrasy of dubbing in Poland and Russia. Here, SP are generally dubbed by a single male voice known as the *Lektor*, who interprets all parts, regardless of whether they are male or female, with a style of intonation which is, to say the least, monotonous to foreign ears. Furthermore, no attention whatsoever is paid to lip sync, while the underlying dialogue in the original language is fairly perceptible. Arguably, this style of dubbing is closer to voice-over (section 9.3.1) simply because of the slight audibility of the underlying code. Although this style of screen translation may seem odd to audiences elsewhere, it nevertheless appears to be appreciated in Poland and Russia.

9.1.2 ADVANTAGES AND DISADVANTAGES OF DUBBING

Bollettieri Bosinelli argues that those in favour of dubbing have traditionally stressed the association of dubbing with 'doubling' and hence the 'opportunity of making films available to larger audiences ('increase the sales')' while privileging the semantic trait of 'exact likeness'. Those against dubbing stress the negative meaning of 'double' such as 'ambiguous, fake, deceitful, false, other than original, phoney, artificial'(1994: 8).

It would not be unfair to say that dubbing has a worse reputation in subtitling countries than subtitling has in dubbing countries. Furthermore, there appears to be a certain element of supremacy attached to subtitles that escapes dubbing, possibly because of its link with art-house movies and artistically renowned directors. Unlike subtitling, dubbing is often condemned for spoiling the original soundtrack and denying audiences the opportunity of hearing the voices of the original actors. Yet, in a sense, dubbing is the screen translation modality which is able to fulfil the greatest filmic uniformity with the original simply by virtue of the fact that there is no need to reduce or condense the source dialogues as in subtitling (section 9.2.1). In other words, there is less textual reduction. With dubbing, audiences can actually watch the film in its entirety as they are not distracted by also having to concentrate on reading the dialogues. In fact, dubbing is a language service that is consumed automatically and in a sense goes by unnoticed by audiences that are used to this modality. However, subtitles too are consumed without audiences being unduly aware of or disturbed by them. In fact, audiences get used to what they see and hear and by and large they accept it simply because 'viewers are creatures of habit' (Ivarsson 1992: 66). Significantly, even the issue of imperfect lip sync, which is frequently raised as one of dubbing's negative points, appears to pass unnoticed by audiences in dubbing countries, presumably because perfect or near-perfect sync is only vital in close-up shots (Herbst 1994).

Nevertheless, dubbing is far more complex, time-consuming and, consequently, more costly than subtitling, simply because of the number of operators involved in dubbing a film from start to finish: dubbing director, translator, dubbing translator, actors, sound engineers, etc. Digital technology can reduce both time and cost factors (see section 9.1.1), but whether it achieves the same quality as that of 'artisan' style dubbing still remains to be seen.

Since the beginning of the twenty-first century, the dubbing countries have begun to be swamped by cost-effective subtitled products, especially the newly invented DVD. This is because the market is in need of very fast (and cheap) translations to deal with the continuous large numbers of new productions for both cinema and TV, as well as an autonomous DVD market. Apart from the real risk of reducing work in the dubbing industry (a significant European market sector which employs thousands of people), there is a real danger of stamping out a singular European craft. Ironically, while the USA filmic and television markets are extremely protectionist, with foreign products exclusively subtitled, it is Hollywood that oversees the dubbing (rather than subtitling) process of their goods in several developing countries. At present, Hollywood supervises dubbing in 33 territories, including Afghanistan and Iraq, to which the USA has sold its 'dubbing expertise' (Chiaro forthcoming a).

9.2 Subtitling

Subtitling can be defined as *'the rendering in a different language* of verbal messages in filmic media, in the shape of one or more lines of written text presented on the screen *in sync with the original written message'* (Gottlieb 2001b: 87, emphasis added).

9.2.1 The subtitling process

Subtitling consists of incorporating on the screen a written text which is a condensed version in the target text of what can be heard on screen. Depending on the mode of projection, subtitles can either be printed on the film itself ('closed' subtitles), selected by the viewer from a DVD or teletext menu ('open subtitles') or projected on to the screen, although the latter mode is largely restricted to film festivals where subtitles are displayed in real time.

The written, subtitled text has to be shorter than the audio, simply because the viewer needs the necessary time to read the captions while at the same time remaining unaware that he or she is actually reading. According to Antonini (2005: 213), the words contained in the original dialogues tend to be reduced by between 40 and 75 per cent in order to give viewers the chance of reading the subtitles while watching the film at the same time. Especially, where an SP is thick with dialogue, the subtitling translator is forced to reduce and condense the original so that viewers have the chance to read, watch and, hopefully, enjoy the film.

Antonini (213–14) identifies three principal operations that the translator must carry out in order to obtain effective subtitles: elimination, rendering and simplification. Elimination consists of cutting out elements that do not modify the meaning of the original dialogue but only the form (e.g. hesitations, false starts, redundancies, etc.) as well as removing any information that can be understood from the visuals (e.g. a nod or shake of the head). Rendering refers to dealing with (in most cases eliminating) features such as slang, dialect and taboo language, while condensation indicates the simplification and fragmentation of the original syntax so as to promote comfortable reading.

Just like dubbing, the subtitling process may also involve several operators. The first stage in subtitling is known as spotting or cueing and involves marking the transcript or the dialogue list according to where subtitles should start and stop. Traditionally, this stage in the process is carried out by a technician, who calculates the length of the subtitles according to the cueing times of each frame. With the aid of the dialogue list annotated for cueing, the translator will then take over and carry out the actual translation. In addition, it is not unusual for a third operator to be employed to perfect the final subtitles, checking language but also technical aspects, such as ensuring that subtitles are in sync with changes of frame. However, as with the dubbing process, thanks to technology it has become quite normal nowadays for a single operator to carry out all three steps of the entire procedure (see the report of a workshop by Díaz Cintas[8]). Nevertheless, while subtitling translators working with SP for the cinema tend to create a new transcript from the original transcript in writing alone (i.e. their end product will be in written form), those working for DVD and TV are likely to work from computer-based workstations that allow them to receive all the necessary information, including the time-coded transcription or dialogue list, from which they devise, cue, check and even edit the subtitles. In other words, they will work directly on to electronic files and produce a complete product.

Traditionally, subtitles consist of one or two lines of 30 to 40 characters (including spaces) that are displayed at the bottom of the picture, either centred or left-aligned (Gottlieb 2001b). However, films for the big screen tend to have longer lines with more characters compared to TV screens because of movie audiences' greater concentration and DVDs also have longer lines, presumably because viewers can rewind and re-read anything they may not have read (Díaz Cintas and Ramael 2007: 24). According to Díaz Cintas, such restrictions are bound to disappear in the future as many subtitling programmes work with pixels that are able to manage space according to the shape and size of letters.[9]

Naturally, subtitles in languages which read from right to left (e.g. Hebrew, Arabic) are, of course, right-aligned, and scripts can also be placed vertically, as for Japanese. Normally, the letters are white, spaced proportionally with a grey-coloured shadow or background box that darkens if the underlying picture becomes darker. Furthermore, nowadays it is also fairly common to find subtitles both at the top of the screen and the bottom, (e.g. MTV television) as well as moving or 'crawling' subtitles in the lower screen (seen by the writer in Taiwan). The exposure time for each subtitle should be long enough to permit comfortable reading; three to five seconds for one line and four to six for two lines (Linde and Kay 1999: 7). Subtitles cannot remain on screen too long because the original dialogue continues and this would lead to further reduction in the following 'sub'. Studies also show that, if they are left on the screen too long, viewers tend to re-read them, which does not appear to lead to better comprehension (Linde and Kay 1999). However, at present subtitles adhere to what Gottlieb has defined as the 'one-size-fits-all' rule of thumb (1994: 118), based on the assumption that slower readers who are not familiar with the source language set the pace. This has led to the established length/timing conventions. Yet different languages use varying amounts of verbal content to express the same meaning. For example, the average German word is longer than the average English word and the syntax of Italian is notoriously complex and hypotactic compared to English, but subtitling conventions are the same for all.

Subtitles can also be either open, meaning that they cannot be turned off and controlled by the viewer (i.e. at cinemas), or closed, which means that they are optional and accessed by the user (i.e. subtitles for hard of hearing, subtitles on pay TV channels and DVDs).

9.2.2 ADVANTAGES AND DISADVANTAGES OF SUBTITLING

Generally speaking, subtitling seems to enjoy a more positive reputation than dubbing (see section 9.1.2.). In fact, the type of film that is subtitled in both English-speaking countries and within the dubbing block will tend to be associated with a more élite and possibly highbrow audience. In addition, the fact that dubbing in countries such as Italy was originally introduced, amongst other things, to meet the needs of the high incidence of illiteracy within the population, associates the mode even further with less intellectual audiences. Moreover, it is not only scholars from subtitling countries who have supported this modality. An abundance of case studies comparing source and target versions of SP have been produced by scholars working within FIGS countries; underscore the weakness of the dubs. In contrast, it would appear that research on subtitling has focused on wider issues such as source language interference in naturally occurring language (Gottlieb 1999, 2001a) and reading speeds (Linde and Kay 1999) as well as more general theoretical aspects (Titford 1982; Delabastita 1989).

The fact that the source language is not distorted in any way is surely the most significant benefit of subtitles. Furthermore, an important advantage is that the original dialogue is always present and potentially accessible. Thus, audiences who are familiar with the original language of the film can also follow the acoustics. A popular argument in favour of subtitling is that it promotes the learning of foreign languages, but whether this is really true has never been established empirically. Certainly, a significant advantage is the prospect of its use as a language-teaching tool in the classroom. However, the fact that the original dialogues can be heard is double-edged as this severely limits translators' choices, especially when translating from English. Censorship is a clear example of this and is exemplified in the manipulation of films in Francoist Spain (Vandaele 2002: 267) and of series such as *The Simpsons* and *South Park* produced for the Arab world (see 'Taboo' in section 9.4.2.2). Yet, as Weissbrod highlights, on Israeli TV the subs in both Hebrew and Arabic retain references to sex and the sacrilegious expressions of the original (2007: 30). Internationally well-known taboo swear words in English films may be reduced in foreign subtitles but they will still be clearly audible and therefore recognized by audiences. And, through comparisons of subtitles and dubs of the same products, it would appear that subtitles reduce taboo language more than dubbing (Bucaria 2007), presumably because of the belief that these words in writing have a stronger effect than speech (Roffe 1995), but again, this is still to be proven empirically.

In addition, the effort of reading and listening at the same time may be disorienting for some viewers. However, this challenge should not be overstated, because (1) there is reason to believe that subtitling audiences pay less attention to the spoken dialogue than dubbing audiences; (2) subtitles are becoming more and more 'readable' and user-friendly. Apart from the greatly improved aesthetics of layout (i.e. 'bleeding'), pale-coloured subtitles are a thing of the past and have been widely replaced by modern black boxes filled with bold characters. Texts are now segmented so that grammatical units are respected across and within a subtitle, with line-breaks occurring after a clause or a sentence (Wildblood 2002). Also, simple lexis is preferred to more complex words, punctuation is conventionalized, with a tendency to avoid hyphenation, and care is taken for the upper line in two-line subtitles to be shorter than the lower line so as to keep eye movement to a minimum (Ivarsson 1992).

Finally, the fact that subtitles are *added* to the original version, rather than *substituting* part of it (i.e. the verbal code), renders subtitling an uncharacteristic and possibly unique type of translation. Moreover, the translation of subtitles is 'diagonal' (Gottlieb 1994) in the sense that, unlike literary translation, for example, in which transfer is 'written to written', or interpreting, in which transfer is 'spoken to spoken', in subtitling spoken language is transformed into writing. Consequently, all the elements that are unacceptable in standard, or even informal written language (e.g. hesitations, false starts, taboo, language, etc.) are inevitably omitted in the streamlining that the modality necessitates. So, paradoxically, subtitles, a form of writing, are unable to conform to 'real' writing by virtue of the fact that they are reflecting speech. To sum up, the bonus of viewers able to hear the original voices and dialogue is traded off not only against the textual reduction of the subtitles but also against the missing elements of 'real' writing such as explicitness, elaborateness, formality, etc.

9.2.2.1 FANSUBS

A fansub is a 'fan-produced, translated, subtitled version of a Japanese anime programme' (Díaz Cintas and Muñoz Sánchez 2006). The production of a fansub involves teamwork, in which different members are responsible for different steps in the procedure, from initially downloading the original video from the web to processes such as timing, editing and distribution. However, the translation element is often carried out separately from the other technical processes and mostly uses the English version (translated by a Japanese) as a pivot language. Fansubs differ significantly from professional subtitling in that they are more daring and flout many conventions by introducing features such as the use of different colours for different actors, the glossing of unfamiliar features on different parts of the screen as well as giving operators more visibility by naming them in the credits, which, unlike most mainstream subs, are also translated (ibid.). Possibly because many fansubbers are information technology experts, many of the innovations adopted, such as use of coloured subs and special fonts, have been borrowed from video game localization that involves expertise in software engineering combined with translational skills (cf. section 9.3.2). Today, however, as well as cartoons, fansubbers create translations for a wide variety of television genres which, once subtitled, are subsequently made available over the internet.

9.3 OTHER SCREEN TRANSLATION MODALITIES

9.3.1 *Voice-over*

Voice-over can be defined as a technique in which a disembodied voice can be heard over the original soundtrack, which remains audible but indecipherable to audiences. To date, this modality of screen translation has been very much overlooked and under-researched by academics. The only study of which the author is aware is Grigaravičiūtė and Gottlieb (2001).

Voice-over consists of a narrator who begins speaking in the target language following the initial utterance in the original and subsequently remains slightly out of step with the underlying soundtrack for the entire recording. Despite the fact that audiences may be familiar with the source language, the underlying speech cannot be clearly perceived apart from the initial and final utterances of the original narrator and the insertion of the odd sound bite. A sound bite is a very short piece of footage of the original soundtrack which is not covered by the new target language audio. For example, a chunk of speech may be given prominence by being made perceptible through a short and temporary silencing of the voice-over. Normally, sound bites are discernible at the beginning and end of a voice-over.

This modality is generally linked to the sober narrative style adopted in traditional historical and wildlife documentaries as well as news broadcasts. However, it would be wrong to believe that voice-over is limited to these particular genres and to factual products alone. In Italy, for example, advertisements and shopping channels make frequent use of voice-over, albeit with an intonation which is less sober than that adopted for traditional documentaries. People acting as testimonials for products advertised are voiced over 'theatrically', as are celebrity chef programmes (e.g. *Jamie at Home*, Channel 4, 2007 broadcast on *Gambero Rosso* pay TV channel) and eyewitnesses in several historical documentaries (e.g. History Channel's *Decoding The Past*, A&E Television Networks, 1995; *Opus Dei Unveiled*,

George Tzimopoulos and Bill Brummel Productions, 2006; etc). Theatrical voice-over refers to a histrionic, 'acted-up' recitation. On Italian news programmes, while interpreters (see Key Concepts: Media interpreting) and/or voice-over narrators adopt a serious stance to translate prominent politicians and other personalities, citizens belonging to underprivileged ethnic minorities are typically voiced over theatrically (Chiaro forthcoming a).

9.3.2 LOCALIZATION FOR VIDEO GAMES

Video games can be defined as 'computer-based entertainment software, using any electronic platform ..., involving one or multiple players in a physical or networked environment' (Frasca 2001: 4).

A wide variety of video games can be accessed and played from computers, television sets, hand-held consoles, machines in dedicated arcades and mobile phones. These games can be fairly simple, involving a single player (e.g. solitaire) or else complex and interactive with more players (e.g. role-play games). Similarly to other SP, video games are audiovisual in nature, but they are created using cutting-edge technology, making great use of creativity that is continually evolving to produce newer, brighter and more lifelike visual and sound effects. Video games incorporate human voices, thus products tend to be both dubbed and subtitled. However, language translation and software engineering go hand in hand in the localization of these products for individual markets, and, unlike for other SP, translation is considered an integral part of the localization process of each product. In terms of revenue, the video game industry has clearly overtaken cinema and television (Bernal Merino 2006) and this may well be due to the quality control that companies exert on each product. In fact, the video game industry is a rare example of the way translation is not seen just as something to be carried out once production has been completed as a sort of unrelated and unimportant appendage. Game publishers are usually also responsible for localizing their products, a process in which both functional and linguistic testing are part of quality assurance (Chandler 2005). Furthermore, translators are involved in each stage of projects. Of course, the negative side is that translators work with 'unstable work models' that are continually changing (O'Hagan and Mangiron 2006).

O'Hagan and Mangiron highlight a number of similarities and diversities between video game localization and audiovisual translation. Firstly, while most SP are dubbed or subtitled from English into other languages, video games are mainly dubbed and subtitled into English from Japanese. The dubbing process for video games is similar to that of other SP; subtitling, however, differs. Most subtitled games make use of intralingual subtitles. Players are able to control them, by pausing for example, as when watching a DVD. Furthermore, in order to keep up with the rapid speed of a video game, subtitles appear at a faster speed than at the cinema or on TV.

Above all, however, the aim of video games is to provide entertainment and to be enjoyed. It is thus paramount that translators bear in mind the importance of the 'look and feel' of the original. Although this involves taking into account culture-specific features and especially humorous effects, it also means that the translator should be familiar with the game genre itself and the specific type of register it employs. In fact, translators are usually given total freedom to accommodate sub and dub so as to come up with a product that is as enjoyable as possible for each locale. Translators are given the freedom to make use as much as possible of local features, such as jokes and references to popular culture, so as to enhance the target product. This kind of translation is often termed 'transcreation' (cf. section 1.7 and Chapter 6).

9.3.3 *Real-time subtitling and respeaking*

Real-time subtitling is 'real time transcription using speaker-dependant speech recognition of the voice of a trained narrating interpreter in order to provide near simultaneous subtitles with a minimum of errors' (Lambourne 2006).

Originally developed to provide intralingual subtitles for the deaf and hard of hearing, real-time subtitling is also widely used for interlingual subtitling in many countries worldwide (see Sheng-Jie Chen 2006 for an overview). Whether inter- or intra-lingual, real-time subtitles are produced with a speaker/interpreter who reads and reduces and, in the case of interlingual subtitles, translates speech flow in the original language while a stenographer creates the subtitles. Korte (2006) reports that Dutch television companies have been regularly adopting real-time subtitles, not only for international affairs, state weddings and funerals etc., but also for live programmes in a foreign language since the late 1990s.

However, more recently the practice of respeaking has been rapidly gaining ground. Thanks to speech recognition software able to transform oral speech into written subtitles with a certain degree of accuracy, the respeaker remains the only human operator in the entire process. Basically, the respeaker reduces the source message, software recognizes his or her voice and automatically translates this into written subtitles. At present, speech recognition software is able to transform oral speech into written subtitles with some accuracy, and there is reason to believe that future advances will eliminate existing technical shortcomings.

9.4 Translating audiovisual products: linguistic and cultural issues

Whether the chosen mode of translation is subtitling, dubbing or voice-over, the screen translator will face a series of common problems. As we have seen, unlike both written texts and purely oral discourse, filmic products contain both oral and visual elements. However, what makes audiovisuals especially complex in translational terms is the fact that the acoustic and visual codes are so tightly combined as to create an inseparable whole. Therefore, although translation operates on the verbal level alone (i.e. the translator can only modify the words of an audiovisual product), it still remains inextricably linked to the visuals of the film itself, which remain intact. Moreover, if we consider the process of dubbing, translation will involve facing the basic difficulty of the synchronization of lip movement in the original language with lip movement in the target language (see 9.1.2). On the other hand, the process of subtitling requires dialogues to be condensed in order for them to fit into short captions which appear on the screen that can only be left on display for a limited time (see 9.2.2). These are difficulties that are specific to each modality. In addition to these, both dubbing translators and subtitling translators have to contend with three basic categories of translational hurdles:

1. highly culture-specific references (e.g. place names, references to sports and festivities, famous people, monetary systems, institutions, etc.);
2. language-specific features (terms of address, taboo language, etc.);
3. areas of overlap between language and culture (songs, rhymes, jokes, etc.).

Of course, the features specified above are problematic in written translation too and in interpreting, but in audiovisual products audiences will be able to match what they see on screen (the visuals) with what they hear in a dub or read in a subtitle. For example, in a novel, no matter how such features are conveyed for the target reader, the *idea* of the objects in question will remain in the reader's mind and imagination; in contrast, with filmic products many references are in full view on the screen, leaving the translator with little room for manoeuvre. Additionally, in the case of subtitling, this leads to what Díaz Cintas (2003: 43) labels 'vulnerable translation' since the possibility of comparing soundtrack and subs renders the latter subject to criticism by audiences who may identify what they perceive to be discrepancies, omissions and unexpected equivalents (see also section 9.2.2 above).

9.4.1 CULTURE-SPECIFIC REFERENCES

Naturally, when watching many audiovisual products, viewers must suspend their disbelief. However, when watching in translation, disbelief must be suspended even further. If French viewers see a well-known American actor on screen climbing into a New York cab and hear him speaking to the driver in impeccable French, they will know that what they are hearing is an artefact. They will be well aware of the fact that the actor normally speaks English and that New York taxi drivers would normally expect to be addressed in English too. However, viewers' acceptance is often stretched to extreme limits, especially because of the presence of a series of highly culture-specific references (CSRs). CSRs are entities that are typical of one particular culture, and that culture alone, and they can be either exclusively or predominantly visual (an image of a local or national figure, a local dance, pet funerals, baby showers), exclusively verbal or else both visual and verbal in nature.

National institutions in film and TV genres are an example of CSRs: there are numerous North American screen products pertaining to 'legal' (e.g. *Ally McBeal*), 'police' (e.g. *CSI* and *Cold Case*) and 'hospital' (e.g. *ER* and *Grey's Anatomy*)[10] which are translated for audiences worldwide.[11] These institutions rarely correspond to those in other countries but, while in English-speaking countries such as the UK the viewer simply 'learns' the additional procedures, practices and above all the specific language of different judiciary, police, health and school systems, elsewhere these are conveyed through diverse translational norms that accommodate these institutions to each target culture. Thus, in Italian dubs and the subtitles of legal filmic genres, for example, a figure such as a 'district attorney' regularly becomes a *procuratore distrettuale* – a nonce term in naturally occurring Italian; similarly, a schoolchild's 'F' grade would be translated literally despite the absence of a corresponding marking system in Italy. In other words, audiences see a foreign reality (e.g. wigs and gowns of French and British judiciary, costume and behaviour of North American cheer leaders, etc.), yet hear some sort of compensatory source language to convey it. Antonini and Chiaro (2005: 39) have identified ten areas in which what they have labelled 'lingua-cultural drops in translational voltage' may occur:

1. **Institutions** (including judiciary, police, military)
    a. Legal formulae: e.g. 'This court is now in session', 'All rise', 'Objection, your Honour', 'Objection overruled/sustained', 'You may be seated';
    b. Courtroom forms of address: e.g. 'Your Honour', 'My Lord', 'Members of the jury';
    c. Legal topography: Supreme Court, Grand Jury, Court, etc.;
    d. Agents: lawyers, solicitors, attorneys, barristers, etc.; hospital hierarchies such as consultants, interns, paramedics; military hierarchies, etc.
2. **Educational** references to 'high school' culture, tests, grading systems, sororities, cheer leaders, etc.
3. **Place names:** The District of Columbia, The Country Club, 42nd Street, etc.
4. **Units of measurement:** Two ounces of meat, 150 pounds, twenty yards, etc.
5. **Monetary systems:** Dollars, soles, pounds, etc.
6. **National sports and pastimes:** American football, baseball, basketball teams: *The Nicks, Boston, Brooklyn Dodgers*, etc.

7. **Food and drink:** Mississippi Mud Pie, pancakes, BLT, etc.
8. **Holidays and festivities:** Halloween, St Patrick's, July 4th, Thanksgiving, Bar Mitzvah, Chinese New Year, The Festival of Light, etc.
9. **Books, films and TV programmes:** 'Did you watch the Brady Bunch?'; 'Welcome to the road Dorothy'.
10. **Celebrities and personalities:** Ringo Starr; Toppy; The Cookie Monster, etc.

Adopting a wavering supply of electricity as a metaphor, 'lingua-cultural drops in translational voltage' (ibid.) refer to the inevitable perceived uneasiness and turbulence in the verbal code with respect to the visuals. The previous examples are mainly taken from US filmic products and, although translations are not provided, it is clear to see why they may create difficulty. Furthermore, the abundance of examples from US SP reflects their dominance in the Italian, and indeed all European, media (see European Audiovisual Observatory data[12]) as well as more internationally.

In order to handle such references, as in written translation, translators opt for either: a) 'chunking up' and making CSR in the target language more general than those in the source language through the adoption of hyperonymy; b) 'chunking down' by replacing them with more specific references in the target language; or c) 'chunking sideways' and replacing CSR with same level equivalents (Katan 1999/2004: 147).

9.4.1.1 CHUNKING UPWARDS AND DOWNWARDS

Chunking a CSR upwards involves replacing it with a more general example of the same object in the target language, while chunking downwards involves substitution with an example of an extremely culture-specific and (therefore) extremely different item, in the target language. For example, in a breakfast scene from a well-known US sitcom *The Nanny*, there is a reference to three foodstuffs that are typically North American, namely muffins, cereals and puddings. Both Italian and German translations (dubs) have been domesticated for respective audiences. However, the original US 'muffins' have been chunked down for Italian audiences to be replaced by *maritozzi*, a type of bun that is typically Roman, while in German they have been chunked up to become generic *Kuchen* – 'cakes'. Again, the non-specific 'cereal' in the original becomes specific *Müsli* – 'muesli' in German. Significantly, in the Italian dub the cereal and puddings are respectively transformed into highly specific *savoiardi* and *pasticcini* ('sponge fingers' and 'petits fours') while in the German version the puddings specifically become *Pralinen* ('chocolates'). Alert viewers in Italy and Germany may well be able to spot the differences as the original muffins, cereal and puddings are likely to be discernible on screen.

9.4.1.2 CHUNKING SIDEWAYS

Chunking sideways occurs when a CSR is replaced with a target feature which is neither more general nor more specific than the original, but of the same level. In a well-known sketch from an episode (Series 2, Episode 1) of *Little Britain*, featuring Lou and Andy subtitled in Italian, the off-screen narrator is heard to say that Lou has just been spending a 'busy morning taking all the K's out of Andy's Alphabet Spaghetti'. Despite the fact that *Alphabet Spaghetti* are not available in Italy, the subtitles supply a word-for-word translation: *una mattinata passata a rimuovere tutte le 'K' dall'Alphabetti Spaghetti di Andy.* The translator has chunked sideways.[13] Similarly, in another sketch in the same episode, the Prime Minister's aide offers the shadow minister a 'chocolate finger'. This time the biscuits can be clearly seen on screen, yet the subtitles refer to *Dito di cioccolato* (literally: a real [chocolate] finger of a hand) despite the fact that similar biscuits in Italy go by the name of *Togo*. Admittedly, translating with *Togo* would have left no room for the sexual innuendo which follows, but the visual/verbal mismatch remains.

9.4.2 LINGUA-SPECIFIC FEATURES

9.4.2.1 LINGUISTIC VARIATION

Sociolinguistic markers such as accent, variety and slang (Pavesi 1996; Chiaro 1996, 2000a) tend to disappear in screen translations. In fact, the 'homogenizing convention' (Sternberg 1981) typical also of literary translation, in which all characters adopt a standard variety of the target language, tends to be the general norm. In the case of subtitles, the translator can attempt to connote those pertaining to the speech of certain characters so that the reader will understand that the vocalizations of a particular person are different from that of others, but transcribing the subtitles of an entire film in any variety other than the standard would be unprecedented.

In the Italian subtitles of *My Cousin Vinnie* (1992, Jonathan Lynn, USA) the odd (deliberate) grammatical mistake underscores teddy-boy Vinnie's (Joe Pesci) poor command of standard American English as well as his Italo-American inarticulateness. For example, Vinnie's inability to correctly pronounce the final fricative of the word 'youths' is reflected in the misspelt *ragassi* instead of *ragazzi* but the inclusion of these mistakes in the subs is not consistent throughout the film. Similarly, in dubbing it is quite unusual to connote all characters in terms of their geographic, ethnic or social origin. In the dubbed version, Vinnie speaks with a Sicilian accent from start to finish. However, he is the only character whose language is marked in the translations (both sub and dub) despite the strong Alabama drawl of most of the other characters. Assis Rosa (2001: 217) provides examples of two film adaptations of Shaw's *Pygmalion* subtitled for Portuguese TV channels. As is well-known, language is a central theme of the plot and Assis Rosa shows how one version simply adopted the odd example of non-standard vocabulary while the other consistently inserted informal lexis, deviant spelling and other oral features.

However, comedies constitute an exception to the homogenizing convention. In fact, it is not at all unusual for comic or cartoon characters to be dubbed with stereotypical accents. In Dreamworks productions such as *Shark Tale* (2004, Bibo Bergeron and Vicky Jenson, USA), the mobster-shark Don Vito (Robert De Niro) and his henchman Sykes (Martin Scorsese) are dubbed with Sicilian accents, while Ernie and Bernie, two Jamaican jelly-fish thugs, are transformed into speakers of Italian teenspeak, voiced by two well-known comedians, thus paralleling, in part, the voices of Ziggy Marley and comedian Doug E. Doug in the original. So, laid-back, vaguely Roman-sounding teenage gobbledygook compensates for the Rasta speech of the jelly-fish and crosscuts dialect and sociolect. Again, in *Chicken Run* (2000, V.G., USA) the Scottish hen is dubbed with a marked German accent. The audience's perception of the hen is no longer that of the strict Scottish spinster but of the stereotypical cruel German. Therefore, the Italian version gives the character a completely different connotation from the intended one, although the comic *skopos* remains.

Nevertheless, on rare occasions, 'serious' genres also choose to insert sociolinguistic markers in translation, as in the Italian dub of *The Da Vinci Code* (2006, Ron Howard, USA) that includes characters speaking Italian with French, Spanish and English accents, but this is an exception rather than the rule. Similarly, educational History Channel documentaries such as *The Plague* (2005) and *The Scourge of the Black Death* (2005) are voiced over by actors speaking English (or the language of each interlingual voice-over) with the imaginary accents of writers at the time.

MULTILINGUAL FILMS

Products containing characters speaking in a language other than the main film language present another translational quandary when the film is dubbed. In the case of multilingual films, the strategy in dubbing countries tends to be to adopt a mixture of dubbing and subtitling although, if one of the foreign languages in question happens to be the one into which the film is being translated, this will create additional difficulties. Thus, in the Italian version of *A Fish Called Wanda* (1988, Charles Crichton, UK) in which Wanda's lovers must speak to her in any language other than English, Otto's Italian is transformed into Spanish. Subtitling is, of course, the most obvious solution in such cases. However, in both Spain and Italy the DVD version of *Babel* (2006, Alejandro González Iñárritu, France, USA, Mexico), a film originally shot in five languages (English, Mexican Spanish, Arabic, Japanese and Japanese sign language), was released completely dubbed, whitewashing the overall effect and missing the point of the film, which concerns the wider issue of the lack of dialogue in contemporary society.

9.4.2.2 Pragmatic features

FORMS OF ADDRESS AND DISCOURSE MARKERS

Language-specific pragmatic features such as politeness and forms of address also create problems. Standard modern English has a single 'you' form, which requires differentiation in languages that have both informal and polite forms of address (e.g. French *tu/vous*) (Pavesi 1994), not to mention languages such as Japanese with a more complex system of honorifies. Thus, amongst the issues faced by screen translators is the means of conveying the explicit shift from formality to intimacy in the French *on se tutoie?* Or the use of the given names in an utterance such as 'You can call me Jane'.

Similarly, translators also need to overcome the hurdle posed by discourse markers and fillers. With the severe restrictions required in subtitling, such markers are an obvious choice when it comes to choosing which parts of the dialogues to eliminate. However, dubs also tend to restrict such markers. Interjections such as 'Oh!' and 'Ah!', as well as hesitations like 'um', 'er' 'mmm' etc. in English tend to disappear in the Spanish subtitles of *Four Weddings and a Funeral* (1994, Richard Curtis, UK). For example, when the main character, played by Hugh Grant, stammers: ' It's that girl, um … Carrie. You remember the uh … The American', in the Spanish version it becomes *Es aquella chica. Carrie. ¿Te acuerdas? La americana.* ('It's that girl. Do you remember? The American'.) Yet Hugh Grant's character is also totally transformed in the Italian dubbed version where his hesitations and false starts are also severely reduced (Chiaro 2000b).

TABOO

Screen translators increasingly have to deal with what many consider to be offensive language. According to Roffe (1995: 221) 'the audience will be more offended by written crudeness than by actual oral usage'. Whether this is true or not remains to be proved, but in matters of censorship, subtitles do appear to be weaker than the original. But again, so does dubbing (Bucaria 2007; Chiaro 2007). However, it is certainly much easier to disguise what may seem distasteful to regimes, commissioners and translators themselves through dubbing than subtitling (Vandaele 2002; Hargan 2006). On the other hand, the adaptation of *The Simpsons* for Arabic speaking audiences has been purged of references to alcohol and sex and the family's lifestyle has been generally sobered up. This, however, appears to have angered those Arab Simpsons fans who want Omar to be as politically incorrect as his original US counterpart Homer. With the ease of accessibility of film and TV materials, as well as information about them, audiences have become extremely knowledgeable and this may cause producers to think twice before censoring.[14]

9.4.2.3 VISUAL VERBAL VERSUS SPOKEN

Anything written on screen, especially elements which are read aloud by the actors, is problematic to convey in another language. In *The Da Vinci Code*, the main characters need to unravel a number of anagrams and cryptic rhymes which can be clearly seen, in English, on the screen. For example, viewers see the anagrams 'O Draconian devil!' and 'So dark the con of Man' and are aided in unravelling them (respectively Leonardo Da Vinci and Madonna of the Rocks) through the visualization of the code-breaking process by lighting up certain portions of the letters. Obviously this requires radical adaptations for both a convincing dub and subtitle. Denton (1994: 31) provides an example of a complex interaction of written and spoken signs from *A Fish Called Wanda*. Otto, Wanda's lover, is in the bathroom making a series of loud invectives against the British: '[the British] ... counting the seconds to the ... weekend, so they can dress up as ballerinas and whip themselves into a frenzy at the ...'. At this point Otto comes across a note from Archie (with whom Wanda is about to have an affair), which he opens. The letter contains an address that is shown on screen:

> So see you at the flat at 4.
> It's 2B St. Trevor's Wharf E.1.
> All my love,
> Archie

Otto reads the note aloud so that the entire dialogue becomes:

> [the British] ... counting the seconds to the ... weekend, so they can dress up as ballerinas and whip themselves into a frenzy at the ... [*reads note that audience can see*] ... flat at four, 2B St ... **To be honest** I ... er ... hate them.

It would not be possible to transpose the phonological connection between the flat number '2B' and 'to be' so the Italian repair strategy becomes:

> ... *contano i secondi che mancano all'arrivo del fine settimana per potersi vestire come delle ballerine e andarsi ad ubriacare* ... [*reads*] *nell'appartamento Quattro al* **2B** ... **due bi** ... **cchieri** *e poi crollano*.
> [lit. they count the seconds till the weekend so they can dress up like ballerinas and get drunk ... in apartment 2B ... two gl ... glasses and they drop].

The translation of *manga* (Japanese comic books, see section 9.0) creates a related problem. In the original these comic books are written from top to bottom and right to left, as this is the natural reading pattern of Japanese. Although some translations are kept in this original format, others are 'flipped' from left to right in translation so as not to confuse foreign readers. Naturally, this practice can lead to inconsistencies with the real world, such as all characters being left-handed. A culturally specific example is that people wearing kimonos in the original *manga*, where it would be shaped like a y, would be depicted wearing them the other way around in the flipped version. In Japan, the left side overlaps the right (from the viewer's perspective) when the person is dead.

9.4.3 FUZZY AREAS

Allusions, songs, rhymes, metaphors, idiomaticity and verbally expressed humour are also extremely problematic. These features have been labelled as fuzzy because they cross strictly linguistic features with cultural references.

9.4.3.1 SONGS

In musicals, as well as films, the words of the songs often contribute to the storyline. In the case of dubbing, the songs are often translated and sung in the target language, but they are just as often left in the original, subtitled or left untranslated. The latter is especially typical of Japanese cartoons in which audiences suddenly hear a song in Japanese when the rest of the audio is dubbed in another language.

9.4.3.2 VERBALLY EXPRESSED HUMOUR

Verbally expressed humour is notoriously difficult to translate when it is simply written or spoken, but on screen it can become especially complex when visuals and vocals coalesce. A clear example of this difficulty can be found in a scene in *The Big Chill* (1983, Lawrence Kasdan, USA) in which one of the main characters, Sam, on being asked by Meg to father her child, replies : 'You're giving me a massive headache!', to which Meg replies: 'You're not gonna use that old excuse, are you? You've got genes!' In response, Sam looks down at his trousers and touches the jeans he is wearing, a bemused expression on his face. The Italian version of Meg's final utterance becomes *perché hai dei buoni geni* [lit. 'because you have good genes'] but the word *geni* is monosemous and can only refer to chemically patterned information ('genes'). Furthermore, it bears no phonological resemblance to the universal word for denim trousers, 'jeans'. Thus, Italian audiences must have wondered why Berenger should touch and glare at his jeans as he does.

Subtitling does not escape the snares of verbally expressed humour either. The main character in *The Pianist* (2002, Roman Polanski, USA) is called Wladyslaw Szpilman. The language of the film is mainly English with some

German that is subtitled. In one of the final scenes of the film, Gestapo captain Wilm Hosenfeld finds Szpilman in hiding. The dialogues between the two men are in German and subtitled in English as follows:

>Captain: What is your name? So I can listen for you.
>Szpilman: My name is Szpilman.
>Captain: Spielmann? That is a good name, for a pianist.

Unless readers know German they will be unable to understand that the surname 'Szpilman' sounds like 'Spielmann' which literally means 'the man who plays' or 'the player'.

However, not all verbally expressed humour based on the visuals fares so badly. In the Marx Brothers' film *Horse Feathers* (1932, Norman McLeod, USA), Groucho is signing a document and asks someone to give him a seal to make it official. At this, Harpo quite typically produces a live (animal) seal that is clearly visible on screen. In Italian, *sigillo* ('seal/stamp') is monosemous so the film's dubbing-scriptwriters were faced with running the risk of puzzling spectators with a word-to-word translation. Long before the days of digitalization, the visual code could not be modified in any way but the dubbing director came up with *Focalizziamo* as a solution, meaning literally, 'Let's focus on it' playing on the term *foca* meaning 'seal' and the verb *focalizzare* meaning 'to focus on something' (see Chiaro 2006). However, a very common strategy adopted to translate a particularly difficult instance of verbally expressed humour is simply to ignore it and subsequently omit it in translation (see Delabastita 1996; Chiaro 2008).

Naturally, problems referred to in this section, together with the strategies adopted to solve them, are not restricted to screen translation alone but can be applied to all types of translation. It is however, important to remember that what is particular about translating for the screen is the existence of a close interplay of visuals and acoustics combined with words. The screen translator can only operate on a linguistic level; he or she is limited to translating the verbal code, yet close attention must be paid to elements that are not strictly linguistic (i.e. gestures, visuals, music, etc.) when transferring the words from one language to another, simply because, by virtue of the fact that these words are 'on screen', they are neither self-sufficient nor independent.

9.5 Conclusions

The twenty-first century is witnessing the advent of new technological devices for people's entertainment and interaction and the future is likely to bring new forms of translation which will be able to cope with the constraints of small, portable screens. These futuristic modalities are, at present, almost unimaginable. Another increasingly important consideration is inclusion (also known as 'accessibility'), namely intralingual translations for the deaf and hard of hearing and audiodescriptions for the blind and visually impaired, which deserves a dedicated space (see the Key concepts entry for Inclusion). However, it is worth stressing that the world's large ageing population will be ever more in need of translation modalities to allow them easy access to SP given the inevitable hearing and reading difficulties that increase with age. This also highlights that screen translation is a service. It is only right that consumers of this service receive high-quality products. The quantity of SP that are produced and translated is incalculable and in today's world the speed at which they are translated is paramount to business. New technologies can indeed speed up the processes of dubbing and subtitling, but it is the quality of the translation itself which is crucial. All the subtitling and dubbing software imaginable cannot replace a good translation. Therefore, training is an essential tool and academia has a duty to interact with screen translation industries to sensitize both them and governmental agencies to the importance of this overlooked and undervalued service.

NOTES

1 The nouns 'dub' and 'sub' are used respectively to refer to translated utterances in dubbed and subtitled form, i.e. the final verbal product in the target language.
2 http://ec.europa.eu/public_opinion/index_en.htm
3 Source: UK Film Council Statistical Yearbook: http://www.rsu.ukfilmcouncil.org.uk
4 Whether dubbed or subtitled, the screen translation of a product first screened at the cinema or on TV is likely to be translated again for VHS formats (where they are still used) for home viewing, and once more for the DVD version. This can obviously lead to three dissimilar translations.
5 Chaume (2007) reports on the slight operational differences in the dubbing process in the different FIGS countries.
6 According to Chaume (2007) *Video Rewrite* appears to have been developed by researchers at New York University. Amongst its more obvious applications is the sync of the speech of computer-generated characters such as those in productions like *Shrek, Ratatouille, Bee Movie*, etc.
7 Gambier (2008) discusses the implications of *ReelVoice*.
8 British Council workshop on subtitling at: http://www.literarytranslation.com/workshops/almodovar/
9 Pixel is short for Picture Element. 'Pixels are the smallest point of light or colour that make up a digital image. The more pixels, the higher the image resolution will be. In subtitling, it is being used to work out the maximum length of a subtitle line, taking over the traditional number of characters per line and allowing greater rationalization of the available space' (Díaz Cintas and Ramael 2007: 250).
10 *Ally McBeal* (Fox, 1997–2002); *CSI* (CBS, 2000 to present); *Cold Case* (CBS, 2003 to present); *ER* (NBC, 1994 to present); *Grey's Anatomy* (CBS, 2005 to present).
11 Most examples provided are taken from US filmic/TV products simply because North America is the chief producer and exporter of these goods worldwide

(data continually updated by the European Audiovisual Observatory, accessible at http://www.obs.coe.int).
12 http://www.obs.coe.int/
13 The translator has chunked sideways despite the fact that just as easy an option was to chunk downwards by translating with *pastina alfabeto*, alphabet-shaped pasta eaten by toddlers, especially since the dish is not visible on screen. It is unlikely that Italian viewers will be familiar with the tinned product and will therefore probably miss the joke (Chiaro forthcoming b).
14 'Homer becomes Omar for Arab makeover of Simpsons'; http://www.independent.co.uk/news/media/homer-becomes-omar-for-arab-makeover-of-simpsons-511733.html (accessed February 2008).

KEY CONCEPTS

Terms in **lower-case bold type** cross-refer to separate entries, Initials denote authors (see list of contributors).

ABUSIVE TRANSLATION

This term was introduced by Lewis (1985), following Derrida, to denote a radical approach to literary translation. The term 'abusive' refers to the fact that all translations require some form of interpretation, which somehow brings about gains and losses. For Lewis, abusive translation is a 'strong, forceful translation that values experimentation, tampers with usage, seeks to match the polyvalencies or plurivocities or expressive stresses of the original by producing its own' (ibid.: 41). This term implies some kind of compromise between the reproduction of ST abuse and the resistance to dominant cultural values in the TL. (**VL**)

FURTHER READING: Lewis (1985); Venuti (2003).

ACCEPTABLE TRANSLATION, SEE NORMS

ACCESSIBILITY, SEE INCLUSION

ADAPTATION

1. In general terms, adaptation denotes a TT that draws on an ST but which has extensively modified it for a new cultural context. This occurs, for example, with the adaptations of classical plays, such as Eugene O'Neill's *Mourning Becomes Electra* or Wole Soyinka's *The Bacchae after Euripedes* (Walton 2006), which develop the plot of the Greek plays but do not purport to be translations of the original dialogue. Irrespective of whether adaptation is considered a form of translation, it demands different criteria for the assessment of its equivalence with the source.
2. The seventh of Vinay and Darbelnet's **translation procedures**. A type of **oblique translation**, it aims at 'situational equivalence'. Vinay and Darbelnet's example (1958: 39) is of the English *cricket* being translated by the French *Tour de France* since they purportedly perform similar functions in the different cultures. This kind of cultural substitution is open to

challenge since it erases the foreign cultural item and replaces it with an item that denotatively is very different. **(JM)**

FURTHER READING: Bastin (1998); Shuttleworth and Cowie (1997); Vinay and Darbelnet (1958, 1958/2004).

ADEQUATE TRANSLATION, SEE NORMS

ADJUSTMENT

A translation technique relating to textual units smaller than a whole text. Suggested by Nida (1964) as a means of producing **equivalence** in translation, this technique can affect textual units at three levels: morphology/syntax, lexis and message (by which he understands the entire meaning of a text, i.e. the ideas and feelings the ST author wants to communicate). Adjustment ensures semantically and stylistically correct TL equivalents as well as **dynamic equivalence**. Though a variety of terms is in use to describe adjustment, three main types can be identified: (1) *addition* (information that is not specified in the ST is inserted into the TT), (2) *subtraction* (information in the ST is omitted in the TT), and (3) *alteration* (changes are required when SL and TL exhibit different semantic and grammatical structures). **(BB)**

FURTHER READING: Molina and Hurtado Albir (2002); Newmark (1988); Nida (1964); Vinay and Darbelnet (1958).

ADVERTISING

In order for an advertisement to be successful transculturally, the verbal message it contains, the accompanying visuals and the product itself, need to be perceived as though they originated in the target culture. Thus, as well as good quality translations of the verbal text in each ad (i.e. the copy in print ads and voice-over and/or dialogue in film ads), international advertising campaigns by multinational stakeholders also require the accompanying visuals to be meaningful to the end user in the target culture. Stecconi (2000) has identified three translational strategies adopted in promotional texts on the internet: (1) *intrasemiotic* translations, in which only the verbal text is translated from one language to another; (2) *intersemiotic* translations, in which the verbal content is translated and the visuals (i.e. photographs, pictures, layout, graphics, colours, etc.) also change from source to target campaign; and (3) *syncretic* translations, in which the verbal content is translated and only some of the visuals are adapted to the target culture while others remain unchanged (see also Munday 2004).

Language affects the creation of advertisements. Thus, if the original ad is in English, a major problem will occur for the copy in, say, French or Spanish because these languages will typically require a third more space. Furthermore, catchphrases that play on words or themes in one culture can be severely distorted in translation; thus, international campaigns tend to rewrite advertisements in the TL rather than translate them in the strict sense of the word (Wells *et al*. 1992). Finally, although the function of advertising is the same all over the world, the expression of the message varies according to whether the target culture belongs to a 'high-context culture' or a 'low-context culture' (Hall 1976; see also Katan, Chapter 5 this volume). Cultures can be placed on a sliding scale regarding the degree of context required in communication. Most Asian cultures are high-context and most western cultures low-context. A message couched in the language of a high-context culture requires very specific contextualization for it to be understood. On the other hand, low-context cultures are more likely to understand messages independently of context. An awareness of the latter leads to very different marketing and therefore promotional styles according to the culture (Mooij 2004). **(DC)**

FURTHER READING: Adab and Valdés (2004); Hall (1976); Mooij (2004 a/b); Stecconi (2000); Wells *et al*. (1992).

AIIC

The International Association of Conference Interpreters, known by its French acronym AIIC (*Association Internationale des Interprètes de Conférence*), was founded in Paris in 1953. Unlike **FIT**, it is based on individual membership, and has grown to some 2,800 members worldwide. AIIC has been vital in shaping working conditions and training for conference interpreters. It adopted a code of ethics and professional practice as early as 1957, and has introduced a generally adopted classification of interpreters' working languages (A, B and C languages). With stringent requirements for the admission of new members (including proof of extensive working experience and endorsement by several members), AIIC established itself as the interlocutor of international bodies such as the United Nations and the European Union, with which it negotiates agreements governing the employment of interpreters. **(FP)**

FURTHER READING: http://www.aiic.net

ANALYSIS

The first of three stages in Nida and Taber's (1969/1974) model of the translation process, preceding the **transfer** and **restructuring** phases. Influenced by generative-transformational grammar, Nida and Taber's analysis involved the identification of events, objects, abstracts and relationals in **kernel** structures. **(JM)**

FURTHER READING: Hatim and Munday (2004); Munday (2001/2008); Nida (1964); Nida and Taber (1969/1974).

Appropriation

This term has been employed to refer to the act of taking possession of an original text from one culture by another culture. In this respect the term 'appropriation' equals that of 'domination ' or 'cultural domination'. One of the most obvious motivations for this act is undoubtedly to gain power over something or someone. Due to its association with the concept of **power**, this term has begun to acquire a negative connotation in cultural studies and in all of its related fields. Recent work in the field of translation studies has addressed the issue of cultural domination as a means by which political and economic power can be exerted by a developed culture over a less-developed culture through the act of translation. **(VL)**

Audience

The readership of a TT. A central concept in translation theory since Nida's work on **equivalence** and **equivalent effect** (1964), as part of which he suggested that translations should produce similar communicative effects to their STs. Between the 1960s and 1980s, Nida's work was pivotal to the development of various translation theories (e.g. functional, communicative and **relevance theory**), resulting in the recognition that texts are dynamic and need to be seen within their cultural and societal contexts. Knowledge of the type of audience of a translation together with the ST type and the function of the translation are drivers in selecting the overall translation method. Types of audience are, for instance, experts, fledgling experts, students, educated laypersons and so on, and combinations of these. **(BB)**

Further reading: Hoffmann (1985); Newmark (1991, 1988); Nida (1964, 2004); Nida and Taber (1969/1974); Nord (1997); Reiss (1971/2000).

Audio description

Audio description is the term used to refer to a special soundtrack recorded for the use of blind and visually impaired people to assist in following audio-visual performances and screenings. On the soundtrack, during breaks in the dialogue, a narrator describes what is happening on-screen. Audio description is also common in museums and art galleries to guide the public through exhibitions, supplying information which they otherwise may not possess. **(DC)**

Further reading: http://www.ofcom.org.uk/static/archive/itc/itc_publications/codes_guidance/audio_description/Index.asp.html

Audiovisual translation

Audiovisual products can be defined as '[a] semiotic construct comprising several signifying codes that operate simultaneously in the production of meaning' (Chaume 2004: 16). Films, plays, opera, video games and hypertexts are examples of audiovisual products that are intended to be both seen and heard at the same time by end users. What is particular about audiovisual translation is that the verbal component will tend to be highly dependent on the visuals, and while the translator operates on the verbal level alone, the translational process will be frequently constrained by the visual code. Dubbing, voice-over and subtitling are the most common modalities adopted in audiovisual translation. (**DC**)

FURTHER READING: Chaume (2004); Chiaro (Chapter 9, this volume); Díaz Cintas and Remael (2007).

BACK TRANSLATION

In its contrastive linguistics sense, it is a translation that sets out to demonstrate the morphological, lexical and syntactic structure of an example, for instance the Spanish *no lo he visto* by the English *no it have-I seen*. (**JM**)

BILATERAL INTERPRETING, SEE LIAISON INTERPRETING

BORROWING

Borrowing is the first of Vinay and Darbelnet's (1958) translation procedures, a form of direct translation which they describe as 'the simplest of all translation methods' (1958: 31). The procedure involves the transference of the ST word into the TT, e.g. *tequila* or *tortilla* from Mexican Spanish or the use of *DVD*, *CD-ROM*, etc. in information technology internationally. This may either be to fill a **lacuna** or to exoticize the TT. As Vinay and Darbelnet point out (ibid.: 31), some borrowings establish themselves so well that they become accepted TL terms: *menu*, *chic*, *enfant terrible*, etc., in English. (**JM**)

FURTHER READING: Baker (1992); Vinay and Darbelnet (1958, 1958/2004).

BRIEF

The instructions that are given to the translator by the commissioner and which guide the translator's understanding of the purpose and function of the TT. (**JM**)

FURTHER READING: Nord (1997, 1998/2001/2005).

CALQUE

Vinay and Darbelnet's second translation procedure, defined as 'a special kind of borrowing whereby a language borrows an expression from another, but then translates literally each of its elements' (1958: 32). This may result in (1) a 'lexical calque', where the syntactic structure of the TL is respected in the new coinage (e.g. Spanish *disco duro* for English *hard disk* or *cambio climático* for *climate change*) or (2) a 'structural calque' where the source structure is imported into the TL. In either case, calque initially differs from **literal translation** because it involves the importation of a new expression or construction into the TL, although these may over time become fixed (e.g. French *thérapie occupationnelle* for English *occupational therapy*). (**JM**)

FURTHER READING: Vinay and Darbelnet (1958, 1958/2004).

CANNIBALISM

A movement in **postcolonial translation studies** in Brazil starting in the 1980s and 1990s. It drew on the metaphor of cannibalism in the 1928 manifesto of Oswald de Andrade (1890–1954) and the prominent work of the poet and translator Haroldo de Campos (1929–2003) to cast the assimilation of the foreign through translation as a form of nourishment for postcolonial Brazilian culture and as a means of subverting the colonialist cultural influences of Europe. (**JM**)

FURTHER READING: Vieira (1999).

COGNITION AND TRANSLATION

Translation, in all its modalities, is a cognitive activity that requires the unfolding of a mental process (the **translation process**) and the existence of a specific competence (**translation competence**). Translation has been studied within cognitive approaches to translation from different perspectives, focusing on the **translation process**, on **translation competence** and on its acquisition. Studies draw on other disciplines, such as cognitive psychology, expertise studies, neurophysiology and cognitive science. In the field of translation studies, **empirical-experimental research** has been carried out mostly on translation as a cognitive activity. (**AHA** and **FA**).

FURTHER READING: Bell (1991); Gutt (1991, 2000); Hurtado Albir and Alves (Chapter 4, this volume); Kiraly (1995); Lederer (1981, 1994/2003); Seleskovitch (1968, 1975); Seleskovitch and Lederer (1984).

COHERENCE

Coherence refers to the accessibility, relevance and logic of the concepts and relations underlying the surface texture of a text. It is thus a psychological concept, but to some extent it is produced by and depends on the textual **cohesion** of the text. (**JM**)

FURTHER READING: Beaugrande and Dressler (1981); Blum-Kulka (1986/2004).

COHESION

Part of the textual function of language, cohesion covers 'relations of meaning that exist within a text' (Halliday and Hasan 1976: 4). A single instance of cohesion is termed a 'tie', and, in Halliday and Hasan's seminal model, there are five types: (1) reference (pronouns such as *she*, *our*, demonstratives such as *this*, comparatives such as *the same*); (2) substitution and ellipsis; (3) conjunction (*and*, *but*, etc.); (4) **collocation**; and (5) lexical cohesion (repetition, synonymy and the use of words related in a lexical field). Such textual devices enable a text to hold together linguistically and contribute to the maintenance of **coherence**. In a well-known study of cohesion and coherence in translation, Blum-Kulka (1986/2004) demonstrates how changes in cohesion cause functional shifts in TTs. **(JM)**

FURTHER READING: Beaugrande and Dressler (1981); Blum-Kulka (1986/2004); Halliday and Hasan (1976); Halliday and Matthiessen (2004); Hoey (2005).

COLLOCATION

The phenomenon of co-occurrence of two lexical items, known as 'collocates' (e.g. *held* our *breath*, *human being*, *in winter*, *wage war*); this is a major building block of lexical and syntactic structure. It shows the paradigmatic axis of language and is a category of **cohesion**. It may be calculated statistically using computer corpora (Sinclair 1991; Church *et al.* 1991) or psychologically (Halliday and Hasan 1976; Partington 1998). Hoey (2005: 5) defines it as 'a psychological association between words (rather than lemmas) up to four words apart and ... evidenced by their occurrence together in corpora more often than is explicable in terms of random distribution'. Incorrect or unusual collocation (e.g. *sustained* our *breath*) often occurs in the speech of language learners and may be a feature of **translationese**. **(JM)**

FURTHER READING: Halliday and Hasan (1976); Hoey (2005); Partington (1998); Sinclair (1991).

COLONIZATION

This term implies some kind of **appropriation** and the establishment of (political) control over something or someone. Within the field of translation studies, translation is generally assumed to have played a very important and active role in the communication exchange process between colonizers and colonized people. The concept of 'colony' is used as a kind of metaphor to draw a parallel between authority and inferiority, between original texts and translations, between colonizers and colonized people.

This link between colonization and translation gave rise to so-called **postcolonial translation studies**, where the central intersection of translation studies and postcolonial theory is that of power relations. **(VL)**

FURTHER READING: Cheyfitz (1991); Rafael (1993, 2005); Robinson (1997b).

COMMISSION, SEE BRIEF

COMMISSIONER

The individual or agency which requests a translation. **(JM)**

FURTHER READING: Nord (1997, 1998/2001/2005).

COMMUNICATIVE TRANSLATION

One of Newmark's two translation categories (1988, 1991) by which he understands that a translation should try to create as much as possible the same effect on its TT readership as the ST has on the ST audience. Newmark's communicative translation is similar to Nida's **dynamic equivalence** (1964) inasmuch as both types try to produce equivalent effects on the TT audiences, but Newmark rejects Nida's idea of a full equivalent effect being achievable. He views it as unrealistic (e.g. in the case of very old texts) and not helpful in resolving the dilemma of whether to be more faithful to the SL or to the TL. Newmark argues that using the concepts of communicative translation and **semantic translation** could lessen this conflict. In recent years, however, he has moved away from these concepts and instead speaks of correlative translation theory (see Anderman and Rogers 2003). **(BB)**

FURTHER READING: Anderman and Rogers (2003); Hatim (2001); Munday (2001/2008); Newmark (1988, 1991, 1988); Nida (1964).

COMMUNITY INTERPRETING

Broadly speaking, community interpreting, also known as community-based and **public service interpreting**, refers to interpreting practices within a given (multi-ethnic) social and institutional context, as distinct from communication at the international level. Typically, one of the parties involved in community interpreting is an individual human being, usually a migrant or deaf person, speaking and acting on his or her own behalf (e.g. as a patient, defendant or asylum seeker) whereas the other is a representative of an institution empowered to provide a service or issue decisions or sanctions (e.g. a doctor, judge or adjudicator). Thus, community-based interpreting includes such domains as **court interpreting** and **healthcare interpreting**, where interpreting, in either language modality, is usually performed as **dialogue interpreting**. **(FP)**

FURTHER READING: Hertog and van der Veer (2006); Roberts (1997); Shackman (1984).

COMPENSATION

1. A technique with which loss of meaning or style in an ST brought upon by translation is made up for in the TT using devices that are characteristic of the TL. A typical example would be the German formal form of address *Sie*, for which in English, depending on the context, the informal *you*, or the *first name*, or even the *surname* would have to be used. Hervey and Higgins (1992) identify four types of compensation: (a) *compensation in place* (an ST item or a particular stylistic feature in the ST cannot be rendered at the same point in the TT but needs to be placed somewhere else in the TT). This type corresponds to Vinay and Darbelnet's (1958) compensation procedure; (b) *compensation in kind* (various linguistic strategies in the TL are used to produce an effect that is as similar as possible to the one in the ST); (c) *compensation by merging* (abridged versions of ST elements and characteristics are produced in the TT); and (d) *compensation by splitting* (the TT creates extended versions of ST meanings so that even the subtlest of meanings can be conveyed). However, the last two types are under criticism (e.g. Harvey 1995).
2. Steiner's fourth stage in his hermeneutic motion model of translation (1975/98). **(BB)**

FURTHER READING: (1) Baker (1992); Crisafulli (1996); Harvey (1995); Hatim (2001); Hatim and Mason (1990); Hervey and Higgins (1992); Newmark (1988); Vinay and Darbelnet (1958). (2) Steiner (1975/1998).

COMPONENTIAL ANALYSIS

A type of contrastive **disambiguation** technique, adapted by Nida (1964) from semantics (the technique was originally conceived by anthropologists for describing kinship terms). It functions as a translation aid for analysing the meanings of different lexical items on the basis of their elementary semantic features, i.e. components, which usually have binary character ($\pm$). For instance, the noun *woman* can be broken down into the meaning components +human, +adult, +female, and on the basis of these the item can be contrasted with other lexical items, in particular with those that are related, e.g. *man, child, baby* and so on. As with **semantic structure analysis**, another **disambiguation** technique, componential analysis results can be represented graphically, e.g. in tables, to support the comparison of word meanings. **(BB)**

FURTHER READING: Bell (1991); Hatim and Munday (2004); Larson (1998); Newmark (1988); Nida (1964, 1975).

COMPUTER-ASSISTED TRANSLATION TOOLS (CAT TOOLS)

A bundle of software functions that may include alignment, **concordancing**, term extraction, workflow management, etc., to assist translation and **localization**. **(JM)**

FURTHER READING: Hartley (Chapter 7, this volume).

CONCORDANCE

An on-screen or printed display of textual examples featuring a specific search term or word. Working on electronic corpora, the keyword under examination appears in the centre of the screen, and all the concordance lines can be sorted alphabetically according to the words which occur either to the right or the left of the keyword. **(JM)**

FURTHER READING: Hartley (Chapter 7, this volume).

CONFERENCE INTERPRETING

Conference interpreting is generally understood as the most prestigious and highly professionalized form of interpreting, usually in the **simultaneous** mode, as represented globally by **AIIC**, valued most highly by **NAATI**, and practised in international fora such as the UN and EU institutions. The term as such, however, specifies only a particular type of formal, if not ritualized, multi-party interaction rather than an international context, a particular mode of interpreting or level of interpreting skills. It is because 'conference interpreters' in fact define themselves by their level of qualification that they also consider **diplomatic interpreting** and **media interpreting** as part of their professional territory. **(FP)**

FURTHER READING: Diriker (2004); Seleskovitch (1968/1978).

CONNOTATION (CONNOTATIVE MEANING)

A term employed in semantics for organizing types of meaning and explored by Nida (1964) and Nida and Taber (1969/1974) in their analyses of meaning as part of their scientific approach to translation. Connotation, or connotative meaning, refers to the associative and emotive meanings of lexical items (words, phrases and expressions) and of other aspects of language (e.g. pronunciation) that can be generated in people's minds. Connotative meanings of, for instance, a lexical item exist in addition to its **denotation** (denotative meaning), i.e. the relationship between a non-linguistic object in the real world and the linguistic unit which labels this object. For example, the adjective *black* in the sense of *the darkest colour in our known world* (denotative meaning) may also invoke negative connotations beyond this primary sense, including *dark*, *depressive* and *sinister*, but also positive ones, e.g. *slimming*, *elegant*, *cool*, etc. (**BB**)

FURTHER READING: Bell (1991); Hatim and Mason (1990); Hatim and Munday (2004); Leech (1983); Newmark (1988); Nida (1964); Nida and Taber (1969/1974).

CONSECUTIVE INTERPRETING

Consecutive interpreting, in the broader sense, is the basic mode in which interpreting must have been practised since ancient times. In consecutive, the interpreter gives his or her rendering after the speaker has ended, with the length of the original utterance ranging anywhere from a single word to a half-hour speech or more. It is in the latter scenario, attested since early-twentieth-century conferences in the League of Nations, that **note taking** becomes crucial to the technique of consecutive interpreting. Unlike this 'classic' form, 'short consecutive' as typically used in dialogic interaction (**liaison interpreting**) requires less emphasis on notes, as the interpreter has some measure of control over turn-taking. (**FP**)

CONTENT, SEE FORM

CONTEXT

While 'co-text' refers to the linguistic elements around a particular item (e.g. in the sentence *Riot police intervened yesterday morning at La Junquera*, the co-text of *intervened* would be *Riot police* and *yesterday morning at La Junquera*), the context is more abstract. Non-technical uses of the term would restrict themselves to indicating that the context of the above was a truckers' strike in Spain, but, as House (2006) details, there are many more sophisticated models of context that have been adopted by linguists. In **relevance theory**, for example, a central feature is the 'communicative clues' in the utterance and the cognitive assumptions used by the receiver in order to infer the speaker's intention. In pragmatics (Leech 1983), the notion of context has been analysed to encompass the hearer's assumptions and beliefs about the world, and language parameters associated with geographical location, status of the participants, the domain and formality of the communication and the **register** of the language. Register analysis is related to the concept of 'context of situation' (Halliday and Hasan 1989; Halliday and Matthiessen 2004) used in translation studies by House (1977/1981, 1997) and Hatim and Mason (1990, 1997) amongst others. House (2006: 343–5) proposes a theory of translation as 're-contextualization', with a translation being 'doubly contextually bound' (to the ST and the TT communicative context) and its function being determined by its use in a specific target context. The higher-level concept of 'context of culture' in systemic-functional linguistics is less well defined; its function covers some of the areas analysed by those interested in translation and **ideology**. **(JM)**

FURTHER READING: House (2006).

CONTROLLED LANGUAGE (CL)

A version of a human language that embodies explicit restrictions on vocabulary, grammar and style for the purpose of authoring technical documentation, making it more readily assimilated for translation purposes (including **machine translation**). **(JM)**

FURTHER READING: Hartley (Chapter 7, this volume).

CORPUS (PLURAL CORPORA)

A corpus ('body') is 'a collection of naturally occurring language data' (McEnery 2003: 449), which can be simply the STs and TTs under investigation. In **corpus-based translation studies**, the corpus is in electronic format and thus analysable by special computer software. **(JM)**

CORPUS-BASED TRANSLATION STUDIES

An area of the discipline that derives from monolingual corpus linguistics originally initiated as a lexicographical tool for the COBUILD dictionaries (Sinclair 1987, 1991). The electronically-readable **corpora** referred to are electronic collections of texts that have been selected and gathered for a specific purpose: these can be individual ST–TT pairs, corpora of **parallel texts** in a specific genre or comparable corpora such as the British National Corpus, which aim to be representative of the language as a whole. Such corpora can be analysed using software to search for phenomena such as lexical frequency, **collocation** and distinctive **stylistic** features. The corpus-based approach links with methodology centred in **descriptive translation studies** and to analyse typical features of translation such as **universals of translation, explicitation**, etc. **(JM)**

FURTHER READING: Baker (1993); Zanettin *et al.* (2003); Hartley (Chapter 7, this volume); Laviosa (1998, 2002); Olohan (2004).

CORRESPONDENCE

1. A concept in contrastive linguistics to describe the resemblance and difference between words and structures in terms of their linguistic form.

The investigation of correspondence takes place at the level of the language system, i.e. Saussure's *langue* (1993, 1996, 1997). Correspondences are naturally higher in related languages, e.g. there is a clear relationship in terms of sound and spelling between English *house* and German *Haus*. Correspondences of words and expressions between language systems often cause language learners problems, in particular loan words such as **false friends** (English *handy* versus German *Handy* = mobile phone) or syntactic interferences in the form of word order problems. The term *correspondence* needs to be differentiated from **equivalence**, which defines the various degrees of equivalence between SL and TL words/expressions (Saussure's *parole*).

2. Correspondence in the above sense equates to Catford's (1965) **formal correspondence**. **(BB)**

FURTHER READING: Crystal (2003); Hatim and Munday (2004); Koller (2004); Munday (2001/2008); Nida (2004); Saussure (1993, 1996, 1997); Venuti (2004).

COURT INTERPRETING

Court interpreting is a very broad and ill-defined concept. Since it is practised mainly – except for international tribunals – within a given national ('intra-social') and institutional context, it comes under the heading of **community interpreting** and constitutes one of its largest domains. In a generic sense, the term court interpreting is used as a synonym of 'legal interpreting', that is, interpreting at any stage or level of the legal process, from police interviews and lawyer–client consultations to jury trials in open court. The latter would be labelled more precisely as 'courtroom interpreting', or court interpreting in the narrower sense. Covering part or all of this broad spectrum are notions like 'forensic interpreting' or 'judicial interpreting'. This conceptual diversity has to do with the fact that many jurisdictions have legal provisions stipulating the requirements and tasks an interpreter serving the judiciary (and the police or administrative tribunals) needs to fulfil. Thus, so-called court interpreters may also serve as sworn public translators or hold a particular type of certification required for work in some but not all legal settings. Court interpreting is therefore defined by legally mandated (or institutionally required) qualifications much more than by the nature of the particular task or setting. The fact that the use of interpreters, at least in criminal proceedings, is generally mandated by law, together with legislation specifying the required qualifications, has favoured the view, in some countries, of court interpreting as an autonomous profession, distinct from international **conference interpreting** as well as from **community interpreting**. **(FP)**

FURTHER READING: Berk-Seligson (1990/2002); Hale (2004); Mikkelson (1998).

COVERT TRANSLATION

A term for one of the two types of translation introduced by House (1977/1981), the other being **overt translation**. Both terms can be traced back to Schleiermacher (1813/2004, see **Overt translation**, **Domestication** and **Foreignization**). Covert translation, which is similar to Schleiermacher's domesticating strategy, describes a translation which is equivalent to the ST in terms of the function it has in its discourse environment. In House's translation model, this type of translation focuses on 'language use', as a result of which anything which might remind the TT readership of the origin and discourse environment of the ST is suppressed. While a covert translation has to be equivalent to the ST at the **genre** and function level, it does not need to be equivalent at the **register** and language/text level. A covert translation approach works well with, for instance, tourist brochures. **(BB)**

FURTHER READING: Hatim (2001); Hatim and Munday (2004); House (1981, 1997, 2001, 2003a/b); Schleiermacher (1813/2004).

CULTURAL FILTER

A term and concept used by House (1977, 1997). As part of **covert translation**, a cultural filter is applied to the ST, or items of it, in order to identify and reduce cognitive and sociocultural differences and expectations between source and target cultures (House 2006). **(JM)**

FURTHER READING: Hervey and Higgins (1992); House (1977, 1997, 2006); Katan (1999/2004). See also Katan (Chapter 5, this volume).

CULTURAL TURN

A term used in translation studies to refer to a phenomenon which helped the theory of translation expand its boundaries beyond the linguistic, particularly from the 1990s onwards. The link between translation studies and cultural studies became stronger and a translation was no longer perceived merely as a transaction between two languages, but rather as a more complex process of negotiation between two cultures. In 1990 Susan Bassnett and André Lefevere described this phenomenon as 'the cultural turn in Translation Studies' claiming that 'neither the word, nor the text, but the culture becomes the operational "unit" of translation' (1990: 8). **(VL)**

FURTHER READING: Bassnett and Lefevere (1990); Bhabha (1994); Gentzler (2001).

CULTURE

See Katan (Chapter 5, this volume).

DENOTATION (DENOTATIVE MEANING)

A term from semantics adopted by Nida (1964) and Nida and Taber (1969/1974) for their analyses of meaning. In contrast to its counterpart **connotation**, denotation (denotative/referential meaning) describes the relationship between a non-linguistic object in the real world and the linguistic unit (a lexical item such as a word, phrase, or expression) which labels this object. For instance, the denotative meaning of *blizzard* is 'a severe snowstorm with high winds'. Linguistically, denotative meanings are conditioned by two major facts: (1) people often do not agree on the referential meaning of even the simplest objects (e.g. the borders between *plates* and *bowls* are fuzzy), and (2) lexical items can have several meanings (polysemy), e.g. *bridge* can mean (a) *a dental device*, (b) *the upper part of the nose*, (c) *area on a ship where the captain and his officers operate*, and so on. Polysemy problems can be solved by **disambiguation** on the basis of a contrasting **semantic structure analysis**. (BB)

FURTHER READING: Bell (1991); Hatim and Mason (1990); Hatim and Munday (2004); Newmark (1988); Nida (1964); Nida and Taber (1969/1974).

DESCRIPTIVE TRANSLATION STUDIES (DTS)

In James S. Holmes' 'map', descriptive translation studies is part of the 'pure' side of the field. This was developed by Gideon Toury in his seminal *Descriptive Translation Studies and Beyond*, where he proposes a systematic methodology for DTS in order to 'ensure that the findings of individual studies will be intersubjectively testable and comparable, and the studies themselves replicable' (Toury 1995: 3). Without such an approach, says Toury, the proliferation of small-scale case studies (of individual texts or authors or translators) leads to a dead end since there is no way of comparing results or making generalizations about translation. By emphasizing testability, comparability and replicability, Toury is advancing science-based methods for the analysis of ST–TT pairs.

In DTS, a TT is taken to be a translation if it is considered by the TT culture to be so (if it is considered to be a 'fact' of the target culture). This removes the problem of differentiating between **adaptation**, translation, version, etc. In the methodology, first the role of the TT in the target culture system is described, the ST and TT are then compared for **shifts**, trends are identified, some generalizations are drawn about the translation strategy and the results are compared with other studies. The idea is that, gradually, as more studies take place, the refinement of such generalizations leads to the establishment of probabilistic **laws of translation**.

The most controversial issues in DTS revolve around why the description should only cover the TT system (many theorists would also compare the position of the ST within its own system) and the form of comparison of ST–TT elements, specifically what these elements should be (word, phrase, syntax, text, etc.) and how **shifts** are ascertained (Toury [1980] originally proposed the use of a *tertium comparationis*, which he later abandoned). **(JM)**

FURTHER READING: Pym *et al.* (2008); Toury (1980, 1995, 1995/2004, 2004).

DIALECT TRANSLATION

The norm for translating dialect, slang and social variation tends to be that of adopting the 'homogenizing convention' (Sternberg 1981). This involves replacing non-standard forms in the SL with standard forms, typical of the written language, in the target version. However, in translation, non-standard language can also be connoted through the insertion of linguistic features common in colloquial speech, such as fillers and discourse markers (e.g. *like*; *you know*; *I mean*, etc.) as well as deliberate mistakes. Replacing dialect in the SL with a dialect of the TL is not usual, although comedy in translation is sometimes an exception, especially on screen. **(DC)**

FURTHER READING: Sternberg (1981).

DIALOGUE INTERPRETING

The concept of dialogue interpreting highlights that interpreter-mediated interaction takes place in a dialogic format, in an exchange between two parties (individuals or groups) as opposed to multilateral interaction in conference-like settings. More so than **liaison interpreting**, the notion of dialogue interpreting foregrounds the dynamics of interactive discourse in triadic (i.e. interpreter-mediated) encounters. Dialogue interpreting is typically conceived of as on-site face-to-face communication, though it may also be carried out as **remote interpreting**. Nor is it limited to intra-social settings, even though the term dialogue interpreting is mainly used in connection with **community interpreting**. **(FP)**

FURTHER READING: Roy (2000); Wadensjö (1998).

DIPLOMATIC INTERPRETING

For most of recorded history, **liaison interpreting** in contacts between official representatives of sovereign powers, states or nations (i.e. 'inter-social'/international interpreting) enjoyed pride of place, except in periods and regions with an established lingua franca such as Aramaic, Latin or French. Those interpreting in (mostly bilateral) affairs of state were often involved in diplomacy themselves, often subsequent to a career as interpreters. With the advent of multilateral international conferencing and the professionalization of international **conference interpreting** in the early twentieth century, diplomatic interpreting, in dialogic as well as conference-like settings, largely merged into the professional territory of conference interpreters. (**FP**)

FURTHER READING: Roland (1999); Thiéry (1990).

DIRECT TRANSLATION

1. One of Vinay and Darbelnet's (1958) two types of translation procedure, the other being **oblique translation**. Both types together cover seven sub-procedures that concern three levels of language: lexis, grammar and meaning. Direct translation (or **literal translation**) is present when two (closely related) languages exhibit perfect equivalence in terms of lexis, morphology and structure. There are three direct translation procedures: (1) **borrowing** (an SL word is used directly in a TL, e.g. German *Kindergarten* → English *kindergarten*), (2) **calque** (the morphemes of an SL item are translated literally into equivalent TL morphemes, e.g. English *skyscraper* → German *Wolkenkratzer*), and (3) **literal translation** (a word-for-word rendering which uses the same number of TL words in the form of established equivalents as well as the same word order and word classes, e.g. English *my cat is hungry* → German *meine Katze ist hungrig*).
2. In the relevance model, which has its origins in **relevance theory**, a linguistically based theory of communication put forward by Sperber and Wilson (1986/1995), direct translation means that the interpretation of a TT is as similar as possible to that of the ST as long as the TT has been dealt with within the context of the ST. The more comparable the context of a direct translation is to the ST context, the closer its interpretation will be to that one of the ST. Opposed to indirect translation.
3. In **machine translation**, the term refers (a) to translation systems which do not perform any linguistic analyses on SL texts beyond the morphological level (direct translations are word-by-word translations which employ only simple grammatical adjustments), and (b) to machine translations that do not require a **pivot** language for translations between a language pair. (**BB**)

FURTHER READING: Gutt (1992, 2000, 2005a); Hatim (2001); Hatim and Munday (2004); Sperber and Wilson (1986/1995); Vinay and Darbelnet (1958, 1958/2004).

DIRECTION OF TRANSLATION

Refers to the direction in which the translation process takes place. For instance, in Polish–German translation the direction could be Polish to German or German to Polish. (**JM**)

DISAMBIGUATION

A term for an analysis which establishes the potential referential meanings of a lexical item in an SL text with a view to determining the proper TL word. For example, in the sentence *The aircraft's bank had increased dangerously* the term *bank* requires disambiguation since it can have various meanings, including *financial establishment, row of similar objects, margin of a river,* and so on; but it can also be an aviation term describing *the lateral, slanting turn of an aircraft*, which is what is meant in this example. Techniques of disambiguation include **componential analysis** and **semantic structure analysis**. Disambiguation also includes the clarification of the context (situational environment) and of the co-text (linguistic environment) an SL item is found in, e.g. in the above example the situation can be described as 'an aircraft is flying and seems to be in trouble' whereas the linguistic environment consists of the words preceding (*the aircraft's*) and succeeding (*had increased*) the noun *bank*. **(BB)**

FURTHER READING: Hatim and Munday (2004); Larson (1998); Nida (1964).

DOCUMENTARY TRANSLATION

One of two basic types of TT in the functional model of text analysis proposed by Christiane Nord, the other being **instrumental translation**. A documentary translation 'serves as a document of a source culture communication between author and ST recipient' (Nord 1991/2005: 72). That is, it documents the original communication, granting the TT reader access to the source and making no attempt to conceal that it is a translation. Typical examples would be: literary translations which borrow or exoticize ST items; the translation of legal documents (e.g. witness statements) for the purpose of analysis in a court of law; and where the purpose would be to demonstrate the structure and peculiarities of the ST. **(JM)**

FURTHER READING: Nord (1991/2005, 1997).

DOMESTICATION (DOMESTICATING TRANSLATION STRATEGY)

A term introduced by Venuti (1995/2008), although it is drawn from the nineteenth-century German philosopher and classicist Friedrich Schleiermacher (1813/2004), who established the dichotomy of **foreignizing translation** (*verfremdende Übersetzung*) and domesticating translation (*einbürgernde Übersetzung*) to refer to the question of whether translators should 'move the reader toward the writer' or 'move the writer toward the reader'. Venuti considers the Anglo-American translation tradition to be primarily one of domestication. This strategy is closely related to fluent translation which is intelligible and familiarized but, at the same time, such transparent translation may lead to the invisibility of translators and may equate to **appropriation** of the text where some source culture features are partially or totally erased. **(VL)**

FURTHER READING: Schleiermacher (1813/2004); Venuti (1995/2008); Venuti (1998a). See also **Foreignization**.

DUBBING

Dubbing is a form of audiovisual translation adopted for cinema and television products (e.g. films, series, sitcoms, etc.) in which the original verbal track (i.e. the dialogue) is replaced by a fresh verbal track in the TL. In Europe, dubbing is the preferred mode of screen translation in the highly populated countries of central and southern Europe, i.e. France, Italy, Germany and Spain. Dubbing in these countries involves careful synchronization of the new verbal track with the lip and facial movements of the actors. In Poland and Russia, the dubbing of all characters (whether male or female) is carried out by a single male voice known as the *Lektor*, who reads the translated dialogue over the original soundtrack with no regard for lip-sync. **(DC)**

FURTHER READING: See also Chiaro (Chapter 9, this volume).

DYNAMIC EQUIVALENCE

A type of **equivalence** introduced by Nida (1964) and Nida and Taber (1969/1974), by means of which the message of the ST is transferred in such a way that the effect on the target readers is as similar as possible to the effect on the ST readership. Nida conceived this concept, together with its counterpart **formal equivalence** (note that in Nida and Taber (1969/1974) they use the term **formal correspondence**), in a move away from notions such as **literal** and **free translation**. The dynamic equivalence model focuses on the receptor of the TT, i.e. the **audience**. This focus requires translators to adjust their texts to the target culture, to harmonize them linguistically in terms of grammar and lexis, and to make them sound 'natural'. Dynamic equivalence can be achieved using various **adjustment** techniques such as additions, subtractions and alterations. **(BB)**

FURTHER READING: Bassnett (1980/2002); Hatim (2001); Hatim and Munday (2004); Newmark (1988); Nida (1964); Nida and Taber (1969/1974).

EMPIRICAL-EXPERIMENTAL RESEARCH

Empirical-experimental research in the field of translation studies has been carried out mostly on the study of translation as a cognitive activity, starting in the 1980s in the case of written translation. For interpreting, empirical-experimental research goes back to an early phase in the 1960s and 1970s. Empirical investigation aims at collecting and analysing data using both quantitative and qualitative methods. There are several proposals to classify empirical investigation.

Gile (1998) distinguishes between two different perspectives: experimental and observational. Experimental investigation aims at a systematic observation of situations created deliberately by researchers to be analysed under pre-defined conditions. There are experimental studies aimed at the statistical validation of hypotheses and open experiments when there are no pre-defined hypotheses. Observational investigation consists of the rigorous observation of a situation as it occurs spontaneously, by means of direct observation, questionnaires, etc. There are three types of observational research: (1) an exploratory approach without previously determined goals, which can lead to the formulation of hypotheses; (2) an analytical approach used for the investigation of specific phenomena; and (3) an approach aimed at the validation of hypotheses which is similar to the experimental method but uses data from real situations.

It is accepted, at present, that empirical-experimental research can use a combination of methods or tools when, depending on the object of study and the expected goals, a combination of relevant methods is selected (see **Triangulation**). (**AHA** and **FA**)

FURTHER READING: Gile (1998).

EQUIVALENCE

1. A key concept in modern translation theory which defines the translational relationship between either an entire ST and a TT or between an ST unit and a TT unit in terms of the degree of correspondence between the texts or the text units. For instance, a full degree of (referential/**denotative**) equivalence at the word level would mean that an SL word and a TL word refer to the same (non-linguistic) object in the real world (e.g. English *apple* – German *Apfel*). Although the notion of equivalence is normally relative owing to language-dependent characteristics and cultural influences, full equivalence of concepts/terms is not uncommon in subject-specific translations in areas such as medicine, chemistry and physics (cf. Arntz, Picht and Mayer 2004; Stolze 2001).

    The concept of equivalence is one of the most controversial issues discussed in translation studies, where scholars disagree on its validity and usefulness. Some reject the notion more or less entirely (e.g. Gentzler 2001; Snell-Hornby 1988/1995), others see it as a helpful tool in translation theory and teaching (e.g. Baker 1992; Kenny 1998), and there are also those who argue that without it translation would not be possible (e.g. Nida and Taber 1969/1974; Koller 1989, 1995).

Over the decades, a variety of types of equivalence have been formulated. For example, equivalence can be described in terms of (a) whether it relates to words, phrases, clauses, sentences or entire texts, (b) the types of meaning lexical items can assume (**denotative**, **connotative**), (c) the communicative effect produced by equivalence (**dynamic equivalence**), (d) the similarity of linguistic features (**formal equivalence**) and (e) the situation, i.e. purpose, function, audience and so on, of a translation (functional equivalence).

2. Vinay and Darbelnet (1958) use the term for one of their translation procedures. By equivalence they understand the practice of employing an established equivalent idiom in the TL, e.g. the now-dated English expression *It's raining cats and dogs* would be incomprehensible if translated literally into German as this language has its own equivalent version–*Es regnet wie aus Kübeln* (lit. 'It's raining as if from buckets'). (**BB**)

FURTHER READING: Arntz, Picht and Mayer (2004); Baker (1992); Bassnett (1980/2002); Gentzler (2001); Hatim (2001); Kenny (1998); Koller (1989, 1995); Nida and Taber (1969/1974); Snell-Hornby (1988/1995); Stolze (2001); Vinay and Darbelnet (1958).

EQUIVALENT EFFECT

The principle of producing a translation on the basis of **dynamic equivalence**, where the translation creates substantially the same effect on the TT readership as the ST does on the ST audience. Nida (1964) formulated this principle as one of his four translation aims: (1) adapting the entire ST meaning to the individual properties of the TL structures; (2) generating TL structures which are semantically as similar as possible; (3) producing a fitting equivalent style; and (4) delivering an equivalent effect on the receptor audience. To achieve these aims, Nida suggests various techniques of **adjustment**, such as additions, subtractions and alterations. (**BB**)

FURTHER READING: Bassnett (1986/2002); Koller (1990/2004); Newmark (1988); Nida (1964, 2004).

ETHNOGRAPHY

This is the branch of anthropology which deals with the study or scientific description of the customs of individual peoples and cultures. In the field of translation studies, the term 'ethnographic translation' is one of four categories proposed by Casagrande in 1954. Casagrande claimed that a translation implied the maintenance and explication of the ST cultural background in the TT, so that translation becomes a 'cultural translation'. The connection between ethnographers and translators lies in the fact that both of them need to observe, analyse and understand the **culture** of a given society before producing a text about it. This kind of research includes socio-economic and political conditions, time of production and readership. **(VL)**

FURTHER READING: Casagrande (1954); Sturge (2007).

EXEGESIS

The science of Bible interpretation. The term derives from the Greek word *exēgēsis* (*exēgeomai* – interpret). In particular, exegesis refers to the critical analysis and explanation of a Bible text or scripture to ascertain its meaning, i.e. the meaning of its vocabulary and syntax. Exegesis needs to take place before a Bible text can be translated. Exegetical accuracy is determined by how closely a translation of a Bible text retains the meaning of the source Bible text. While many scholars use the terms *exegesis* and *hermeneutics* (the science of text interpretation) virtually synonymously, Nida (e.g. Nida and Reyburn 1981) clearly differentiates between them and views them as two discrete features of the broader category of interpretation. **(BB)**

FURTHER READING: Carson (1996); Louw (1991); Nida (1964); Nida and Reyburn (1981); Nida and Taber (1969/1974), Toussaint (1966), Waard and Nida (1986).

EXPLICITATION

One of Vinay and Darbelnet's (1958) supplementary translation procedures, which they list in addition to their **direct translation** and **oblique translation** procedures. In contrast to implicitation, explicitation (or explication) means that information that is only implicitly mentioned in the ST is expressed clearly in the TT. Making information explicit in the TT can take place at least at three levels of language: grammar, semantics and pragmatics/discourse. Techniques include using explicatory words or phrases, employing cohesive devices, clearing up grammatical ambiguities and so on. Explicitation can be compulsory, non-compulsory or pragmatic, or be induced by the translation process itself. An example of compulsory explicitation is the translation of the English gender-neutral noun phrase *the doctor who* (m/f) into gender-specific languages such as German where one of two options, depending on the context, needs to be chosen: i.e. *der Arzt* (m) or *die Ärztin* (f). The most interesting area is non-compulsory explicitation of pragmatic/discourse features in the TT, which has been posited as a **universal of translation**. **(BB)**

FURTHER READING: Blum-Kulka (1986/2004); Hatim (2001); Klaudy (1993, 1998); Olohan and Baker (2000); Toury (1995); Vinay and Darbelnet (1958).

Expressive Text-Type, see Text Types
Faithfulness, see Fidelity
False Friend

A word in a TL which, because of similarities in form or pronunciation to a word in an SL, leads language users to believe that they have the same meaning. False friends, often also called *faux amis*, tend to occur in related languages (e.g. Swedish and Norwegian) or in languages which have been in close contact with each other (e.g. German and French). There are lexical and grammatical false friends, the former being the more frequent and important type. For example, the French *librairie* does not mean *library* in English but *bookshop* – *library* is *bibliothèque* in French; likewise, the Spanish *decepción* means *disappointment* in English, not *deception*, which would be *engaño*. Grammatical false friends often involve (1) countable/uncountable nouns, e.g. English *research* (uncountable) versus French *les recherches* (plural), (2) different parts of speech, e.g. English *tentative* (adjective) versus French *tentative* (noun, with the sense of *attempt*), and (3) grammatical **collocation**s, such as verbs that may have similar form and meaning but connect differently, e.g. English *depend on* versus French *dépendre de*. **(BB)**

Further reading: Baker (1992); Chamizo Domínguez (2007); Chamizo Domínguez and Nerlich (2002); Newmark (1988, 1991).

Feminist Translation Studies, see Gender and Translation
Fidelity (Faithfulness, Loyalty)

1. A term referring to the close reproduction of ST meaning in the TT within the requirements of the TL without **gain** or **loss** in meaning. Also called *loyalty* or *faithfulness*. Translations characterized by fidelity usually exhibit the following features: (a) transferred cultural words, (b) no unnecessary deviation from the grammatical and lexical ST structures, unless stipulated by TL constraints, and (c) loyalty to the ST author's textual objectives.
2. In *skopos* **theory**, loyalty (cf. Nord 1991/2005, 1991) describes the interrelationships of participants in a translation process, including the ST author, the ST sender, the translator and the recipient of the TT. Hence, translators bear a responsibility to both the ST author and the TT receiver.
3. The *fidelity rule* in *skopos* **theory** describes the requirement for intertextual **coherence** between ST and TT. This **coherence** is upheld if there is a correlation between what the ST author has intended, what the translator's interpretation of this is, and how the ST information is reproduced in the TT. **(BB)**

FURTHER READING: Hatim (2001); Hatim and Munday (2004); Nord (1991/2005, 1991, 1997, 2003).

(FIT) FÉDÉRATION INTERNATIONALE DES TRADUCTEURS / INTERNATIONAL FEDERATION OF TRANSLATORS (IFT)

FIT was founded in 1953 on the initiative of the Société française des traducteurs and its President Pierre-François Caillé under the auspices of UNESCO (the United Nations Educational, Scientific and Cultural Organization); it is a worldwide gathering of professional translator associations (now numbering over one hundred). With UNESCO, FIT produced two landmark documents on the status of literary translators. The first, the *Translator's Charter*, was passed at the FIT Congress in Dubrovnik in 1963 and amended in Oslo in 1994; amongst other things, it set out the obligations, rights and economic and social position of the translator. The second document was the seminal **Nairobi Declaration**, adopted in 1976.

In the words of the FIT website, 'FIT is ... concerned with the conditions of professional practice in various countries and strives to defend translators' rights in particular and freedom of expression in general', although for many translators the goals in its *Charter* and *Declaration* remain an aspiration rather than a reality. **(JM)**

FURTHER READING: http://www.fit-ift.org/

FOREIGNIZATION (FOREIGNIZING TRANSLATION STRATEGY)

A concept that owes its origins to the German scholar Friedrich Schleiermacher (1813/2004) and refers to the question of whether translators should 'move the reader toward the writer or the writer toward the reader'. The twentieth-century French theorist and translator Antoine Berman disapproved of the tendency to avoid the sense of foreignness in translation, claiming instead that 'the properly *ethical* aim of the translating act is receiving the foreign as foreign' (Berman 1985/2004: 277). However, Berman also recognized that this foreignness in translated texts is unable to come through because of a 'system of textual deformation', which he calls 'negative analytic' (ibid.: 278). Opposite to this concept is Berman's elaboration of a 'positive analytic' of 'literal translation' (ibid.: 288–9), through which translators can bring the sense of the 'foreign' into the TT.

'Foreignization' is the term used by Venuti (1995/2008) and is opposed to **domestication**. Foreignization, which may involve lexical and syntactic borrowings and calques, reflects the SL norms and reminds the target culture readers that they are dealing with a translation, thus in some ways bringing them closer to the experience of the foreign text. These strategies retain a sense of foreignness of the original and have the advantage of resisting the '**appropriation**' of the original text. Foreignization, however, may make a text more cryptic and thus harder to access by readers. (**VL**)

FURTHER READING: Berman (1985/2004); Schleiermacher (1813/2004); Venuti (1995/2008, 1998a).

FORM-CONTENT

The contrast between the outward aspect of a linguistic unit with regard to its grammar and style (form) and the **meaning** intended by it (content). The content is that which the author wants to communicate to the reader and in order to do this the author can use various forms of conveying this meaning. For instance, if the author wants to pass on the information that he had just had dinner prepared by a three-star chef he could use the ST form *A three-star chef cooked my dinner today* or he could use the form *Today my dinner was prepared by a chef with three stars*, and so on. In translation studies, the contrast between form and content has its origin in the age-old debate – stretching back as far as Cicero (106–43 BCE) and St Jerome (ca. 347–420 CE) – of whether to favour **literal** or **free translation**, i.e. **word-for-word** versus **sense-for-sense** translation. (**BB**)

FURTHER READING: Hatim and Munday (2004); Nida and Taber (1969/1974).

FORMAL CORRESPONDENCE

A term introduced by Catford (1965) in his approach to translation equivalence for describing the purely theoretical relationships between linguistic units of an SL system and units in a TL system. Such relationships are characterized by the fact that a TL item that substitutes an SL item during translation acts linguistically in the same way as the source item does in its language system. Seen in this way, formal correspondence relates to Saussure's *langue* while Catford's other type of correspondence, which he calls **textual equivalence**, links to Saussure's *parole*. For instance, although there is a formal correspondence between the English noun *cat* and the French *chat* in the respective language systems, actual translations of *cat* may differ depending on the TT context, e.g. *animal*, *créature* and so on.

Note that Nida and Taber (1969/1974) use the term *formal correspondence* to refer to what Nida (1964) called **formal equivalence** (versus **dynamic equivalence**). (**BB**)

FURTHER READING: Baker (1998); Catford (1965); Hatim (2001); Hatim and Munday (2004); Nida (1964); Nida and Taber (1969/1974); Saussure (1993, 1996, 1997).

FORMAL EQUIVALENCE

A type of **equivalence** which, alongside **dynamic equivalence**, forms one of the two general orientations in Nida's (1964) and Nida and Taber's (1969/1974) model of translation. Formal equivalence considers the message of the ST to be the focal point, resulting in a TT which follows the content as well as the linguistic structures of the ST as closely as possible. Formal equivalence can be seen in terms of the formal relationships existing between ST and TT structures, e.g. when a noun phrase in the ST is substituted by a noun phrase in the TT, an adverb by an adverb, and so on.

Formal equivalence must not be confused with **literal translation** (cf. Hatim and Munday 2004: 41). **(BB)**

FURTHER READING: Bassnett (1980/2002); Hatim (2001); Hatim and Munday (2004); Munday (2001/2008); Nida (1964, 2004); Nida and Taber (1969/1974).

FREE TRANSLATION

A translation strategy which is usually contrasted with **literal translation** – a distinction which can be traced back to Cicero's (106–43 BCE) and St Jerome's (ca. 347–420 CE) **sense-for-sense** versus **word-for-word** debate. In translation literature, free translation is treated as a broad category comprising virtually any type of translation that is not faithful to the original, hence defining it depends on what individual scholars understand by it. A general definition of free translation conceives it as a strategy which is more concerned with creating a TT that sounds natural in the TL than with conforming to ST elements and structures. In contrast to **literal translation**, free translation tends to go beyond the word level, which means that the **unit of translation** can be a phrase, clause, sentence or even a larger unit.

The distinction between free and literal translation has been the subject of many studies and has undergone various developments. One of the most famous attempts at providing new descriptions of literal versus free translation can be found with Catford (1965). He differentiates between *bound* and *unbounded* translation: the former type is bound by rank (e.g. a word needs to be translated by a word, a phrase by a phrase, and so on); the latter type, which corresponds to free translation, can render an ST text segment with a TL segment of a different length (e.g. an ST phrase may become a TL clause). Other scholars view free translation as a kind of higher-level translation that renders the ST meaning without necessarily altering it while fully adhering to TL requirements (e.g. Barkhudarov 1969 as cited in Shuttleworth and Cowie 2007). Vinay and Darbelnet (1958) describe free translation within the framework of **oblique translation**, which applies when **word-for-word** renderings are not possible. **(BB)**

FURTHER READING: Barkhudarov (1969); Catford (1965); Hatim and Munday (2004); Munday (2001/2008); Newmark (1988, 1991); Robinson (1991, 1998a); Shuttleworth and Cowie (1997); Steiner (1975/1998).

FUZZY MATCH

A term used to denote an equivalent in the translation memory which *partially* matches the segment in the ST. **(JM)**

FURTHER READING: Hartley (Chapter 7, this volume).

GAIN/LOSS

When ST features cannot be rendered in the TT at the same place as in the ST (loss), they need to be moved to another place in the TT, resulting in a compensating addition (gain). This procedure corresponds to one of Hervey and Higgins's (1992) four types of **compensation** (i.e. 'compensation in place') as well as to Vinay and Darbelnet's (1958) **compensation** procedure. For example, the sentence *The House of Representatives' Chief Administrative Officer, Daniel Beard, sworn in on 15th February 2007, is employed by the House of Representatives and elected every two years*, can only be translated into German by moving some parts of the ST information to other places in the TT as not all the information would fit into one meaningful and natural sounding German sentence. On some occasions, gain occurs with no loss, when additional information is included in the TT in the form of **explicitation**. **(BB)**

FURTHER READING: Bassnett (1980/2002); Hatim and Munday (2004); Hervey and Higgins (1992); Vinay and Darbelnet (1958).

GENDER AND TRANSLATION

Since both women and translation have tended to be allocated a subordinate role in society in terms of authority, many scholars became interested in the intersection between gender and translation. This relationship is usually referred to as 'feminist translation studies', the focus of which has been on challenging the traditional metaphors of translation, les belles infidèles, or George Steiner's (1998) **hermeneutic motion** of penetration – see Chamberlain (1988/1992), and on feminist translators' work (e.g. Simon 1996). Such studies grew out of the feminist protest movements which had developed in Western Europe and North America by the mid-1960s as a reaction to the dominance of the so-called 'patriarchal world'; in these terms, translation was understood as a form of communication, power and manipulation. Through a series of strategies, including the selection of texts, the feminist translators in, for example, the Canadian translation 'project' (see Lotbinière-Harwood 1991; Simon 1996) manipulated words and meanings in order to mark their presence in society since they had been silenced and oppressed for too long.

More recent work on gender (Harvey 1998/2004; Santaemilia 2005) has looked at the translation of gay writers and texts. **(VL)**

FURTHER READING: Arrojo (1994, 1995); Flotow (1991, 1997); Krontiris (1992); Levine (1991); Maier (1998); Massardier-Kenney (1997); Robinson (1995); Spivak (1992/2004).

GENRE

Conventional forms of text associated with particular types of social occasion or communicative events (e.g. the news report, the editorial, the cooking recipe). There are various forms of genre analysis based on the monolingual study of English, much from a systemic-functional perspective (e.g. Martin 1993), in which genre mediates between the overarching 'context of culture' and the expression of social communication through **register**. Much occurs within a language for specific purposes (LSP) framework, which has begun to influence translator training. In translation studies, genre (or *Textsorte*, as she called them) is also linked to **text types**, which, according to Reiss (1971/2000), determine translation strategy. **(JM)**

FURTHER READING: Bruce (2007); Hatim and Mason (1990, 1997); Hyland (2005); Reiss (1971/2000).

GIST TRANSLATION

A translation that is a summary or otherwise shortened version of the ST. A gist translation may be requested by the commissioner because of time constraints or because it is less expensive than a full translation. **(JM)**

GLOSS

A term used by Nida (1964) for a type of translation, by means of which the **form** (e.g. syntax, word order, idiomatic expressions) and **content** (e.g. the subject matter) of the SL text are recreated in the TT as closely as possible and in such a way that they are comprehensible to the TT reader. According to Nida, a gloss translation presents a typical example of **formal equivalence** (one of his translation orientations). Since a gloss translation stays very close to the structure of the ST in terms of form and content, Nida points out that for TL readers to be able to understand such translations they may have to be annotated heavily, e.g. with footnotes. Gloss translations allow the reader to focus largely on the source language and culture.

Less technically, a gloss is descriptive information that is added to the TT to explain an ST item. **(BB)**

FURTHER READING: Bassnett (1980/2002); Hatim (2001); Nida (1964).

HABITUS

A term, taken from the French ethnographer and sociologist Pierre Bourdieu, which he defines (1990) as a 'system of durable and transposable dispositions', structures that are both 'structured' and 'structuring' and which tend to organize often unconsciously a field of human activity. First used in translation studies by Daniel Simeoni (1998), it has become popular within sociological approaches to translation (see **Sociology of translation**) that investigate the professional role of the translator, where it typically refers to a translator's 'mindset' or 'cultural mind' (Chesterman 2007: 177). Habitus is personal and is acquired through experiences, not learnt or taught. It derives from the assimilation of accepted forms of social practice (Inghilleri 2005), which, in the view of Simeoni, may account for translators' general undervaluing of their role.

FURTHER READING: Chesterman (2007); Gouanvic (2005); Simeoni (1998).

HEALTHCARE INTERPRETING

Healthcare settings constitute one of the most important domains of **community interpreting**. Healthcare or 'medical interpreting' emerged in the 1970s in countries receiving a strong influx of foreign-language-speaking immigrants, such as Australia and Sweden. Subject to legal provisions for access to healthcare regardless of language barriers, healthcare interpreting in some countries, not least in some states of the USA, has undergone considerable professionalization, with specialized professional associations, codes of professional conduct and training programmes. In addition to interpreter-mediated clinical interviews (doctor–patient communication), mental health settings and emergency departments have received particular attention. **(FP)**

FURTHER READING: Angelelli (2004); Pöchhacker (2006).

HERMENEUTIC MOTION

Steiner's term (1975/1998) stems from his efforts to feel himself into the activity of translation, thus viewing it as an art and not a science. Steiner's hermeneutic motion (i.e. the recovering of ST meaning and the subsequent transfer of it to the TT) comprises four stages: trust, aggression, incorporation and **compensation**. During the first stage, the translator has to trust and believe that he will find something in the ST that can be understood and translated. In the aggression stage, the translator 'enters' the text, extracts meaning and takes it away. Incorporation then means that this 'take-away' meaning is brought into the TL. By compensation, which takes place last, Steiner understands the upholding of the equality in status between an ST and its TT, which becomes necessary after a translator has interpreted and appropriated the ST meaning, leaving behind an ST which has lost something. Only when this **loss** has been compensated is the translation process complete. In Steiner's view, the status of every ST is heightened if it qualifies for translation. **(BB)**

FURTHER READING: Steiner (1975/1998).

HERMENEUTICS

A term derived from the Greek verb *hermeneuein* – *to interpret*. Originally, hermeneutics only referred to the interpretation of the Bible. The more modern use of the term is broader and can be traced back to the German Romanticists Schleiermacher (1768–1834) and Dilthey (1833–1911). Hermeneutics refers to the theory, methodology and processes involved in interpreting all types of text with the aim of discovering the meaning of a text, i.e. to gain an understanding of it. As hermeneutics presupposes that texts are distant in time and culture, interpretive methods focus on how the recovery of text meaning is influenced by these factors. In addition, the interpreter tries to feel him/herself into the activity of text production, making the attempt to interpret textual meaning from an inside point of view.

Note that many scholars use the terms '**exegesis**' and 'hermeneutics' synonymously. **(BB)**

FURTHER READING: Bassnett (1980/2002); Dilthey (1996); Gadamer (2004); Nida and Reyburn (1981); Palmer (1969); Ricoeur (1981/1998); Robinson (1998b); Schleiermacher (1813/2004); Steiner (1975/1998).

HUMOUR

The translation of humour can be compared to the translation of traditional poetry as both exploit to extremes a variety of options inherent in languages such as sounds and semantic ambiguities. Furthermore, the translation of both poetry and humour activate a conflict with two tenets of translation theory, namely **equivalence** and translatability, notions that have been debated at length over the centuries. It is generally agreed that **formal equivalence** cannot be obtained because of the very nature of languages, which are all unalike. The notion of translatability is closely linked to that of equivalence and refers to some kind of meaning being transferred from one language to another without undergoing radical changes. It accordingly follows that the less referential a text, the more radical the changes will be. In other words, if equivalence is at issue in the translation of a highly referential text such as an instruction leaflet, the problem is clearly magnified in the case of a poetic or humorous text. However, the comparison of humour with poetry can be taken no further because, while traditional poetry is highly governed by rules (i.e. metre, rhyme, stanzas, etc.) humour tends to break rules by deliberately exploiting areas of linguistic and semantic duplicity (Attardo and Raskin 1991; Raskin 1985).

For example, jokes are often based upon puns. It is highly unlikely that a single item will be ambiguous in the same manner (i.e. graphically, morphologically, phonetically, lexically, syntactically, semantically or pragmatically) across languages; thus, the possibility of **formal equivalence** of the same pun in another language is remote. Similarly, humour that pivots on culture-specific features may be likely to respond easily to adequate translation, but the target culture may be lacking in a corresponding cultural reference necessary to understand it. Paradoxically, despite being untranslatable, humour is indeed translated (i.e. in literature and for cinema and TV). Accordingly, translational **norms** suggest that humorous features in the SL will tend to be substituted with different, albeit humorous, features in the TT. However, sometimes the extreme exploitation of language required to create humour in the original requires extreme solutions in order to allow the text to function in translation. If the function of a text is to amuse, yet it by default poses difficult translation problems, it is not unusual to find that text either eliminated altogether or else substituted with a completely different humorous text which will be equally entertaining in the TL (Chiaro 2008). (**DC**)

FURTHER READING: Attardo and Raskin (1991); Chiaro (2005, 2008); Delabastita (1996, 1997); Vandale (2002).

HYPONYM

A term from semantics for describing the **meaning** relationship between a lexical item with a specific meaning and an item with a more general meaning where the meaning of the specific item is included in the meaning of the general item. For instance, *river* is a hyponym of the superordinate *flowing body of water* as its meaning is included in the meaning of the latter. Hence, the word *stream*, also a hyponym of *flowing body of water*, is a co-hyponym to *river* as it is at the same level of abstraction. In translation, the problem often consists in finding equivalent TL terms at the same semantic level. For example, in German the semantic field of 'flowing body of water' includes lexical items such as *Fluss, Flüsschen, Strom, Bach, Bächlein* and so on, for which it may not always be straightforward to determine the appropriate English equivalents in certain contexts (e.g. a *Strom* is a very large river). (**BB**)

FURTHER READING: Baker (1992); Bell (1991); Jackson and Ze Amvela (2007); Lutzeier (1995); Lyons (1977/1993).

IDEOLOGY

Many scholars seem to agree that translation is not a neutral activity but a form of 'political' intervention aimed at negotiating meanings through the use of language. Translation reflects **power** relations since it involves different cultures and its main communication channel is language. Language is not only a tool for communication but is also a potentially manipulative instrument which reflects ideologies through lexical, syntactic and discoursal choices employed by translators (Hatim and Mason 1997). These linguistic strategies can partly be influenced by the translators' own background and are a clear sign of mediation within their work. More recent studies have focused on the selection and framing of texts in translation (Baker 2006) and on the role of censorship (Billiani 2007; Sturge 2004).

It is sometimes difficult, however, to define 'ideology', which could be considered as '**culture**' (cf. Faiq 2004) and therefore it is an open question whether translations are 'ideologically slanted' or 'culturally mediated' by translators. (**VL**)

FURTHER READING: Álvarez and Vidal (1996); Calzada-Pérez (2003); Cunico and Munday (2007); Hatim and Mason (1990, 1997); Mason (1994); Munday and Fawcett (2008); Venuti (1992).

IDIOMATIC TRANSLATION

The translation of the meaning of an ST unit by employing an equivalent TL unit which expresses the ST meaning as closely as possible. For example, the idiom *He's getting up my nose* (he's annoying me) would be rendered into German idiomatically by an equivalent unit which is naturally present in this language, i.e. *Er geht mir auf den Wecker* (He's going around my alarm clock), since a literal translation would be marked or even incomprehensible. Nida (1964) classifies the translation of idiomatic expressions as one of three subtypes of his translation technique of alteration, an **adjustment** technique. Vinay and Darbelnet mention it as an example of **equivalence**, which is one of their translation procedures (1958).

Note that in **machine translation**, the translation of idioms is considered a problematic area (e.g. Volk 1998). (**BB**)

FURTHER READING: Baker (1992); Bassnett (1980/2002); Molina and Hurtado Albir (2002); Newmark (1991); Nida (1964); Nida and Taber (1969/1974); Vinay and Darbelnet (1958); Volk (1998).

ILLOCUTIONARY ACT, SEE SPEECH ACTS

IMITATION

The third of Dryden's (1680/1992) three categories of translation, corresponding to a very free translation or **adaptation**. (**JM**)

IMPLIED MEANING

The study of implied meaning is another influential development in the discipline of pragmatics. The trend was led by American language philosopher Paul Grice (e.g. 1975); rather than elaborating rules for successful communication, he preferred to concentrate on where, how and why the smooth ongoingness of interaction is intentionally thwarted. Disturbance of cooperativeness can be a case of lack of knowledge (breaking the rule), failure on the part of a speaker to secure the hearer's 'uptake' or acceptance (a case of violation of the rule) or, more significantly, disobeying the rules in a motivated, deliberate manner. This 'flouting' of the 'cooperative principle' may be achieved through deviating from total adherence to any one of four maxims: quantity (be succinct), quality (do not tell falsehoods), relevance, manner (be communicatively orderly). Underlying these maxims is, of course, the assumption that participants normally pursue their goals in communication in accordance with such 'default' conventions. However, deviations do occur and the floutings are interpreted in terms of the 'good reason' principle which helps participants make sense via the notion of 'implicature' of what is being implied and not stated. This has proven extremely helpful to practising translators and interpreters. In purely receptive terms, appreciation of implied meaning facilitates comprehension, which would otherwise be blurred. In terms of re-producing the message in the TL, on the other hand, the meanings which are implied and not stated could be the last court of appeal in assessing adequate equivalence. This last point is particularly relevant in working with languages which are both culturally and linguistically remote one from the other, and where different pragmatic means may have to be opted for to achieve a given ultimate effect. (**BH**)

FURTHER READING: Baker (1992); Grice (1975); Hatim and Mason (1997).

INCLUSION

The term inclusion (sometimes known as 'accessibility') refers to the prospect of providing audiovisual products such as plays, opera, films, TV programmes and videogames that can be consumed and enjoyed by all members of the public, including those who are in some way physically challenged. Thus, inclusion promotes intra-lingual translations for the Deaf and hard of hearing as well as audio-descriptions for the Blind and the visually challenged.

Technically speaking, access to audiovisual products for hearing impaired viewers can occur either with the aid of **sign-language interpreting**, or else through subtitles. Television news programmes, for example, can be translated into **sign language** by an interpreter who appears in a corner of the screen, while for plays and opera, the interpreter stands in one of the front corners of the stage. **Subtitles** for the Deaf and hard of hearing are accessible on TV across Europe via individual Teletext services. They differ from mainstream subtitles as they contain added information regarding music and sound effects. (See also **Audio description**). (**DC**)

INFORMATIVE TEXT TYPES, SEE TEXT TYPES

INSTRUMENTAL TRANSLATION

One of two basic types of TT in the functional model of text analysis proposed by Christiane Nord (1991/2005), the other being **documentary translation**. With an instrumental translation, the TT is usually read by receivers as though it were an original ST, fulfilling a communicative purpose in the target culture without the readers' being aware that it was originally written in another language and for another communicative situation. Typical examples are translations of technical texts where the function is preserved in the TL. **(JM)**

FURTHER READING: Nord (1991/2005, 1997).

INTENDED MEANING, INTENTION, SEE SPEECH ACTS

INTERFERENCE

Interference refers to the influence of linguistic and other elements of the ST on the TT. Toury (1995: 274–9) sees interference as a 'default' of translation, occurring either 'negatively' (creating unusual TT patterns, for example **false friends** such as French *actuel* and English *actual* or other cognates such as French *comprendre* and English *comprehend*), or 'positively'. In the latter case, the appearance of elements in the ST makes them more likely to be used in the TT and these may not create unusual patterns in the TL – thus, the order of major elements in a French ST may be followed in the TL, or a word such as *incroyable* may be more likely to be translated as *incredible* than *unbelievable*. One of Toury's two probabilistic **laws** is the law of interference. **(JM)**

FURTHER READING: Duff (1981); Toury (1995).

INTERLINEAR TRANSLATION

A translation that appears above or below the ST items. It is often used to indicate the lexical and syntactic structure of the ST, for the purposes of analysis or in order to enable the TT reader access to a sensitive text. Walter Benjamin (1923/2004) describes interlinear translation of the Bible as the 'ideal of all translation' because it gives fresh vigour to the ST. See also **Logos**. **(JM)**

FURTHER READING: Benjamin (1923/2004); Shuttleworth and Cowie (1997).

INTERLINGUAL TRANSLATION

Jakobson's (1959/2004) second type of translation, which he also calls 'translation proper', 'an interpretation of verbal signs by means of some other [verbal] language', for example, Malay to Arabic, Portuguese to Greek.

Interlingual translation forms the main, but no longer the exclusive, object of translation studies. **(JM)**

INTERPRETATION

1. A term, used in the United States amongst others, to refer to **interpreting**.
2. A term referring to the elucidation of the meaning contained in a text segment during the translation process. In translation studies, the notion of interpretation is discussed from two viewpoints: (a) to look for what the ST author intended to say, or (b) to look for what the ST author actually expressed in the text. Yet the initial basis of either of these types of interpretation is the general meaning of a lexical item, i.e. its **sense** (the meaning that is listed in a dictionary).

FURTHER READING: Bassnett (1980/2002); Eco (1992); Hatim and Mason (1997); Newmark (1988, 1991). **(BB)**

INTERPRETING

Sometimes loosely described as oral translation of speech. The more precise definition proposed by Otto Kade (1968) sees interpreting as a form of 'Translation' (in the wider sense), the characteristics of which are that (1) the SL text is presented only once and thus cannot be reviewed or replayed, and (2) the TL text is produced under time pressure, with little chance for correction and revision. **(JM)**

FURTHER READING: Pöchhacker (Chapter 8, this volume).

INTERPRETIVE THEORY

An account of the translation and interpreting process championed by Danica **Seleskovitch** and the **Paris School**. Originally developed with reference to interpreting, it is based on a triangular model in which the crucial stage between SL input and TL output is '**sense**', that is, the cognitive result of the translator/interpreter's comprehension process, in which SL words are discarded and their meaning fused with prior knowledge ('cognitive complements'). Having applied this process of 'deverbalization' to capture the speaker's intended meaning, or *vouloir dire*, the sense can then be expressed in the TL with little regard for divergent lexical patterns or syntactic structures in a given language pair. Allowing for direct SL to TL conversion ('transcoding') only for such items as numbers and technical terms, Seleskovitch conceived of interpreting as knowledge-based comprehension followed by sense-based (re)expression. Though a bold cognitivist move at the time, the interpretive theory proved too 'true' to generate and solve many new research problems in the study of interpreting. It has been particular for pedagogical purposes and is at the heart of the studies by **Seleskovitch** on **note taking** in **consecutive interpreting** and by Marianne Lederer to the process of **simultaneous interpreting** among others. (**FP**)

FURTHER READING: Israël and Lederer (2005); Lederer (1994); Seleskovitch and Lederer (1984/2001); Seleskovitch and Lederer (1989). See also Hurtado Albir and Alves (Chapter 4, this volume); Pöchhacker (Chapter 8, this volume).

INTERSEMIOTIC TRANSLATION

Jakobson's (1959/2004) third type of translation, also known as 'transmutation', 'an interpretation of verbal signs by means of signs of non-verbal sign systems'. Typical examples would be a film version of a novel, or an advertisement that represents in images a concept elsewhere represented by the written word. (**JM**)

FURTHER READING: Oittinen and Kaindl (2008); Susam-Sarajeva (2008)

INTRALINGUAL TRANSLATION

Jakobson's (1959/2004) first type of translation, also known as 'rewording', 'an interpretation of verbal signs by means of other signs of the same language'. In some cases this may be similar to **paraphrase 2**; in others it may refer to a rewriting for another SL audience, e.g. a children's version of a classic text. (**JM**)

INVARIANCE

A term for that which stays constant when an SL text undergoes translation, e.g. the ST **content**, the ST **meaning**, the function of the ST, its textual characteristics and so on. The transformation brought about by the process of translation can be described on the basis of the changes, i.e. **shifts,** that occur. Invariants and **shifts** are hence interrelated inasmuch as the description of one conditions the description of the other. In the relevant literature, invariance is looked at in two ways: (1) it is seen as a requirement before translation, or (2) it is a concept that becomes relevant after translation. In the first case, invariance corresponds to the *tertium comparationis*, against which texts can be measured to judge variation. In the second case, invariance additionally serves as a means of describing translations which have already been carried out. (**BB**)

FURTHER READING: Bassnett (1980/2002); Catford (1965); Munday (2001/2008); Popovič (1970, 1976); Steiner (1975/1998); Toury (1980, 1995).

INVERSE TRANSLATION

A term used in some languages to refer to translation into the foreign language, e.g. French–Chinese translation taught to French university students. (**JM**)

INVISIBILITY

A term used to refer to the role of the translator in the translation process. Venuti (1995/2008) employs it in relation to the translation strategy of **domestication**, through which the translator adopts a fluent and natural style to reduce the sense of 'otherness' of the foreign text for the TL audience and thus make it more easily assimilated. According to Venuti, it is the translator's invisibility that concurrently 'enacts and masks an insidious domestication of foreign texts' (1995: 16–17). This 'invisibility' raises questions of violent translation practices of dominant cultures around the world 'accustomed to fluent translations that invisibly inscribe foreign texts with [TL] values and provides readers with the narcissistic experience of recognizing their own culture in a cultural other' (ibid.: 15). In Venuti's analysis, invisibility has been prevalent in the Anglo-American translation tradition, not only in the preferred translation strategies but in the selection and scarcity of books translated and in the absence of recognition of the translator (in reviews, copyright assignation, contracts, etc.). **(VL)**

FURTHER READING: Venuti (1995/2008, 1998a).

KERNEL

A term taken from generative grammar by Nida (1964) and Nida and Taber (1969/1974) to describe the most elementary syntactic structures to which a sentence can be minimized during the analysis stage of their three-part **translation process**. Kernel sentences can be made up of a mixture of semantic categories: (1) objects (represented by nouns), (2) events (e.g. verbs), (3) abstracts such as quantities and qualities (e.g. adjectives), and (4) relationals (e.g. conjunctions, gender markers). The main means of distilling an ST sentence to a kernel sentence is by **back-translation**, during which the grammatical relationships between the ST items are made explicit. This allows the surface structures to be represented by way of formulae which coalesce any of the semantic categories. For instance, the ST sentence *The cat caught the mouse* can be reduced to the following formulae: A (object = cat) carries out B (event = catch, object = mouse). In Nida's view, kernels are relatively constant cross-linguistically. **(BB)**

FURTHER READING: Hatim and Munday (2004); Munday (2001/2008); Nida (1964); Nida and Taber (1969/1974).

KINSHIP TERMS

The terms within a language for labelling the relationships between family members, which are usually based on blood and marriage, but they can also include adoption and fosterage. Kinship terms have been the object of numerous cross-linguistic analyses, often on the basis of

componential analysis since the binary contrast provided by this type of analysis facilitates the diagrammatic representation of such terms. For **componential analysis** to work, the terms to be analysed must be interrelated, e.g. on the basis of characteristics they have in common. *Mother* and *daughter* share, for example, the feature *+female*. Although componential analysis is useful for systematizing kinship terms, translating them can still be problematic since kinship concepts in one language may not be lexicalized in another language, e.g. Russian has separate words to distinguish a *wife's father* from a *husband's father* whereas English has only the word *father-in-law*. **(BB)**

FURTHER READING: Goodenough (1956, 1965); Hatim and Munday (2004); Larson (1998); Lyons (1977/1993); Scheffler (2002).

LACUNA (PLURAL *LACUNAE*)

A lexical gap in the TL with respect to the SL, i.e. the concept has a specific lexical term in the SL but not in the TL. These may be cultural items (e.g. English *porridge*, *A-levels*, *April Fool's Day*, Arabic *wadi*, *Eid*, *hajj*, etc.) that may be translated by **borrowing** or **explicitation**, or they may simply be concepts that are lexicalized differently in different languages (e.g. English *shallow* > French *peu profound* ['little deep']). **(JM)**

FURTHER READING: Shuttleworth and Cowie (1997); Vinay and Darbelnet (1958).

LAWS OF TRANSLATION

The goal of **descriptive translation studies** (Toury 1995) was to establish probabilistic 'scientific' laws of translation, that is, a statement of the characteristics that distinguish the **translation process** and product. Toury (ibid.: 267–74) proposes two laws: 'the law of standardization' and 'the law of **interference**'. As Pym (2008) points out, these two laws seem somewhat contradictory: the law of standardization states that items in the ST are 'often ignored' in favour of more frequent, more natural TL combinations (e.g. a translator might choose a more frequent **collocation** or **idiom** in the TL), while the law of interference states that the lexical, syntactic etc. form of the ST influences the TT and produces non-normal patterns (e.g. a word might be calqued into a deviant TL form). Pym (2008) suggests a reconciliation of these laws by stressing their dependence on the sociocultural context. See also **Norms**, **Universals of translation**. **(JM)**

FURTHER READING: Pym (2008); Toury (1995, 2004).

LEXICOGRAMMAR

A term used by the systemic functional linguist Halliday (e.g. Halliday 1985/1994; Halliday and Mathiessen 2004) for describing the integrated system of lexicon and grammar (morphology and syntax). The reason for Halliday's argument that lexis and grammar have to be viewed and examined as one entity lies in the way he explains what language is, namely a layered whole consisting of semantics and lexicogrammar. He points out that the word 'semantics' refers to all the meaning systems within a particular language, which are represented by lexicon and grammar. Meaning itself is expressed by what he calls 'wordings', such as grammatical patterns (e.g. clauses, phrases), function words and so on. Halliday hence believes that the term 'lexicogrammar' helps to highlight the fact that both lexicon and grammar are at the same level of language, or 'code', as he calls it. **(BB)**

FURTHER READING: Halliday (1985/1994); Halliday and Mathiessen (2004); Hatim and Mason (1990, 1997), Mathiessen (1995, 2002); Munday (2001/2008).

LIAISON INTERPRETING

The term 'liaison interpreting' foregrounds the prototypical function of interpreters as communication-enabling links between two (or more) interacting parties using different languages. As such it is closely related to 'bilateral interpreting', which denotes that an interpreter works in both directions, that is, back and forth between a given pair of languages (though this occurs also in **conference interpreting**, as when UN interpreters in the Chinese booth work into their A language as well as *retour*). Liaison interpreting typically implies dialogic, face-to-face interaction and is therefore often used interchangeably with **dialogue interpreting**. While liaison interpreting has been taken to refer to business settings ('business interpreting') and other authors use it in connection with **community interpreting**, it clearly applies to international as well as intra-social communication scenarios. **(FP)**

FURTHER READING: Gentile, Ozolins and Vasilakakos (1996).

LITERAL TRANSLATION

The distinction between literal and **free translation** can already be found with Cicero (106–43 BCE) and St Jerome (ca. 347–420 CE) in the **sense-for-sense** versus **word-for-word** debate. Literal translation is in essence concerned with the level of words, i.e. a word is the **unit of translation**. A narrow interpretation of literal translation conceives it as the one-by-one rendering of individual ST words into a TL. This, however, usually turns out to be unfeasible, e.g. the German sentence *Er ging nach Hause* cannot be rendered into English using the same number of words, instead it requires one less, i.e. *He went home*. A more broad definition of literal translation describes it as the close adherence to the surface structures of the ST message both in terms of semantics and syntax.

The term 'literal translation' is understood by translation scholars in varying ways. For instance, it can be conceived as a word-for-word rendering, e.g. by Vinay and Darbelnet (1958), who use the term as another label for their **direct translation** procedure (confusingly, they also use this term for one of the three procedures subsumed under **direct translation**). Others (e.g. Catford 1965) view it as some form of draft or pre-translation – a kind of lower-level translation that is adequate enough to transfer the ST message within TL requirements (e.g. Barkhudarov 1969, as cited in Shuttleworth and Cowie 1997). **(BB)**

FURTHER READING: Barkhudarov (1969); Bassnett (1980/2002); Catford (1965); Hatim and Munday (2004); Newmark (1988, 1991); Nida and Taber (1969/1974); Robinson (1998c); Shuttleworth and Cowie (1997); Vinay and Darbelnet (1958).

LOCALE

A term used in **localization**, the locale refers to the geographical region and language in which a text operates. Thus, France and Québec are different locales. In localization, the requirements of the target locale determine the translation strategy employed. **(JM)**

FURTHER READING: Hartley (Chapter 7, this volume).

LOCALIZATION

The adaptation of a product to the linguistic and cultural expectations of the target **locale**. In the translation industry localization is sometimes used as a synonym for translation. **(JM)**

FURTHER READING: Hartley (Chapter 7, this volume).

LOGOS

1. Another label for 'pure language', which is a term going back to W. Benjamin (1923/2004). He claims that it is in translations that the relationship between two languages becomes evident in the form of a pure language (*reine Sprache*). This relationship, or '*kinship*', as he calls it, manifests itself as the intention that is fundamental to each language as a whole; pure language is hence the sum of both the intentions, which are extending each other. In other words, pure language is thus the result of some kind of synthesis of the SL and of the language into which the original was translated, with the result that both languages are strengthened. Benjamin argues that pure language can be released by **literal translation**s of syntax and by focusing on translating words instead of sentences.

2. Logos is also the name for one of the old-generation **machine translation** (MT) systems that are still in use. The current generation model, however, includes a grammar that differs considerably from the one in the original system. **(BB)**

FURTHER READING: Benjamin (1923/2004); Bennett (1996); Bush (1998); Quine (1960), Schmid and Gdaniec (1996); Shuttleworth and Cowie (1997).

LOSS, SEE GAIN/LOSS

MACHINE TRANSLATION

Translation automatically generated by computer software. **(JM)**

FURTHER READING: Hartley (Chapter 7, this volume).

MANIPULATION SCHOOL

A group of scholars, centred in Belgium, the Netherlands and Israel, working within the field of **descriptive translation studies** (DTS). The name was coined further to the seminal publication *The Manipulation of Literature: Studies in literary translation*, edited by Theo Hermans (1985); this work included a number of essays about translation, which was viewed as a primary literary **genre** and as a fundamental aspect in the evolution of cultural systems. According to this group, 'all translation implies a degree of manipulation of the ST for a certain purpose' (Hermans 1985: 11). Their methodology was based on a search for translational **norms**, proposed by Toury (1980), and their research on translation was understood as a product of interdisciplinary studies. **(VL)**

FURTHER READING: Hermans (1985, 1991); Lambert (1991); Leuven-Zwart and Naaijkens (1991), Snell-Hornby (1988/1995); Toury (1980).

MEANING

The notion of meaning is studied by many disciplines, ranging from linguistics, psychology and theology to philosophy. What all these disciplines have in common is that they are interested in finding out what it is that allows meaning (e.g. in a text) to be elucidated and brought out. All these disciplines have varying objectives in investigating meaning, and linguistics examines this notion within the framework of semantics. Here, the focus is on studying meaning in everyday speech, how meaning is systematized in other languages, and how it relates to other elements of language, mainly to grammar.

In translation studies, meaning is seen as the meaning a word takes on within a particular context and that meaning is culture-dependent. Nida's writings (1964) were pivotal in this context as he instigated the move away from viewing the meaning of a word as being fixed.

In translation, various types of meaning play an important role. Apart from linguistic meaning (**sense**), there are also **denotation** (or denotative, referential, extensional meaning) and **connotation** (or connotative, emotive, expressive meaning). Extra-linguistic meaning relates to factors such as situation, intention, the author's knowledge, the reader's knowledge and so on. Some translation scholars, however, classify types of meaning in different ways, e.g. Newmark (1991), who distinguishes three broad types of meaning: cognitive, communicative and associative. The first includes linguistic, referential, implicit and thematic meaning; the second subsumes illocutionary, performative, inferential and prognostic meaning; and associative meaning deals with pragmatic issues.

Note that in translation studies, it is not entirely clear how the terms 'meaning' and 'message' relate to each other. Some scholars, e.g. Nida (1964) and Nida and Taber (1969/1974) view 'meaning' as equating to 'message' since they define the latter as consisting of the entire meaning (**content**) of a text, by which they understand both the **content** (concepts) and the feelings that the ST author wishes to communicate to the readers. In contrast, Newmark (1988) makes a clear distinction between 'message' and 'meaning', defining the former as what the author wants the reader to think and feel, and the latter as the entire meaning of the ST text, including all denotative and connotative meanings. However, there is also the more general definition (e.g. Weston 2003) that the meaning of the ST consists of what the ST author wants to communicate, which does not clarify whether the author's intentions refer to both the text **content** and the author's feelings, or just to one of these notions. (**BB**)

FURTHER READING: Baker (1992); Bassnett (1980/2002); Bell (1991); Benjamin (1923/2004); Crystal (2003); Hatim (2001); Malmkjær (2005); Munday (2001/2008); Newmark (1988, 1991); Nida (1964); Nida and Taber (1969/1974); Vinay and Darbelnet (1958/2004); Weston (2003).

MEDICAL INTERPRETING, SEE HEALTHCARE INTERPRETING

MEDIA INTERPRETING

The notion of media interpreting subsumes various forms of interpreting in media settings, which mainly include broadcast mass media (i.e. radio and television) but also newer types of electronic media and transmission such as webcasting.

Irrespective of transmission mode, a distinction must be made between live and pre-recorded media content, and between different communicative scenarios, such as **liaison interpreting** in talkshows with a studio audience, **simultaneous interpreting** of previewed news broadcasts, and live broadcast interpreting of televised communication events, such as press conferences, speeches by international dignitaries, sporting events, royal weddings, Oscar ceremonies, etc.,

For other audiovisual scenarios a translation is **voiced over** at a later stage. In fact, it is not at all unusual for there to be more than one translation of the same event, namely an initial live interpretation and a subsequent tidier, voiced-over version normally based on a written translation. (**FP** and **DC**)

FURTHER READING: Chiaro (2002); Kurz (1997); Mack (2002); Russo (1995).

METAPHRASE

Dryden's (1680/1992) first category of translation, which corresponds to **word-for-word translation** or extreme **literal translation**. (**JM**)

MILITARY INTERPRETING

Since earliest times, interpreters have played a significant role in situations of armed conflict and their aftermath. Whether in reconnaissance, liaising with allies, the interrogation of prisoners of war, or truce negotiations, language and interpreting skills are an undisputed asset. While modern-day military interpreters are likely to serve also peacekeeping and humanitarian relief efforts, the loyalty required of them may put them at great risk, whether they are soldiers or locals recruited to serve a military force. (**FP**)

FURTHER READING: Thomas (1997).

MINORITIZING TRANSLATION

Minoritizing translation is related to '**foreignizing translation**' and was introduced by Venuti (1995/2008; 1998a) to refer to a kind of translation that challenges the powerful standard language and cultural forms of American English (1998a: 10). According to Venuti (ibid.: 108), minoritizing translation allows the translator to break free from the linguistic and textual conventions of the TL through the release of the unpredictable variable of the 'remainder', "the collective force of linguistic forms that outstrips any individual's control and complicates intended meanings". This produces an 'alien reading experience' (1995: 20; 1998a 11). A minoritizing translation strategy also encompasses the selection of texts (those occupying a 'minor' or marginal position because of their genre, provenance, stylistic innovation, etc.) which can disrupt the target culture and language. Venuti emphasizes the 'translation ethics' of such a strategy: it makes the translation visible and subverts, but does not seek to replace, the dominant power relations of the TL by the release of foreign textual elements. (**VL and JM**)

FURTHER READING: Venuti (1995/2008, 1998a).

MODULATION

One of Vinay and Darbelnet's (1958) four **oblique translation** procedures. Modulation involves a shift in perspective and changes the semantics in the TT, even though the basic meaning of the ST segment remains unchanged. In contrast to **transposition** (grammatical shifts), modulation constitutes a shift at the cognitive rank. Modulation can be classified according to whether the shift in perspective is necessary because of TL requirements, e.g. *lost property office* translates as *Fundsachenstelle* ('Foundthingsplace') in German (property is viewed as being *lost* in English while German considers it as being *found*). The change in perspective can also be optional, e.g. German *Diese Sportart ist schwierig* ('This sport-type is difficult') → English *This type of sport is not easy* (negation of opposite). In total, Vinay and Darbelnet divide modulation into eleven types: abstract/concrete, cause/effect, active/passive, negation of the opposite, space/time, part/whole, part for another part, reversal of viewpoint, intervals and limits, change of symbols, and geographical change. **(BB)**

FURTHER READING: Hatim and Munday (2004); Munday (2001/2008), Newmark (1995), Vinay and Darbelnet (1958, 1958/2004).

MULTIMEDIA TRANSLATION

Multimedia products are both produced and consumed by means of several media. In other words, typical multimedia products, such as a films and hypertexts, will be created through the implementation of diverse technological equipment (i.e. cameras, computers, software programs, etc.) and subsequently consumed by end users via some sort of electronic device such as a television, a computer screen or a console. Translation for such products varies greatly. **Dubbing** and **subtitling** are most popular in cinema, television, DVD and video game translation while hypertexts on the internet (e.g. promotional websites, institutional websites), tend to be **localized** through the translation of the verbal text and through the insertion of visuals which are meaningful in the target culture. **(DC)**

NAATI

The National Accreditation Authority for Translators and Interpreters, established in 1977, is a standards and credentialing body which tests and accredits individuals in Australia and overseas at four different levels of vocational linguistic qualification (Paraprofessional Interpreter, Interpreter, Conference Interpreter, Senior Conference Interpreter). Though not necessarily requiring training, NAATI's elaborate testing and newly introduced revalidation system for some fifty languages is a prime example of the role of certification in establishing and maintaining professional standards in interpreting. **(FP)**

FURTHER READING: http://www.naati.com.au

NAIROBI DECLARATION/RECOMMENDATION

The *UNESCO Recommendation on the Protection and Improvement of the Legal and Social Status of Translations and Translators* is known as the Nairobi

Declaration since it was adopted at the UNESCO General Conference in Nairobi in 1976. The document states the ethical responsibilities of the translator, the rights of the translator to copyright and decent remuneration and conditions, and the goal of the associations in providing training and maintaining standards. **(JM)**

NATURALNESS

A core concept in Nida's (1964) **dynamic equivalence** model. In this translation orientation, which focuses on recreating essentially the same effect on the TT readership as the ST does on the ST audience, naturalness in translation means that there are no apparent signs of foreignness of expression present in the TT. Naturalness can be achieved, or put another way, foreignness can be avoided by making appropriate lexical and grammatical adjustments and by taking the TL culture requirements well into account. A natural translation does not have the appearance of a translation at all. Instead, it looks like an original TL text to the readership. **(BB)**

FURTHER READING: Larson (1998); Munday (2001/2008); Newmark (1988); Nida (1964); Nida and Taber (1969/1974); Thomas (1985).

NEOLOGISM

A label for a recently created word, term or phrase, or for an already existing word, term or phrase which has taken on a new meaning. Examples of the first type of neologism are names for newly discovered, invented or created objects, e.g. the new Boeing 787, for which the name *Dreamliner* was coined. An example of the second type is the general-language word *mouse*, which took on a new meaning when the computer mouse was created. Beyond these two types, which are the most common types of neologism, Newmark (1988) also distinguishes the following types: derived words, abbreviations, collocations, eponyms, phrasal words, transferred words, acronyms and pseudo-neologisms. **(BB)**

FURTHER READING: Baker (1992); Lehrer (1996, 1997, 2003); Newmark (1988, 1991).

NORMS

In **descriptive translation studies**, the term 'norm' is non-prescriptive and is said by Toury (1995/2004) to occupy a point on a continuum of 'socio-cultural constraints' between the extremes of 'idiosyncrasies' and 'absolute rules'. Norm is used to refer to 'regularities of translation behaviour' (ibid.: 206) as determined by observation of translation products and processes and the identification of tendencies, since translation as a 'norm-governed activity' is not completely systematic.

Toury proposes observation of three different kinds of norm: (1) the basic initial norm, concerning the translator's orientation towards the norms of the ST (in which case the translator will aim for an 'adequate translation') or towards the norms of the TT (and to aim for an 'acceptable translation'); (2) preliminary norms, relating to translation policy (the selection of texts) and the directness of translation (whether translation occurs through a **pivot language**); (3) operational norms which are matricial norms (whether the text is complete, abridged or otherwise modified) and text-linguistic norms (governing the choice of lexis, syntax and other wording).

Different classifications of norms have been proposed. Thus, Chesterman (1997a) suggests (1) product/expectancy norms, which refer to the TT reader's concept of translation and expectations regarding the translation product (for instance, in countries with a **dubbing** tradition a TV viewer is likely to expect a blockbuster film to be dubbed rather than **subtitled**) and (2) professional norms of 'accountability' (the translator accepts responsibility for the work), 'communication' (the translator seeks to ensure satisfactory communication) and 'relation' (the ST should bear relation to the TT). **(JM)**

FURTHER READING: Baker (1998); Chesterman (1997a); Hermans (1999); Toury (1995/2004, 1995).

NOTE TAKING

Note taking is used in **consecutive interpreting** when the source utterance is too long or dense (e.g. with names or numbers) for the interpreter to render by relying on memory alone. It therefore serves to support and complement an interpreter's memory in a given situation rather than constituting a shorthand-like transcription of the ST. Though some basic principles for note taking in consecutive interpreting (such as a vertical arrangement and a focus on message sense rather than words) evolved among the first generation of conference interpreters in the early twentieth century and have remained valid to this day, interpreters are expected to develop their own 'personal technique, using a variable extent and repertoire of abbreviations and/or symbols, with more or less reliance on their A language or the source versus target language in a given assignment. **(FP)**

FURTHER READING: Herbert (1952); Ilg and Lambert (1996); Rozan (1956); Seleskovitch (1975/2002).

OBLIQUE TRANSLATION

One of Vinay and Darbelnet's (1958) two broad types of translation procedure. Opposed to **direct translation**. Both types cover a total of seven specific procedures at three levels: lexis, grammar and **meaning**. Oblique translation strategies are applied when **word-for-word** renderings do not work. To these strategies belong: (1) **transposition**, which concerns grammatical shifts such as word class changes, e.g. German noun *Materialisierung* → English verb *to materialise*; (2) **modulation**, which is a shift in focus that may either be required by TL constraints (e.g. <u>at</u> my desk becomes <u>on</u> my desk in Arabic ‏على مكتبي‎ (ɛalā maktabi)) or else be an option (e.g. English *Das ist nicht richtig* [That is not right] → English *This is wrong*); (3) **equivalence**, which is the use of an established equivalent in the TL for describing the same situation as in the ST, e.g. *Das bringt mich auf die Palme* would not be comprehensible if rendered literally as 'this is sending me up the palm tree' as the English language has its own equivalent, i.e. *This is driving me up the wall*; and (4) **adaptation**, which involves changing the cultural setting if the one in the ST is unfamiliar to the target culture, e.g. the traditional turkey dinners served by the British at Christmas are still largely unknown to most Germans. **(BB)**

FURTHER READING: Fawcett (1997); Hatim and Munday (2004); Munday (2001/2008); Vinay and Darbelnet (1958, 1958/2004).

OMISSION

The intentional or unintentional non-inclusion of an ST segment or meaning aspect in the TT. Opposed to addition. Intentional omissions are mainly carried out to avoid repetitions, e.g. by using pronouns for nouns, or to avoid redundancy in TL texts, e.g. the verb *to fail* in the sentence *Their son failed to come home* can be considered redundant in the German translation *Ihr Sohn kam nicht nach Hause* ('Their son came not to house'). Unintentional omissions tend to be oversights, e.g. in the translation of the noun phrase *the cluster of five engines* as *die fünf Triebwerke* ('five fire engines') in German, in which the noun *cluster* has been left out. **(BB)**

FURTHER READING: Baker (1992); Hatim and Munday (2004).

OPERA TRANSLATION

Opera consists of the union of words and music brought together by a performance on stage in which casting, voices, costume, gesture, lighting, ballet and scenarios are inter-connected to the music and lyrics to create an artistic whole. Many operatic works are intersemiotic translations of literary and theatrical works (e.g. Verdi's *Macbeth*; Puccini's *La Bohème*, etc.) which are transformed into a 'script' written both in the conventionalized language of the libretto and in the musical notations of the score. Traditional print librettos have been largely substituted with electronic librettos positioned in front of each theatre seat that provide simultaneous translations in several languages for patrons who wish to use them. Surtitles provide a translation of the lyrics which are projected on to the top arch or sides of the stage. Unlike electronic librettos, which are controlled by each individual member of the audience, surtitles are 'closed' and can be seen by the entire audience. **(DC)**

OVERT TRANSLATION

One of two types of translation in House's translation model (1977, 1997), the other being **covert translation**. This dichotomy originally stems from the nineteenth century German philosopher and classicist F. Schleiermacher (1813/1973), who distinguished between foreignizing translation (*verfremdende Übersetzung*) and domesticating translation (*einbürgernde Übersetzung*). Overt translation (Schleiermacher's first type) refers to a strategy on the basis of which the TT does not have the status of a second original but of an unconcealed (overt) translation because the TT is not specifically directed at the TT audience. In contrast to covert translations, which involve 'language use', overt translations concern 'language mention'. An overt translation has to be equivalent to the ST at the **register**, **genre**, and language/text level, but in general it is not equivalent at the function level. The function of the TT allows the TT audience to access the function of the ST in its discourse environment. Examples of texts for which an overt translation strategy would be appropriate are, for instance, political addresses and most literary texts. **(BB)**

FURTHER READING: Hatim (2001); Hatim and Munday (2004); House (1977/1981, 1997, 2001, 2003a/b); Munday (2001/2008), Schleiermacher (1813/2004).

OVERT TRANSLATION

A term for the translation of an ST segment resulting in an unnecessarily elaborate and detailed TT version, in which meaning has been added to the originally intended meaning. Opposed to **undertranslation**. Overtranslation occurs, for instance, when there is (1) a focus on the communication of the ST information, rather than on the communicative effect, (2) when undue repetition is present, e.g. if the translator fails to recognize semantically linked units of information in and across clauses and sentences, or (3) when excessive descriptions of cultural concepts are produced that have no or only a partial equivalent in the TL. An example of an overtranslation resulting in excessive and unneeded detail for the audience would be the translation of the cultural acronym *NASA* as *US-Bundesbehörde für Luft- und Raumfahrt (National Aeronautics and Space Administration, NASA)* ('US-Federal-administration for Air and Spacetravel', plus gloss) in a German TT that is specifically addressed to experts. **(BB)**

FURTHER READING: Dussart (2005); Newmark (1988, 1991); Rock (2006); Shuttleworth and Cowie (1997); Vinay and Darbelnet (1958).

PARALLEL TEXT

1. A text in the TL from the same domain as the ST. Such texts assist the translator in finding equivalents for technical terminology, typical rhetorical structures, etc.
2. A TT of an ST that may be compared with the ST to discover the **translation procedures** and translation strategy adopted. Electronic collections of such texts may be aligned to form parallel corpora and to assist descriptive analyses. **(JM)**

PARAPHRASE

1. A term in translation studies, which goes back to Dryden (1680/1992), for an expanded TT version of an ST lexical unit, written in the translator's own words in order to reproduce the ST author's meaning as closely as possible. In this type of translation, adhering to the ST author's original words is secondary to reproducing the intended ST meaning. For example, terms which designate culture-specific or highly complex technical or scientifc concepts may have to be rendered using paraphrases. Thus, depending on the TT text type and readership, an ST abbreviation such as *NSF* may need to rendered with the help of a paraphrase explaining what it is and does: e.g. 'the US National Science Foundation (NSF), a major funding body for science and engineering'.
2. In linguistics, a form of rewording of an ST, '**intralingual translation**', in Jakobson's (1959/2004) terms, which is an alternative version of a text segment without an obvious change in its referential meaning. For example, the sentence *The cat killed the bird* can be paraphrased into *The bird* was *killed by the cat* or into *it was the cat who killed the bird*, and so on. **(BB)**

FURTHER READING: Baker (1992); Bassnett (1980/2002); Dryden (1680/1992); Newmark (1988, 1991); Robinson (1998d); Steiner (1998).

PARATEXT

Paratexts are material additional to a text which comment on, evaluate or otherwise frame it. Genette (1997) describes two kinds of paratext: the 'peritext', which accompanies the text (e.g. foreword, translator's preface, list of contents, acknowledgements, glossary, footnotes, index, cover) and the 'epitext', which appears elsewhere (e.g. publicity material, reviews, critical studies). The importance of paratextual features lies in the evaluation they bring to the text and in their role of guiding the reception of the text by the reader. Thus, Baker (2006) describes how ideological shifts may occur in translation by the use of paratexts such as newspaper headlines and summaries added to a TT that has been otherwise closely translated lexically; Venuti (1995/2008) describes the effect of reviews in conditioning the image of a translated literary work in the target culture. **(JM)**

FURTHER READING: Fawcett (2000); Genette (1997); Nabokov (1955/2004).

PARIS SCHOOL

This label refers to the approach to teaching and research in **conference interpreting** (and translation) championed by Danica **Seleskovitch** and her associates at the the *École Supérieure d'Interprètes et de Traducteurs* (ESIT) at the University of Paris (Sorbonne Nouvelle). Its theoretical underpinning is the '**interpretive theory** of translation', also known as *théorie du sens*, which can be traced to the early 1960s. The Paris School paradigm has remained influential, especially as a training approach. **(FP)**

FURTHER READING: Israël and Lederer (2005); Lederer (1994); Seleskovitch and Lederer (1984/2001); Seleskovitch and Lederer (1989). See also Hurtado Albir and Alves (Chapter 4, this volume).

PATRONAGE, SEE REWRITING

PERLOCUTIONARY ACT, SEE SPEECH ACTS

PIVOT LANGUAGE

An intermediate language through which interpreting or translation sometimes takes place when no interpreter or translator is available to work directly. For instance, English might be used as a pivot language to interpret between Finnish and Greek. See also **Relay interpreting**. **(JM)**

POLYSYSTEM THEORY

Drawing on the work of the Russian Formalists of the 1920s, Itamar Even-Zohar advanced polysystem theory in the 1970s; in this theory, the overall literary (poly)system is considered to be made up of various component systems that interact and evolve dynamically in a hierarchy. Since the polysystem is inherently dynamic, each of its smaller systems may change its position and influence over time, occupying a 'central' or 'peripheral', 'primary' ('innovative') or 'secondary' (conservative') position. Even-Zohar (e.g. 1990/2004: 199–200) considers translated literature to be a distinct system but within the overall literary polysystem of the target culture since (1) the selection of source texts is related to the kinds of text that are published at that time in the target system and (2) the '**norms**, behaviors and policies' adopted are also related to those of the target culture system. Although translated literature may often be peripheral (cf. Venuti's 1995/2008 study of translation in the Anglo-American tradition), Even-Zohar suggests that it can be central and primary when a young system is being established, or it can be weak, importing foreign models (which happened in Hebrew from the 1940s onwards) at critical historical points when the target system's established models are no longer deemed satisfactory. See also **Descriptive translation studies**. **(JM)**

FURTHER READING: Even-Zohar (1990/2004, 1997); Shuttleworth and Cowie (1997); Toury (1995).

POSTCOLONIAL TRANSLATION STUDIES

The explosion of postcolonial studies has contributed to making the so-called '**cultural turn**' in translation become 'intercultural'. Postcolonial scholars began to realize that culture is mediated through language and that translation was an intercultural tool for communication and manipulation. Both postcolonial theories and translation studies share a concern over the issue of **power** relations, and their intersection gave rise to the so-called 'postcolonial translation studies', where translation is often employed as a metaphor to show how it functions as an instrument of colonial domination. Robinson (1997b) sees translation as playing three different roles: in the past it was actively used as a means of colonization to control people; in the present it is a postcolonial act; and in the future it will hopefully be used as a means of decolonization. **(VL)**

FURTHER READING: Bandia (2007); Bassnett and Trivedi (1999); Cheyfitz (1991); Hermans (1985); Niranjana (1992); Rafael (1993); Robinson (1997b); Venuti (1992).

POWER

Since the so-called '**cultural turn**', theorists have become interested in the power relations rooted in textual practice. The issue of power has played an active role in the representation of the source culture, including the selection of STs and the influence and manipulation of the original text in the target culture. Translation is now considered as a powerful and ideological activity which by its very nature cannot be neutral. Further investigations in this field showed how translation has contributed to the construction of textual images influenced by class, gender, race and ethnicity. The growing interest in the issue of power over the years has shifted the boundaries from the '**cultural turn**' to the 'power turn' as claimed by Tymoczko and Gentzler (2002). It has also contributed to the proliferation of studies on **ideology**, how it affects translators' choices and target readers' reception of the ST and perception of the source culture. The issue of power in translation is investigated in many different research fields such as feminist translation studies (see **Gender and translation**), **postcolonial translation studies** and audiovisual translation studies (see Chapter 9). **(VL)**

FURTHER READING: Baker (2006); Tymoczko and Gentzler (2002); Venuti (1992, 1995/2008, 1998a).

PROBLEM SOLVING

A concept used in cognitive psychology and cognitive science which presupposes the interdependence of general cognitive abilities that can potentially be applied to an essentially unlimited range of domains (Holyoak 1990). It involves an initial state, a goal state, a set of operators or actions and path constraints. Problem solving can be viewed as a process of heuristic search (Newell and Simon 1972) with means–ends analysis being a productive search method guided by the detection of differences between an initial or current state and a goal state. As such, problem solving is inextricably connected to decision making as it moves from an initial state towards a goal state in which decisions are made. In translation studies, Wilss (1998) has pointed to the relevance of considering problem solving and decision making in a cognitive approach aimed at understanding translators' performance and translation competence. An entire translation commission or task can be considered as a problem. When solving a translation problem, translators look for a way to a goal to find a solution which they consider most adequate. Therefore, problem solving in translation can be defined as potentially consisting of all procedures that are employed when advancing from an ST to a TT, or from commission to delivery. (**AHA** and **FA**)

FURTHER READING: Wilss (1998); Sirén and Hakkarainen (2002).

PSEUDO-TRANSLATION

1. Generally used in literary translation studies to refer to a text which is overtly published as a translation but for which there is no ST, sometimes to avoid censorship or to increase **acceptability** in the target culture. Perhaps the most famous case is James Macpherson's *Ossian* poems, published 1760–63 as purported translations from Gaelic to English, which achieved a prominent reception as examples of an ancient folk culture.
2. In **localization**, it refers to text that mimics a foreign language (using accent marks, etc., enlarging a text box for languages that typically require more space). It is generated automatically as a pre-translation phase to test a software's functionality and to identify potential problems. (**JM**)

FURTHER READING: Du Pont (2005); Robinson (1998e); Toury (1995).

PUBLIC SERVICE INTERPRETING

Public service interpreting (PSI) is the preferred term in the United Kingdom and some other countries for what is generally known as **community interpreting**.

Though the latter term was coined in Britain in the 1980s and is still in use, albeit with a more activist connotation, PSI has become institutionalized in the UK thanks to the Diploma in Public Service Interpreting (offered with specializations in healthcare, legal and local government services) and the National Register for Public Service Interpreters (NRPSI), a subsidiary non-profit-making company owned by the Chartered Institute of Linguists. **(FP)**

PURE LANGUAGE, SEE LOGOS

PURPOSE

Generally used to refer to the purpose of a text, that is, how and for what purpose it will be used (e.g. for information, for publication). *Skopos* **theory** sees the purpose of the TT as taking priority and determining the translation strategy. **(JM)**

RECEIVER

The **audience** to whom a translation is addressed. The term tends to be used in the context of texts being seen as communicative events. The receiver of a translation, together with its sender/producer, form the key notions in the analysis of texts within this framework. In the communicative model of the translation process, promoted by Nida (1964, 2004) and Nida and Taber (1969/1974), the role of the receiver (they use the term 'receptor') becomes the focal point while the sender steps into the background but is still taken into account. However, there are also theories that pay little attention to the relationship the TT has with the ST (e.g. Holz-Mäntärri 1984). Pym (1992) distinguishes three types of receiver: (a) excluded (a receiver who can only partially respond to the TT), (b) participative (a receiver who is able to respond to the TT), and (c) observational (a receiver who cannot respond to the TT). **(BB)**

FURTHER READING: Hatim (2001); Holz-Mäntärri (1984); Nida (1964, 2004); Nida and Taber (1969/1974); Pym (1992); Reiss (2004).

RECEPTION

1. The manner in which a translation comes over to the TT readership. An important means of gauging how a translation has been received is by way of reviews (of translated books, short stories, essays, articles, plays, advertisements and so on). Some of the criteria involved in judging the reception of a TT have been adopted from reception theory (e.g. Brown 1994) and concern the ways in which a translation complies with what a readership would normally expect, or gives them something to think about,

or lets them down. Criticisms about how reviews of translations are carried out centre around the problem that translations are often read and judged as if they were original TL texts. Reviewers often do not have access to the ST, and hence neither the process of the translation nor the ST are taken into account.
2. In interpreting, reception refers to the text reception phase, which, for instance, in **simultaneous interpreting** takes place more or less at the same time as the text production. **(BB)**

FURTHER READING: Brown (1994); Hardwick (2003); Holub (1984); Iser (1978); Jauss (1982); Munday (2001/2008); Venuti (1995/2008).

REDUNDANCY

1. The amount of information provided in a TT segment over and above that which is essential. Redundant information in the TT may, for instance, be caused if a translator who decides to use **explicitation** as a translation procedure overdoes it in order to clarify a particular ST meaning in the TT. For example, a non-essential **explicitation** would be present if, in the translation of the instruction *Connect the USB cable to the USB port on your computer*, the acronym USB were explained.
2. In simultaneous interpreting, redundancy is a necessary element without which this kind of interpretation cannot take place. Hence, the amount of redundancy is here considerably higher than in an equivalent written translation (cf. Chernov 1979). **(BB)**

FURTHER READING: Blum-Kulka (1986/2004); Chernov (1979, 1994); Hatim (2001); Hatim and Munday (2004); Newmark (1988); Nida (1964).

REFERENTIAL MEANING, SEE DENOTATION

REFRACTION, SEE REWRITING

REGISTER

The set of features which distinguishes one stretch of language from another in terms of variation in **context**, relating to the language user (geographical dialect, idiolect, etc.) and/or language use ('field', which is subject matter, 'tenor', which is the level of formality and the relationship between writer and reader, and 'mode', which is whether the text is spoken or written, formal or informal). Examination of a text using these parameters, and looking at the way in which they are conveyed by the **lexicogrammar**, is known as Register Analysis and draws on the Hallidayan systemic-functional linguistic tradition. **(BH)**

FURTHER READING: Hatim and Mason (1990, 1997); House (1997, 2006).

Relay interpreting

Relay interpreting is used when no interpreter is available to cover a given source–TL combination directly. Interpreting then proceeds indirectly via a third language (**pivot** language), with the output of one interpreter (**pivot**) serving as the source for another. With team interpreting during the Spanish conquest of the Aztec Empire (Spanish–Maya and Maya–Nahuatl, by Doña Marina) serving as a famous historical precedent, such 'double' interpreting is used in international **conference interpreting** (e.g. to interpret from Arabic and Chinese into other UN languages via English or French) as well as in community-based settings and in **signed-language interpreting**, also including Deaf relay interpreters. (**FP**)

Relevance theory

Relevance theory, developed by Sperber and Wilson (1986/1995; see also Wilson and Sperber 2004) and building on the work of Grice in pragmatics (see **implied meaning**), focuses on the importance of intention in human communication. Two central principles of relevance theory are (1) the 'cognitive principle' of maximization of relevance (by the listener) and (2) the 'communicative principle', which states that participants in an interaction expect an utterance to be relevant and a communicative interaction to perform a specific act (cf. **speech acts**). Thus, a listener will attempt to use 'communicative clues' in an utterance and his/her own assumptions about the interaction to establish such relevance and to 'infer' from the context the speaker's intention.

In translation studies, relevance theory has been prominently used by Ernst-August Gutt (1991/2000), who, borrowing the relevance theory concepts of 'descriptive' and 'interpretive' language use, develops the idea of 'indirect' and '**direct**' translation. An indirect translation is considered to be designed to function on its own (e.g. a tourist brochure) and may be modified in order to achieve maximal relevance for the TT user, while a direct translation seeks 'interpretive resemblance', that is, close resemblance with the ST. (Compare **covert** and **overt translation**). (**JM**)

FURTHER READING: Gutt (1991/2000, 2005a); Hatim and Munday (2004); Sperber and Wilson (1986/1995, 2004). See also Hurtado Albir and Alves (Chapter 4, this volume).

Remote interpreting

Remote interpreting refers to a scenario in which the interpreter is not in the same location as the communicating parties, interacting via the telephone, the internet or various forms of videoconferencing. While its increasing use in community-based settings (**healthcare**, legal) mostly involves interpreters working in the **consecutive** (**liaison**) mode, its adoption for international conference settings implies booth-style **simultaneous interpreting**, with special equipment for image capture and display to compensate for the lack of a direct view of the meeting room. (**FP**)

FURTHER READING: Mouzourakis (2006).

RESISTANCE

A term used by Venuti (1998a) as a counter to the tendency towards domestication in the Anglo-American translation tradition. It is related to the strategy of **minoritizing translation**. (**JM**)

FURTHER READING: Venuti (1998a).

RESTRUCTURING

The third of three phases in Nida and Taber's (1969/1974) model of the translation process. Following the **analysis** and the **transfer** phase, the restructuring phase focuses on reorganizing the SL meaning, which is transferred in the form of **kernel** sentences. During this phase the TT readership becomes the focal point and the SL meaning is restructured in terms of register, style, additions and so on. Apart from modifying the transferred SL meaning into a style that is expected by the TT readership, this phase also has as its goal to make sure that the intended ST effect on the ST audience is recreated with regard to the TT audience (cf. Nida 1969). (**BB**)

FURTHER READING: Hatim (2001); Hatim and Munday (2004); Munday (2001/2008); Nida (1969); Nida and Taber (1969/1974).

REWRITING

Lefevere coined this term (initially he had used the term 'refraction') to denote activities such as literary criticism, reviewing, anthologizing and translation, which in some way manipulate original texts. In rewriting, it is the institutions or powerful individuals involved in the process which hold power within a specific community. These political and literary power institutions exert control over the work that circulates in their own cultural system and may bestow patronage, for example to fund translation and publication. For Lefevere (1992: 9), translation is the 'most obviously recognizable type of rewriting' and manipulates the ST due to ideology (of translator and institutions) and the dominant poetics in the target culture, though these remained unproblematized in Lefevere's work. (**VL**)

FURTHER READING: Bassnett and Lefevere (1990); Hermans (1985, 1994); Lefevere (1985, 1992).

RID

The Registry of Interpreters for the Deaf, founded in the mid-1960s to help meet the demand for **signed-language interpreting** in vocational rehabilitation mandated by US legislation, is the world's largest professional association of interpreters. It has thousands of members, many of whom hold certification according to the organization's own national evaluation system developed since the early 1970s, recently in cooperation with the National Association of the Deaf. The RID *Code of Ethics* has proved a source of inspiration for similar documents on community-based interpreting in spoken languages. Its revised version, the *NAD-RID Code of Professional Conduct*, effective since 2005, is comprised of seven tenets, including confidentiality, professional skills, respect and continuing education. **(FP)**

FURTHER READING: http://www.rid.org

ROLE (OF THE INTERPRETER)

The notion of role, defined by sociologists as a set of more or less normative behavioural expectations associated with a social position, denotes a fundamental challenge for interpreters, given their intermediate position between two parties or groups representing different cultural backgrounds, social status, power and value systems. Where such unequal clients have conflicting goals and expectations, particularly in face-to-face interaction, the traditional principle of the interpreter's neutrality, if not 'invisibility', becomes an ultimately impossible challenge. The appropriate degree of interpreters' visibility or 'agency' – as clarifiers, discourse managers, culture brokers or even advocates – is thus a perennial subject of debate, both within the profession and in relation to its clients, especially in legal and **court interpreting**. **(FP)**

FURTHER READING: Anderson and Bruce (1976/2002); Roy (2000).

SCIENCE OF TRANSLATION

A term which refers to the development of translation studies from the 1960s (e.g. by Nida 1964) in the form of linguistic-oriented theories of translation. Various translation concepts play an important role in the science of translation, e.g. **equivalence**, **equivalent effect**, types of translation **shift**, discourse, ST and TT cultural aspects and so on. The science of translation is still pursued in Germany, except for a change in viewpoint regarding **equivalence**. Linguistic theories of translation are seen as useful tools in translation teaching since the linguistic level comes into play at some point during the translation process. **(BB)**

FURTHER READING: Bassnett (1980/2002); Fawcett (1997); Munday (2001/2008), Nida (1964, 1969); Wilss (1982); Zaixi (1997).

SELESKOVITCH

A pioneer practitioner of conference interpreting after World War II, Danica Seleskovitch (1921–2001) is the most widely known scholar and educator in the field of interpreting and has shaped the field of interpreting studies as nobody else. Born to a Serbian father and a French mother, she spent her youth in Berlin before starting a distinguished career in the profession as well as in academia. She served as Secretary-General of **AIIC** and for many years headed the School of Interpreters and Translators at the University of Paris, where she established a doctoral research programme in *traductologie* in 1974. Her interpretive theory of translation (dubbed *théorie du sens*) has had a lasting impact and informs the research and teaching approach of what is known as the **Paris School**. **(FP)**

FURTHER READING: Seleskovitch (1968/1978, 1975/2002); Widlund-Fantini (2007).

SEMANTIC STRUCTURE ANALYSIS

A type of contrastive **disambiguation** technique which was adapted by Nida (1964) from linguistics. It is a translation aid for establishing the different referential meanings of a linguistic item by highlighting individual meaning characteristics of the item. For example, one way of systematizing and at the same time disambiguating the English noun *fire* would be in terms of whether human beings (e.g. emotions, enthusiasm, energy) or objects (e.g. fireplace, weapons) are involved. In particular, Nida developed this analysis technique to sensitize novice translators to the fact that a word can have varying meanings and that it is the context of a word that governs its meaning. For example, the German noun *Verfahren* often poses problems as it covers two similar concepts in English, *process* and *procedure*. Only by disambiguating the referential meanings and by taking the context into account can the correct target word be selected. Disambiguation can be carried out schematically using tree or bracket diagrams as this facilitates the comparison of meanings. **(BB)**

FURTHER READING: Hatim and Munday (2004); Larson (1998); Munday (2008); Nida (1964).

SEMANTIC TRANSLATION

One of Newmark's two translation categories (1988, 1991), by which he understands the strategy of recreating as far as possible the contextual meaning of an ST in a TT within the syntactic and semantic limitations of the TL. In the same way that Newmark's second type, **communicative translation,** is comparable to Nida's **dynamic equivalence,** so semantic translation is reminiscent of Nida's **formal equivalence**. Newmark believes that the conflict of whether translators should be more faithful to the ST or to the TT will continue, but that the notions of semantic and communicative translation could lessen this conflict. In other words, the gap between putting more focus on the ST or the TT would be smaller. Nowadays, however, Newmark does not employ the terms 'semantic' and 'communicative translation' any longer and instead speaks of 'correlative translation theory' (see Anderman and Rogers 2003). **(BB)**

FURTHER READING: Anderman and Rogers (2003); Hatim (2001); Hatim and Munday (2004); Munday (2001/2008); Newmark (1988, 1991).

SEMANTIC VOID, SEE LACUNA

SENSE

In semantics, a word's sense is distinguished from its **meaning**. Sense refers to the 'general' meaning that is always connected to a word. For example, the word *cat* always has the same general meaning, namely *a small, furry domesticated animal with four legs*. It is these general meanings, i.e. the senses of words, that are recorded in dictionaries. The sense of a word helps us to establish what kind of object, person and so on is meant. In a particular context, such as *The vet gave Mary's cat an injection* the word *cat* refers to a 'specific feline creature', namely 'Mary's cat'. In this case, 'Mary's cat' is the 'referent'.

In **machine translation** (MT) and in natural language processing (NLP), word sense disambiguation is considered to be a problematic area. **(BB)**

FURTHER READING: Bell (1991); Hudson (1995); Kilgarriff (1993, 1997); Lyons (1977/1993); Newmark (1988).

SENSE-FOR-SENSE

A term for a translation approach by means of which the **content**, i.e. the **sense** of an ST, is translated. The **meanings** of ST words are translated within their **context** and within TL requirements. It is opposed to **word-for-word** translation, which renders ST words by their closest TL forms, thereby producing a translation that is difficult to understand. The notion of sense-for-sense translation was first conceived by St Jerome (ca. 347–420 CE) in an attempt to find an approach which is in-between Cicero's (106 to 43 BCE) extremely free interpretations of texts and the radically literal and faithful renderings of texts criticized by Cicero and Horace (65 to 8 BCE). St Jerome believed that the translation method is conditioned by the function of a translation. The dichotomy of sense-for-sense and **word-for-word** translation can be seen as the beginning of the long-standing debate about **literal** and **free translation**, i.e. **form-content**, among writers on translation. **(BB)**

FURTHER READING: Baker (1992); Bassnett (1980/2002); Munday (2001/2008); Robinson (1997a).

SHIFTS IN TRANSLATION

Catford (1965:73) was the first to use the term 'shift' to denote 'departures from formal correspondence in the process of going from the SL to the TL'. For Catford, then, shifts are structural and linguistic, similar to the procedures analysed by Vinay and Darbelnet in their comparative stylistics of French and English. Subsequently, the concept of shift has most notably been used by Leuven-Zwart (1989, 1990), who attempts a complex classification of micro-level changes in extracts of Latin American novels translated into Dutch, and Toury (1995) who sees shifts as being either or non-obligatory and motivated by sociocultural factors obligatory, due to systemic differences between languages (e.g. English *skimmed milk* > French *lait écrémé* or, a more complex example, Spanish *se implementó la ley* ['self implemented the law'] > English *the law was implemented*). **(JM)**

FURTHER READING: Catford (1965); Leuven-Zwart (1989, 1990); Shuttleworth and Cowie (1997); Toury (1995, 2004).

SIGHT TRANSLATION

Ostensibly a hybrid between translation and interpreting, translating a written text 'at sight' for a live audience is in fact a form of (**simultaneous**) interpreting. In healthcare and legal as well as business settings, interpreters called upon to render documents are expected to work at the pace of speech, producing their TL output while reading the text, even without a prior overview. Though visual ST reception makes it a specific processing mode, 'sight interpreting' is frequently used as a preliminary exercise in the training of simultaneous interpreters and practised in the composite mode of 'simultaneous with text' in the booth. **(FP)**

FURTHER READING: Pöchhacker (1994); Weber (1990).

SIGN

A unit of signifier and signified, in which the linguistic form (signifier) stands for a concrete object or concept (signified). When the notion of sign is extended to include anything which means something to somebody in some respect or capacity, signs could then be used to refer to cultural objects such as *honour* (micro-sign), as well as to more global structures such as text, **genre** and discourse (macro-sign), and to even more global structures such as that of the myth. **(BH)**

SIGNED-LANGUAGE INTERPRETING

Sign(ed)-language interpreting is a form of interpreting distinguished by the modality (visual-gestural) of one, or both, of the languages involved.

Signed languages being the natural means of communication developed by the Deaf (as a group with its own cultural identity within a hearing mainstream society), interpreting for the Deaf is typically between a given sign language (American Sign Language, British Sign Language, French Sign Language, etc.) and the (spoken) national language of the respective country or region. As signed-languages are no less distinct from one another than different national spoken languages, and hence not mutually intelligible, signed-language interpreting is also required in international contacts, that is, between different Deaf communities and their languages. In addition to a sign language proper, signed-language interpreters also use secondary sign systems based on spoken and written languages (e.g. Signed English) as preferred by the hard of hearing and by deafened adults. Signing in these manual codes is also referred to as '**transliteration**'. Given its social context, interpreting for the Deaf mostly takes place in (a wide variety of) community-based settings, from kindergarten to doctor's offices, police stations and the theatre, including face-to-face as well as conference-like situations ('platform interpreting'). Given the lack of acoustic interference, professional signed-language interpreters mostly work in the simultaneous mode. However, the professional status of signed-language interpreting largely depends on legal provisions regarding minority language rights or the social integration of persons with disabilities, and hence varies widely from country to country. (**FP**)

FURTHER READING: Janzen (2005); Stewart, Schein and Cartwright (1998).

SIMULTANEOUS INTERPRETING

In the simultaneous mode of interpreting, the TT (interpretation) is produced concurrently with the interpreter's reception of the ST, with a processing-related delay (known as 'time lag' or *décalage*) of only a few seconds. When a **signed language** is involved, the absence of acoustic source–target overlap makes simultaneous interpreting the mode of choice, whereas simultaneous interpreting between spoken languages – except for **whispered interpreting** – is provided with electro-acoustic transmission equipment from a sound-insulated booth. In all its manifestations, including 'live' **sight translation**, simultaneous interpreting implies a high load on the interpreter's attentional resources (working memory) and requires appropriate cognitive and linguistic coping strategies. (**FP**)

FURTHER READING: Gile (1997/2002).

SKOPOS THEORY

The Greek word *skopos* means 'purpose'. *Skopos* theory was developed in Germany first by Hans Vermeer and then in conjunction with Katharina Reiss (see also **Text Types**) in the 1970s and 1980s and shares concepts with the theory of **translatorial action** (Holz-Mänttäri 1984). *Skopos* theory is TT-oriented in the sense that it gives priority to the purpose of the envisaged TT ('translatum' or 'translat') and the function it is to play in the target culture as stipulated by the client or 'initiator'. Thus, if a Beijing-based client commissions the translation of an advertisement for publication in a national newspaper in South Africa in order to promote a positive image of a product and therefore boost sales, the specific *skopos* will determine the translation strategy. The focus on achieving the *skopos* of the communication means that criteria based on close **equivalence** with the ST are not necessarily appropriate for assessing the TT. Instead, a **coherence** rule and a loyalty/**fidelity** rule are invoked: the TT should be coherent enough for it to be understood by the target audience, yet sufficiently loyal to the ST. The fuzzy nature of such loyalty, and the difficulty in determining the conditions under which such loyalty is achieved, is one of the criticisms of *skopos* theory, but its consideration of the cultural role of the TT was a significant advance in the 1980s and presaged the **cultural turn**. **(JM)**

FURTHER READING: Nord (1997, 2003, 1998/2001/2005); Reiss and Vermeer (1984); Schäffner (1998b); Vermeer (1989).

SL, SEE SOURCE LANGUAGE

SOCIOLOGY OF TRANSLATION

A recent growth area in translation studies, the sociology of translation has attempted systematically to investigate translation as social practice, focusing on the study of the professional role of the translator and of other agents involved in the process. Work in the late 1990s (e.g. Gouanvic 1999; Simeoni 1998) began to apply particularly the sociology of Pierre Bourdieu (1990, 1992) and his concepts of 'field', '**habitus**', 'capital' and 'illusio' to understanding the economic and cultural exchanges and hierarchies at work in translation. The link with translation and **power** is clear. Other sociological theories that have been imported have been used to research translation as a social system (the work of Niklas Luhmann in Hermans 1999, 2007) and as a network (Bruno Latour's actor–network theory, in Buzelin 2005). Interest in the 'discourse of translation', self-reflexivity around the translation profession and the academic discipline of translation studies, has also become more prominent. **(JM)**

FURTHER READING: Hermans (1999); Inghilleri (2005); Simeoni (1998); Wolf and Fukari (2007).

SOURCE LANGUAGE (SL)

The language of the **Source text**.

Source text (ST)

The 'original text' which is the source for a translation. **(JM)**

Soviet school

Represented chiefly by Ghelly V. Chernov (1929–2000) at the Maurice Thorez Institute of Foreign Languages in Moscow, the Soviet School of interpreting research focused on the psycholinguistic process of **simultaneous interpreting**. In cooperation with psychologist Irina Zimnyaya, Chernov, who worked for twelve years as a conference interpreter at the United Nations in New York, conducted experimental research in the 1970s to demonstrate the crucial role of predictive understanding in the simultaneous mode. In the professional sphere, the Soviet School (unlike the **Paris School**) favoured interpreting from the A into the B language, with Russian serving as the pivot language for **relay interpreting** in multilingual meetings. **(FP)**

Further reading: Chernov (1979/2002, 2004).

Speech acts

In attempting to express themselves, people do not just only produce sentences that are well-formed, they perform actions via utterances that are intended to achieve specific purposes. Consider, for example, 'Lecturer to students: You might read Chapter 5 for our next meeting on Tuesday'. This utterance has little if anything to do with the modality of 'possibility'; it is an 'order'. Speech act theory, proposed by Oxford language philosopher John Austin (1962), holds that, while sentences can be used to report states of affairs, some sentences are uttered to perform certain acts in specific circumstances. Actions performed via utterances (e.g. apology, complaint, compliment, invitation, promise, request) are related to the speaker's communicative intention in producing an utterance. Both speaker and hearer are usually helped by the circumstances surrounding the utterance or speech event (e.g. classroom interaction). Yule (1996: 48) states that 'it is the nature of the speech event that determines the interpretation of an utterance as performing a particular speech act', which in turn is determined by **culture**.

Speech acts function at three levels of **meaning** or action. First, the locutionary level, the basic act of producing a meaningful linguistic expression (i.e. grammatical and lexically well-formed). Second, in the illocutionary act, we utter a linguistic expression with some kind of function in mind. Each illocutionary act is the force of the utterance (e.g. promise, order, warn). Finally, the perlocutionary act, is the effect we intend the illocutionary act to have on the recipient (e.g. authority). The communication circumstances will determine what and how an utterance is made in order to force the hearer to recognize the intended effect. The third, perlocutionary, level is perhaps the most significant in the area of translation because the circumstances that govern the hearer/**receiver** would be determined by the translator's ability to preserve the speaker's ultimate intention as expressed in the linguistic **context**.

As Yule (1996: 59–60) makes abundantly clear, a great deal of what we communicate is determined by our social relationships (social conventions). A linguistic interaction between a speaker and a hearer is necessarily a social interaction, which is also part of our general sociocultural knowledge. To achieve better understanding of what goes on in a text or to make sense of what is uttered, we have to think of the various factors related to social distance and closeness. Some of these factors are external, being established before an interaction. They involve the relative status of the participants, which is based on social values to such things as age and power. Others are internal and negotiated during an interaction, such as the amount of imposition or degree of friendliness. Both the internal and the external factors influence what we say. More importantly, they influence how we interpret what is said. Cultures do not follow a single set of values when it comes to ways of negotiating social relations. In the light of such norms, a translator needs to observe the influence of these cultural ways before arriving at an interpretation of the speaker's intended meaning. (**BH**)

FURTHER READING: Austin (1962); Yule (1996).

SPIRIT

A term in translation studies, derived from the Latin word *spiritus*. The word *spirit* can be understood in two ways: St Augustine (354–430 CE) employed it to denote the Holy Spirit, but it can also refer to the creativity or inspiration involved in writing literary texts (cf. Kelly 1979). So, the translation of a literary text is said by some to be dependent on the transfer of the artistic spirit contained in the original text. However, St Jerome (ca. 347–420 CE) used the term to denote both the Holy Spirit and creative energy. For Kelly (1979), the term *spirit* is intricately linked with the terms **fidelity** and truth (**content**). (**BB**)

FURTHER READING: Amos (1920/1973); Bassnett (1980/2002); Kelly (1979); Robinson (1991); Steiner (1975/1998).

ST, SEE SOURCE TEXT

STYLE

Style has sometimes been used as a very general term that covers some of the ground of **form** and contrasts with **content** or **meaning**. Nida and Taber

(1969/1974: 12), for instance, saw the translator's role as being to translate the meaning first and then the style, which they defined as 'the patterning of choices made by a particular author within the resources and limitations of the language and of the literary **genre** in which he is working' (ibid.: 207). Since then, developments in the analysis of style (e.g. Leech and Short 1981) have attempted to analyse that patterning of choices as deviance from a **norm**, as deliberate artistic foregrounding or as a psychological phenomenon of prominence, and as both a collective and individual phenomenon (e.g. the style of nineteenth-century Russian novels, or of Dostoevski). Work in translation studies has examined, amongst others, the artistic (Parks 2007), cognitive (Boase-Beier 2006) and ideological (Munday 2001/2008) reasons behind the variation in linguistic style and has studied both different variations of the same text and tried to identify the style of individual translators. Other work (e.g. Baker 2000) has adopted corpus-based methods or has looked at the translation of the narrative point of view (Bosseaux 2007). The development of stylistics (the linguistic analysis of style) has influenced many theorists; Malmkjær has coined the term 'translational stylistics' for this type of study since 'it is concerned to explain why, *given the source text*, the translation has been shaped in such a way that it comes to mean what it does' (2003: 39, emphasis in original). **(JM)**

FURTHER READING: Baker (2000); Boase-Beier (2004, 2006); Bosseaux (2007); Malmkjær (2003); Munday (2008); Parks (2007).

SUBTITLING

Subtitling can be defined as *'the rendering in a different language* of verbal messages in filmic media, in the shape of one or more lines of written text presented on the screen *in sync with the original written message'* (Gottlieb 2001b: 87, emphasis in original). Subtitling is extremely cost-effective and, unlike dubbing, leaves the original soundtrack intact. However, the process involves a significant reduction of the original dialogues, resulting in a written text that is shorter than the audio because the viewer needs the necessary time to read the captions, as well as simultaneously follow the action of the film itself. **(DC)**

FURTHER READING: Gottlieb (2001b). See also Chiaro (Chapter 9, this volume).

SUPERORDINATE, SEE HYPONYM

SURTITLES, SEE OPERA TRANSLATION

TARGET LANGUAGE (TL)

The language of the **TT**.

TARGET TEXT (TT)

The translated text, or the text that is to be created in translation. (**JM**)

TELEPHONE INTERPRETING

The most basic form of **remote interpreting**, 'over-the-phone interpreting' has come into widespread use, particularly in community-based settings (e.g. healthcare, police, emergency services) but also in business communication. With minimal technological requirements, it permits **consecutive interpreting** (audio only) from any location for short encounters (5–10 minutes), for which clients (institutional subscribers) are usually billed by the minute. Whether using a three-way phone connection or a speaker-phone, the interpreter is invariably deprived of visual contact with the callers, unless more advanced technology (video telephony) is available. (**FP**)

FURTHER READING: Ko (2006); Rosenberg (2007).

TERTIUM COMPARATIONIS

A term used in contrastive linguistic studies to describe the basis of comparison between two objects of analysis (SL and TL units) in terms of a shared criterion. This criterion, the *tertium comparationis* (lit. 'the third [element] of the comparison') is a text-independent meaning (**invariant**) shared by both the SL and TL unit, by means of which the variation in equivalence between the two units can be established. For instance, an assessment of the transfer of meaning from the English expression *You can't mix apples and oranges* (*comparandum*) to the German saying *Man kann Äpfel nicht mit Birnen vergleichen* (*comparatum*) can be carried out using a *tertium comparationis*. In both idioms, the objects of comparison are 'two things that cannot, or at least not easily, be compared with each other'. The *tertium comparationis* between these objects can be formulated intralingually as well as cross-linguistically as the 'fundamental differences in quality, value, and appearance in spite of seeming similarities'. Note that translation scholars consider the *tertium comparationis* to be a controversial issue since it carries with it an inevitable element of subjectivity. (**BB**)

FURTHER READING: Chesterman (2005); Hatim and Munday (2004); Hoey and Houghton (1998); Krzeszowski (1984, 1990); Leuven-Zwart (1989, 1990); Munday (2001/2008); Toury (1980, 1995).

TEXT

A sequence of cohesive and coherent sentences realizing a set of mutually relevant intentions. A text exhibits features which serve a particular contextual focus and identify the text as a token of a given **text type**. (**BH**)

TEXT TYPES

The seminal work of Katharina Reiss (1971/2000) on text typology was based on the three functions of language proposed by Karl Bühler (1934/1965). Reiss's three text types are (1) the informative text type, with the focus on the referential content; (2) the expressive text type, with the focus on the author and the form of the message; and (3) the operative text type, where the function is to appeal to or persuade the reader. Typical examples of 'text varieties' associated with each text type are: (1) encyclopaedias, manuals, etc.; (2) novels, poems and other literary works; and (3) advertisements. In Reiss's opinion, each text type demands a different translation 'method' or strategy. In the case of (1) it is 'plain prose' and **explicitation** of referential content; in (2) it is an 'identifying method', where the translator adopts the perspective of the ST author; and for (3) it is the **'adaptive'** method, with the aim of achieving similarly persuasive effect on the TT audience. There is a fourth text type, audio-medial, which Reiss leaves undeveloped but which might now be termed **audiovisual translation**. In addition, as Reiss herself began to note (1977/1989), many if not all texts are characterized by some degree of hybridity. Nevertheless, text typology of some kind still forms the basis of much specialized translator training. **(JM)**

FURTHER READING: Hatim (Chapter 7, this volume); Hatim and Mason (1990, 1997); Reiss (1971/2000, 1977/1989, 2004); Trosberg (1997, 2000).

TEXTUAL EQUIVALENCE

1. A term used by Catford (1965) in his approach to translation equivalence for the real-world relationships between ST and TT linguistic units. In other words, textual equivalence holds between text segments that are existing translations of each other. Hence, textual equivalence concerns Saussure's language level of *parole* while its counterpart **formal correspondence** is linked to *langue*. According to Catford, textual equivalence comes into play when translation on the basis of **formal correspondence** is not possible, resulting in translation **shifts** (level, category). For example, class shifts from verbs to nouns are a common type of category **shift** between English and German: thus, English *The employment was terminated by the employer* – German *Die Auflösung des Arbeitsverhältnisses fand durch den Arbeitgeber statt* ['The ending of the employment took place through the employer'].
2. Baker (1992) uses the term 'textual equivalence' for both the **correspondences** between ST and TT with regard to the way information flows in the respective texts and to the cohesiveness created by devices that are each specific to the ST and TT. **(BB)**

FURTHER READING: Baker (1992); Catford (1965); Hatim (2001); Hatim and Munday (2004); Saussure (1993, 1996, 1997).

THICK TRANSLATION

A term coined by Appiah (1993/2004), drawing on the use of 'thick description' by the philosopher Gilbert Ryle (1971, as quoted in Hermans 2003) and, more prominently, the ethnographer Clifford Geertz (1973). In ethnography, thick description emphasized that interpretation was a 'self-conscious' (i.e. deliberate) action of the ethnographer, negotiating an understanding and at the same time forming a representation of the foreign object and culture, not a purely objective, impartial observation of reality; in translation studies, thick translation stresses that the source culture is being investigated by the use of foreign terms and concepts and consciously accepts that the form of investigation and interpretation may be manifold. No one interpretation holds the whole truth. Hermans (2003: 386) sees thick translation as a means of countering 'the universalizing urge of theory' that, in translation studies, has tended to be grounded in European-oriented languages, disciplines and methodologies. **(JM)**

FURTHER READING: Appiah (1993/2004); Hermans (2003).

THINK-ALOUD PROTOCOLS (TAPS)

Think-Aloud Protocols (TAPs), also known as introspective verbal reports, are a type of data source stemming from psychology which consists of recording verbalizations about mental processes while or after a task is performed. In the application of TAPs to the investigation of the translation processes, subjects are asked to verbalize their thoughts, which are then recorded and later transcribed. Most TAPs are concurrent reports collected while a translation task is performed, but retrospective protocols, collected immediately after the translation task has been completed, and dialogued protocols, collected with direct intervention of researchers in the questioning of events, have also been used. The first TAPs used in translation studies go back to the mid-1980s for the study of written translation. (**AHA** and **FA**)

FURTHER READING: Krings (1986); Sandrock (1982); Tirkkonen-Condit and Jääskeläinen (2000). See also Hurtado Albir and Alves (Chapter 4, this volume).

THIRD CODE/LANGUAGE

A term used to describe translations as a language product existing between SL and TL texts; in this sense a translation is a sub-code to the ST code and the codes of TL texts. According to Frawley (1984), a translation is written in its own style, i.e. it is a code displaying typical lexical, syntactic and textual characteristics, including **explicitation**, simplification and so on. In the case of these features being required by the process of translation (e.g. adjustments to the TT culture) they are perceived as positive, but if there is an unusually high frequency of occurrences present, the translation is perceived negatively (e.g. Baker 1993). The latter case is usually referred to as '**translationese**' (e.g. Gellerstam 1986). **(BB)**

FURTHER READING: Baker (1993, 1998); Baroni and Bernardini (2006); Frawley (1984); Gellerstam (1986); Laviosa (1998); Lind (2007); Olohan and Baker (2000); Øverås (1998); Toury (1995).

TL, SEE TARGET LANGUAGE

TRANSCRIPTION

In translation studies, this term is generally used to refer to the written version of an oral text, for example of the screen dialogue in **audiovisual translation** or of the output in an **interpreting** scenario. **(JM)**

TRANSFER

The second of three phases in Nida and Taber's (1969/1974) outline of the translation process. The first stage concerns the **analysis** of the meaning of the SL text, during which **kernel** sentences are determined. During the subsequent transfer phase, which serves as a connection between the ST and the TT, the SL meanings are mentally 'taken across' by the translator to the TL, whereby it is important that the SL meanings are preserved. The focus in the third phase is on the TT readership and on the restructuring of the transferred kernel sentences in terms of **register**, **style**, additions and so on. **(BB)**

FURTHER READING: Beekman and Callow (1974); Glassman (1981); Hatim (2001); Hatim and Munday (2004); Nida (1969); Nida and Taber (1969/1974); Shuttleworth and Cowie (1997).

TRANSLATESE, SEE TRANSLATIONESE

TRANSLATION COMPETENCE

The set of knowledge, abilities and attitudes that a translator/interpreter must possess in order to perform adequately his/her professional activity. It is a type of expert knowledge combining declarative knowledge (knowing what) and procedural knowledge (knowing how), being predominantly procedural. Translation competence is formed by several interrelated components or sub-competences, the most important of which are communicative and textual competence in two (or more) languages; extra-linguistic competence (encyclopaedic, cultural and content knowledge as well as knowledge about translation); instrumental competence (the ability to use relevant documentation sources and technological tools applied to translation); professional competence (knowledge about the work market); and strategic competence (related to problem solving and decision making). Translation competence is an acquired skill which undergoes different phases, evolving from novice to expert knowledge.

There are several models of translation competence, most of which are componential models aimed at describing the components of this specific competence (PACTE 2000, 2003, 2005; D. Kelly 2002, 2005; Shreve 2006; Alves and Gonçalves 2007, etc.). Some authors criticize these componential models and adopt a minimalist perspective for a definition of translation competence (Pym 1992, 2003).

Other models attempt to explain the acquisition of translation competence (Alves and Gonçalves 2007; Chesterman 1997a; PACTE 2000; Shreve 1997, 2006, etc.). They all agree that translation competence is an acquired skill and that there are several phases in the acquisition process. (**AHA** and **FA**)

FURTHER READING: Hurtado Albir and Alves (Chapter 4, this volume).

TRANSLATION PROCEDURE

A term used by Vinay and Darbelnet to describe the linguistic means adopted by translators to change ST items into TT items. Vinay and Darbelnet's seven procedures are **borrowing**, **calque**, **literal translation**, **transposition**, **modulation**, **equivalence and adaptation**. These are divided into two general strategies: **literal translation** and **oblique translation**. (**JM**)

FURTHER READING: Vinay and Darbelnet (1958, 1958/2004); Munday (2001/2008).

TRANSLATION PROCESS

A mental activity performed by a translator/interpreter allowing him/her to render an ST (oral, written, audiovisual, etc.), formulated in an SL, into a TT using the resources of a TL. It is a complex cognitive process which has an interactive and non-linear nature, encompassing controlled and uncontrolled processes, and requiring processes of **problem solving** and decision making, and the use of strategies. Its specific characteristics vary according to the type of translation (written, oral, audiovisual, etc.).

The translation process has basic phases related to the processes of comprehension and re-expression. Both phases require the association of linguistic knowledge (pragmatic, sociolinguistic, textual, morph-syntactic and lexical knowledge) and extra-linguistic knowledge (encyclopaedic, cultural and content knowledge as well as knowledge about translation) available in the translator's memory. Strategies of internal support (including different cognitive operations) and external support (including the use of relevant documentation sources and technological tools applied to translation) play a role in the unfolding of the translation process to allow for the solution of comprehension/re-expression problems and decision making.

These basic phases are similar to the functioning of comprehension/ expression processes in monolingual communication. Nevertheless, the comprehension phase in the translation process requires from a translator/ interpreter a more deliberate and analytical process, which is determined by the fact that one has to produce a new text in another language and in another sociocultural context. As far as the process of re-expression is concerned, the translator/interpreter must take into consideration the meaning conveyed by the ST, the characteristics and expectations of the audience of the TT and its goals. There are several models of the translation process. (**AHA** and **FA**)

FURTHER READING: Hurtado Albir and Alves (Chapter 4, this volume).

TRANSLATION SHIFTS, SEE SHIFTS IN TRANSLATION

TRANSLATION UNIVERSALS, SEE UNIVERSALS OF TRANSLATION

TRANSLATIONESE

A pejorative general term for the language of translation (cf. Duff's 'third language'), often indicating a stilted form of the TL resulting from the influence of ST lexical or syntactic patterning. It is thus linked to the concept of **interference**. (**JM**)

FURTHER READING: Duff (1981); Gellerstam (1986); Spivak (1992/2004).

TRANSLATORIAL ACTION

A model proposed by Holz-Mänttäri. Using concepts from communication theory and action theory, she views translation as a form of human interaction that focuses on the purpose and outcome. This emphasis on the outcome and the TT links translatorial action with the *skopos* **theory** of the time. Holz-Mänttäri investigates the roles of initiator, commissioner, ST producer, TT producer, TT user and TT receiver. (**JM**)

FURTHER READING: Holz-Mänttäri (1984); Munday (2001/2008); Schäffner (1998a); Snell-Hornby (2006).

TRANSLITERATION

1. The one-by-one rendering of individual letters and signs of an SL item in one alphabet with the closest corresponding letters and signs of another alphabet. For instance, the Arabic letters ب (bā'), ن (nūn) and ي (yā') can be transliterated using the Latin letters *b*, *n* and *y* respectively. Words consisting of a combination of letters and signs are transliterated

character by character. For example, the Arabic word for *female cat* → هِرَّة can be transliterated into English as *hirra*, whereby the letter *h* corresponds to the Arabic letter ﻫ (hā'), *r* to ر (rā'), the second *r* to the sign ˜, and the letter *a* to ة (tā' marbūta). The diacritical mark ˜ (shadda) above the letter ر (rā') indicates that this consonant is emphatic. Transliteration should not be confused with *transcription*, which takes the phonology of a language into account.
2. In American Sign Language (ASL) transliteration refers to one of the two tasks signed-language interpreters are proficient in, the other being **interpreting**. Transliteration means that spoken English words are translated into Signed Exact English (SEE) or Cued Speech (which combines hand shapes with mouth movements). Interpretation occurs when spoken English is translated into ASL and vice versa. **(BB)**

FURTHER READING: Barry (1997); Isham Wellisch (1975, 1976, 1978).

TRANSPOSITION

One of Vinay and Darbelnet's (1958) four **oblique translation** procedures. Transposition concerns grammatical shifts in the TT without changing the meaning of the ST segment, which means that the meaning of the ST expression or parts of it are assumed by different grammatical TL elements. Vinay and Darbelnet, who consider transposition as the most commonly occurring **translation procedure**, classify it according to whether the grammatical shifts are required due to TL constraints, e.g. German *die Möbel* (pl.) → English *furniture* (sing.), or whether they are optional, e.g. German *Die Arbeit im Garten hellte seine Stimmung auf* → English *Working in the garden, his mood lifted; His mood lifted when he worked in the garden; The gardening work lifted his mood*). Vinay and Darbelnet distinguish various types of transposition, including verb–noun, adverb–verb, noun–adverb, noun–preposition, crossed shifts and so on. **(BB)**

FURTHER READING: Hatim and Munday (2004); Munday (2001/2008); Newmark (1988); Vinay and Darbelnet (1958, 1958/2004).

TRIANGULATION

A multi-methodological perspective which aims at explaining a given phenomenon from several vantage points combining quantitative and qualitative methods. Data can thus be cross-analysed and researchers can overcome the limitations caused by the use of a sole method of investigation (distortion of results, artificiality, etc.). For an object of study as complex as translation, triangulation appears to be a productive way of conducting experimental research. See also **Empirical-experimental research**. **(AHA** and **FA)**

FURTHER READING: Alves (2003).

TT, see **Target Text**

Undertranslation

A term for the translation of an ST segment which results in an oversimplified TT version, in which meaning aspects of the ST have been generalized or even been lost during the process of **meaning** transfer from ST to TT. Opposed to **overtranslation**. Undertranslation tends to occur when the rendering of the communicative effect of the ST is in the foreground rather than the pure communication of the ST information, or when translators fail to comprehend ST meaning, either partially or in full. It is possible to detect undertranslation through the lack of idioms in the TL, the use of a style that adheres too closely to the ST style in terms of word order and syntax, and the use of inexact terms and phrases. For example, in the TT sentence *Das SSR-Projekt, das in diesem Forschungszentrum durchgeführt wird, wurde letztes Jahr begonnen* ('The SSR-Project, which will be carried out in this research centre, was begun last year'), the English source term *SSR-Project* is undertranslated as the German audience is likely to require some explanation of what this is and does. **(BB)**

Further reading: Dussart (2005); Newmark (1988, 1991); Rock (2006); Shuttleworth and Cowie (2007); Vinay and Darbelnet (1958).

Unit of Translation

Communicative and cognitive unity employed by a translator/interpreter in the performance of a translation task. The translation unit can be considered from two perspectives: as a (bi)textual unit, and as a cognitive unit. From a textual perspective, it is embedded in a complex relationship with all the other units in a given text. Hurtado Albir (2001) distinguishes between micro-units (communicative units conveying sense), intermediate units, differing according to the type of translation (paragraph and chapter in written translation; the take in **dubbing**; the subtitle in **subtitling**; callouts in comic strips, etc.), and macro-units (the whole text). Cognitively speaking, the translation unit is considered as a comprehension unit and as a processing unit, i.e. as a dynamic segment of the ST, independent of specific size or form, to which, at a given moment, the translator's focus of attention is directed, enabling the translator to process the unit according to his/her cognitive needs (Alves 1997). (**AHA** and **FA**)

Universals of Translation

Features that are considered to characterize translated language and texts in whatever language pair. Universals that have been proposed include lexical and syntactic simplification, **explicitation** and normalization to TL patterns.

Such universals are linked to the concept of **laws of translation** such as growing standardization and **interference** (Toury 1995). Methods from **corpus-based translation studies** are useful in investigating large amounts of data but the concept of a true universal (i.e. a feature that occurs in every translated text) is doubtful; Toury (2004), for example, emphasizes the probabilistic nature of the concept since the only true translation universal would be **shifts in translation**. **(JM)**

FURTHER READING: Baker (1993); Blum-Kulka and Levenston (1983); Laviosa (1998); Toury (1995, 2004).

VOICE-OVER

Voice-over generally tends to be used as a translational modality in informative, non-fictional screen products such as news programmes, advertisements and documentaries. In voice-over the underlying original language will be slightly noticeable, apart from the initial and final utterances of the original narrator and the insertion of the odd sound bite, i.e. a short piece of footage of the original soundtrack which is not covered by the new TL audio. For example, a chunk of speech may be given prominence by being made perceptible through a short and temporary silencing of the voice-over but it cannot be clearly perceived. **(DC)**

WHISPERED INTERPRETING

Whispered interpreting, also known by the French term *chuchotage*, is **simultaneous interpreting** without an interpreting booth. It is practised in **liaison interpreting** as well as conference settings to provide simultaneous interpreting for one or two listeners, by an interpreter seated next to them and speaking in a low voice so as not to disturb other participants. While acoustic conditions make traditional whispering very strenuous, the use of 'whispering' for small groups has been facilitated by portable equipment (referred to by the French word *bidule*) that enables the interpreter to speak into a microphone and listeners to receive the interpretation via cordless headsets, ideally with the interpreter receiving the original speech via a headset as well. **(FP)**

WORD-FOR-WORD TRANSLATION

A form of translation in which each ST linguistic element is replaced by its closest target-language correspondent. It is therefore sometimes used, as by Cicero (46 BCE), to mean a close **literal** translation (cf. Vinay and Darbelnet 1958: *les lunettes son sur la table – the spectacles are on the table*). It is the opposite of **sense-for-sense** translation. However, it is also sometimes used in the sense of **back translation**. **(JM)**

ZERO TRANSLATION

A type of deliberate **omission**. It characterizes a translation situation in which an ST item is not translated by an established TT equivalent because the **meaning** of the ST item is assumed or implied by another or several other TT items. During pre-translation analysis, translators typically break down an ST segment (e.g. phrase, clause or sentence) into several meaningful **units of translation**. For example, the sentence *Please read these safety instructions and the operation instructions provided in this booklet* may be subdivided into the units *please – read – these safety instructions – and – the operation instructions – provided – in the booklet*. A juxtaposition of these units with those from the German translation *Lesen Sie diese Sicherheits- und Betriebshinweise* ('Read you these safety- and operation instructions') results in the following pairs, where the symbol Ø indicates a zero translation: *Please – Ø; read – Lesen Sie; these safety instructions – diese Sicherheits-/Ø; und – and; the operation instructions – Betriebshinweise; provided – Ø; in this booklet – Ø*. **(BB)**

FURTHER READING: Aijmer and Altenberg (2002); Hatim and Munday (2004); Nida (1964); Vinay and Darbelnet (1958).

BIBLIOGRAPHY

Adab, B. and C. Valdés (eds) (2004) *Key Debates in the Translation of Advertising Material*, Special issue of *The Translator* 10(2).
Agar, M. (1994) *Language Shock: Understanding the culture of conversation*, New York: William Morrow.
Agar, M. (2006) 'Culture: can you take it anywhere?', *International Journal of Qualitative Methods*, 5(2): 1–12.
Aijmer, K. and B. Altenberg (2002) 'Zero translations and cross-linguistic equivalence: evidence from the English-Swedish parallel corpus', in L. E. Breivik and A. Hasselgren (eds) *From the COLT's Mouth ... and Others: Language corpora studies, in honour of Anna-Brita Stenström*, Amsterdam and New York: Rodopi, pp. 19–41.
Allen, G. (2000) *Intertextuality*, London and New York: Routledge.
Allen, J. (2003) 'Post-editing', in H. Somers (ed.) *Computers and Translation: A translator's guide*, Amsterdam and Philadelphia: John Benjamins, pp. 297–317.
Álvarez, R. and C.-A. Vidal (eds) (1996) *Translation, Power, Subversion*, Clevedon: Multilingual Matters.
Alves, F. (1995) *Zwischen Schweigen und Sprechen: Wie bildet sich eine transkulturelle Brücke? Eine psycholinguistisch orientierte Untersuchung von Übersetzungsvorgängen zwischen portugiesischen und brasilianischen Übersetzern*, Hamburg: Dr. Kovac.
Alves, F. (1997) 'A formação de tradutores a partir de uma abordagem cognitiva: reflexões de um projeto de ensino', *TradTerm*, 4(2): 19–40.
Alves, F. (ed.) (2003) *Triangulating Translation: Perspectives in process oriented research*, Amsterdam and Philadelphia: John Benjamins.
Alves, F. (2005) 'Ritmo cognitivo, meta-reflexão e experiência: parâmetros de análise processual no desempenho de tradutores novatos e experientes', in F. Alves, C. Magalhães and A. Pagano (eds) *Competência em tradução: cognição e discurso*, Belo Horizonte: Ed. UFMG, pp. 109–69.
Alves, F. and J. L. Gonçalves (2007) 'Modelling translator's competence: Relevance and expertise under scrutiny', in Y. Gambier, M. Shlesinger and R. Stolze (eds) *Translation Studies: Doubts and directions: Selected papers from the IV Congress of the European Society for Translation Studies*, Amsterdam and Philadelphia: John Benjamins, pp. 41–55.
Amos, F. R. (1920/1973) *Early Theories of Translation*, New York: Octagon.
Anderman, G. and M. Rogers (eds) (2003) *Translation Today: Trends and perspectives*, Clevedon: Multilingual Matters.
Anderson, R. W. B. (1976/2002) 'Perspectives on the role of interpreter', in F. Pöchhacker and M. Shlesinger (eds) (2002) *The Interpreting Studies Reader*, London and New York: Routledge, pp. 209–17.

Angelelli, Claudia V. (2004) *Medical Interpreting and Cross-cultural Communication*, Cambridge: Cambridge University Press.

Antonini, R. (2005) 'The perception of subtitled humour in Italy: An empirical study', in D. Chiaro (ed.) *Humor International Journal of Humor Research*, Special Issue *Humor and Translation*, 18(2): 209–25.

Antonini, R. and D. Chiaro (2005) 'The quality of dubbed television programmes in Italy: The experimental design of an empirical study', in M. Bondi and N. Maxwell (eds) *Cross-Cultural Encounters: Linguistic perspectives*, Roma: Officina Edizioni, pp. 33–44.

Appiah, K. (1993/2004) 'Thick translation', *Callaloo*, 16: 808–19, reprinted in L. Venuti (2004) *The Translation Studies Reader*, 2nd edition, London and New York: Routledge, pp. 389–401.

Archer, C. M. (1986) 'Culture bump and beyond', in J. M. Valdes (ed.) *Culture Bound: Bridging the cultural gap in language teaching*, Cambridge: Cambridge University Press, pp. 170–78.

Arnold, D. (2003) 'Why translation is difficult for computers', in H. Somers (ed.) *Computers and Translation: A translator's guide*, Amsterdam and Philadelphia: John Benjamins, pp. 119–42.

Arnold, D., L. Balkan, R. L. Humphreys, S. Meijer and L. Sadler (1994) *Machine Translation: An introductory guide*, Oxford: Blackwell, available online http://www.essex.ac.uk/linguistics/clmt/MTbook/, visited 15/08/2008.

Arnold, M. ([1861]1978) *On Translating Homer*, London: AMS Press.

Arntz, R., Picht, H. and F. Mayer (2004) *Einführung in die Terminologiearbeit*, 5th edition, Studien zu Sprache und Technik, Hildesheim: Georg Olms.

Arrojo, R. (1994) 'Fidelity and the gendered translation', *TTR (Traduction, terminologie, rédaction)*, 7(2): 142–63.

Arrojo, R. (1995) '"Feminist Orgasmic": Theories of translation and their contradictions', *TradTerm* 2: 67–75.

Assis Rosa, A. (2001) 'Features of oral and written communication in subtitling', in Y. Gambier and H. Gottlieb (eds) *(Multi)Media Translation: Concepts, practices and research*, Amsterdam and Philadelphia: John Benjamins, pp. 213–21.

Attardo, S. and V. Raskin (1991) 'Script theory revis(it)ed: joke similarity and joke representation model', *Humor, International Journal of Humor Research*, 4(3–4): 293–347.

Augustine (Aurelius Augustinus) (428/1997) 'The use of translations', in D. Robinson (ed.) (1997) *Western Translation Theory: From Herodotus to Nietzsche*, Manchester: St. Jerome, pp. 30–34.

Austermühl, F. (2001) *Electronic Tools for Translators*, Manchester: St Jerome.

Austin, J. L. (1962) *How to do Things with Words*, Oxford: Clarendon Press, 2nd edition, Cambridge, MA: Harvard University Press, 1975.

Baigorri-Jalón, J. (2004) *De Paris à Nuremberg: Naissance de l'interprétation de conférence*, Ottawa, ON: University of Ottawa Press.

Bair, D. (1990) *Simone de Beauvoir: A biography*, London: Jonathan Cape.

Baker, M. (1992) *In Other Words: A coursebook on translation*, London and New York: Routledge.

BIBLIOGRAPHY

Baker, M. (1993) 'Corpus linguistics and translation studies: implications and applications', in M. Baker, G. Francis and E. Tognini-Bonelli (eds) *Text and Technology: In honour of John Sinclair*, Amsterdam and Philadelphia: John Benjamins, pp. 233–50.

Baker, M. (1997) 'Non-cognitive constraints and interpreter strategies in political interviews', in K. Simms (ed.) *Translating Sensitive Texts: Linguistic aspects*, Amsterdam and Atlanta, GA: Rodopi, pp. 111–29.

Baker, M. (1998) 'Réexplorer la langue de la traduction: une approche par corpus', *Meta*, 43(4): 480–85.

Baker, M. (2000) 'Towards a methodology for investigating the style of a literary translator', *Target*, 12: 241–66.

Baker, M. (2006) *Translation and Conflict: A narrative account*, London and New York: Routledge.

Baker, M. and K. Malmkjær (eds) (1998) *Routledge Encyclopedia of Translation Studies*, 1st edition, London and New York: Routledge.

Baker, M. and G. Saldanha (eds) (2008) *Routledge Encyclopedia of Translation Studies*, 2nd edition, London and New York: Routledge.

Bakhtin, M. (1981) *The Dialogic Imagination: Four Essays*, ed. M. Holquist, trans. C. Emerson and M. Holquist, Austin, Texas: University of Texas Press.

Bakhtin, M. M. (1986) *Speech Genres and Other Late Essays*, trans. V. W. McGee, Austin, Texas: University of Texas Press.

Bandia, P. (2007) *Translation as Reparation: Orality, writing and translation in postcolonial Africa*, Manchester: St. Jerome.

Bandler, R. and J. Grindler (1975) *The Structure of Magic I*, Palo Alto, CA: Science and Behavior Books.

Barik, H. C. (1975/2002) 'Simultaneous interpretation: qualitative and linguistic data', in F. Pöchhacker and M. Shlesinger (eds) (2002) *The Interpreting Studies Reader*, London and New York: Routledge, pp. 79–91.

Barkhudarov, L. (1969) 'Urovni yazykovoy iyerarkhii i perevod' [Levels of language hierarchy and translation], *Tetradi perevodchika* [The Translator's Notebooks], 6: 3–12.

Baroni, M. and S. Bernardini (2006) 'A new approach to the study of translationese: machine-learning the difference between original and translated text', *Literary and Linguistic Computing*, 21(3): 259–74.

Barry, R. K. (ed.) (1997) *ALA-LC Romanization Tables: Transliteration schemes for non-Roman scripts*, Washington, DC: Library of Congress and American Library Association.

Bartlett, F. C. (1932) *Remembering: A study in experimental and social psychology*, Cambridge: Cambridge University Press.

Bassnett, S. (1980/2002) *Translation Studies*, London and New York: Routledge.

Bassnett, S. and A. Lefevere (eds) (1990) *Translation, History and Culture*, London and New York: Pinter.

Bassnett, S. and A. Lefevere (1998) *Constructing Cultures: Essays on literary translation*, Clevedon: Multilingual Matters.

Bassnett, S. and H. Trivedi (eds) (1999) *Post-Colonial Translation: Theory and practice*, London and New York: Routledge.

Bastin, G. (1998) 'Adaptation', in M. Baker and K. Malmkjær (eds), *Routledge Encyclopedia of Translation Studies*, 1st edition, London and New York: Routledge pp. 5–8.

Bateson, G. (1972) *Steps to an Ecology of Mind*, New York: Ballantine Books.

Beaugrande, R. de (1980) *Text, Discourse and Process*, London and New York: Longman.

Beaugrande, R. de and W. Dressler (1981) *Introduction to Text Linguistics*, London and New York: Longman.

Beeby, A. (1996) *Teaching Translation from Spanish to English*, Ottawa, ON: University of Ottawa Press.

Beekman, J. and J. Callow (1974) *Translating the Word of God*, Grand Rapids, MI: Zondervan Publishing House.

Bell, R. T. (1991) *Translation and Translating: Theory and practice*, London and New York: Longman.

Bell, R. T. (1998) 'Psycholinguistic/cognitive approaches', in M. Baker and K. Malmkjær (eds) *Routledge Encyclopedia of Translation Studies*, 1st edition, London and New York: Routledge, pp. 185–90.

Benjamin, W. (1923/2004) 'The task of the translator: an introduction to the translation of Baudelaire's *Tableaux Parisiens*', trans. H. Zohn, in L. Venuti (ed.) *The Translation Studies Reader*, 2nd edition, London and New York: Routledge, pp. 75–85.

Bennett, K. (2007) 'Epistemicide! The Tale of a Predatory Discourse', *The Translator* 13.2: 151–69.

Bennett, M. J. (1993) 'Towards ethnorelativism: a developmental model of intercultural sensitivity', in M. R. Paige (ed.) *Education for the Intercultural Experience*, Yarmouth, ME: Intercultural Press Inc., pp. 22–73.

Bennett, M. J. (1998) 'Intercultural communication: a current perspective', in M. J. Bennett (ed.) *Basic Concepts of Intercultural Communication: Selected readings*, Yarmouth, ME: Intercultural Press Inc., pp. 1–34.

Bennett, W. S. (1996) 'System demonstration: logos intelligent translation system', in *Expanding MT Horizons*, Proceedings of the Second Conference of the Association for Machine Translation in the Americas, 2–5 October 1996, Montreal, QC, Washington, DC: AMTA, pp. 264–67.

Bentahila, A. (2004) 'The transfer of cultural and pragmatic norms: examples from letter-writing', in *Interaction entre culture et traduction*, Actes du symposium international organisé à Tanger les 13, 14 et 15 mars 2002 par l'Ecole Supérieure Roi Fahd de Traduction, Tangiers: l'Ecole Supérieure Roi Fahd de Traduction, pp. 75–82.

Berk-Seligson, S. (1988/2002) 'The impact of politeness in witness testimony: the influence of the court interpreter', in F. Pöchhacker and M. Shlesinger (eds) (2002) *The Interpreting Studies Reader*, London and New York: Routledge, pp. 279–92.

Berk-Seligson, S. (1990/2002) *The Bilingual Courtroom: Court interpreters in the judicial process*, Chicago: The University of Chicago Press.

Berman, A. (1985/2004) 'Translations and the trials of the foreign', in L. Venuti (ed.) (2004) *The Translation Studies Reader*, 2nd edition, London and New York: Routledge, pp. 276–89.

Berman, A. (1992) *The Experience of the Foreign: Culture and translation in Romantic Germany*, trans. S. Heyvaert, Albany, NY: State University of New York Press.

Berman, A. (1995) *Pour une critique des traductions: John Donne*, Paris: Gallimard.

Bermann, S. and M. Wood (eds) (2005) *Nation, Language, and the Ethics of Translation*, Princeton, NJ, and Oxford: Princeton University Press.

Bernal Merino, M. (2006) 'On the translation of video games', *JoSTrans: Journal of Specialized Translation*, 6: 22–36.

Bhabha, H. K. (1994) *The Location of Culture*, London and New York: Routledge.

Bhatia, V. K. (1993) *Analysing Genre: Language use in professional settings*, London and New York: Longman.

Billiani, F. (ed.) (2007) *Modes of Censorship and Translation: National context and diverse media*, Manchester: St Jerome.

Blench, M. (2007) 'Global Public Health Intelligence Network (GPHIN)', in *Proceedings of MT Summit XI*, pp. 45–9, http://www.mt-archive.info/MTS-2007-Blench.pdf, visited 15/08/2008.

Blum-Kulka, S. (1986/2004) 'Shifts of cohesion and coherence in translation', in L. Venuti (ed.) (2004) *The Translation Studies Reader*, 2nd edition, London and New York: Routledge, pp. 290–305.

Blum-Kulka, S. and E. Levenston (1983) 'Universals of lexical simplification', in C. Faerch and G. Kasper (eds) *Strategies in Interlanguage Communication*, London and New York: Longman, pp. 119–39.

Boase-Beier, J. (ed.) (2004) *Translation and Style*, Special issue of *Language and Literature*, 13(1).

Boase-Beier, J. (2006) *Stylistic Approaches to Translation*, Manchester: St Jerome.

Bollettieri Bosinelli, R. M. (1994) 'Film dubbing: linguistic and cultural issues', *Il traduttore nuovo*, XLII(1): 7–28.

Bosseaux, C. (2007) *How Does It Feel? Point of view in translation*, Amsterdam: Rodopi.

Boucau, F. (2006) *The European Translation Markets: Updated facts and figures 2006–2010*, Brussels: EUATC.

Bourdieu, P. (1990) *The Logic of Practice*, Stanford: Stanford University Press.

Bourdieu, P. (1992) *The Field of Cultural Production: Essays in art and literature*, Cambridge: Polity.

Bowen, M. (1995) 'Interpreters and the making of history', in J. Delisle and J. Woodsworth (eds) *Translators Through History*, Amsterdam and Philadelphia: John Benjamins, pp. 245–73.

Bowker, L. (2002) *Computer-Aided Techology: A practical introduction*, Ottawa: Ottawa University Press.

Bowker, L. and J. Pearson (2002) *Working with Specialized Languages: A practical guide to using corpora*, London and New York: Routledge.

Braden, G., R. Cummings, and T. Hermans (eds) (2004) *The Oxford History of Literary Translation in English. Volume II: 1550–1660*, Oxford: Oxford University Press.

Brisset, A. (1996) *A Sociocritique of Translation: Theatre and alterity in Quebec, 1968–1988*, trans. R. Gill and R. Gannon, Toronto: University of Toronto Press, originally published (1990) *Sociocritique de la traduction*.

Brisset, A. (2003) 'Alterity in translation: an overview of theories and practices', in S. Petrilli (ed.) *Translation Translation*, Amsterdam and New York: Rodopi, pp. 101–32.

Britten, B. (1964) *On Receiving the First Aspen Award*, London: Faber and Faber.

Brown, M. H. (1994) *The Reception of Spanish American Fiction in West Germany 1981–91*, Tübingen: Niemeyer.

Bruce, D. (1994) 'Translating the commune: cultural politics and the historical specificity of the anarchist text', *TTR (Traduction, terminologie, rédaction)*, 1(1): 47–76.

Bruce, I. (2007) *Academic Writing and Genre: A systematic analysis*, London: Continuum.

Brunette, L., G. Bastin, I. Hemlin, and H. Clarke (eds) (2003) *The Critical Link 3: Interpreters in the community*, Amsterdam and Philadelphia: John Benjamins.

Bucaria, C. (2007) 'Humour and other catastrophes: dealing with the translation of mixed TV genres', *Linguistica Antverpiensia New Series*, Special Issue *Audiovisual Translation: A tool for social integration*, 6: 235–54.

Buchweitz, A. (2006) 'Two languages, two input modalities, one brain: An fMRI study of Portuguese-English bilinguals and Portuguese listening and reading comprehension effects on brain activation', unpublished PhD thesis, Universidade Federal de Santa Catarina (UFSC), Brazil.

Bühler, K. (1934/1965) *Sprachtheorie: Die Darstellungsfunktion der Sprache*, Stuttgart: Gustav Fischer.

Bush, P. (1998) 'Pure language', in M. Baker and K. Malmkjær (eds) (1998) *Routledge Encyclopedia of Translation Studies*, 1st edition, London and New York: Routledge, pp. 194–96.

Buzelin, H. (2005) 'Unexpected allies: how Latour's network theory could complement Bourdieusian analyses in translation studies', *The Translator*, 11(2): 193–218.

Calvino, I (1993) *Gli amori difficili*, Milan: Mondadori.

Calzada Pérez, M. (ed.) (2003) *Apropos of Ideology: Translation studies on ideology – Ideologies in translation studies*, Manchester: St. Jerome.

Campbell, S. (1998) *Translation into the Second Language*, London and New York: Longman.

Candlin, C. N. (1985) 'Preface', in M. Coulthard, *Introduction to Discourse Analysis*, London and New York: Longman, pp. vii–x.

Candlin, C. N. and M. Gotti (2004) *Intercultural Aspects of Specialized Communication*, Frankfurt am Main, Berlin and Bern: Peter Lang.

Carl, M. and A. Way (eds) (2006/7) Special issue on example-based Machine Translation, *Machine Translation* 19(3–4) and 20(1).

Carr, S. E., R. Roberts, A. Dufour and D. Steyn (eds) (1997) *The Critical Link: Interpreters in the community*, Amsterdam and Philadelphia: John Benjamins.

Carson, D. A. (1996) *Exegetical Fallacies*, 2nd edition, Grand Rapids, MI: Baker Academic.

Carter, R., A. Goddard, D. Reah, K. Sanger and M. Bowring (1997) *Working with Texts: A core book for language analysis*, London and New York: Routledge.

Casagrande, J. (1954) 'The ends of translation', *International Journal of American Linguistics*, 20: 335–40.
Catford, J. C. (1965) *A Linguistic Theory of Translation*, Oxford: Oxford University Press.
Cenkova, I. (1989) 'L'importance des pauses en interprétation simultanée', in *Mélanges de phonétique générale et expérimentale*, Publications de l'Institut de Phonétique de Strasbourg, pp. 249–60.
Chamberlain, L. (1988/1992) 'Gender and the metaphorics of translation', in L. Venuti (ed.) *Rethinking Translation: Discourse, subjectivity, ideology*, London and New York: Routledge, pp. 57–74, originally published (1988) in *Signs: Journal of Women and Culture and Society*, 13(3): 454–72.
Chamizo Domínguez, P. J. (2007) *Semantics and Pragmatics of False Friends*, London and New York: Routledge.
Chamizo Domínguez, P. J. and B. Nerlich (2002) 'False friends: their origin and semantics in some selected languages', *Journal of Pragmatics*, 34(12): 1833–49.
Chan, Leo Takhung (ed.) (2004) *Twentieth-century Chinese Translation Theory*, Amsterdam and Philadelphia: John Benjamins.
Chan, S.-W. and D. Pollard (eds) (1995) *An Encyclopaedia of Translation: Chinese-English, English-Chines*, Hong Kong: Chinese University Press.
Chandler, H. (2005) *The Game Localization Handbook*, Hingham, MA: Charles River Media.
Chaume, F. (2004) 'Film Studies and Translation Studies: Two Disciplines at Stake in Audiovisual Translation', *Meta*, 49(1): 12–24.
Chaume, F. (2006) 'Interview with Frederic Chaume', *JoSTrans: Journal of Specialized Translation*, 6(July), http://www.jostrans.org/issue06/int_chaume.php, visited 15/08/2008.
Chaume, F. (2007) 'Dubbing practices in Europe: localisation beats globalization', *Linguistica Antverpiensia New Series*, Special Issue *Audiovisual Translation: A tool for social integration*, 6: 154–67.
Chen, S.J. (2006) 'Real-time subtitling in Taiwan', *Intralinea*, Special Issue *Respeaking*, www.intralinea.it/specials/respeaking/eng_more.php?id=455_0_41_0_M, visited 15/08/2008.
Chernov, G. V. (1979/2002) 'Semantic aspects of psycholinguistic research in simultaneous interpretation', *Language and Speech*, 22(3): 277–96, reprinted in F. Pöchhacker and M. Shlesinger (eds) (2002) *The Interpreting Studies Reader*, London and New York: Routledge, pp. 99–109.
Chernov, G. V. (1994) 'English message redundancy and message anticipation in simultaneous interpreting', in S. Lambert and B. Moser-Mercer (eds) *Bridging the Gap: Empirical research in simultaneous interpretation*, Amsterdam and New York: John Benjamins, pp. 139–53.
Chernov, G. V. (2004) *Inference and Anticipation in Simultaneous Interpreting: A probability-prediction model*, Amsterdam and Philadelphia: John Benjamins.
Chesterman, A. (ed.) (1989) *Readings in Translation Theory*, Helsinki: Oy Finn Lectura Ab.

Chesterman, A. (1993) 'From "is" to "ought": translation laws, norms and strategies', *Target*, 5(1): 1–20.
Chesterman, A. (1997a) *Memes of Translation: The spread of ideas in translation theory*, Amsterdam and Philadelphia: John Benjamins.
Chesterman, A. (1997b) 'Ethics of translation', in M. Snell-Hornby, Z. Jettmarová and K. Kaindl (eds) (1997) *Translation as Intercultural Communication: Selected papers from the EST Congress, Prague 1995*, Amsterdam and Philadelphia: John Benjamins, pp. 147–57.
Chesterman, A. (2001) 'Proposal for a Hieronymic oath', *The Translator*, 7: 139–54.
Chesterman, A. (2002) 'On the interdisciplinarity of translation studies', *Logos* 3(1): 1–9.
Chesterman, A. (2005) *On Definiteness: A study with special reference to English and Finnish*, Cambridge: Cambridge University Press.
Chesterman, A. (2007) 'Bridge concepts in translation sociology', in M. Wolf and A. Fukari (eds) *Constructing a sociology of translation*, Amsterdam and Philadelphia: John Benjamins, pp. 171–83.
Chesterman, A. and R. Arrojo (2000) 'Shared ground in translation studies', *Target* 12(1): 151–60.
Cheung, M. (ed.) (2006) *An Anthology of Chinese Discourse on Translation: From earliest times to the Buddhist project*, Vol. 1, Manchester: St. Jerome.
Cheyfitz, E. (1991) *The Poetics of Imperialism: Translation and colonization from 'The Tempest' to 'Tarzan'*, Oxford: Oxford University Press.
Chiaro, D. (1996) 'The translation game/La moglie del soldato – dubbing Neil Jordan', in C. Heiss and R. M. Bollettieri Bosinelli (eds) *Traduzione multimediale per il cinema, la televisione e la scena*, Bologna: CLUEB, pp. 131–8.
Chiaro, D. (2000a) 'Servizio completo: on the (un)translatability of puns on screen', in R. M. Bollettieri Bosinelli, C. Heiss, M. Soffritti and S. Bernardini (eds) *La Traduzione Multimediale: Quale traduzione per quale testo?* Bologna: CLUEB, pp. 27–42.
Chiaro, D. (2000b) 'The British will use tag questions, won't they? The case of Four Weddings and a Funeral', in C. Taylor (ed.) *Tradurre il Cinema*, Trieste: Università degli Studi di Trieste, pp. 27–39.
Chiaro, D. (2002) 'Linguistic mediation on Italian television: when the interpreter is not an interpreter – a case study', in G. Garzone and M. Viezzi (eds) *Interpreting in the 21st Century: Challenges and opportunities*, Amsterdam and New York: John Benjamins, pp. 215–25.
Chiaro, D. (ed.) (2005) *Humor, International Journal of Humor Research*, Special Issue *Humor and Translation*, 18(2).
Chiaro, D. (2006) 'Verbally expressed humour on screen: Reflections on translation and reception', *JoSTrans: Journal of Specialized Translation*, 6: 198–208, http://www.jostrans.org/issue06/art_chiaro.php, visited 15/08/2008.
Chiaro, D. (2007) 'Not in front of the children? An analysis of sex on screen in Italy', *Linguistica Antverpiensia New Series*, Special Issue *Audiovisual Translation: A tool for social integration*, 6: 255–76.

Chiaro, D. (2008) 'Humor and translation', in V. Raskin (ed.) *The Primer of Humor Research*, Berlin and New York: Mouton de Gruyter, pp. 573–612.

Chiaro, D. (forthcoming a) 'The politics of screen translation', in F. Federici (ed.) Selected papers from *Translating Voices, Translating Regions*, Second International Conference held at the University of Durham, UK, September 2007, Rome: Aracne.

Chiaro, D. (forthcoming b) 'In English please!' Lost in Translation: 'Little Britain' and Italian Audiences', in S. Lockyer (ed.) *Reading Little Britain*, London: I. B. Tauris.

Church, K., W. Gale, P. Hanks and D. Hindl (1991) 'Using statistics in lexical analysis', in U. Zernik (ed.) Lexical Acquisition, Englewood Cliff: Lawrence Erlbaum, pp. 115–64.

Cicero, M. T. (46 BCE/1997 CE) 'The best kind of orator', trans. H. M. Hubbell, in D. Robinson (ed.) 1997, *Western Translation Theory: From Herodotus to Nietzsche*, Manchester: St. Jerome, 7–10.

Clark, B., J. Drugan, T. Hartley and D. Wu (2006) 'Training for localization', in A. Pym et al. (eds) *Translation Technology and its Teaching*, Tarragona: Intercultural Studies Group, pp. 45–7.

Classe, O. (ed.) (2000) *Encyclopedia of Literary Translation into English*, Chicago: Fitzroy.

Clifford, J. and G. Marcus (eds) (1986) *Writing Culture: The poetics and politics of ethnography*, Berkeley, CA: University of California Press.

Cohen, E. (1972) 'Towards a sociology of international tourism', *Social Research*, 39(1): 164–82.

Cohen, L. and L. Manion (1980) *Research Methods in Education*, London: Croom Helm.

Collados Aís, Á. (1998) *La evaluación de la calidad en interpretación simultánea: la importancia de la comunicación no verbal*, Granada: Comares.

Collados Aís, Á. (1998/2002) 'Quality assessment in simultaneous interpreting: the importance of nonverbal communication', in F. Pöchhacker and M. Shlesinger (eds) (2002), *The Interpreting Studies Reader*, London and New York: Routledge, pp. 327–36.

Collados Aís, Á., M. Fernández Sánchez, and D. Gile (eds) (2003) *La evaluación de la calidad en interpretación: investigación*, Granada: Comares.

Collados Aís, Á., O. García Becerra, E. M. Pradas Macías and E. Stévaux (eds) (2007) *La evaluación de la calidad en interpretación simultánea: parámetros de incidencia*, Granada: Comares.

Connor, U. (1996) *Contrastive Rhetoric: Cross-cultural aspects of second-language writing*, Cambridge: Cambridge University Press.

Corbin, R. M. (1980) 'Decisions that might not get made', in T. E. Wallsten (ed.) *Cognitive Processes in Choice and Decision Behaviour*, Hillsdale, NJ: Erlbaum, pp. 47–67.

Coulthard, M. (1985) *Introduction to Discourse Analysis*, London and New York: Longman.

Crisafulli, E. (1996) 'Dante's puns and the question of compensation', in D. Delabastita (ed.) *The Translator*, Extended Special Issue *Wordplay and Translation*, 2(2): 259–76.

Cronin, M. (1996) *Translating Ireland: Translation, languages, cultures*, Cork: Cork University Press.
Cronin, M. (2003) *Translation and Globalization*, London and New York: Routledge.
Cronin, M. (2006) *Translation and Identity*, London and New York: Routledge.
Crystal, D. (2003) *A Dictionary of Linguistics and Phonetics*, 5th edition, Oxford: Blackwell Publishing Ltd.
Cunico, S. and J. Munday (eds) (2007) *Translation and Ideology: Encounters and clashes*, Special Issue of *The Translator*, 13(2).
Dancette, J. (1994) 'Comprehension in the translation process: an analysis of think-aloud protocols', in C. Dollerup and A. Lindegaard (eds) *Teaching Translation and Interpreting 2*, Amsterdam and Philadelphia: John Benjamins, pp. 113–20.
Darò, V. (1989) 'The role of memory and attention in simultaneous interpretation: a neurolinguistic approach', *The Interpreter's Newsletter*, 2: 50–56.
Darò, V. (1994) 'Non-linguistic factors influencing simultaneous interpretation', in S. Lambert and B. Moser-Mercer (eds) *Bridging the Gap: Empirical research in simultaneous interpretation*, Amsterdam and Philadelphia: John Benjamins, pp. 249–72.
Darò, V. (1997) 'Experimental studies on memory in conference interpretation', *Meta*, 42(4): 622–8.
Darò, V. and F. Fabbro (1994) 'Verbal memory during simultaneous interpretation: effects of phonological interference', *Applied Linguistics*, 15: 337–41.
Darò, V., S. Lambert and F. Fabbro (1996) 'Conscious monitoring of attention during simultaneous interpretation', *Interpreting*, 1(1): 101–24.
Delabastita (1989) 'Translation and mass-communication: Film- and T.V.-translation as evidence of cultural dynamics', *Babel*, 35.4: 193–218.
Delabastita, D. (1990) 'Translation and the mass media', in S. Bassnett and A. Lefevere (eds) *Translation, History and Culture*, London and New York: Printer, pp. 97–109.
Delabastita, D. (ed.) (1996) *Wordplay and Translation*, Special Issue of *The Translator*, 2(2).
Delabastita, D. (1997) *Traductio: Essays on punning and translation*, Manchester: St. Jerome.
Deleuze, G. and F. Guattari (1988) *A Thousand Plateaus: Capitalism and schizophrenia*, trans. B. Massumi, London: Athlone.
Delisle, J. (1980/1988) *L'analyse du discours comme méthode de traduction*, Ottawa, ON: University of Ottawa Press, Part I trans. by P. Logan and M. Creery (1988) as *Translation: An Interpretive Approach*, Ottawa: University of Ottawa Press.
Delisle, J. and J. Woodsworth (1995) *Translators through History*, Amsterdam and Philadelphia: John Benjamins, UNESCO Publishing.
DeLozier, J. and J. Grinder (1987) *Turtles All the Way Down*, Santa Cruz, CA: Grinder, DeLozier & Associates.
Denton, J. (1994) 'How a fish called Wanda became Un pesce di nome Wanda', *Il traduttore nuovo*, XLII(1): 29–34.
Denzin, N. K. (1970) *The Research Act in Sociology: A theoretical introduction to sociological methods*, London: The Butterworth Group.

Désilets, A., Gonzalez, L., Paquet, S. and M. Stojanovic (2006) 'Translation the wiki way', in *Proceedings of the WIKISym 2006*, online http://www.wikisym.org/ws2006/proceedings/p19.pdf, visited 15/08/2008.

Díaz Cintas, J. (1999) 'Dubbing or subtitling: the eternal dilemma', *Perspectives: Studies in Translatology*, 7(1): 31–40.

Díaz Cintas, J. (2003) *Teoría y práctica de la subtitulación: inglés – español*, Barcelona: Ariel.

Díaz Cintas, J. and P. Muñoz Sánchez (2006) 'Fansubs: audiovisual translation in an amateur environment', *JoSTrans: The Journal of Specialised Translation*, 6 (July): 37–52.

Díaz Cintas, J. and A. Ramael (2007) *Audiovisual Translation: Subtitling* (Translation practices explained), Manchester: St. Jerome.

Diaz-Guerrero, R. and L. B. Szalay (1991) *Understanding Mexicans and Americans: Cultural perspectives in conflict*, New York: Plenum Press.

Dillinger, M. (1989) *Component processes of simultaneous interpreting*, unpublished doctoral thesis, Montreal: McGill University.

Dillinger, M. (1990) 'Comprehension during interpreting: what do interpreters know that bilinguals don't', *The Interpreters' Newsletter*, 3: 41–58.

Dillon, G. (1992) 'Insider reading and linguistic form: Contextual knowledge and the reading of linguistic discourse', in M. Toolan (ed.) *Language, Text and Context*, London and New York: Routledge, pp. 39–52.

Dilthey, W. (1996) 'Hermeneutics and its history', in R. A. Makkreel and F. Rodi (eds) *Wilhelm Dilthey – Selected Works, Vol. 4: Hermeneutics and the study of history*, Princeton, NJ: Princeton University Press, pp. 233–58.

Dilts, R. (1990) *Changing Belief Systems with NLP*, Cupertino, CA: Meta Publications.

Dingwaney, A. and C. Maier (eds) (1995) *Between Languages and Cultures: Translation and cross-cultural texts*, Pittsburgh, PA: University of Pittsburgh Press.

Diriker, E. (2004) *De-/Re-Contextualizing Conference Interpreting: Interpreters in the ivory tower?* Amsterdam and Philadelphia: John Benjamins.

Dolet, E. (1540/1997) *La manière de bien traduire d'une langue en aultre*, Paris: J. de Marnef, trans. D. G. Ross as 'How to translate well from one language into another', in D. Robinson (ed.) (1997b), pp. 95–7.

Dreyfus, H. L. and S. E. Dreyfus (1986) *Mind over Machine: The power of human intuition and expertise in the era of the computer*, Oxford: Blackwell Publishing Ltd.

Dries, J. (1996) 'Circulation des programmes télévisés et des films en Europe', in Y. Gambier (ed.) *Les transferts linguistiques dans les médias audiovisuels*, Villeneuve d'Ascq: PU du Septentrion, pp. 15–32.

Dryden, J. (1680/1697/1992) 'Metaphrase, paraphrase and imitation'. Extracts of 'Preface to Ovid's Epistles' (1680), and 'Dedication of the Aeneis' (1697), in R. Schulte and J. Biguenet (eds.) (1992) *Theories of Translation*, Chicago and London: University of Chicago Press, pp. 17–31.

Du Pont, O. (2005) 'Robert Graves's Claudian novels: A case of pseudotranslation', *Target*, 17(2): 327–47.

Duff, A. (1981) *Third Language: Recurrent problems of translation into English*, Oxford: Pergamon.

Duranti, A. (1997) *Cultural Linguistics*, Cambridge: Cambridge University Press.
Dussart, A. (2005) 'Faux sens, contresens, non-sens ... un faux débat?', *Meta*, 50(1): 107–119.
Eco, U. (1992*) Les limites de l'interprétation*, Paris: Grasset.
Ellis, R. (ed.) (2003) *The Oxford History of Literary Translation in English. Volume I: to 1550*, Oxford: Oxford University Press.
Ellis, R. and L. Oakley-Brown (eds) (2001) *Translation and Nation: Towards a cultural politics of Englishness*, Clevedon: Multilingual Matters.
Englund-Dimitrova, B. (2005) *Expertise and Explicitation in the Translation Process*, Amsterdam and Philadelphia: John Benjamins.
Ericsson, K. A. and H. A. Simon (1984) *Protocol Analysis: Verbal reports as data*, Cambridge, MA: MIT Press.
Esselink, B. (2000) *A Practical Guide to Localization*, Amsterdam and Philadelphia: John Benjamins.
Esselink, B. (2003) 'Localisation and translation', in H. Somers (ed.) *Computers and Translation: A translator's guide*, Amsterdam and Philadelphia: John Benjamins, pp. 67–86.
Esselink, B. (2006) 'The evolution of localization', in A. Pym *et al.* (eds) *Translation Technology and its Teaching*, Tarragona: Intercultural Studies Group, pp. 21–9.
Even-Zohar, I. (1978) 'Papers in historical poetics', in B. Hrushovski and I. Even-Zohar (eds) *Papers on Poetics and Semiotics*, Vol. 8, Tel Aviv: University Publishing Projects.
Even-Zohar, I. (1990/2004) *Poetics Today*, Special Issue *Polysystem Studies*, 11(1), reprinted in L. Venuti (ed.) (2004) *The Translation Studies Reader*, 2nd edition, London and New York: Routledge, pp. 199–204.
Even-Zohar, I. (1997/2005) 'Polysystem theory revised', in I. Even-Zohar *Papers in Culture Research*, pp. 38–49, http://www.tau.ac.il/~itamarez/works/books/EZ-CR-2005.pdf, visited 15/08/2008.
Faiq, S. (ed.) (2004) *Cultural Encounters in Arabic Translation*, Clevedon: Multilingual Mattters.
Fairclough, N. (1989/2001) *Language and Power*, London: Longman.
Fairclough, N. (2003) *Analysing Discourse: Textual analysis for social research*, London and New York: Routledge.
Fanon, Frantz (1952/1967) *Peau noire masques blancs*, Paris: Seuil, trans. C.L. Markmann (1967) as *Black Skin, White Masks*, New York: Grove Weidenfeld.
Fanon, Frantz (1961/1963) *Les damnés de la terre*, Paris: F. Maspero, trans. C. Farrington (1963) as *The Wretched of the Earth*, New York: Grove Weidenfeld.
Fawcett, P. (1997) *Translation and Language*, Manchester: St Jerome.
Fawcett, P. (2000) 'Translation in the broadsheets', *The Translator*, 6(2): 295–307.
Fédération Internationale des Traducteurs (International Federation of Translators) *Bylaws, Article 6*, http://www.fit-ift.org/en/bylaws.php, visited 05/08/2008.
Firth, J. R. (1957) *Papers in Linguistics 1934–1951*, Oxford: Oxford University Press.

Flotow, L. von (1991) 'Feminist translation: context, practices, theories', *TTR* 4(2): 69–84.

Flotow, L. von (1997) *Translation and Gender: Translating in the 'era of feminism'*, Manchester and Ottawa: St. Jerome and University of Ottawa Press.

Folkart, B. (1991) *Le conflit des énonciations: traduction et discours rapporté*, Québec: Balzac.

Fowler, R. (1981) *Literature as Social Discourse*, London: Chrysalis; Bloomington: Indiana University Press.

France, P. (ed.) (2000) *Literature in English Translation*, Oxford: Oxford University Press.

France, P. and K. Haynes (eds) (2006) *The Oxford History of Literary Translation in English. Volume I: to 1550*, Oxford: Oxford University Press.

Francis, G. and A. Kramer-Dahl (1992) 'Grammaticalizing the medical case history', in M. Toolan (ed.) *Language, Text and Context: Essays in stylistics*, London and New York: Routledge, pp. 56–89.

Frasca, G. (2001) 'Rethinking agency and immersion: video games as a means of consciousness-raising', SIGGRAPH 2001, http://siggraph.org/artdesign/gallery/S01/essays/0378.pdf, visited 22/08/2008.

Fraser, J. (1993) 'Public accounts: using verbal protocols to investigate community translation', *Applied Linguistics*, 14(4): 325–43.

Fraser, J. (1996) 'The translator investigated: learning from translation process analysis', *The Translator*, 2(1): 65–79.

Frawley, W. (1984) *Translation: Literary, linguistic and philosophical perspectives*, Newark, NJ: University of Delaware Press.

Friederich, W. (1977) *Die Technik des Übersetzens*, 4th edition, Munich: Max Hueber Verlag.

Gadamer, H.-G. (2004) *Truth and Method*, London: Continuum.

Gaiba, F. (1998) *The Origins of Simultaneous Interpretation: The Nuremberg trial*, Ottawa, ON: University of Ottawa Press.

Gambier, Y. (ed.) (2003) 'Introduction – Screen translation: Perception and reception', *The Translator*, Special Issue, 9(2): 171–89.

Gambier, Y. (ed.) (2004) 'La traduction audiovisuelle', *Meta*, Special Issue, 49(1), www.erudit.org/revue/meta/2004/v49/n1/009015ar.html, visited 15/08/2008.

Gambier, Y. (2008) 'Recent developments and challenges in audiovisual translation research', in D. Chiaro, C. Heiss and C. Bucaria (eds) *Between Text and Image: Updating research in screen translation*, Amsterdam and Philadelphia: John Benjamins, pp. 6–25.

Garzone, G. and M. Viezzi (2002) 'Introduction', in G. Garzone and M. Viezzi (eds) *Interpreting in the 21st Century: Challenges and opportunities*, Amsterdam and Philadelphia: John Benjamins, pp. 1–11.

Geertz, C. (1973) *The Interpretation of Cultures*, New York: Basic Books.

Geest, D. de (1992) 'The notion of "system": its theoretical importance and its methodological implications for a functionalist translation theory', in H. Kittel (ed.) *Geschichte, System, literarische Übersetzung [Histories, Systems, Literary Translations]*, Berlin: Erich Schmidt, pp. 32–45.

Gellerstam, M. (1986) 'Translationese in Swedish novels translated from English', in L. Wollin and H. Lindquist (eds) *Translation Studies in Scandinavia*, Lund: CWK Gleerup, pp. 88–95.

Genette, G. (1997) *Paratexts: Thresholds of interpretation*, Cambridge: Cambridge University Press.

Gentile, A., U. Ozolins and M. Vasilakakos (1996) *Liaison Interpreting: A handbook*, Melbourne: Melbourne University Press.

Gentzler, E. (2001) *Contemporary Translation Theories*, 2nd edition, London and New York: Routledge.

Gerloff, P. (1988) *From French to English: A look at the translation process in students, bilinguals and professional translators*, Cambridge, MA: Harvard University Press.

Gerver, D. (1969/2002) 'The effects of source language presentation rate on the performance of simultaneous conference interpreters', in F. Pöchhacker and M. Shlesinger (eds) (2002) *The Interpreting Studies Reader*, London and New York: Routledge, pp. 53–66.

Gerzymisch-Arbogast, H. (ed.) *MuTra 2005 – Challenges of Multidimensional Translation: Conference Proceedings*, Manchester: St. Jerome; see also http://www.euroconferences.info/proceedings/2005_Proceedings/2005_proceedings.html, visited 15/08/2008.

Ghadessy, M. (ed.) (1988) *Registers in Written English: Situational factors and linguistic features*, London: Pinter Publishers.

Gibbons, S. (1932/2000) *Cold Comfort Farm*, Harmondsworth: Penguin.

Gile, D. (1995a) *Basic Concepts and Models for Interpreter and Translator Training*, Amsterdam and Philadelphia: John Benjamins.

Gile, D. (1995b) *Regards sur la recherche en Interprétation de conférence*, Lille: Presses Universitaires de Lille.

Gile, D. (1997/2002) 'Conference interpreting as a cognitive management problem', in F. Pöchhacker and M. Shlesinger (eds) (2002) *The Interpreting Studies Reader*, London and New York: Routledge, pp. 163–76.

Gile, D. (1998) 'Observational studies and experimental studies in the investigation of conference interpretation', *Target*, 10(1): 69–93.

Gile, D. and G. Hansen (2004) 'The editorial process through the looking glass', in G. Hansen, K. Malmkjær and D. Gile (eds) *Claims, Changes and Challenges in Translation Studies*, Amsterdam and Philadelphia: John Benjamins, pp. 297–306.

Gillespie, S. and D. Hopkins (eds) (2005) *The Oxford History of Literary Translation in English. Volume III: to 1660–1790*, Oxford: Oxford University Press.

Glassman, E. H. (1981) *The Translation Debate*, Downers Grove, Illinois: InterVarsity Press.

Goffman, E. (1974) *Frame Analysis*, New York: Harper and Row.

Goldhagen, D. (1996) *Hitler's Willing Executioners*, New York: Knopf.

Gonçalves, J. L. (2005) 'O desenvolvimiento da competência do tradutor: em busca de parâmetros cognitivos', in F. Alves, C. Magalhães and A. Pagano (eds) *Competência em tradução: cognição e discurso*, Belo Horizonte: Editora da UFMG, pp. 59–90.

Goodenough, W. H. (1956) 'Componential analysis and the study of meaning', *Language*, 32(1): 195–216.

Goodenough, W. H. (1957/1964) 'Cultural anthropology and linguistics, in D. Hymes (ed.) *Language in Culture and Society*, New York: Harper and Row, pp. 36–9.

Goodenough, W. H. (1965) 'Yankee kinship terminology: a problem in componential analysis', *American Anthropologist*, Special Issue, *Formal Semantic Analysis*, 67(5): 259–97.

Gottlieb, H. (1994) 'Subtitling: diagonal translation', *Perspectives*, 2(1): 101–21.

Gottlieb, H. (1999) 'The impact of English: Danish TV subtitles as mediators of Anglicisms', *Zeitschrift für Anglistik und Amerikanistik*, 47(2): 133–53.

Gottlieb, H. (2001a) 'Anglicisms and TV subtitles in an anglified world', in Y. Gambier and H. Gottlieb (eds) *(Multi) Media Translation*, Amsterdam and Philadelphia: John Benjamins.

Gottlieb, H. (2001b) 'Subtitling: visualizing filmic dialogue', in L. Garcia and A. M. Pereira Rodríguez (eds) *Traducción subordinada (II). El subtitulado*, Vigo: Servicio de la Universidad de Vigo, pp. 85–110.

Gottlieb, H. (2004) 'Subtitles and international anglification', *Nordic Journal of English Studies*, Special Issue *Worlds of Words: A Tribute to Arne Zettersten*, 3(1): 219–30.

Gottlieb, H. (2005) 'Multidimensional translation: semantics turned semiotics', in H. Gerzymisch-Arbogast (ed.) *MuTra 2005 – Challenges of Multidimensional Translation: Conference Proceedings*, Manchester: St. Jerome, pp. 1–29.

Gouadec, D. (2005) 'Modélisation du processus d'exécution des traductions', *Meta*, 50(2): 643–55.

Gouadec, D. (2007) *Translation as a Profession*, Amsterdam and Philadelphia: John Benjamins.

Gouanvic, J-M. (1999) Sociologie de la traduction. La science-fiction américaine dans lespace culturel français des années 1950, Arras: Artois University Press.

Gouanvic, J.-M. (2005) 'A Bourdieusian theory of translation, or the coincidence of practical instances: Field, "habitus", capital and "illusio", *The Translator* 11(2): 147–66.

Graham, J. (ed.) (1985) *Difference in Translation*, Ithaca and London: Cornell University Press.

Gran, L. and F. Fabbro (1988) 'The role of neuroscience in the teaching of interpretation', *The Interpreter's Newsletter*, 1: 23–41.

Green, A., J. Vaid, N. White and R. Steiner (1990) 'Hemispheric involvement in shadowing vs. interpretation: a time sharing study of simultaneous interpreters with matched bilingual and monolingual controls', *Brain and Language*, 39: 107–33.

Grice, P. (1975) 'Logic and conversation', in P. Cole and J. L. Morgan (eds) *Speech Acts* (Syntax and semantics, 3), New York: Academic Press, pp. 41–58.

Grigaravičiūtė, I. and H. Gottlieb (2001) 'Danish voices, Lithuanian voice-over: the mechanics of non-synchronous translation', H. Gottlieb, in *Screen Translation*, CTS, University of Copenhagen, pp. 75–114.

Grossman, V. (1980) *Life and Fate*, trans. R. Chandler, New York: Harper and Row.

Gutt, E.-A. (1991/2000) *Translation and Relevance: Cognition and context*, Oxford: Blackwell Publishing Ltd; Manchester: St. Jerome.

Gutt, E.-A. (1992) *Relevance Theory: A guide to successful communication in translation*, Dallas: Summer Institute of Linguistics.

Gutt, E.-A. (2000) 'Issues of translation research in the inferential paradigm of communication', in M. Olohan (ed.) *Intercultural Faultlines – Research models in translation studies 1: Textual and cognitive aspects*, Manchester: St. Jerome, pp. 161–79.

Gutt, E.-A. (2005a) 'On the impossibility of practising translation without theory', in J. Peeters (ed.) *On the Relationships between Translation Theory and Translation Practice*, Vol. 19, Frankfurt am Main, Berlin; Bern: Peter Lang, pp. 13–21.

Gutt, E.-A. (2005b) 'On the significance of the cognitive core of translation', *The Translator*, 11(1): 25–49.

Hale, S. (2004) *The Discourse of Court Interpreting*, Amsterdam and Philadelphia: John Benjamins.

Hall, E. T. (1959/1990) *The Silent Language*, New York: Doubleday.

Hall, E. T. (1976/1989) *Beyond Culture*, New York: Doubleday.

Hall, E. T. (1983) *The Dance of Life*, New York: Doubleday.

Halliday, M. A. K. (1978) *Language as Social Semiotic*, London: Edward Arnold.

Halliday, M. A. K. (1985/1994) *An Introduction to Functional Grammar*, London: Edward Arnold.

Halliday, M. A. K. and R. Hasan (1976) *Cohesion in English*, London and New York: Longman.

Halliday, M. A. K. and R. Hasan (1989) *Language, Context, and Text: Aspects of language in a social-semiotic perspective*, Oxford: Oxford University Press.

Halliday, M. A. K. and C. M. I. M. Matthiessen (2004) *An Introduction to Functional Grammar*, 3rd revised edition, London: Hodder Arnold.

Halliday, M. A. K., A. McIntosh and P. Strevens (1964) *The Linguistic Sciences and Language Teaching*, London and New York: Longman.

Halverson, S. (1999) 'Conceptual work and the "translation" concept', *Target* 11(1): 1–31.

Hampden-Turner, C. and F. Trompenaars (1983) *The Seven Cultures of Capitalism*, London: Piatkus.

Hansen, G. (ed.) (1999) *Probing the Process in Translation*: Methods and results, Copenhagen: Samfundslitteratur.

Hansen, G. (ed.) (2002) *Empirical Translation Studies*: Process and product, Copenhagen: Samfundslitteratur.

Hansen, G. (2006) *Erfolgreich Übersetzen: Entdecken und Beheben von Störquellen*, Tübingen: Gunter Narr Verlag.

Hardwick, L. (2003) *Reception Studies: Greece and Rome* (New Surveys in the Classics, No. 33), Oxford: Oxford University Press.

Hargan, N. (2006) 'The foreignness of subtitles: the case of *Roma, città aperta* in English', in N. Armstrong and F. Federici (eds) *Translating Voices, Translating Regions*, Proceedings of International Conference held at the University of Durham, September 2007, Rome: Aracne, pp. 53–71.

Harris, B. (1977) 'The importance of natural translation', *Working Papers on Bilingualism*, 12: 96–114.

Harris, B. (1980) 'How a three-year-old translates', in E. A. Afrendas (ed.) *Patterns of Bilingualism*, Singapore: National University of Singapore Press, pp. 370–93.

Harris, B. and B. Sherwood (1978) 'Translating as an innate skill', in D. Gerver and H. Wallace Sinaiko (eds) *Language, Interpretation and Communication*, Oxford: Plenum Press, pp. 155–70.

Harvey, K. (1995) 'A descriptive framework for compensation', *The Translator,* 1(1): 56–86.

Harvey, K. (1998) 'Compensation', in M. Baker and K. Malmkjær (eds) (1998) *Routledge Encyclopedia of Translation Studies*, 1st edition, London and New York: Routledge, pp. 37–40.

Harvey, K. (1998/2004) 'Translating camp talk: gay identities and culture transfer', *The Translator* 4(2): 295–320, reprinted in L. Venuti (ed.) (2004) *The Translation Studies Reader*, 2nd edition, London and New York: Routledge, pp. 402–22.

Harwood, R. (1977) *Did Six Million Really Die?* Toronto, ON: Samisdat.

Hasan, R. (1985) *Linguistics, Language and Verbal Art*, Deakin: Deakin University Press.

Hatim, B. (2001) *Teaching and Researching Translation*, London and New York: Longman.

Hatim, B. and I. Mason (1990) *Discourse and the Translator*, London and New York: Longman.

Hatim, B. and I. Mason (1997) *The Translator as Communicator*, London and New York: Routledge.

Hatim, B. and J. Munday (2004) *Translation: An advanced resource book*, London and New York: Routledge.

Headland T. N., K. L. Pike and M. Harris (eds) (1990) *Emics and Etics: The insider/outsider debate,* London: Sage Publications.

Heaney, S. (1990) *The Cure at Troy*, London: Faber.

Helbig, G. and W. Schenkel (1969) *Wörterbuch zur Valenz und Distribution deutscher Verben*, Leipzig: Veb Enzyklopadie.

Herbert, J. (1952) *The Interpreter's Handbook: How to become a conference interpreter*, Geneva: Georg.

Herbst, T. (1994) *Linguistische Aspekte der Synchronisation von Fernsehserien*, Tübingen: Niemeyer.

Hermann, A. (1956/2002) 'Interpreting in antiquity', in F. Pöchhacker and M. Shlesinger (eds) (2002) *The Interpreting Studies Reader*, London and New York: Routledge, pp. 15–22.

Hermans, T. (ed.) (1985) *The Manipulation of Literature: Studies in literary translation*, London and Sydney: Croom Helm.

Hermans, T. (1991) 'Translational norms and correct translations', in K. Van Leuven-Zwart and T. Naaijkens (eds) *Translation Studies: The state of the art – proceedings of the First James S. Holmes Symposium on Translation Studies*, Amsterdam: Rodopi, pp. 155–69.

Hermans, T. (1994) 'Translation between poetics and ideology', *Translation and Literature*, 3: 138–45.

Hermans, T. (1999) *Translation in Systems: Descriptive and systemic approaches explained*, Manchester: St. Jerome.

Hermans, T. (ed.) (2002) *Crosscultural Transgressions – Research models in translation Studies II: Historical and ideological issues*, Manchester: St. Jerome.

Hermans, T. (2003) 'Cross-cultural translation studies as thick translation', *Bulletin of SOAS*, 66 (3), 380–89.

Hermans, T. (ed.) (2006) *Translating Others*, 2 vols, Manchester: St. Jerome.

Hermans, T. (2007) *The Conference of the Tongues*, Manchester: St. Jerome.

Hertog, E. and B. van der Veer (eds) (2006) *Taking Stock: Research and methodology in community interpreting*, Antwerp: Hogeschool Antwerpen.

Hervey, S. and I. Higgins (1992) *Thinking Translation – A course in translation method: French–English*, London and New York: Routledge.

Hirschman, L. and I. Mani (2003) 'Evaluation', in R. Mitkov (ed.) *The Oxford Handbook of Computational Linguistics*, Oxford: Oxford University Press, pp. 414–29.

Hodge, R. and G. Kress (1979/1993) *Language as Ideology*, London and New York: Routledge.

Hoey, M. (2005) *Lexical Priming: A new theory of words and language*, London and New York: Routledge.

Hoey, M. and D. Houghton (1998) 'Contrasive analysis and translation', in M. Baker and K. Malmkjær (eds) *Routledge Encyclopedia of Translation Studies*, 1st edition, London and New York: Routledge, pp. 45–9.

Hoffmann, L. (1985) *Kommunikationsmittel Fachsprache: Eine Einführung* (Forum für Fachsprachen-Forschung Vol. 1), 2nd edition, Tübingen: Gunter Narr Verlag.

Hofstede, G. (1991) *Cultures and Organizations: Software of the mind*, London: McGraw-Hill.

Hofstede, G. (2001) *Culture's Consequences: Comparing values, behaviors, institutions, and organizations across nations*, Newbury Park, CA: Sage Publications.

Holmes, J. S. (1988) *Translated: Papers on literary translation and translation studies*, Amsterdam: Rodopi.

Holmes, J. S. (1988/2004) 'The name and nature of translation studies', in L. Venuti (ed.) (2004) *The Translation Studies Reader*, 2nd edition, London and New York: Routledge, pp. 180–92.

Holub, R. C. (1984) *Reception Theory: A critical introduction*, London and New York: Routledge.

Holub, R. C. (1992) *Crossing Borders: Reception theory, poststructuralism, deconstruction*, Madison, WI: The University of Wisconsin Press.

Holyoak, K. J. (1990) 'Problem solving', in D. Osherson and E. E. Smith (eds) *Thinking: An invitation to cognitive science*, Cambridge, MA: MIT Press, pp. 117–46.

Holz-Mänttäri, J. (1984) *Translatorisches Handeln: Theorie und Methode*, Helsinki: Suomalainen Tiedeakademia.

House, J. (1977/1981) *A Model for Translation Quality Assessment*, Tübingen: Gunter Narr Verlag.

House, J. (1997) *Translation Quality Assessment: A model re-visited*, Tübingen: Gunter Narr Verlag.
House, J. (2001) 'Translation quality assessment: linguistic description versus social evaluation', *Meta*, 46(2): 243–56.
House, J. (2003a) 'English as lingua franca and its influence on discourse norms in other languages', in G. Anderman and M. Rogers (eds) *Translation Today: Trends and perspectives*, Clevedon: Multilingual Matters, pp. 168–79.
House, J. (2003b) 'Misunderstanding in intercultural communication', in C. Inchaurralde and C. Florén (eds) *Interaction and Cognition in Linguistics*, Frankfurt am Main, Berlin and Bern: Peter Lang, pp. 15–38.
House, J. (2006) 'Text and context in translation', *Journal of Pragmatics*, 38: 338–58.
House, J., R. Martín, Ruano and N. Baumgarten (eds) (2005) *Translation and the Construction of Identity*, Seoul: International Association for Translation and Intercultural Studies.
Howard Parshley (Beauvoir, S. de (1953)) *The Second Sex*, trans. H. M. Parshley, New York: Knopf.
Hudson, R. (1995) *Word Meaning*, London and New York: Routledge.
Hughes, T. (1999) *The Oresteia*, London: Faber.
Humboldt, W. von (1816/1997) 'Introduction to the translation of Aeschylus' *Agamemnon*', excerpted and translated in D. Robinson (ed.) (1997) *Western Translation Theory: From Herodotus to Nietzsche*, Manchester: St. Jerome, pp. 238–40.
Hung, E. and J. Wakabayashi (eds) (2005) *Asian Translation Traditions*, Manchester: St. Jerome.
Hurtado Albir, A. (1996) 'La enseñanza de la traducción directa "general". Objetivos de aprendizaje y metodología', in A. Hurtado Albir (ed.) *La enseñanza de la traducción* (Coll. Estudis sobre la traducció 3), Castellón: Universitat Jaume I, pp. 31–55.
Hurtado Albir, A. (ed.) (1999) *Enseñar a traducir. Metodología en la formación de traductores e intérpretes*, Madrid: Edelsa.
Hurtado Albir, A. (2001) *Traducción y traductología. Introducción a la traductología*, Madrid: Cátedra.
Hutchins, J. (2003) 'Machine translation: general overview', in R. Mitkov (ed.) *The Oxford Handbook of Computational Linguistics*, Oxford: Oxford University Press, pp. 501–11.
Hyland, K. (2005) *Metadiscourse*, London: Continuum.
Ilg, G. and S. Lambert (1996) 'Teaching consecutive interpreting', *Interpreting*, 1(1): 69–99.
Ilic, I. (1990) 'Cerebral lateralization for linguistic functions in professional interpreters', in L. Gran and C. Taylor (eds) *Aspects of Applied and Experimental Research on Conference Interpretation Research*, Udine: Campanotto Editore, pp. 101–10.
Inghilleri, M. (ed.) (2005) *Bourdieu and the Sociology of Translation and Interpreting*, Special Issue of *The Translator*, 11(2).

Iser, W. (1978) *The Act of Reading: A theory of aesthetic response*, London and New York: Longman.

Isham, W. P. (1998) 'Signed language interpreting', in M. Baker and K. Malmkjær (eds) *Routledge Encyclopedia of Translation Studies*, 1st edition, London and New York: Routledge, pp. 231–5.

Israël, F. and M. Lederer (eds) (2005) *La théorie interprétative de la traduction*, 3 vols, Paris/Caen: Minard Lettres Modernes.

Ivarsson, J. (1992) *Subtitling for the Media: A handbook of an art.* Stockholm: Transedit.

Izard, N. (2000) 'La traducció i la normalització de la llengua catalana: el cas de la televisió', in A. Englebert (ed.) *Actes du XXIIe Congrès International de Linguistique et de Philologie Romane*, Vol. III, Tübingen: Niemeyer.

Jääskeläinen, R. (2000) 'Focus on methodology in think-aloud studies on translation', in S. Tirkkonen-Condit and R. Jääskeläinen (eds) *Tapping and Mapping the Process of Translation: Outlooks on empirical research*, Amsterdam and Philadelphia: John Benjamins, pp. 71–82.

Jackson, H. and E. Ze Amvela (2007) *Words, Meaning and Vocabulary: An introduction to modern English lexicology*, 2nd revised edition, London: Continuum.

Jacquemin, C. and D. Bourigault (2003) 'Term extraction and automatic indexing', in R. Mitkov (ed.) *The Oxford Handbook of Computational Linguistics*, Oxford: Oxford University Press, pp. 599–615.

Jacquemond, R. (1992) 'Translation and cultural hegemony', in L. Venuti (ed.) *Rethinking Translation: Discourse, subjectivity, ideology*, London and New York: Routledge, pp. 139–58.

Jakobsen, A. L. (2002) 'Orientation, segmentation, and revision in translation', in G. Hansen (ed.) *Empirical Translation Studies: Process and product*, Copenhagen: Samfundslitteratur, pp. 191–204.

Jakobsen, A. L. (2003) 'Effects of think aloud on translation speed, revision and segmentation', in F. Alves (ed.) *Triangulating Translation: Perspectives in process oriented research*, Amsterdam and Philadelphia: John Benjamins, pp. 69–95.

Jakobsen, A. L. and L. Schou (1999) 'Translog documentation', in G. Hansen (ed.) *Probing the Process in Translation: Methods and results*, Copenhagen: Samfundslitteratur, pp. 73–101.

Jakobson, R. (1959/2004) 'On linguistic aspects of translation', in L. Venuti (ed.) (2004) *The Translation Studies Reader*, 2nd edition, London and New York: Routledge, pp. 138–43.

James, C. (1989) 'Genre analysis and the translator', *Target*, 1(1): 21–41.

Janzen, T. (ed.) (2005) *Topics in Signed Language Interpreting*, Amsterdam and Philadelphia: John Benjamins.

Jauss, H. R. (1982) *Toward an Aesthetic of Reception*, trans. T. Bahlti, Brighton: Harvester Press.

Jenks, C. (1993) *Culture*, London and New York: Routledge.

Jerome, E. H. (St. Jerome) (395 CE/1997) 'On the best kind of translator', trans. P. Carroll, in D. Robinson (ed.) (1997) *Western Translation Theory: From Herodotus to Nietzsche*, Manchester: St. Jerome, pp. 22–30.

Jiménez, A. (2000) 'El reto de investigar en interpretación', *Sendebar*, 10(11): 43–66.

Johnson, B. (1985) 'Taking fidelity philosophically', in J. Graham (ed.) *Difference in Translation*, Ithaca and London: Cornell University Press, pp. 142–48.

Kade, O. (1968) *Zufall und Gesetzmässigkeit in der Übersetzung*, Leipzig: Verlag Enzyklopädie.

Katan, D. (1993) 'The English Translation of *Il Nome della Rosa* and the Cultural Filter' *Umberto Eco, Claudio Magris: Autori e Traduttori a Confronto*, in L. Avirovic and J. Dodds (eds) Campanotto Editore, Udine, pp. 149–65.

Katan, D. (1999) 'What is it that's going on here? Mediating cultural frames in translation', *Textus: Translation Studies Revisited*, XII(2): 409–26.

Katan, D. (1999/2004) *Translating Cultures: An introduction for translators, interpreters and mediators*, Manchester: St. Jerome.

Katan, D. (2001) 'When difference is not dangerous: modelling intercultural competence for business', *Textus* XIV(2): 287–306.

Katan, D. (2002) 'Mediating the point of refraction and playing with the perlocutionary effect: a translator's choice?', in S. Herbrechter (ed.) *Cultural Studies: Interdisciplinarity and translation* (Critical Studies: Vol. 20), Amsterdam and New York: Rodopi, pp. 177–95.

Katan, D. (2006) 'It's a question of life or death: cultural differences in advertising private pensions', in N. Vasta (ed.) *Forms of Promotion: Texts, contexts and cultures*, Bologna: Pàtron Editore, pp. 55–80.

Katan, D. (2008) 'Translation theory and professional practice: a global survey of the great divide' *Hermes* Special Issue *Translation Studies: Focus on the Translator*.

Katan, D. and F. Straniero Sergio (2003) 'Submerged ideologies in media translating', in M. Calzada Pérez (ed.) *Apropos of Ideology: Translation studies on ideology – Ideologies in Translation Studies*, Manchester: St. Jerome, pp. 131–44.

Kay, M. (1980) *The Proper Place of Men and Machines in Language Translation*, Research Report CSL-80-11, Palo Alto: Xerox. Reprinted in *Machine Translation* vol. 12 (1997).

Kelly, D. (2002) 'Un modelo de competencia traductora: bases para el diseño curricular', *Puentes. Hacia nuevas investigaciones en la mediactión intercultural* 1: 9–20.

Kelly, D. (2005) *A Handbook for Translator Trainers*, Manchester: St. Jerome.

Kelly, L. (1979) *The True Interpreter: History of translation theory and practice in the West*, New York: St Martin's Press.

Kelly, L. (2005) 'Theories of translation: the eighteenth century to Tytler', in S. Gillespie and D. Hopkins (eds) *The Oxford History of Literary Translation in English, Volume 3: 1660–1790*, Oxford: Oxford University Press, pp. 67–78.

Kenny, D. (1998) 'Equivalence', in M. Bakers and K. Malmkjær (eds) *Routledge Encyclopedia of Translation Studies*, 1st edition, London and New York: Routledge, pp. 77–80.

Kertesz, A. (1979) 'Visual agnosia: the dual deficit of perception and recognition', *Cortex*, 15: 403–19.

Kilborn, R. (1989) 'They don't speak proper English: a new look at the dubbing and subtitling debate', *Journal of Multilingual and Multicultural Development*, 10(5): 421–34.

Kilgarriff, A. (1993) 'Dictionary word sense distinctions: an enquiry into their nature', *Computers and the Humanities,* 26: 365–87.

Kilgarriff, A. (1997) 'I don't believe in word senses', *Computers and the Humanities,* 31(2): 91–113.

Kiraly, D. (1995) *Pathways to Translation: Pedagogy and process,* Kent, OH: Kent State University Press.

Kittredge, R. (2003) 'Sublanguages and controlled languages', in R. Mitkov (ed.) *The Oxford Handbook of Computational Linguistics,* Oxford: Oxford University Press, pp. 430–47.

Klaudy, K. (1993) 'On explicitation hypothesis', in K. Klaudy and J. Kohn (eds) *Transferre necesse est ... Current Issues of Translation Theory,* Proceedings of Symposium in honour of György Radó on his 80th birthday, Szombathely: Dániel Berzsenyi College, pp. 69–77.

Klaudy, K. (1998) 'Explicitation', in M. Baker and K. Malmkjær (eds) *Routledge Encyclopedia of Translation Studies,* 1st edition, London and New York: Routledge, pp. 80–84.

Ko, Leong (2006) 'The need for long-term empirical studies in remote interpreting research: a case study of telephone interpreting', in E. Hertog and B. van der Veer (eds) *Taking Stock: Research and methodology in community interpreting,* Antwerp: Hogeschool Antwerpen, pp. 325–38.

Koller, W. (1971) 'Übersetzen, Übersetzung und Übersetzer: zu schwedischen Symposien über Probleme der Übersetzung', *Babel,* 17: 3–11.

Koller, W. (1979/2004) *Einführung in die Übersetzungswissenschaft,* Heidelberg: Quelle und Meyer.

Koller, W. (1989) 'Equivalence in translation theory', in A. Chesterman (ed.) *Readings in Translation Theory,* Helsinki: Finn Lectura, pp. 99–104.

Koller, W. (1995) 'The concept of equivalence and the object of translation studies', *Target,* 7(2): 191–222.

Kondo, M. and H. Tebble (1997) 'Intercultural communication, negotiation and interpreting', in C. J. Taylor, Y. Gambier and D. Gile (eds) *Conference Interpreting: Current trends in research,* Amsterdam and Philadelphia: John Benjamins, pp. 149–66.

Königs, F. G. (1987) 'Was beim Übersetzen passiert: Theoretische Aspekte, empirische Befunde und praktische Konsequenzen', *Die Neueren Sprachen,* 86: 162–85.

Korte, T. de (2006) 'Live inter-lingual subtitling in the Netherlands: historical background and current practice', *Intralinea,* Special Issue *Respeaking,* http://www.intralinea.it/specials/respeaking/eng-more.php?id=454_0.41_0_M, visited 15/08/2008.

Korzybski, A. (1933/1958) *Science and Sanity,* 4th edition, Lakeville, CT: The International Non-Aristotelian Library Publishing Company.

Kress, G. R. (1985) *Linguistic Processes in Sociocultural Practice,* Victoria, Australia: Deakin University Press.

Krings, H. P. (1986) *Was in den Köpfen von Übersetzern vorgeht: Eine empirische Untersuchung zur Struktur des Übersetzungsprozesses an fortgeschrittenen Französischlernern,* Tübingen: Gunter Narr Verlag.

Kroeber, A. L. and C. Kluckhohn (1952) *Cultures: A critical review of concepts and definitions* (Peabody Museum Papers Vol. 47, 1), Cambridge, MA: Harvard University Press.

Krontiris, T. (1992) *Oppositional Voices: Women as writers and translators of literature in the English Renaissance*, London and New York: Routledge.

Kruger, A. (1997) 'The translator as agent of reconciliation: translating an eye-witness report in a historical text', in K. Simms (ed.) *Translating Sensitive Texts: Linguistic aspects*, Amsterdam and Atlanta, GA: Rodopi, pp. 77–86.

Krzeszowski, T. P. (1984) 'Tertium comparationis', in J. Fisiak (ed.) *Contrastive Linguistics: Prospects and problems*, Berlin and New York: Mouton de Gruyter, pp. 301–12.

Krzeszowski, T. P. (1990) *Contrasting Languages: The scope of contrastive linguistics*, Berlin and New York: Mouton de Gruyter.

Kuhiwczak, P. (1990) 'Translation as appropriation: the case of Milan Kundera's *The Joke*', in S. Bassnett and A. Lefevere (eds) *Translation, History and Culture*, London and New York: Pinter, pp. 118–30.

Kuhiwczak, P. and K. Littau (eds) (2007) *A Companion to Translation Studies*, Clevedon: Multilingual Matters.

Kuhn, T. (1962/1970/1996) *The Structure of Scientific Revolutions*, Chicago: University of Chicago Press.

Kurz, I. (1993) 'EEG probability mapping: detecting cerebral pocesses during mental simultaneous interpreting', *The Jerome Quarterly*, 8(2): 3–5.

Kurz, I. (1993/2002) 'Conference interpretation: expectations of different user groups', in F. Pöchhacker and M. Shlesinger (eds) (2002) *The Interpreting Studies Reader*, London and New York: Routledge, pp. 313–24.

Kurz, I. (1997) 'Getting the message across: simultaneous interpreting for the media', in M. Snell-Hornby, Z. Jettmarová and K. Kaindl (eds) *Translation as Intercultural Communication*, Amsterdam and Philadelphia: John Benjamins, pp. 195–205.

Kussmaul, P. (1991) 'Creativity in the translation process: empirical approaches', in K. M. van Leuven-Zwart and T. Naaijkens (eds) *Translation Studies: The state of the art*, Amsterdam and Atlanta, GA: Rodopi, pp. 91–101.

Kussmaul, P. (1995) *Training the Translator*, Amsterdam and Philadelphia: John Benjamins.

Kuznik, A. (2007) 'Les "tâches de traduction" en tant qu'indicateurs de la compétence de traduction dans une approche comportementale', in D. Gouadec (ed.) *Quelle qualification universitaire pour les traducteurs?*, Paris: La Maison du Dictionnaire, pp. 117–32.

Kwieciński. P. (2001) *Disturbing Strangeness*, Toruń, Poland: Wydawnictwo EDYTOR.

Ladmiral, J.-R. (1979) *Traduire: theoremes pour la traduction*, Paris: Payot.

Lajoie, S. (2003) 'Transitions and trajectories for studies of expertise', *Educational Researcher*, 32(8): 21–5.

Lambert, J. (1991) 'Shifts, oppositions and goals in translation studies: towards a genealogy of concepts', in K. Van Leuven-Zwart and T. Naaijkens (eds) *Translation Studies: The state of the art*, Amsterdam: Rodopi, pp. 25–37.

Lambert, J. (2006) *Functional Approaches to Culture and Translation: Selected papers by José Lambert*, D. Delabastita, L. D'hulst and R. Meylaerts (eds), Amsterdam and Philadelphia: John Benjamins.

Lambert, S. (1989) 'Simultaneous interpreters: one ear may be better than two', *The Interpreter's Newsletter*, 2: 11–16.

Lambourne, A. (2006) 'Subtitle respeaking: a new skill for a new age', *Intralinea*, Special Issue *Respeaking*, http://www.intralinea.it/specials/respeaking/eng_more.php?id=447_0_41_0_M, visited 15/08/2008.

Larson, M. L. (1998) *Meaning-Based Translation: A guide to cross-language equivalence*, 2nd edition, Lanham, MD: University Press of America.

Lathey, G. (ed.) (2006) *Children's Literature in Translation: A reader*, Clevedon: Multilingual Matters.

Laviosa, S. (1998) 'Universals of translation', in M. Baker and K. Malmkjær (eds) *Routledge Encyclopedia of Translation Studies*, 1st edition, London and New York: Routledge, pp. 288–91.

Laviosa, S. (2002) *Corpus-based Translation Studies: Theory, findings, applications*, Amsterdam: Rodopi.

Laviosa, S. (2003) 'Corpora and the translator', in H. Somers (ed.) *Computers and Translation: A translator's guide*, Amsterdam and Philadelphia: John Benjamins, pp. 105–17.

Lecercle, J.-J. (1990) *The Violence of Language*, London and New York: Routledge.

Lederer, M. (1981) *La traduction simultanée*, Paris: Minard.

Lederer, M. (1994/2003) *La traduction aujourd'hui: Le modèle interprétatif*, Paris: Hachette, trans. N. Larché as *Translation: The interpretive model* (2003), Manchester: St Jerome.

Leech, G. N. (1983) *Principles of Pragmatics*, London and New York: Longman.

Leech, G. and M. Short (1981) *Style in Fiction*, London: Longman.

Lefevere, A. (1977) *Translating Literature: The German tradition from Luther to Rosenzweig*, Assen: Van Gorcum.

Lefevere, A. (1982/2004) 'Mother Courage's cucumbers', in L. Venuti (ed.) (2004) *The Translation Studies Reader*, 2nd edition, London and New York: Routledge, pp. 239–55.

Lefevere, A. (1985) 'Why waste our time on rewrites? The trouble with interpretation and the role of rewriting in an alternative paradigm', in T. Hermans (ed.) *The Manipulation of Literature: Studies in Literary Translation*, London and Sydney: Croom Helm, pp. 215–43.

Lefevere, A. (1992) *Translation, Rewriting and the Manipulation of Literary Fame*, London and New York: Routledge.

Lefevere, A. and S. Bassnett (1990) 'Introduction: Proust's grandmother and the Thousand and One Nights: the "cultural turn" in translation studies', Preface to S. Bassnett and A. Lefevere (eds) *Translation, History and Culture*, London: Pinter, pp. 1–13.

Lehrer, A. (1996) 'Why neologisms are important to study', *Lexicology*, 2(1): 63–73.

Lehrer, A. (1997) 'Problems in the translation of creative neologisms', in B. Lewandowska-Tomaszczyk and M. Thelen (eds) *Translation and Meaning*, Part 4, Maastricht: Hogeschool Maastricht Press, pp. 141–7.

Lehrer, A. (2003) 'Understanding trendy neologisms', *Italian Journal of Linguistics/Revista di Linguistica*, 15(2): 369–82.

Leppihalme, R. (1997) *Culture Bumps*, Clevedon: Multilingual Matters.

Leuven-Zwart, K. van (1989) 'Translation and original: similarities and dissimilarities, I', *Target*, 1(2): 69–95.

Leuven-Zwart, K. van (1990) 'Translation and original: similarities and dissimilarities, II', *Target*, 2(1): 151–81.

Leuven-Zwart, K. van and T. Naaijkens (eds) (1991) *Translation Studies: The state of the art – proceedings of the First James S. Holmes Symposium on Translation Studies*, Amsterdam: Rodopi.

Levine, S. J. (1991) *The Subversive Scribe: Translating Latin American fiction*, Saint Paul, MN: Graywolf.

Lewis, P. (1985) 'The measure of translation effects', in J. Graham (ed.), *Difference in Translation*, Ithaca and London: Cornell University Press, pp. 31–62, reprinted in L. Venuti (ed.) The Translation Studies Reader, 2nd edition, London and New York: Routledge, pp. 256–75.

Lianeri, A. (2002) 'Translation and the establishment of liberal democracy in nineteenth century England: constructing the political as an interpretive act', in M. Tymozcko and E. Gentzler, *Translation and Power, Amherst* and *Boston*, MA: University of Massachusetts Press, pp. 1–24.

Lind, S. (2007) 'Translation universals (or laws, or tendencies, or …?)', *TIC Talk, Newsletter of the United Bible Societies*, 63: 1–10.

Linde, Z. de and N. Kay (1999) *The Semiotics of Subtitling*, Manchester: St. Jerome.

Liu, L. (1995) *Translingual Practice: Literature, national culture and translated modernity – China 1900–1937*, Stanford, CA: Stanford University Press.

Liu, L. (ed.) (1999) *Tokens of Exchange: The problem of translation in global circulations*, Durham, NC, and London: Duke University Press.

Lodge, D. (1992) *The Art of Fiction: Illustrated from classic and modern texts*, Penguin: London.

Lörscher, W. (1991) *Translation Performance, Translation Process, and Translation Strategies: A psycholinguistic investigation*, Tübingen: Gunter Narr Verlag.

Lotbinière-Harwood, S. de (1991) *Re-belle et infidèle: la traduction comme pratique de réécriture au féminin [The Body Bilingual: Translation as a rewriting in the feminine]*, Montréal and Toronto: Éditions du remue-ménage and Women's Press.

Louw, J. P. (ed.) (1991) *Meaningful Translation: Its implications for the reader*, Reading and New York: UBS.

Luther, M. (1530/1963) 'Sendbrief vom Dolmetschen', in H. Störig (ed.) (1963) *Das Problem des Übersetzens*, Darmstadt: Wissenchaftliche Buchgemeinschaft pp. 14–32.

Lutzeier, P. R. (1995) *Lexikologie*, Tübingen: Stauffenburg Verlag.

Luyken, G. M., T. Herbst, J. Langham-Brown, H. Reid and H. Spinhof (1991) *Overcoming Language Barriers in Television: Dubbing and subtitling for the European audience*, Manchester: European Institute for the Media.

Lyons, J. (1977/1993) *Semantics*, Vol. 1, Cambridge: Cambridge University Press.

McEnery, A. (2003) 'Corpus linguistics', in R. Mitkov (ed.) *The Oxford Handbook of Computational Linguistics*, Oxford: Oxford University Press, pp. 448–63.

Mack, G. (2002) 'New perspectives and challenges for interpretation: the example of television', in G. Garzone and M. Viezzi (eds) *Interpreting in the 21st Century: Challenges and Opportunities*, Amsterdam and Philadelphia: John Benjamins, pp. 203–13.

Maier, C. (1998) 'Issues in the practice of translating women's fiction', *Bulletin of Hispanic Studies*, 75: 95–108.

Makoushina, J. (2007) 'Translation quality assurance tools: current state and future approaches', in *Translating and the Computer 29*, London: Aslib, pp. 1–39.

Malblanc, A. (1963) *Stylistique comparée du français et de l'allemand*, Paris: Didier.

Malinowski, B. (1923/1938) 'The Problem of meaning in primitive languages', in C. K. Ogden and I. A. Richards (eds) *The Meaning of Meaning: A study of the influence of language upon thought and of the science of symbolism*, Supplement 1, 5th edition, New York: Harcourt, Brace, and World, pp. 296–336.

Malinowski, B. (1935/1967) *The Language of Magic and Gardening*, Bloomington: Indiana University Press.

Malmkjær, K. (2003) 'What happened to God and the angels: H. W. Dulken's translations of Hans Christian Andersen's stories in Victorian Britain OR An exercise in translational stylistics', *Target*, 15(1): 37–58.

Malmkjær, K. (2005) *Linguistics and the Language of Translation*, Edinburgh: Edinburgh University Press.

Manca, E. (2008) 'From phraseology to culture: Qualifying adjectives in the language of tourism', in U. Römer and R. Schulze (eds) *Patterns, meaningful units and specialized discourses*, Special issue of *International Journal of Corpus Linguistics*, 368–85.

Mann, H. (1914/1997) *Der Untertan*, Frankfurt: Fischer.

Marcus, G. and M. Fischer (1986) *Anthropology as Cultural Critique: An experimental moment in the human sciences*, Chicago IL and London: University of Chicago Press.

Martin, J. R. (1985) *Factual Writing: Exploring and challenging social reality*, Victoria, Australia: Deakin University Press.

Martin, J. R. (1993) 'Genre and literacy: Modeling context in educational linguistics', *Annual Review of Applied Linguistics*, 13: 141–72.

Mason, I. (1994) 'Discourse, ideology and translation', in R. de Beaugrande, A. Shunnaq and M. Helmy Heliel (eds) *Language, Discourse and Translation in the West and Middle East*, Amsterdam and Philadelphia: John Benjamins, pp. 23–34.

Mason, I. (ed.) (2001) *Triadic Exchanges: Studies in dialogue interpreting*, Manchester: St. Jerome.

Massardier-Kenney, F. (1997) 'Towards a redefinition of feminist translation practice', *The Translator*, 3(1): 55–69.

Matthiessen, C. M. I. M. (1995) *Lexicogrammatical Cartography: English systems*, Tokyo: International Language Sciences Publishers.

Matthiessen, C. M. I. M. (2002) 'Lexicogrammar in discourse development: logogenetic patterns of wording', in G. Huang and Z. Wang (eds) *Discourse and Language Functions*, Shanghai: Foreign Language Teaching and Research Press, pp. 2–25.

Mikkelson, H. (1998) 'Towards a redefinition of the role of the court interpreter', *Interpreting*, 3(1): 21–45.

Mitkov, R. (ed.) (2003) *The Oxford Handbook of Computational Linguistics*, Oxford: Oxford University Press.

Molina, L. and A. Hurtado Albir (2002) 'Translation techniques revisited: a dynamic and functionalist approach', *Meta*, 47(4): 498–512.

Mooij, M. de (2004a) *Consumer Behaviour and Culture*, Thousand Oaks, NJ: Sage.

Mooij, M. de (2004b) 'Translating advertising: painting the tip of an iceberg', *The Translator*, 10(2): 179–98.

Moser-Mercer, B. (1997) 'Methodological issues in interpreting research: an introduction to the Ascona workshops', *Interpreting*, 2: 1–11.

Moser-Mercer, B. (1997/2002) 'Process models in simultaneous interpretation', in F. Pöchhacker and M. Shlesinger (eds) (2002) *The Interpreting Studies Reader*, London and New York: Routledge, pp. 149–61.

Moser-Mercer, B. (2005) 'Remote interpreting: issues of multi-sensory integration in a multilingual task', *Meta*, 50(2): 727–38.

Mossop, B. (1983) 'The translator as rapporteur: a concept for training and self-improvement', *Meta*, 28(3), 244–78.

Mossop, B. (1998) 'What is a translating translator doing?', *Target*, 10(1): 231–66.

Mossop, B. (2007) 'The translator's intervention through voice selection', in J. Munday (ed.) Translation as Intervention, London: Continuum.

Mouzourakis, P. (2006) 'Remote interpreting: a technical perspective on recent experiments', *Interpreting*, 8(1): 45–66.

Mukherjee, S. (1981) *Translation as Discovery and Other Essays on Indian Literature in English Translation*, Delhi: Allied.

Mukherjee, S. (1996) 'The technique of translation and transcreation from English to Tamil'. in A. K. Singh (ed.) *Translation, Its Theory and Practice*, New Delhi: Creative Books, pp. 89–103.

Mukherjee, S. (2004) *Translation as Recovery*, Delhi: Pencraft International.

Munday, J. (2001/2008) *Introducing Translation Studies: Theories and applications*, London and New York: Routledge.

Munday, J. (2004) 'Advertising: some challenges to translation theory', *The Translator*, 10(2): 199–219.

Munday, J. (2008) *Style and Ideology in Translation: Latin American writing in English*, London and New York: Routledge.

Munday, J. and P. Fawcett (2008) 'Ideology', in M. Baker and G. Saldanha (eds) *Routledge Encyclopedia of Translation Studies*, 2nd edition, London and New York: Routledge.

Muñoz, R. (2007) 'Traductología cognitiva y traductología empírica', in G. Wotjak (ed.) *Quo vadis, translatologie?* Berlin: Franck und Timme, pp. 267–78.

Nabokov, V. (1955/2004) 'Problems of translation: *Onegin* in English', *Partisan Review*, 22: 496–512, reprinted in L. Venuti (ed.) (2004) *The Translation Studies Reader*, 2nd edition, London and New York: Routledge, pp. 115–27.

Nabokov, V. (1959) 'The servile path', in R. Brower (ed.) *On Translation*, Cambridge, MA: Harvard University Press, pp. 97–110.

Nabokov, V. (1964) 'Translator's introduction' to A. S. Pushkin *Eugene Onegin: A novel in verse*, trans. with commentary by V. Nabokov, pp. i–xxvi.

Neisser, U. (1967) *Cognitive Psychology*, New York: Appleton.

Neubert, A. (2000) 'Competence in language, in languages, and in translation', in C. Schäffner and B. Adab (eds) *Developing Translation Competence*, Amsterdam and Philadelphia: John Benjamins, pp. 3–18.

Neunzig, W. (1997a) 'Der Computer als Hilfsmittel beim Erwerben kognitiver Übersetzungsstrategien', in E. Fleischmann, W. Kutz and P. A. Schmitt (eds) *Translationsdidaktik: Grundfragen der Übersetzungswissenschaft*, Tübingen: Gunter Narr Verlag, pp. 377–84.

Neunzig, W. (1997b) 'Die Effizienz computergestützter Übungsformen: eine Untersuchung im Rahmen des Übersetzungsunterrichts', in J. Kohn, B. Rueschoff and D. Wolff (eds) *New Horizons in CALL*, Szombathely: Berzsenyi Daniel, pp. 303–12.

Neunzig, W. (2002) 'Estudios empíricos en traducción: apuntes metodológicos', *Cadernos de Tradução*, 10: 75–96.

Neunzig, W. and H. Tanqueiro (2007) *Estudios empíricos en traducción: enfoques y métodos*, (Col. Vademecum 2), Bellaterra, Girona: Departament de Traducció i d'Interpretació Universitat Autònoma de Barcelona – Documenta Universitaria.

Newell, A. and H. A. Simon (1972) *Human Problem Solving*, Englewood Cliffs, NJ: Prentice Hall.

Newman, F. (1861) *Homeric Translation in Theory and Practice*, London: Williams and Norgate.

Newmark, P. (1981) *Approaches to Translation*, Oxford: Pergamon Press, reprinted (2001) Shanghai: Shanghai University Press.

Newmark, P. (1988) *A Textbook of Translation*, Hemel Hempstead: Prentice Hall, reprinted (2001) Shanghai: Shanghai University Press.

Newmark, P. (1991) *About Translation*, Clevedon: Multilingual Matters.

Nida, E. A. (1964) *Toward a Science of Translating with Special Reference to Principles and Procedures Involved in Bible Translating*, Leiden: E. J. Brill.

Nida, E. A. (1969) 'Science of translation', *Language*, 45(3): 483–98.

Nida, E. A. (1975) *Componential Analysis of Meaning: An introduction to semantic structures*, The Hague: Mouton de Gruyter.

Nida, E. A. (1997) 'The principles of discourse structure and content in relation to translating', in K. Klaudy and J. Kohn (eds) *Transferre necesse Est ... Current issues of translation theory*, Budapest: Scholastica, pp. 37–42.

Nida, E. A. (2002) *Contexts in Translating*, Amsterdam and Philadelphia: John Benjamins.

Nida, E. A. (2004) 'Principles of correspondence', in L. Venuti (ed.) *The Translation Studies Reader*, 2nd edition, London and New York: Routledge, pp. 153–67.

Nida, E. A. and C. R. Taber (1969/1974) *The Theory and Practice of Translation*, Leiden: E. J. Brill.

Nida, E. A. and W. D. Reyburn (1981) *Meaning Across Culture*, Maryknoll, NY: Orbis.

Niranjana, T. (1992) *Siting Translation: History, post-structuralism and the colonial context*, Berkeley, CA: University of California Press.

Nord, C. (1988) *Textanalyze and Übersetzen: Theoretische Grundlagen, Methode und didaktische Answendung einer übersetzungsrelevanten Textanalyze*, Heidelberg: J. Groos, translated (1st edition 1991; 2nd edition 2005) as *Text Analysis in Translation: Theory, Methodology and Didactic Application of a Model for Translation-Oriented Text Analysis*, Amsterdam: Rodopi.

Nord, C. (1991) 'Skopos, loyalty and translational conventions', *Target*, 3(1): 91–109.

Nord, C. (1995) 'Text-functions in translation: titles and headings as a case in point', *Target*, 7(2): 261–84.

Nord, C. (1997) *Translating as a Purposeful Activity: Functionalist approaches explained*, Manchester: St Jerome.

Nord, C. (2000) 'What do we know about the target-text receiver?', in A. Beeby, D. Ensinger and M. Presas (eds) *Investigating Translation*, Amsterdam and Philadelphia: John Benjamins, pp. 195–212.

Nord, C. (2003) 'Function and loyalty in Bible translation', in M. Calzada Pérez (ed.) *Apropos of Ideology: Translation studies on ideology – Ideologies in translation studies*, Manchester: St. Jerome, pp. 89–112.

Nyberg, E., T. Mitamura and W-O. Huijsen (2003) 'Controlled language for authoring and translation', in H. Somers (ed.) *Computers and Translation: A translator's guide*, Amsterdam and Philadelphia: John Benjamins, pp. 245–82.

O'Brien, S. (2006) 'Eye-tracking and translation memory matches', *Perspectives: Studies in Translatology*, 14(3): 185–205.

O'Connell, E. (1996) 'Media translation and translation studies', in T. Hickey and J. Williams (eds) *Language, Education and Society in a Changing World*, Clevedon: Multilingual Matters, pp. 151–56.

O'Connor, J. (2001) *The NLP Workbook*, London: Thorsons.

Ogden, C. (1932) *Basic English: A general introduction with rules and grammar*, New York: W. W. Norton and Co.

O'Hagan, M. and C. Mangiron (2006) 'Game localisation: unleashing imagination with "restricted" translation', *The Journal of Specialised Translation*, 6: 10–21.

Oittinen, R. and K. Kaindl (2008) *Le verbal, le visuel, le traducteur / The Verbal, the Visual, the Translator*, Special issue of META 53(1).

Oksaar, E. (1989) 'Psycholinguistic aspects of bilingualism', *Journal of Multilingual and Multicultural Development*, 10(1): 33–46.

Olohan, M. (2004) *Introducing Corpora in Translation Studies*, London and New York: Routledge.

Olohan, M. and M. Baker (2000) 'Reporting *that* in translated English: evidence for subconscious processes of explicitation?', *Across Languages and Cultures*, 1(2): 141–58.

O'Neill, E. (1931) *Mourning becomes Electra*, New York: Liveright.

Orozco, M. and A. Hurtado Albir (2002) 'Measuring translation competence acquisition', *Meta*, 47(3): 375–402.

Ortiz, F. (1940) *Contrapunto cubano del tabaco y el azúcar*, Havana: Universidad Central de las Valles, trans. H. Onis (1947) as *Cuban Counterpoint: Tobacco and Sugar*, New York: Knopf.

Osborne, H. (2001) 'Hooked on classics: discourses of allusion in the mid-Victorian novel', in R. Ellis and L. Oakley-Brown (eds) *Translation and Nation: Towards a cultural politics of Englishness*, Clevedon: Multilingual Matters, pp. 120–66.

Øverås, L. (1998) 'In search of the third code: an investigation of norms in literary translation', *Meta*, 48(4): 571–88.

PACTE (2000) 'Acquiring translation competence: hypotheses and methodological problems in a research project', in A. Beeby, D. Ensinger and M. Presas (eds) *Investigating Translation*, Amsterdam and Philadelphia: John Benjamins, pp. 99–106.

PACTE (2003) 'Building a translation competence model', in F. Alves (ed.) *Triangulating Translation: Perspectives in process oriented research*, Amsterdam and Philadelphia: John Benjamins, pp. 43–66.

PACTE (2005) 'Investigating translation competence: conceptual and methodological issues', *Meta*, 50(2): 609–19.

PACTE (2007) 'Zum Wesen der Übersetzungskompetenz: Grundlagen für die experimentelle Validierung einesÜk-Modells', in G. Wotjak (ed.) *Quo vadis Translatologie? Ein halbes Jahrhundert universitärer Ausbildung von Dolmetschern und Übersetzern in Leipzig: Rückschau, Zwischenbilanz und Perspektiven aus der Aussensicht*, Berlin: Frank und Timme, pp. 327–42.

Padilla, P. and T. Bajo (1998) 'Hacia un modelo de memoria y atención en interpretación simultánea', *Quaderns*, 2: 107–17.

Paige, M. R. (1993) 'On the nature of intercultural experiences and intercultural education', in M. R. Paige (ed.) *Education for the Intercultural Experience*, Yarmouth, ME: Intercultural Press, pp. 1–21.

Paine, T. (1791/1984) *The Rights of Man*, Harmondsworth: Penguin.

Palmer, R. E. (1969) *Hermeneutics: Interpretation theory in Schleiermacher, Dilthey, Heidegger, and Gadamer*, Evanston, IL: Northwestern University Press.

Paolinelli, M. and E. Di Fortunato (2005) *Tradurre per il Doppiaggio*, Milano: Hoepli.

Parks, T. (2007) *Translating Style: The English Modernists and their Italian translations*, Manchester: St Jerome, 2nd edition.

Partington, A. (1998) *Patterns and Meanings: Using corpora for English language research and teaching*, Amsterdam and Philadelphia: John Benjamins.

Pavesi, M. (1994) 'Osservazioni sulla (socio)linguistica del doppiaggio', in R. Baccolini, R. M. Bollettieri Bosinelli and L. Gavioli (eds) *Il Doppiaggio: Trasposizioni Linguistiche e Culturali*, Bologna: CLUEB, pp. 129–42.

Pavesi, M. (1996) 'L'allocuzione nel doppiaggio dall'inglese all'italiano', in C. Heiss and R. M. Bollettieri Bosinelli (eds) *La traduzione multimediale per il cinema, la televisione e la scena*, Bologna: CLUEB, pp. 117–30.

Perrot d'Ablancourt, N. (1654/1997) Dedication of translation of Lucian, translated by D. Ross, in D. Robinson (ed.) (1997) *Western Translation Theory: From Herodotus to Nietzsche*, Manchester: St. Jerome, pp. 156–61.

Perteghella, M. and E. Loffredo (eds) (2006) *Translation and Creativity*, London: Continuum.

Peters, F. E. (2007) *The Voice, the Word, the Books: The sacred scripture of the Jews, Christians and Muslims*, Princeton: Princeton University Press.

Philo Judaeus (20 BCE/1997) 'The creation of the Septuagint', in D. Robinson (ed.) (1997) *Western Translation Theory: From Herodotus to Nietzsche*, Manchester: St. Jerome, pp. 12–14.

Pike, K. L. (1967) *Tone Languages*, Anne Arbor, MI: University of Michigan Press.

Pisek, G. (1994) *Die Grosse Illusion: Probleme und Möglichkeiten der Filmsynchronisation. Dargestellt an Woody Allens "Annie Hall", "Manhattan" und "Hannah and Her Sisters"*, Trier: Wissenschaftlicher Verlag Trier.

Pöchhacker, F. (1994) 'Sight translation and interpreter training', in Y. Gambier and M. Snell-Hornby (eds) (1994) *Problems and Trends in the Teaching of Interpreting and Translation*, Misano Adriatico: Istituto San Pellegrino, pp. 127–37.

Pöchhacker, F. (1998) 'Unity in diversity: the case of interpreting studies', in L. Bowker, M. Cronin, D. Kenny and J. Pearson (eds) *Unity in Diversity: Current trends in translation studies,* Manchester: St. Jerome, pp. 169–76.

Pöchhacker, F. (2004) *Introducing Interpreting Studies*, London and New York: Routledge.

Pöchhacker, F. (2006) 'Research and methodology in healthcare interpreting', in E. Hertog and B. van der Veer (eds) (2006) *Taking Stock: Research and methodology in community interpreting*, Antwerp: Hogeschool Antwerpen, pp. 135–59.

Pöchhacker, F. and M. Shlesinger (eds) (2002) *The Interpreting Studies Reader*, London and New York: Routledge.

Pollard, D. (ed.) (1998) *Translation and Creation: Readings of Western literature in Early Modern China, 1840–1918*, Amsterdam and Philadelphia: John Benjamins.

Popovič, A. (1970) 'The concept "shift of expression" in translation', in J. Holmes, F. de Haan and A. Popovič (eds) *The Nature of Translation: Essays on the theory and practice of literary translation*, The Hague: Mouton de Gruyter, pp. 78–87.

Popovič, A. (1976) *A Dictionary for the Analysis of Literary Translation*, Edmonton, AB: University of Alberta.

Poyatos, F. (1987/2002) 'Nonverbal communication in simultaneous and consecutive interpretation: a theoretical model and new perspectives', in F. Pöchhacker and M. Shlesinger (eds) (2002) *The Interpreting Studies Reader*, London and New York: Routledge, pp. 235–46.

Poyatos, F. (2002) *Nonverbal Communication across Disciplines: Culture, sensory interaction, speech, conversation*, Amsterdam and Philadelphia: John Benjamins.

Pradas Macías, E. M., E. Ortega Arjonilla and P. San Ginés Aguilar (2004) *La fluidez y sus pausas: enfoque desde la interpretación de conferencias*, Granada: Comares.

Presas, M. (2000) 'Bilingual competence and translation competence', in B. Adab and C. Schäffner (eds) *Developing Translation Competence*, Amsterdam and Philadelphia: John Benjamins, pp. 19–31.

Presas, M. (2004) 'Translatorische Kompetenz als Expertenwissen: Eine Annäherung aus kognitiv-psychologischer Sicht', in E. Fleischmann, P. A. Schmitt and G. Wotjak (eds) *Translationskompetenz*, Tübingen: Stauffenburg Verlag, pp. 199–207.

Prins, Y. (2005) 'Metrical translation: nineteenth-century Homers and the hexameter mania', in S. Bermann and M. Wood (eds) *Nation, Language, and the Ethics of Translation*, Princeton, NJ, and Oxford: Princeton University Press, pp. 229–56.

Pushkin, A. (1964) *Eugene Onegin: A Novel in Verse*, translated with a commentary by V. Nabokov, London and New York: Pantheon Books.

Pym, A. (1992) 'The relation between translation and material text transfer', *Target*, 4(2): 171–89.

Pym, A. (1992a) *Translation and Text Transfer: An essay on the principles of intercultural communication*, Frankfurt am Main, Berlin and Bern: Peter Lang.

Pym, A. (1992b) 'Translation error analysis and the interface with language teaching', in C. Dollerup and A. Lindegaard (eds) *Teaching Translation and Interpreting 1*, Amsterdam and Philadelphia: John Benjamins, pp. 279–88.

Pym, A. (1997) *Pour une éthique du traducteur*, Arras, France, and Ottawa, ON: Artois Presses Université and Presses de l'Université d'Ottawa.

Pym, A. (ed.) (2001) *The Translator*, Special Issue *The Return to Ethics*, 7(2).

Pym, A. (2002) 'On cooperation', in M. Olohan (ed.) *Intercultural Faultlines: Research methods in translation studies I: Textual and cognitive aspects*, Manchester: St. Jerome, pp. 181–92.

Pym, A. (2003) 'Redefining translation competence in an electronic age: in defence of a minimalist approach', *Meta*, 48(4): 481–97, http://www.erudit.org/revue/meta/2003/v48/n4/008533ar.html, visited 01/03/08.

Pym, A. (2004) 'Propositions on cross-cultural communication and translation', *Target*, 16(1): 1–28.

Pym, A. (2008) 'On Toury's laws of how translators translate', in A. Pym, M. Shlesinger and D. Simeoni (eds) *Beyond Descriptive Translation Studies*, Amsterdam and Philadelphia: John Benjamins, pp. 311–28.

Pym, A., A. Perekrestenko and B. Starink (eds) (2006) *Translation Technology and its Teaching*, Tarragona: Intercultural Studies Group.

Pym, A, M. Shlesinger and D. Simeoni (eds) (2008) *Beyond Descriptive Translation Studies*, Amsterdam and Philadelphia: John Benjamins.

Quine, W. (1960) *Word and Object*, Cambridge, MA: MIT Press.

Rafael, V. (1993) *Contracting Colonialism: Translation and Christian conversion of Tagalog society under early Spanish rule*, Durham, NC and London: Duke University Press.

Rafael, V. (2005) *The Promise of the Foreign: Nationalism and the technics of translation in the Spanish Philippines*, Durham, NC, and London: Duke University Press.

Rapp, R. (1999) 'Automatic identification of word translations from unrelated English and German corpora', in *Proceedings of the 37th Annual Meeting of the Association for Computational Linguistics*, College Park, MA: University of Maryland, pp. 395–8.

Raskin, V. (1985) *Semantic Mechanisms of Humour*, Dordrecht: D. Reidel.

Reddy, M. J. (1973/1993) 'The conduit metaphor', in A. Ortony (ed.) *Metaphor and Thought*, Cambridge: Cambridge University Press, pp. 164–201.

Reiss, K. (1971/2000) *Möglichkeiten und Grenzen der Übersetzungskritik*, Munich: Max Hueber, trans. E. F. Rhodes as *Translation Criticism: The Potential and limitations*, New York: American Bible Society; Manchester: St. Jerome.

Reiss, K. (1976) *Texttyp und Übersetzungsmethode: Der operative Text*, Kronberg: Scriptor Verlag.

Reiss, K. (1977/1989) 'Text-types, translation types and translation assessment', trans. A. Chesterman, in A. Chesterman (ed.) (1989) *Readings in Translation Theory*, Helsinki: Oy Finn Lectura Ab, pp. 105–15.

Reiss, K. (2004) 'Type, kind, and individuality of text: decision-making in translation', in L. Venuti (ed.) *The Translation Studies Reader*, 2nd edition, London and New York: Routledge, pp. 168–79.

Reiss, K. and H. J. Vermeer (1984) *Grundlegung einer allgemeinen Translationtheorie*, Tübingen: Niemeyer.

Rener, F. (1989) *Interpretatio: Language and translation from Cicero to Tytler*, Amsterdam and Atlanta: Rodopi.

Reynolds, M. (2006) 'Principles and norms of translation', in P. France and K. Haynes (eds) *The Oxford History of Literary Translation in English: Volume 4, 1790–1900*, Oxford: Oxford University Press.

Ricoeur, P. (1981/1998) *Hermeneutics and the Human Sciences*, trans. and ed. J. B. Thompson, Cambridge: Cambridge University Press.

Risager, K. (2006) *Language and Culture*, Clevedon: Multilingual Matters.

Risku, H. (1998) *Translatorische Kompetenz: Kognitive Grundlagen des Übersetzens als Expertentätigkeit*, Tübingen: Stauffenburg Verlag.

Roberts, R. (1997) 'Community interpreting today and tomorrow', in E. S. Carr, R. Roberts, A. Dufour and D. Steyn (eds) (1997) *The Critical Link: Interpreters in the community*, Amsterdam and Philadelphia: John Benjamins, pp. 7–26.

Roberts, R. P., S. E. Carr, D. Abraham and A. Dufour (eds) (2000) *The Critical Link 2: Interpreters in the community*, Amsterdam and Philadelphia: John Benjamins.

Robinson, D. (1991) *The Translator's Turn*, Baltimore, MD, and London: Johns Hopkins University Press.

Robinson, D. (1995) 'Theorizing translation in a woman's voice', *The Translator*, 1(2): 153–75.

Robinson, D. (ed.) (1997a) *Western Translation Theory: From Herodotus to Nietzsche*, Manchester: St. Jerome.

Robinson, D. (1997b) *Translation and Empire: Postcolonial theories explained*, Manchester: St. Jerome.

Robinson, D. (1998a) 'Free translation', in M. Baker and K. Malmkjær (eds) *Routledge Encyclopedia of Translation Studies*, 1st edition, London and New York: Routledge, pp. 87–90.

Robinson, D. (1998b) 'Hermeneutic motion', in M. Baker and K. Malmkjær (eds) *Routledge Encyclopedia of Translation Studies*, 1st edition, London and New York: Routledge, pp. 97–9.

Robinson, D. (1998c) 'Literal translation', in M. Baker and K. Malmkjær (eds) *Routledge Encyclopedia of Translation Studies*, 1st edition, London and New York: Routledge, pp. 125–27.

Robinson, D. (1998d) 'Paraphrase', in M. Baker and K. Malmkjær (eds) *Routledge Encyclopedia of Translation Studies*, 1st edition, London and New York: Routledge, pp. 166–67.

Robinson, D. (1998e) 'Pseudo-translation', in M. Baker and K. Malmkjær (eds) *Routledge Encyclopedia of Translation Studies*, 1st edition, London and New York: Routledge, pp. 183–5.

Rock, J. (2006) 'The translator's tightrope: recognizing and avoiding overtranslation', *The ATA Chronicle*, 35(19) (June).

Roffe, I. (1995) 'Teaching, learning and assessment strategies for interlingual subtitling', *Journal of Multilingual and Multicultural Development*, 16(3): 215–25.

Rogers, E. M., W. B. Hart and Y. Miike (2002) 'Edward T. Hall and the history of intercultural communication: the United States and Japan', *Keio Communication Review*, 24: 3–26.

Roland, R. (1999) *Interpreters as Diplomats*, Ottawa: University of Ottawa Press.

Rosenberg, B. A. (2007) 'A data-driven analysis of telephone interpreting', in C. Wadensjö, B. Englund Dimitrova and A-L. Nilsson (eds) *The Critical Link 4: Professionalisation of interpreting in the community*, Amsterdam and Philadelphia: John Benjamins, pp. 65–76.

Rothe-Neves, R. (2005) 'A abordagem comportamental das competências: aplicabilidade aos estudos da tradução', in F. Alves, C. Magalhães and A. Pagano (eds) *Competência em tradução. Cognição e discurso*, Belo Horizonte: Universidade Federal de Minas Gerais, pp. 91–107.

Rothe-Neves, R. (2007) 'Notes on the concept of "translator's competence"', *Quaderns*, 14: 125–38.

Rowling, J. K. (1997a) *Harry Potter and the Philosopher's Stone*, London: Bloomsbury.

Rowling, J. K. (1997b) *Harry Potter a l'école des sorciers*, trans. J-F. Menard, Paris: Éditions Gallimard.

Roy, C. B. (1993/2002) 'The problem with definitions, descriptions, and the role of metaphors of interpreters', in F. Pöchhacker and M. Shlesinger (eds) (2002) *The Interpreting Studies Reader*, London and New York: Routledge, pp. 345–53.

Roy, C. B. (2000) *Interpreting as a Discourse Process*, Oxford: Oxford University Press.

Rozan, J.-F. (1956) *La prise de notes en interprétation consécutive*, Geneva: Georg.

Rushdie, S. (1988) *The Satanic Verses,* London: Viking Penguin.

Russo, M. (1995) 'Media interpreting: variables and strategies', *Translatio: Nouvelles de la FIT – FIT Newsletter*, 14(3–4): 343–9.

Sacks, O. (1985) *The Man who Mistook his Wife for a Hat*, London: Picador.

Sager, J. C. (1990) *A Practical Course in Terminology Processing*, Amsterdam and Philadelphia: John Benjamins.

Sager, J. C. (1993) *Language Engineering and Translation: Consequences of automation*, Amsterdam and Philadelphia: John Benjamins.

Salkie, R. (2001) 'A new look at modulation', in M. Thelen (ed.) *Translation and Meaning*, Part 5, Maastricht: Translation Institute, pp. 433–41.

Sandrock, U. (1982) Thinking aloud protocols (TAPs) – ein Instrument zur Dekomposition des komplexen Prozesses "Übersetzen" ', unpublished PhD thesis, Universität Kassel.

Santaemilia, J. (ed.) (2005) *Sex and Translation: The manipulation of identities*, Manchester: St Jerome.

Sanz, J. (1931) 'Le travail et les aptitudes des interprètes parlementaires', *Anals d'Orientació Professional*, 4(4): 303–18.

Sapir, E. (1929/1958) *Culture, Language and Personality*, D. G. Mandelbaum (ed.) 1958, Berkeley: University of California Press.

Saussure, F. de (1993) *Troisième cours de linguistique générale (1910–1911): d'après les cahiers d'Émile Constantin* [Saussure's Third Course of Lectures on General Linguistics (1910–1911): From the notebooks of E. Constantin], French text ed. E. Komatsu, English trans. R. Harris, Oxford: Pergamon.

Saussure, F. de (1996) *Premier cours de linguistique générale (1907): d'après les cahiers d'Albert Riedlinger* [Saussure's First Course of Lectures on General Linguistics (1907): From the notebooks of A. Riedlinger], French text ed. E. Komatsu, English trans. G. Wolf, Oxford: Pergamon.

Saussure, F. de (1997) *Deuxième cours de linguistique générale (1908–1909): d'après les cahiers d'Albert Riedlinger et Charles Patois* [Saussure's Second Course of Lectures on General Linguistics (1908–09): From the notebooks of A. Riedlinger and C. Patois], French text ed. E. Komatsu, English trans. G. Wolf, Oxford: Pergamon.

Schäffner, C. (1998a) 'Skopos theory', in M. Baker (ed.) 1998, pp. 235–8.

Schäffner, C. (1998b) 'Action (theory of "translatorial action")', in M. Baker (ed.) 1998, pp. 3–5.

Schäffner, C. and H. Kelly-Holmes (eds) (1995) *Cultural Functions of Translation*, Clevedon: Multilingual Matters.

Scheffler, H. W. (2002) 'Kinship terms', in D. A. Cruse, F. Hundsnurscher, M. Job and P. R. Lutzeier (eds) *Lexikologie: ein Internationales Handbuch zur Natur und Struktur von Wörtern und Wortschätzen / Lexicology: An international handbook on the nature and structure of words and vocabularies*, Vol. 2, Berlin and New York: Walter de Gruyter, pp. 1539–41.

Schleiermacher, F. (1813/1963) 'Über die verschiedenen Methoden des Übersetzens', in J. Störig (ed.) *Das Problem des Übersetzens* (Wege der Forschung 8), Darmstadt: Wissenschaftliche Buchgesellschaft, pp. 38–70.

Schleiermacher, F. (1813/2004) 'On the different methods of translating', in L. Venuti (ed.) (2004) *The Translation Studies Reader*, 2nd edition, London and New York: Routledge, pp. 43–63.

Schleiermacher, F. (1998) *Hermeneutics and Criticisms and Other Writings*, trans. and ed. A. Bowie, Cambridge: Cambridge University Press.

Schmid, P. and C. Gdaniec (1996) 'Evolution of the logos grammar: system design and development methodology', in *Expanding MT Horizons*, Proceedings of the 2nd Conference of the Association for Machine Translation in the Americas, 2–5 October 1996, Montreal, QC, Washington, DC: AMTA, pp. 86–95.

Séguinot, C. (1989) 'Understanding why translators make mistakes', *TTR (Traduction, terminologie, rédaction)*, 2(2): 73–81.

Seleskovitch, D. (1968/1978) *L'interprète dans les conférences internationales: problèmes de langage et de communication*, Paris: Minard, trans. (1978) as *Interpreting for International Conferences*, Washington, DC: Pen and Booth.

Seleskovitch, D. (1975) *Langage, langues et mémoire: étude de la prise de notes en interprétation consécutive*, Paris: Minard.

Seleskovitch, D. (1975/2002) 'Language and memory: a study of note-taking in consecutive interpreting', in Franz Pöchhacker and Miriam Shlesinger (eds) (2002) *The Interpreting Studies Reader*, London and New York: Routledge, pp. 121–9.

Seleskovitch, D. (1986) 'Translation: corresponding words or equivalent texts', *Textcontext*, 2: 128–40.

Seleskovitch, D. (1990) 'La contribution de l'interprétation à la théorie de la traduction', in R. Arntz and G. Thome (eds) *Übersetzungswissenschaft: Ergebnisse und Perspektiven, Festschrift für W. Wilss*, Tübingen: Gunter Narr Verlag, pp. 528–35.

Seleskovitch, D. and M. Lederer (1984/2001) *Interpréter pour traduire*, Paris: Didier Érudition.

Seleskovitch, D. and M. Lederer (1989) *Pédagogie raisonnée de l'interprétation*, Paris: Didier Érudition.

Sengupta, M. (1990) 'Translation, colonialism and poetics: Rabindranath Tagore in two worlds', in S. Bassnett and A. Lefevere (eds), *Translation, History and Culture*, London and New York: Pinter, pp. 56–63.

Shackman, J. (1984) *The Right to Be Understood: A handbook on working with, employing and training community interpreters*, Cambridge: National Extension College.

Sharoff, S. (2006) 'Open-source corpora: using the net to fish for linguistic data', *International Journal of Corpus Linguistics*, 11(4): 435–62.

Sharoff, S., B. Babych and A. Hartley (2008) '"Irrefragable answers": using comparable corpora to retrieve translation equivalents', *Language Resources and Evaluation*, (forthcoming), available online at www.springerlink.com/content/8k6631431pl35381, visited 15/08/2008.

Shelley, P. B. (1821/2003) 'A defence of poetry', in P. B. Shelley (2003) *Major Works*, Oxford: Oxford University Press.

Shlesinger, M. (1994) 'Intonation in the production and perception of simultaneous interpretation', in S. Lambert and B. Moser-Mercer (eds) *Bridging the Gap: Empirical research in simultaneous interpretation*, Amsterdam and Philadelphia: John Benjamins, pp. 225–36.

Shreve, G. M. (1997) 'Cognition and the evolution of translation competence', in J. H. Danks, G. M. Shreve, S. B. Fountain and M. K. McBeath (eds) *Cognitive Processes in Translation and Interpreting*, Thousand Oaks, CA: Sage, pp. 120–36.

Shreve, G. M. (2006) 'The deliberate practice: translation and expertise', *Journal of Translation Studies*, 9(1): 27–42.

Shuttleworth, M. and M. Cowie (1997) *Dictionary of Translation Studies*, Manchester: St. Jerome.

Simeoni, D. (1998) 'The pivotal status of the translator's habitus', *Target*, 10(1): 1–40.
Simms, K. (ed.) (1997) *Translating Sensitive Texts: Linguistic aspects*, Amsterdam and Atlanta, GA: Rodopi.
Simon, S. (1996) *Gender in Translation: Cultural identity and the politics of transmission*, London and New York: Routledge.
Simon, S. and P. St.-Pierre (eds) (2000) *Changing the Terms: Translating in the postcolonial era*, Ottawa: University of Ottawa Press.
Simons, M. (1999) *Beauvoir and The Second Sex: Feminism, race, and the origins of existentialism*, Lanham, MD: Rowman and Littlefield.
Sinclair, J. M. (1987) *Looking Up – An account of the COBUILD project in lexical computing*, London: Collins.
Sinclair, J. M. (1991) *Corpus, Concordance, Collocation*, Oxford: Oxford University Press.
Sirén, S. and K. Hakkarainen (2002) 'The cognitive concept of expertise applied to expertise in translation', Across Languages and Cultures 3(1): 71–82.
Snell-Hornby, M. (1988/1995) *Translation Studies: An integrated approach*, Amsterdam and Philadelphia: John Benjamins.
Snell-Hornby, M. (2006) *The Turns of Translation Studies: New paradigms or shifting viewpoints?*, Amsterdam and Philadelphia: John Benjamins.
Somers, H. (ed.) (2003a) *Computers and Translation: A translator's guide*, Amsterdam and Philadelphia: John Benjamins.
Somers, H. (2003b) 'Machine translation: latest developments', in R. Mitkov (ed.), *The Oxford Handbook of Computational Linguistics*, Oxford: Oxford University Press, pp. 512–28.
Somers, H. (2008) 'Corpora and machine translation', in A. Lüdeling and M. Kytö (eds) *Corpus Linguistics: An international handbook*, Berlin: Mouton de Gruyter, (forthcoming).
Sowerby, R. (2006) *The Augustan Art of Poetry: Augustan translation of the classics*, Oxford: Oxford University Press.
Soyinka, W. (1973) *The 'Bacchae' of Euripides*, London: Eyre Methuen.
Sperber, D. and D. Wilson (1986/1995) *Relevance: Communication and cognition*, Oxford: Blackwell Publishing.
Spiro, R. J. (1980) 'Constructive processes in prose comprehension and recall', in R. J. Spiro, B. C. Bruce and W. F. Brewer (eds) *Theoretical Issues in Reading Comprehension*, Hillsdale, NJ: Erlbaum, pp. 245–78.
Spivak, G. C. (1992/2004) 'The Politics of Translation', in M. Barret and A. Philips (eds) *Destabilizing Theory: Contemporary feminist debates*, Cambridge: Polity, pp. 177–200.
Spivak, G. (1993/2004) 'The politics of translation', in L. Venuti (ed.) (2004) *The Translation Studies Reader*, London and New York: Routledge, pp. 369–88.
Spivak, G. C. (2005) 'Translating into English', in S. Bermann and M. Wood (eds) *Nation, Language, and the Ethics of Translation*, Princeton, NJ, and Oxford: Princeton University Press, pp. 93–110.

Stark, S. (1999) *'Behind Inverted Commas': Translation and Anglo-German cultural relations in the nineteenth century*, Clevedon: Multilingual Matters.

Stecconi, U. (2000) 'Translating like a spider: An empirical study of translated websites', unpublished paper presented at *Research Models in Translation Studies Conference*, Manchester, April 2000.

Stein, G. (1922) *Geography and Plays*, Boston: Four Seas.

Steiner, G. (1967) *Language and Silence: Essays on language, literature, and the inhuman*, New York: Atheneum.

Steiner, G. (1975/1998) *After Babel: Aspect of language and translation*, Oxford: Oxford University Press.

Steiner, G. (2004) 'The hermeneutic motion', in L. Venuti (ed.), *The Translation Studies Reader*, 2nd edition, London and New York: Routledge, pp. 193–98.

Steiner, T. (ed.) (1975) *English Translation Theory: 1650–1800*, Assen and Amsterdam: van Gorcum.

Sternberg, M. (1981) 'Polylingualism as reality and translation as mimesis', *Poetics Today*, 2(4): 221–39.

Stewart, D., Schein, J. and B. Cartwright (1998) *Sign Language Interpreting: Exploring its art and science*, Boston: Allyn and Bacon.

Stolze, R. (1997) *Übersetzungstheorien: Eine Einführung*, Tübingen: Gunter Narr.

Stolze, R. (2001) *Die Fachübersetzung: Eine Einführung*, Tübingen: Gunter Narr Verlag.

Sturge, K. (2004) *'The Alien Within': Translation into German during the Nazi Regime*, Munich: Iudicium.

Sturge, K. (2007) *Representing Others: Translation, ethnography and the museum*, Manchester: St. Jerome.

Susam-Sarajeva, Ş. (2002) 'A "multilingual" and "international" translation studies?', in T. Hermans (ed.), *Crosscultural Transgressions – Research models in translation studies II: Historical and ideological issues*, Manchester: St. Jerome, pp. 193–207.

Susam-Sarajeva, S. (2008) *Translation and Music*, Special issue of *The Translator* 14(2).

Swales, J. (1990) *Genre Analysis*, Cambridge: Cambridge University Press.

Taft, R. (1981) 'The role and personality of the mediator', in S. Bochner (ed.) *The Mediating Person: Bridges between cultures*, Cambridge, MA: Schenkman, pp. 53–88.

Tannen, D. (1979) 'What is a frame – surface evidence for underlying expectations', in R. O. Freedle (ed.) *New Directions in Discourse Processing*, Norwood, NJ: Ablex, pp. 137–81.

Tesnière, L. (1959) *Éléments de syntaxe structurelle*, Paris: Klincksieck.

Thiéry, C. (1990) 'Interprétation diplomatique', in M. Lederer (ed.) *Études traductologiques*, Paris: Minard-Lettres modernes, pp. 45–59.

Thomas, E. (1985) 'How to increase naturalness in translation by mother-tongue translators', *Notes on Translation*, 1(106): 6–9.

Thomas, R. (1997) 'United Nations military observer interpreting in a community setting', in E. Silvana, R. Roberts, A. Dufour and D. Steyn (eds) (1997) *The Critical Link: Interpreters in the Community*, Amsterdam and Philadelphia: John Benjamins, pp. 249–57.

Tirkkonen-Condit, S. (1989) 'Professional versus non-professional translation: a think-aloud protocol study', in C. Séguinot (ed.) *The Translation Process*, Toronto: H. G. Publications, pp. 73–85.

Tirkkonen-Condit, S. and R. Jääskeläinen (eds) (2000) *Tapping and Mapping the Process of Translation: Outlooks on empirical research*, Amsterdam and Philadelphia: John Benjamins.

Titford, C. (1982) 'Subtitling – constrained translation', *Lebende Sprachen*, 17(3): 113–16.

Toolan, M. (ed.) (1992) *Language, Text and Context: Essays in stylistics*, London and New York: Routledge.

Toury, G. (1980) *In Search of a Theory of Translation*, Tel Aviv: The Porter Institute for Poetics and Semiotics.

Toury, G. (1995) *Descriptive Translation Studies and Beyond*, Amsterdam and Philadelphia: John Benjamins.

Toury, G. (1995/2004) 'The nature and role of norms in translation', in L. Venuti (ed.) (2004) *The Translation Studies Reader*, 2nd edition, London and New York: Routledge, pp. 205–18.

Toury, G. (2004) 'Probabilistic explanations in translation studies: welcome as they are, would they qualify as universals?', in A. Mauranen and P. Kujamäki (eds) *Translation Universals: Do They Exist?* Amsterdam and Philadelphia: John Benjamins, pp. 15–32.

Toussaint, S. D. (1966) 'A proper approach to exegesis', *Notes on Translation*, 1(20) (May): 1–6.

Trivedi, H. (2006) 'In our own time, on our own terms', in T. Hermans (ed.) (2006), pp. 102–19.

Trosberg, A. (ed.) (1997) *Text Type and Typology*, Amsterdam and Philadelphia: John Benjamins.

Trosberg, A. (2000) 'Discourse analysis as part of translator training', *Current Issues in Language and Society*, 7(3): 185–228.

Turner, G. H. (2007) 'Exploring inter-subdisciplinary alignment in interpreting studies: sign language interpreting at conferences', in F. Pöchhacker, A. L. Jakobsen and I. M. Mees (eds) *Interpreting Studies and Beyond*, Copenhagen: Samfundslitteratur Press, pp. 191–216.

Tymoczko, M. (1999) *Translation in a Postcolonial Context: Early Irish literature in English translation*, Manchester: St. Jerome.

Tymoczko, M. (2000) 'Translation and political engagement: activism, social change and the role of translation in geopolitical shifts', *The Translator*, 6: 23–47.

Tymoczko, M. (2003) 'Ideology and the position of the translator: in what sense is a translator "in between"?', in M. Calzada Pérez (ed.) *Apropos of Ideology: Translation studies on ideology – Ideologies in translation studies*, Manchester: St. Jerome, pp. 181–201.

Tymoczko, M. (2006) 'Reconceptualizing Western Translation Theory', in Theo Hermans (ed.) (2006) *Translating Others*, Manchester: St. Jerome, Vol. I, pp. 13–22.

Tymoczko, M. and E. Gentzler (eds) (2002) *Translation and Power*, Amherst and Boston, MA: University of Massachusetts Press.

Tytler, A. F. (Lord Woodhouselee) (1797/1978/1997) *Essay on the Principles of Translation*, London: Cadell and Davies, Edinburgh: Creech (1797, second edition); edited with an introduction by J. F. Huntsman, Amsterdam: John Benjamins (1978); extracted in D. Robinson (ed.) (1997), *Western Translation Theory: From Herodotus to Nietzsche*, Manchester: St. Jerome, pp. 208–12.

United Nations (1948) *Universal Declaration of Human Rights*, http://www.un.org/Overview/rights.html, visited 22/08/2008.

Vandaele, J. (2002) ' "Funny fictions": Francoist translation censorship of two Billy Wilder Films', *The Translator*, 8(2): 267–302.

Vandaele, J. (ed.) (2003) *Humour and Translation*, Special Issue of *The Translator* 8(2).

Vásquez Ayora, G. (1977) *Introducción a la traductología*, Washington, DC: Georgetown University Press.

Ventola, E. (ed.) (2000) *Discourse and Community: Doing functional linguistics*, Tübingen: Gunter Narr Verlag.

Venuti, L. (ed.) (1992) *Rethinking Translation: Discourse, subjectivity, ideology*, London and New York: Routledge.

Venuti, L. (1995/2008) *The Translator's Invisibility: A history of translation*, London and New York: Routledge.

Venuti, L. (1998a) *The Scandals of Translation: Towards an ethics of difference*, London and New York: Routledge.

Venuti, L. (ed.) (1998b) *The Translator*, Special Issue *Translation and Minority*, 4(2).

Venuti, L. (2003) 'Translating Derrida on translation: relevance and disciplinary resistance', *The Yale Journal of Criticism*, 16(2): 237–62.

Venuti, L. (ed.) (2004) *The Translation Studies Reader*, 2nd edition, London and New York: Routledge.

Venuti, L. (2005a) 'Local contingencies: translation and national identities', in S. Bermann and M. Wood (eds) *Nation, Language, and the Ethics of Translation*, Princeton, NJ, and Oxford: Princeton University Press, pp. 177–202.

Venuti, L. (2005b) 'Translation, history, narrative', *Meta*, 50(3): 800–16.

Venuti, L. (2007) 'Adaptation, translation, critique', *Journal of Visual Culture*, 6(1): 25–43.

Venuti, L. (ed.) (forthcoming) *The Oxford History of Literary Translation in English. Volume 5: 1900–2000*, Oxford: Oxford University Press.

Vermeer, H. (1978) 'Ein Rahmen für eine allgemeine Translationstheorie', Lebende Sprachen 23(3): 99–102.

Vermeer, H. J. (1986) 'Übersetzen als kultureller Transfer', in M. Snell-Hornby (ed.) *Übersetzungswissenchaft – eine neue Orientierung*, Tübingen: Francke, pp. 30–53.

Vermeer, H. J. (1989/2004) 'Skopos and commission in translational action', trans. A. Chesterman, in A. Chesterman (ed.), *Readings in Translation Theory*, Helsinki: Oy Finn Lectura Ab, pp. 173–87, reprinted in L. Venuti (ed.) *The Translation Studies Reader*, 2nd edition, London and New York: Routledge, pp. 227–38.

Véronis, J. (ed.) (2000) *Parallel Text Processing: Alignment and use of translation corpora*, Dordrecht: Kluwer.

Verschueren, J. (2003) ' "Culture" between interaction and cognition: bridge or gap?', in C. Inchaurralde and C. Florén (eds) *Interaction and Cognition in Linguistics*, Frankfurt am Main, Berlin and Bern: Peter Lang, pp. 3–14.

Vieira, E. (1999) 'Liberating Calibans: readings of Antropofagia and Haroldo de Campos' poetics of transcreation', in S. Bassnett and H. Trivedi (eds), *Post-Colonial Translation: Theory and practice*, London and New York: Routledge, pp. 95–113.

Viezzi, M. (1989) 'Information retention as a parameter for the comparison of sight translation and simultaneous interpretation: an experimental study', *The Interpreter's* Newsletter, 2: 65–9.

Viezzi, M. (1990) 'Sight translation, simultaneous interpretation and information retention', in L. Gran and C. Taylor (eds) *Aspects of Applied and Experimental Research on Conference Interpretation*, Udine: Campanotto, pp. 54–60.

Vinay, J.-P. and J. Darbelnet (1958) *Stylistique comparée du français et de l'anglais*, Paris: Didier, trans. and ed. J. C. Sager and M.-J. Hamel (1995) as *Comparative Stylistics of French and English: A methodology for translation*, Amsterdam and Philadelphia: John Benjamins.

Vinay, J.-P. and J. Darbelnet (1958/2004) 'A methodology for translation', trans. J. C. Sager and M.-J. Hamel, in L. Venuti (ed.) (2004) *The Translation Studies Reader*, 2nd edition, London and New York: Routledge, pp. 128–37.

Volk, M. (1998) 'The automatic translation of idioms: machine translation vs. translation memory systems', in N. Weber (ed.) *Machine Translation: Theory, applications, and evaluation – An assessment of the state of the art*, St. Augustin: Gardez-Verlag, pp. 1–27.

Vygotsky, L. (1962) *Thought and Language*, Cambridge, MA: MIT Press.

Waard, J. de and E. A. Nida (1986) *From One Language to Another: Functional equivalence in Bible translating*, Nashville, TN, Camden, NJ, and New York: Nelson.

Wadensjö, C. (1993/2002) 'The double role of a dialogue interpreter', in F. Pöchhacker and M. Shlesinger (eds) (2002) *The Interpreting Studies Reader*, London and New York: Routledge, pp. 355–70.

Wadensjö, C. (1998) *Interpreting as Interaction*, London and New York: Longman.

Wadensjö, C., B. Englund Dimitrova and A.-L. Nilsson (eds) (2007) *The Critical Link 4: Professionalisation of interpreting in the community*, Amsterdam and Philadelphia: John Benjamins.

Walton, J. M. (2006) *Found in Translation: Greek drama in English*, Cambridge: Cambridge University Press.

Weber, W. (1990) 'The importance of sight translation in an interpreter training program', in D. Bowen and M. Bowen (eds) (1990) *Interpreting – Yesterday, Today, and Tomorrow*, Binghamton: SUNY, pp. 44–52.

Webster, J. (1922) *Daddy Long-Legs*, London: Samuel French.

Weissbrod, R. (2007) 'Translation for Israeli television: the reflection of a hybrid identity', *Linguistica Antverpiensia New Series*, Special Issue *Audiovisual Translation: A tool for social integration*, 6: 23–33.

Wellisch, H. H. (1975) *Transcription and Transliteration: An annotated bibliography on conversion of scripts*, Silver Spring, MD: Institute of Modern Languages.

Wellisch, H. H. (1976) 'Script conversion practices in the world's libraries', *International Library* Review, 8: 55–84.

Wellisch, H. H. (1978) *The Conversion of Scripts, its Nature, History, and Utilization by Language: English*, New York: Wiley.

Wells, W., J. Burnett and S. Moriarty (1992) *Advertising Principles and Practices*, Englewood Cliffs, NJ: Prentice Hall.

Werlich, E. (1976) *A Text Grammar of English*, Heidelberg: Quelle und Meyer.

Weston, M. (2003) 'Meaning, truth and morality in translation', in G. Anderman and M. Rogers (eds) *Translation Today: Trends and perspectives*, Clevedon: Multilingual Matters, pp. 140–51.

White, J. (2003) 'How to evaluate machine translation', in H. Somers (ed.) *Computers and Translation: A translator's guide*, Amsterdam and Philadelphia: John Benjamins, pp. 211–44.

Widlund-Fantini, A-M. (2007) *Danica Seleskovitch: Interprète et témoin du XXe siècle*, Lausanne: L'Age d'Homme.

Wierzbicka, A. (1992) *Semantics, Culture, and Cognition: Universal human concepts in culture-specific configurations*, New York: Oxford University Press.

Wierzbicka, A. (1996) 'Japanese cultural scripts: cultural psychology and "cultural grammar" ', *Ethos*, 24(3) (Sept): 527–55.

Wierzbicka, A. (2006) *English Meaning and Culture*, Oxford: Oxford University Press.

Wildblood, A. (2002) 'A subtitle is not a translation: a day in the life of a subtitler', *Language International*, 14(2): 40–3.

Williams, J. and A. Chesterman (2002) *The Map: A beginner's guide to doing research in translation studies*, Manchester: St. Jerome.

Williams, R. (1976/83) *Keywords: A vocabulary of culture and society*, London: Fontana.

Wilson, D. and W. Sperber (2004) 'Relevance theory', in L. Horn and G. Ward (eds) *Handbook of Pragmatics*, Oxford: Blackwell, pp. 607–32, also online at: http://www.phon.ucl.ac.uk/home/deirdre/papers.html visited 03/11/2008.

Wilss, W. (1976) 'Perspectives and limitations of a didactic framework for the teaching of translation', in R. W. Brislin (ed.) *Translation Applications and Research*, New York: Gardner, pp. 117–37.

Wilss, W. (1982) *The Science of Translation: Problems and methods*, Tübingen: Gunter Narr Verlag.

Wilss, W. (1996) *Knowledge and Skills in Translator Behaviour*, Amsterdam and Philadelphia: John Benjamins.

Wilss, W. (1998) 'Decision making in translation', in M. Baker and Malmkjær (eds) *Routledge Encyclopedia of Translation Studies*, 1st edition, London and New York: Routledge, pp. 57–60.

Wilss, W. (1999) *Translation and Interpreting in the 20th Century: Focus on German*, Amsterdam and Philadelphia: John Benjamins.

Wittgenstein, L. (1958/1973) *Philosophical Investigations*, 3rd edition, trans. G. E. M. Anscombe, Cambridge: Cambridge University Press.

Wolf, M. (2000) 'The 'Third Space' in Postcolonial Representation', in S. Simon and P. St-Pierre (eds.) *Changing the Terms: Translating in the Postcolonial Era*, Ottawa: University of Ottawa Press, pp. 127–45.

Wolf, M. and A. Fukari (eds) (2007) *Constructing a Sociology of Translation*, Amsterdam and Philadelphia: John Benjamins.

Würtz, E. (2005) 'A cross-cultural analysis of websites from high-context cultures and low-context cultures', *Journal of Computer-Mediated Communication*, 11(1), article 13, http://jcmc.indiana.edu/vol11/issue1/wuertz.html, visited 01/03/2008.

Yule, G (1996) *Pragmatics*, Oxford: Oxford University Press.

Zaixi, T. (1997) 'Reflections on the science of translation', *Babel*, 43(4): 331–52.

Zanettin, F. (ed.) (2008) *Comics in Translation*, Manchester: St. Jerome.

Zanettin, F., S. Bernardini and D. Stewart (eds) (2003) *Corpora in Translator Education*, Manchester: St Jerome.

Zuber, R. (1968) *Les 'Belles Infidèles' et la formation du goût classique: Perrot d'Ablancourt et Guez de Balzac*, Paris: Armand Colin.

Zukofsky, L. and C. Zukofsky (1969) *Catullus*, London: Cape Goliard, and New York: Grossman.

INDEX

Numbers in **bold** indicate entry in Key Concepts section.

abusive: fidelity 98; translation **166**
accessibility *see* inclusion
adaptation 32, **166–7**, 180, 197, 212, 232
adequacy 16
adjustment **167**, 184, 186, 197
advertising 87, **167–8**
AIIC (Association Internationale des Interprètes de Conférence) **168**, 223
allusions 81
analysis **168**, 221, 234
anuvad 18
appropriation **169**, 184, 189
audience **169**, 184
audio description **169**, 198
audiovisual translation 17, 141–65, **169–70**, 232; linguistic and cultural issues 154–64; *see also* audio-description, dubbing, subtitling, voice-over
Augustine (Aurelius Augustinius) 2

back translation **170**
belles infidèles 22
Bible translation 2–3, 28
bilateral interpreting *see* liaison interpreting
borrowing 32, **170**, 182, 189, 203
brief **170**
Buddhist scriptures 16

calque 32, **170**, 182, 189
cannibalism 103, **171**
CAT Tools 107, 109, 117–21, **175**
Cicero, M. T. 1–2, 4, 190, 191
cognition 54–73, **171**; and culture 83–6; and interpreting 134, 135
coherence **171**, 188, 227
cohesion **172**
collocation 111, **172**, 203
colonization **172–3**
commissioner **173**
communicative: stage of translation 13, 21, 26–33; translation 30, 43, **173**, 223
community interpreting 137, **173–4**, 178, 204, 217

compensation **174**, 192, 194
componential analysis 29, **174–5**, 183, 203
computer-assisted translation tools *see* CAT Tools
concordance **175**
conference interpreting **175**, 178, 182, 204, 215, 220
connotation **176–7**, 186, 207
consecutive interpreting **176**, 211, 221, 231
content **190**, 191, 201, 207, 224, 229
context 37, 41, 76–7, **176–7**, 229; of culture 14, 77; of situation 77
controlled language 115–17, **177**
corpus, corpora 109–112, **177**, 214
corpus-based translation studies **176**, 239
correspondence **177–8**; formal 28, 178, 184, 186, **190**, 225, 232
court interpreting **178**, 222
covert translation 29, 30, 42, **179**, 213, 220
cultural filter, culture filter 29, 75–6, **179**
cultural references: translation of 155–8
cultural turn 11, **179**, 216, 227
culture 14, 74–92, 187, 197, 228; formal 81–3; grammar of 86–7; iceberg model of 78–9; informal 83–7; logical typing of 77–9; and power 87–8; as system of frames 76–9; technical 79
culturemes 79–81

decision-making 60
denotation, denotative meaning 85, **180**, 185, 186, 207
descriptive translation studies 10–11, 94–6, **180–1**, 203, 206, 210, 216
deverbalization 55
dialect translation **181**
dialogue interpreting **181**, 204
diplomatic interpreting **181–2**
direction of translation **182**
direct translation **182**, 187, 205, 211, 220
disambiguation 180, **183**, 223

INDEX

discourse 37, 47–9, 50–3, 225; and interpreting 134; markers, translation of 160
documentary translation 30, 43, **183**, 199
Dolet, E. 4
domestication 12, 43, 98–9, 179, 189, 202, 208
Dryden, J. 4
dubbing 141, 144–7, **184**, 209, 211, 238; countries 143–4
dynamic equivalence *see* equivalence

École Supérieure d'Interprètes et de Traducteurs (ESIT) 22
empirical-experimental research 68–72, **184–5**, 237; challenges ahead 72–3
equivalence **185–6**, 190, 195, 197, 212, 222, 223, 227; dynamic and functional 28–9, 30, 167, **184**, 190, 191, 210; formal **191**, 193, 195, 223; pragmatic 42; *see also* textual equivalence
equivalent effect **186**, 222
ethics 15, 93–7; ethical stage 21, 33–4, 95–7; and interpreting 137–8
ethnography 103, **186–7**, 233
evaluation: of machine translation 125–7
exegesis 187, 195
explicitation **187**, 192, 203, 219, 232, 233, 238
eye-tracking 71

faithfulness *see* fidelity
false friends 23, **188**, 199
fansubs 151–2
fan yi 18
feminist translation studies 100–2, *see also* gender and translation
fidelity **188**, 227, 229; abusive 98
FIT (Fédération Internationale des Traducteurs) **189**
footnotes 25
foreignization 11, 43, 84, 99, 179, 183, **189**, 208
form **190**, 191, 224, 229
formal equivalence *see* correspondence: formal
free translation 22–3, 184, **191**, 204, 224
functional equivalence *see* equivalence
functionalist: stage of translation 21, 33, 39–41, 94; view of culture 81–3
fuzzy match 192

gain 188, **192**
gender and translation **192–3**, 216
genre 36, **193**, 206, 213, 225, 230; genre shifts 46–7, 50, 179
gist translation **193**

globalization 104–5, 107
gloss **193**

habitus 84, **194**, 227
healthcare interpreting **194**, 220
hermeneutic motion 26, 192, **194**
hermeneutics 187, **195**
history of translation practice and theory 1–4; in Asia 4; challenge to Western presuppositions 18; in China 4, 16, 103; in India 103–4;
humour **195–6**; translation of 162–3
hybridity 102
hyponym **196**

ideology 97, 177, **196–7**, 216
idiomatic translation 22, **197**
imitation **197**
implied meaning **197–8**, 220
inclusion **198–9**
instrumental translation 30, 43, 183, **199**
intentionality 43–4
intercultural communication: translation as 74–92
interference **199**, 203, 236, 239
interlinear translation **199**
interlingual translation 5–6, **199**
interpretation *see* interpreting; (of meaning) *see* meaning
interpreter: as mediator 134; role of 134, 137; training 136–7
interpreting 9, 94, **200**; cognitive processing in 135; history of 138; quality of 135–6; signed 132, 140; *see also* community interpreting, conference interpreting, consecutive interpreting, court interpreting, dialogue interpreting, diplomatic interpreting, healthcare interpreting, liaison interpreting, medical interpreting, military interpreting, public service interpreting, relay interpreting, remote interpreting, simultaneous interpreting, telephone interpreting, whispered interpreting
interpreting studies 9, 16–17; 128–40; empirical research 184–5; evolution of 129–31; memes and models of 133–4; paradigms 132–3, 140; trends 139–40; unity in diversity 131–3
interpretive theory 54–6, 130–1, **200–1**, 215, 223
intersemiotic translation 5–6, **201**
intertextuality 44
intralingual translation 5–6, **201**, 214
invariance **201**, 231
inverse translation **201**
invisibility **201**

285

INDEX

Jerome 1–4, 21, 190

kernel **202**, 221, 234
kinship terms **202–3**
knowledge: encyclopaedic 79–81

lacuna **203**
language service providers 106
laws of translation 180, 199, **203**, 239
lexicogrammar **203–4**
liaison interpreting 181, **204**, 207, 221
linguistics: and translation 13, 26; and subtitling 154
linguistic variation: translation of 158–60
literal translation 22–3, 25, 182, 184, 189, 191, **204–5**, 224, 239
literary vs non-literary translation: 28–31, 34
locale **205**
localization 107, **205**, 209, 217; tools 120–1; of videogames 153–4
logos **205–6**
loss 188, **192**
loyalty *see* fidelity
Luther, M. 3, 4

machine translation (MT) 106–7, 110, 182, 197, **206**, 224; tools 121–3
Manipulation School **206**
meaning 26, 187, 190, 201, **206–7**, 212, 224, 228, 240; connotative, *see* connotation; denotative *see* denotation
media interpreting **207–8**
metaphrase **208**
military interpreting **208**
minoritizing translation 99, **208**
modulation **208–9**, 212
multimedia translation **209**

NAATI (National Accreditation Authority for Translators and Interpreters) **209**
Nairobi Declaration **209–10**
naturalness **210**
neologism **210**
neologistic translation 27
norms 83, 95–7, 196, 206, **210–11**, 215, 230
note taking **211**

oblique translation 182, 187, 195, 208, **211–12**
omission **212**, 240
opera translation **212–13**
otherness 104
overt translation 29, 30, 43, 179, **213**, 220
overtranslation **213**

parallel text **214**
paraphrase 201, **214**
paratext **214–15**
Paris School 14, 130, 132, **215**, 223, 228, *see also* interpretive theory
pivot language **211**, 220
politics 15, 93–105
polysystem theory **215–16**
postcolonial translation studies 101–2, **216**
power 87–8, 101–2, 192, 196, **216**, 227
pragmatic features: translation of 160–1
principles of translation (Tytler) 23–5
problem-solving **217**, 235
procedures *see* translation procedures
process of translation *see* translation process
project management 123–4
proxy 71
pseudo-translation 16, **217**
public service interpreting **217–18**
pure language *see* logos
purpose 218; communicative 134; rhetorical 53

receiver **218**, 229
reception **218–19**
redundancy **219**
referential meaning *see* denotation
refraction *see* rewriting
register analysis 13, 38–9, 41–3, 48–50, 53, 176–7, 179, 193, 213, **219**
relay interpreting 215, **220**, 228
relevance theory 60–1, 176, 182, **220**
remote interpreting **220–1**, 231
representation 19, 97–105
resistance, resistant translation 99, **221**
re-speaking 154
restructuring **221**
rewriting **221**
RID (Register of Interpreters for the Deaf) **222**
role of interpreter 134, 137, **222**
rupantar 18

sacred books 2, 22
science of translation 28, 31, **222**
screen translation *see* audiovisual translation; dubbing; subtitling
Seleskovitch, D. 215, **223**; *see also* interpretive theory, Paris School
semantic: structure analysis 180, **183**, 223; translation 30, 43, **223–4**
sense 200, 207, **224**
sense-for-sense 22, 191, 200, 204, **224**, 239
shifts in translation 180, 181, 201, 222, **225**, 232, 239
sight translation **225**, 226
sign **225**

286

INDEX

signed language 132, 140, 198, 200; interpreting 220, 222, **225–6**
simultaneous interpreting 207, 219, 221, **225**, **226**, 228
skopos theory 13, 39–41, 188, 218, **226–7**, 236
sociology of translation 194, **227**
songs: translation of 162
source-text oriented 33
Soviet School 130, **228**
speech acts 220, **228–9**
spirit **229**
style 190, **229–30**, 234
subtitling 6, 141, 143–4, 209, 211, **230**, 238; fansubs 151–2; for hard of hearing 198; process of 148–51; real-time 154; tools 120–1
surtitles, *see* opera translation

taboo language: translation of 160–1
target-text oriented 33
tarjama 18
technology 15–16, 106–27; authoring tools 114–17; CAT Tools 117–21; collaborative tools 124–5; evaluation techniques 125–7; in interpreting 138–9; infrastructure 108–112; machine translation 121–3; project management tools 123–4; software localization 120–1; subtitling 120–1
telephone interpreting **231**
terminology tools 112–14; term extraction 113–14; term management 114
tertium comparationis 181, 201, **231**
text **231**
text linguistics 36–7
text types 30–1, 40–1, 44–6, 193, 226, **232**
textual equivalence **190**, **232**
textuality 36, 43–6, 51, 53; in interpreting 134
théorie du sens see interpretive theory
thick translation 99–100, **233**
think-aloud protocols (TAPs) 69, 70, **233**
third code, third language **233–4**
transcription **234**
transculturation 19
transfer **234**
transference 19
translation competence 63–72, **234–5**; acquisition of 66–7; components 65–6; definition of 64–5; and expert knowledge 67–8; research on 68–72

translationese 234, **236**
translation memory 117–19
translation procedures 31–3, 35, 214, **235**, 237
translation process 14, 54–63, 202, 203, **235–6**; Bell's psycholinguistic model 56–7, 62, 63; Gile's effort model 61–2, 63; Gutt and relevance theory 60–1, 62; interpretive theory 54–5; Kiraly's sociological and psycholinguistic model 58–9, 52; research on 68–72; Wilss and decision-making 60
translation studies: corpus-based 177; and interpreting studies 128; as interdiscipline 19n1; name of 5, 20; scope of 5–12, 15, 18; *see also* descriptive translation studies, history of translation practice and theory
translation theory 9–10, 17, 20–35; communicative stage 21, 26–33; ethical/aesthetic stage 21; functionalist stage 21; integratedness 26–7; linguistic stage 20–1, 21–6; *see also* history of translation practice and theory
translator: as intervener 100–2; as mediator 88–91; as negotiator 96–7
translatorial action 227
transliteration 200, 226, **236–7**
Translog 70
transposition 209, 212, **237**
triangulation **237**

undertranslation 213, **238**
universals of translation 187
unicode 109
unit of translation 191, 204, **238**, 240
universals of translation **238–9**

visual: translation of 161–2
voice-over **239**; in screen translation 152–3

whispered interpreting 226, **239**
word-for-word translation 22, 191, 204, 212, 224, **239**

XML mark-up language 108

zero translation **240**

287